Natural Language Processing in Mental Health Care

Scrivener Publishing
100 Cummings Center, Suite 541J
Beverly, MA 01915-6106

Publishers at Scrivener
Martin Scrivener (martin@scrivenerpublishing.com)
Phillip Carmical (pcarmical@scrivenerpublishing.com)

Natural Language Processing in Mental Health Care

Methodologies and Clinical Practice

Edited by

Sudesh Yadav

Govt. College, Ateli, Indira Gandhi University Meerpur, Rewari, Haryana, India

Pethuru Raj

Reliance Jio Platforms Ltd., Bangalore, India

Satya Prakash Yadav

Dept. of Computer Science and Engineering, Madan Mohan Malaviya University of Technology, Gorakhpur, U.P., India

and

Victor Hugo C. de Albuquerque

Department of Teleinformatics Engineering, Federal University of Ceará, Brazil

Scrivener Publishing

WILEY

This edition first published 2026 by John Wiley & Sons, Inc., 111 River Street, Hoboken, NJ 07030, USA and Scrivener Publishing LLC, 100 Cummings Center, Suite 541J, Beverly, MA 01915, USA

For more information about Scrivener publications please visit www.scrivenerpublishing.com.

Wiley Global Headquarters
111 River Street, Hoboken, NJ 07030, USA

For details of our global editorial offices, customer services, and more information about Wiley products visit us at www.wiley.com.

The manufacturer's authorized representative according to the EU General Product Safety Regulation is Wiley-VCH GmbH, Boschstr. 12, 69469 Weinheim, Germany, e-mail: Product_Safety@wiley.com.

Library of Congress Cataloging-in-Publication Data

ISBN 978-1-394-39284-1

Cover image: Generated with AI using Adobe Firefly
Cover design by Russell Richardson

Set in size of 11pt and Minion Pro by Manila Typesetting Company, Makati, Philippines

Printed in the USA

10 9 8 7 6 5 4 3 2 1

Contents

Preface

The book delves into the transformative advancements and cutting-edge trends in the application of behavior-based Natural Language Processing (NLP) in mental health care, emphasizing the pivotal role of intelligent computational technologies in addressing the growing global mental health crisis. As psychological well-being emerges as a cornerstone of public health, the increasing prevalence of mental illnesses—ranging from anxiety and depression to psychosis and PTSD—has become a critical concern, especially among youth and vulnerable populations. The pandemic disease has further exacerbated these challenges, leading to unprecedented levels of psychological distress while exposing the limitations of conventional mental health services. To tackle these complex and evolving issues, integrating advanced NLP techniques into mental health research and clinical practice has garnered significant attention. Innovative models such as BioBERT, Med-BERT, and other domain-specific language representations are revolutionizing the landscape by enabling nuanced understanding and early detection of mental health conditions. From identifying suicidal ideation through linguistic patterns to analyzing emotional tone in speech for signs of post-traumatic stress, NLP has proven to be a powerful tool in predictive diagnostics and personalized intervention strategies.

This book offers a comprehensive exploration of state-of-the-art NLP-driven methodologies, including behavior signal processing, computational psycholinguistics, sentiment and emotion analysis, and clinical text mining. The application of deep learning architectures, transformer-based models, and real-time analytics enables the extraction of behavioral cues from multimodal data—such as voice recordings, written narratives, and digital interactions—thereby providing valuable insights into a patient's mental state. Moreover, the development of rule-based and AI-powered conversational agents for therapeutic support and motivational interviewing demonstrates how intelligent systems can supplement human expertise in mental health services. Among the most impactful innovations discussed is the deployment of AI-enhanced virtual platforms for remote mental health monitoring and care delivery. These systems leverage NLP for continuous assessment and behavioral trend analysis, empowering practitioners with actionable intelligence while enhancing accessibility and scalability of services. In addition to diagnostic and monitoring applications, the book also highlights the ethical frameworks, privacy considerations, and algorithmic fairness necessary for the responsible use of AI in sensitive mental health contexts. Artificial intelligence, once used primarily for data mining, has evolved into a generative and context-aware technology that is now instrumental in revolutionizing psychological assessment and therapeutic interventions. When synergized with other digital health innovations—such as mobile health (mHealth), wearable biosensors, and cloud-based health informatics—NLP becomes a cornerstone of next-generation mental healthcare. This book not only showcases the foundational technologies propelling this shift but also explores the latest behaviour-based NLP systems and their role in reshaping the future of mental health services worldwide.

In closing, we extend our sincere thanks to Martin Scrivener and the team at Scrivener Publication for their effort and guidance throughout the development of this publication.

The Editors

Part 1

FOUNDATIONS OF NLP IN MENTAL HEALTH

1

Introduction to NLP in Mental Health

Anandaraj S.P.[1]*, Rakesh Mohanty[2], Trapty Agarwal[3], Taskeen Zaidi[4] and Pratyashi Satapathy[5]

[1]Department of Computer Science & Engineering, Presidency University, Bengaluru, Karnataka, India
[2]Department of Psychiatry, IMS and SUM Hospital, Siksha 'O' Anusandhan (Deemed to be University), Bhubaneswar, Odisha, India
[3]Maharishi School of Engineering and Technology, Maharishi University of Information Technology, Uttar Pradesh, India
[4]Department of CSIT, Jain(Deemed-to-be University), Bangalore, Karnataka, India
[5]Department of Computer Science and Engineering, Siksha 'O' Anusandhan (Deemed to be University), Bhubaneswar, Odisha, India

Abstract

Natural language processing (NLP) has gained significant attention in mental health (MH) research, offering promising advancements in the analyzing, handling, and monitoring of MH conditions. This chapter introduces the role of NLP in MH research, providing an overview of how NLP techniques transform the understanding and management of these conditions. Here, it explains the underlying principles of NLP and how relate to the analysis of textual information. The chapter considers how NLP can expand the understanding of language patterns associated with premature indicators of MH conditions namely depression, anxiety and posttraumatic stress disorder (PTSD). It also discusses its affordance in enhancing MH assessments *via* machine learning algorithms for personalized treatment strategies. Overall, the chapter provides a background for the understanding of the function of NLP in MH research; certainly a way to move toward a broader discussion on its impact and prospects for the future.

**Corresponding author*: anandaraj@presidencyuniversity.in; ORCID: 0000-0003-3660-4503
Rakesh Mohanty: ORCID: 0000-0001-7982-5002
Trapty Agarwal: ORCID: 0009-0007-4081-4999
Taskeen Zaidi: ORCID: 0009-0005-6169-1428
Pratyashi Satapathy: ORCID: 0009-0009-0333-1159

Sudesh Yadav, Pethuru Raj, Satya Prakash Yadav and Victor Hugo C. de Albuquerque (eds.) Natural Language Processing in Mental Health Care: Methodologies and Clinical Practice, (3–14) © 2026 Scrivener Publishing LLC

***Keywords*:** Natural language processing, mental health, textual data analysis, machine learning algorithms, personalized treatment

1.1 Introduction to NLP's Significance in Mental Health Analysis

Globally, neuropsychiatric conditions, such as anxiety and depression, are the main reasons for incapacity. The consequences of poor MH are costly to healthcare systems, disproportionately impact lower socioeconomic groups and minorities, and result in economic losses. A variety of mental health interventions (MHIs), such as behavioral, pharmacological, psychological, and telemedicine techniques, have been shown to be effective in promoting wellbeing. Notwithstanding their advantages, MHIs have structural problems that restrict their effectiveness and capacity to satisfy growing demand. The first is reliable diagnostic methods, objective diagnostics, which add to the already limited clinical workforce by requiring extensive training for diagnostic techniques. The second challenge is variable treatment quality [1]. Reduced effect sizes have been observed with widespread MHI distribution, which cannot be easily addressed by supervision and current quality assurance procedures. Third, there are not enough clinicians, especially in developing nations and rural areas, for a variety of reasons, including the high expense of training. Because of this, MHI quality is still low, which emphasizes the need for the study, development, and implementation of tools that streamline the diagnostic and therapeutic processes [2].

Options for resolving MHI issues are provided by recent developments in the domains of machine learning and artificial intelligence (AI). Numerous medical specialties, including radiology, cancer, ophthalmology, emergency medicine, and of particular significance in this context MH, are developing technological and algorithmic solutions. NLP enables the representation, analysis, and generation of vast corpora of linguistic data, making it a relevant area of AI. NLP makes it possible to analyze unstructured free text quantitatively by transforming words into graphical and numerical representations. Because MHIs rely on language interactions, MHIs are ideally appropriate for NLP analysis, which makes it possible to specify interactional details at the utterance level for incredibly huge numbers of people, something previously unattainable.

Table 1.1 Application of NLP in mental health analysis.

NLP application	Description
Diagnosis assistance	Extracts symptoms, MH conditions, and risk factors from clinical notes and patient interactions.
Treatment quality assessment	Evaluates therapy sessions and adherence to MHIs by analyzing linguistic patterns.
Suicide risk prediction	Identifies linguistic markers indicating suicidal ideation from clinical notes and social media.
Patient-provider interaction analysis	Assesses therapeutic alliance and communication quality using NLP-driven conversation analysis.
MH trend monitoring	Analyzes social media posts and online forums to track MH trends and crises.
Digital health platform integration	Enhances telemedicine and Chabot-based interventions for MH support.

Source: Own elaboration.

NLP can be used to analyze traits of patients and providers that are typically overlooked. The earliest NLP applications in MHI were prepackaged software tools. More computationally demanding deep neural networks (DNNs), especially large language models, and emerged alongside other techniques for finding significant patterns in vast volumes of data. These kinds of details are more widely accessible due to the growth of digital health platforms. Finally, NLP has been used outside of MHI in contexts related to MH, such as electronic health records and social media [3]. Table 1.1 lists important NLP uses in MH analysis, such as predicting suicide risk, assisting with diagnosis, and evaluating the effectiveness of treatment. Examining clinical notes, social media, and patient–provider contacts demonstrates how NLP improves MH interventions.

1.2 Early Mental Health Condition Detection with NLP

Timely and appropriate treatment is essential for MH conditions, like schizophrenia. The time between the appearance of the first psychotic symptoms (onset) and the start of treatment is known as the duration of untreated psychosis (DUP). Longer DUPs have been linked to weaker recovery and global functioning, more long-term social impairment, and worse intervention effects. Population-level prognostic surveillance and a more thorough understanding of illness trajectories are required [4]. Research findings have significantly influenced MH care, resulting in the creation of early intervention teams that support individuals experiencing their First Episode of Psychosis (FEP) to lower DUP. However, conducting extensive investigations of future clinical research is challenging due to the very low prevalence of schizophrenia.

Retrospective clinical research has access to a multitude of patient-related data due to the increasing use of EHRs. However, pertinent disease onset data is primarily recorded in free text in MHEHRs. NLP techniques can be developed to extract clinically significant information from EHR-free text. These methods have shown effectiveness in a range of clinical settings, particularly when it comes to extracting certain clinical entities, such as symptoms, diagnoses, and prescription drugs [5]. However, these methods' generalizability and transferability are rarely assessed in actual clinical contexts, and NLP solutions are required for increasingly difficult tasks, like relation recognition and temporal information extraction. In MHEHRs, clinically relevant data is more often recorded in free text rather than organized fields compared to other medical areas. It can be difficult to unlock these data for patient-level research because there is a lot of variation in the definitions of terms.

Mental health EHRs can be difficult to unlock this data, especially for patient-level research because there is a lot of variation in the definition and documentation of concepts, which could account for the extraction of various informational layers and relationships. While creating a suitable NLP technique, it is crucial to comprehend the background of the documentation processes and the underlying EHR data to collect the required data [6]. Calculating DUP at scale using EHR data requires extracting information from free text about the age or date psychosis started. Finding this construct at the patient level poses several difficulties from an NLP standpoint.

First, a time reference, a temporal relationship, and a symptom mention are the three main elements that are usually present in remarks of the onset of psychosis. To extract each of these components, different NLP approaches could be needed. Second, EHRs do not reliably record information on the start of psychosis. Usually, it is documented in particular EHR record types during specific clinical assessment scenarios; however, it can also appear more than once in different papers for a particular patient, for example, if the patient receives different treatments, if the evaluation is conducted by separate medical professionals, or in other situations affecting the healthcare route [7]. Furthermore, the physician (and the patient, in fact) could not be certain about the details surrounding the outset of the disease, and the records could contain various pertinent references regarding the onset as well as contradicting remarks. Regarding this, there is some clinical ambiguity regarding the reporting and recording of information in clinical notes, in addition to the capability of an NLP technique to distinguish reliable data from obtainable data when determining the onset of a disease. Analyzing temporal relationships within the texts is necessary for the extraction of clinical-temporal characteristics at the patient level. Many NLP studies have focused on temporal information extraction to simulate this issue, treating the identification of entities and temporal correlation categorization as distinct, consecutive responsibilities [8]. Table 1.2 outlines the main obstacles to employing NLP for early

Table 1.2 Key challenges in early mental health condition.

Challenges	Description
Variability in terminology	Different clinicians use different terms and phrasing to describe the same symptoms, making standardization difficult.
Temporal information extraction	Extracting psychosis onset time from unstructured EHR data requires recognizing temporal associations and sequencing events correctly.
Data redundancy and contradictions	Patient records often contain repeated, conflicting, or uncertain information about symptom onset across multiple documents.
Generalizability of NLP models	Most NLP models are trained on specific datasets and could not transfer well to different clinical settings.
Complexity of relation recognition	Identifying relationships between symptoms, treatment initiation, and patient outcomes remains challenging for NLP techniques.

Source: Own elaboration.

MH diagnosis. These include variations in clinical terminology, issues in extracting temporal information, redundant data, and restrictions on the generalizability of the model.

Before identifying the connections between entity pairs, symptoms, and temporal expressions are first extracted as entities. Errors from the entity extraction step can spread and affect the following identification of pertinent temporal correlations, even though this approach makes it possible to break the problem down into smaller parts [9]. An additional strategy could be to map concepts with knowledge bases to identify pertinent entities, then categorize these for relevance in both past and present contexts to develop enduring courses. For ideas that have been documented in a variety of ways, such as positive psychosis symptoms, this poses a challenging issue.

1.3 Enhancing Mental Health Assessments with NLP

The use of AI in healthcare has accompanied an innovative period of accurate diagnosis, principally in the field of mental health, where subjectivity and interpretation variability lead to the failure of traditional evaluation methods. Recent developments in AI technology, particularly in the areas of NLP and machine learning (ML) or deep learning (DL), can transform MH diagnosis. ML and DL broadly known for their ability to classify images—have also shown potential for unraveling complex patterns within brain scans and medical imaging to yield a better understanding of neurobiological bases of different MH disorders [10].

At the same time, NLP makes it possible to make sense of and score huge volumes of unstructured text data, including patient narratives and clinical notes, to offer invaluable insights on symptomatology and course, which are so important for correct diagnosis. The use of ML or DL and NLP in AI-based evaluation tools concedes a range of drawbacks of traditional techniques [11]. Subjective variability and biases have often interfered with diagnostic tools that rely on clinician interpretation of self-reported signs and standard questionnaires. Making use of multimodal data, such as text and neuroimaging, AI-powered technologies are capable of providing objective, repeatable evaluations through the careful analysis of different types of data [12]. Such capability in MH is particularly salient, wherein prognosis and intervention are of paramount importance to outcomes but typically suffer from false and unreasonably delayed diagnoses.

The scalability and accessibility of mental health treatments have been immeasurably improved by the use of AI-enhanced diagnostic tools.

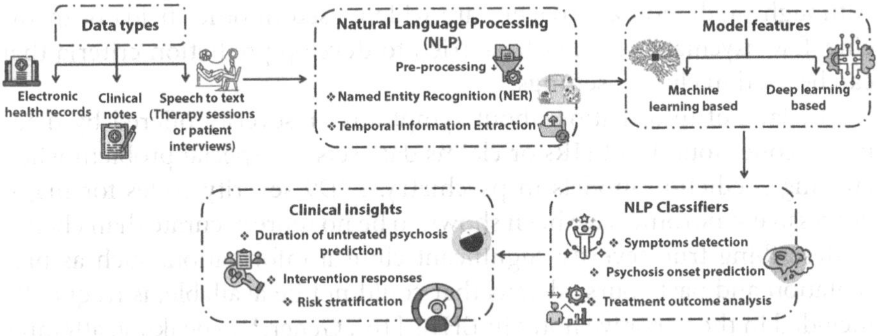

Figure 1.1 NLP structure in mental healthcare. Source: Own elaboration.

These tools automate portions of its diagnostic process, alleviating humans from the incessant burden of work. Research allows real-time feedback and continuous monitoring, which promote proactive and individualized patient treatment. Such effective and scalable treatments are extremely relevant as mental health issues continue to surge globally in numbers, fueled by socioeconomic and environmental pressures. Nevertheless, there are certain difficulties in using ML or DL and NLP in MH diagnosis. Implementation must be done carefully and ethically due to concerns about algorithmic bias, model interpretability, and data privacy [13]. Overall, utilizing NLP with ML or DL capabilities in AI-based MH screening systems is a viable avenue for advancement. These technologies can entirely convert MH care by refining diagnostic efficiency and accuracy. This would lead to more individualized treatment regimens, earlier intervention, and ultimately improved patient outcomes [14]. The NLP framework in mental healthcare is depicted in Figure 1.1, which also highlights important clinical applications, integrated ML/DL approaches, NLP processing processes, and data sources, such as clinical notes and EHRs.

1.4 NLP-Based Customized Therapy Approaches

Early hospital readmission is a major Medicare quality metric and an avoidable cause of health care expenses. Since mental illnesses are often characterized by increased recurrence rates and chronicity, readmission is a significant concern for these individuals; the post-hospitalization phase is known to be a high-risk period for outcomes, like substance use relapse and suicide [15]. Finding the individual most at risk and who could benefit from tailored interventions is crucial in reducing the likelihood of readmission.

Although prediction approaches are widely used in other fields of medicine, few psychiatric studies have tried to develop prediction criteria that can be used in clinical settings.

The lack of information about symptoms or severity offered by diagnostic codes found in EHRs or claims data sets is a special problem when creating prediction models in psychiatry. ICD9 severity codes for major depressive syndrome have been shown to be no more accurate than chance in describing true severity. Significant clinical information, such as presentation and past course details that could not be available, is frequently included in the narrative notes in EHRs [16]. Generally speaking, attempts to interpret description notes in EHR data focus on a single symptom or diagnosis. Typical tactics include identifying the terms that clinicians have manually preselected using information extraction methods; these terms are occasionally complemented by additional terminology.

If the objective is to describe people in terms of general psychopathology rather than the specifics of a single diagnosis or result, approaches that require experts to select each phrase do not scale effectively [17]. However, term-agnostic techniques for automatic clinical concept extraction that are more dependable and widely applicable have shown some promise in other medical domains. However, these approaches continue to rely on conventional diagnostic categories, their ability to resolve psychopathology in general seems to be restricted.

1.5 Advancements and Future Directions in Clinical NLP for Mental Health

Research and the provision of healthcare could be significantly impacted by the appropriate use of massive data sources, such as EHR databases. Research to improve NLP techniques with requests for the medical province has increased in tandem with the substantial quantity of records in text format that is accessible in EHRs. In topical periods, the field has advanced significantly, tackling many of the issues noted. For instance, the aforementioned suggestions address the main issues of poor cooperation, a lack of resources, and evaluation techniques for important jobs, including de-identification, medical concept detection and classification, semantic modifiers, and temporal information. Several shared tasks have been organized to solve these issues [18].

New initiatives center on the aim to encourage resource allocation and progress in the profession by making NLP techniques more visible, replicable, and accessible. The use of NLP techniques and methods has grown rapidly in the field of MH in recent years. The primary reason for the majority of physician records are in free text, but other kinds of files offer clues about how patients are reacting to various illnesses and treatments as well as social, emotional, and cognitive markers. Social media, the internet, doctor-patient contacts, and online treatment are a few examples of these text sources. Additionally, the domain is still more specialized than biological or general clinical NLP, despite a few similar tasks in MH [19]. Advancements in NLP methods and state-of-the-art outcomes have led to a significant increase in the successful implementation of NLP solutions for complex clinical outcomes research. Even though clinical research studies typically rely on NLP technology for data extraction and preparation, the techniques for evaluating and rating these technologies varies slightly. These distinctions must be made clear, and new strategies and techniques must be created to close this gap.

1.6 Conclusion

Natural language processing (NLP) has gained attention as a revolutionary tool in mental health research, offering the creative possibilities to diagnose, treat, and detect early illnesses such as depression, anxiety, and schizophrenia. Through the unstructured text level of analysis of clinical notes, electronic health records, and social media, NLP paves the way for building more scattered knowledge of the patterning and risk factors for mental health. It enhances the accuracy of the diagnosis, facilitates early intervention, and helps create an individualized treatment plan, all through AI-based insight. While challenges like data heterogeneity, temporal information extraction, and model generalizability continue to hinder deep learning NLP advances in mental health assessments, important work is being done. That said, ethical challenges related to bias and data privacy must be addressed to guarantee responsible implementation.

AI disclosure statement: The author confirms that no artificial intelligence (AI)-generated content or AI-assisted writing tools were used in the preparation of this chapter (including summaries and the abstract). All text, analysis, and conclusions are the result of the author's original work.

References

1. Kishimoto, T., *et al.*, Understanding Psychiatric Illness through Natural Language Processing (UNDERPIN): Rationale, Design, and Methodology. *Front. Psychiatry*, 13, 954703, 2022, https://doi.org/10.3389/fpsyt.2022.954703.
2. Marshall, C., *et al.*, Using Natural Language Processing to Explore Mental Health Insights from UK Tweets during the COVID-19 Pandemic: Infodemiology Study. *JMIR Infodemiol.*, 2, 1, e32449, 2022, https://doi.org/10.2196/32449.
3. Spruit, M., *et al.*, Exploring Language Markers of Mental Health in Psychiatric Stories. *Appl. Sci.*, 12, 4, 2179, 2022, https://doi.org/10.3390/app12042179.
4. Anjali, K., *et al.*, Psychological Mental Health Analysis Using NLP and Machine Learning. *2024 International Conference on Electrical Electronics and Computing Technologies (ICEECT)*, vol. 1, pp. 1–6, IEEE, 2024, https://doi.org/10.1109/ICEECT61758.2024.10739022.
5. Marder, S.R., Natural Language Processing: Its Potential Role in Clinical Care and Clinical Research. *Schizophr. Bull.*, 48, 5, 958–959, 2022, https://doi.org/10.1093/schbul/sbac092.
6. Borah, T. and Ganesh Kumar, S., Application of NLP and Machine Learning for Mental Health Improvement, in: *International Conference on Innovative Computing and Communications: Proceedings of ICICC 2022, Volume 3*, pp. 219–228, Springer Nature Singapore, 2022, https://doi.org/10.1007/978-981-19-3679-1_16.
7. Corona Hernández, H., *et al.*, Natural Language Processing Markers for Psychosis and Other Psychiatric Disorders: Emerging Themes and Research Agenda from a Cross-Linguistic Workshop. *Schizophr. Bull.*, 49, Supplement 2, S86–S92, 2023, https://doi.org/10.1093/schbul/sbac215.
8. Singla, A., RoBERTa and BERT: Revolutionizing Mental Healthcare through Natural Language. *Shodh Sagar J. Artif. Intell. Mach. Learn.*, 1, 1, 10–27, 2024, https://orcid.org/0009-0003-2027-0112.
9. Swaminathan, A., *et al.*, Natural Language Processing System for Rapid Detection and Intervention of Mental Health Crisis Chat Messages. *npj Digit. Med.*, 6, 1, 213, 2023, https://doi.org/10.1038/s41746-023-00951-3.
10. Crestani, F., Losada, D.E., Parapar, J., Early Detection of Mental Health Disorders by Social Media Monitoring. *Stud. Comput. Intell.*, 1018, 4, 2022, https://doi.org/10.1007/978-3-031-04431-1.
11. Kerz, E., *et al.*, Toward Explainable AI (XAI) for Mental Health Detection Based on Language Behavior. *Front. Psychiatry*, 14, 1219479, 2023, https://doi.org/10.3389/fpsyt.2023.1219479.
12. Turner, R.J., *et al.*, Information Extraction from Free Text for Aiding Transdiagnostic Psychiatry: Constructing NLP Pipelines Tailored to Clinicians' Needs. *BMC Psychiatry*, 22, 1, 407, 2022, https://doi.org/10.1186/s12888-022-04058-z.

13. Miranda, O., *et al.*, Enhancing Post-Traumatic Stress Disorder Patient Assessment: Leveraging Natural Language Processing for Research of Domain Criteria Identification Using Electronic Medical Records. *BMC Med. Inf. Decis. Making*, 24, 1, 154, 2024, https://doi.org/10.1186/s12911-024-02554-8.
14. Lee, D.Y., *et al.*, Psychosis Relapse Prediction Leveraging Electronic Health Records Data and Natural Language Processing Enrichment Methods. *Front. Psychiatry*, 13, 844442, 2022, https://doi.org/10.3389/fpsyt.2022.844442.
15. Verma, S., *et al.*, AI-Enhanced Mental Health Diagnosis: Leveraging Transformers for Early Detection of Depression Tendency in Textual Data. *2023 15th International Congress on Ultra Modern Telecommunications and Control Systems and Workshops (ICUMT)*, IEEE, pp. 56–61, 2023, https://doi.org/10.1109/ICUMT61075.2023.10333301.
16. Olawade, D.B., *et al.*, Enhancing Mental Health with Artificial Intelligence: Current Trends and Prospects. *J. Med. Surg. Public Health*, 3, 100099, 2024, https://doi.org/10.1016/j.glmedi.2024.100099.
17. Botella, R., *et al.*, Can Natural Language Processing Models Extract and Classify Instances of Interpersonal Violence in Mental Healthcare Electronic Records: An Applied Evaluative Study. *BMJ Open*, 12, 2, e052911, 2022, https://doi.org/10.1136/bmjopen-2021-052911.
18. Cohen, A.S., *et al.*, Natural Language Processing and Psychosis: On the Need for Comprehensive Psychometric Evaluation. *Schizophr. Bull.*, 48, 5, 939–948, 2022, https://doi.org/10.1093/schbul/sbac051.
19. Young, M., *et al.*, Natural Language Processing Diagnosed Behavioral Disturbance vs Confusion Assessment Method for the Intensive Care Unit: Prevalence, Patient Characteristics, Overlap, and Association with Treatment and Outcome. *Intensive Care Med.*, 48, 5, 559–569, 2022, https://doi.org/10.1007/s00134-022-06650-z.

2

Mental Health Issues, Concerns, and Solutions

Y. Narasimha Raja[1]*, Suvendu Narayan Mishra[2], Shweta Bajaj[3] and M. N. Nachappa[4]

[1]*Department of Management, Presidency University, Bengaluru, Karnataka, India*
[2]*Department of Psychiatry, IMS and SUM Hospital, Siksha 'O' Anusandhan (Deemed to be University), Bhubaneswar, Odisha, India*
[3]*Maharishi School of Pharmaceuticals, Maharishi University of Information Technology, Uttar Pradesh, India*
[4]*Department of CSIT, Jain(Deemed-to-be University), Bangalore, Karnataka, India*

Abstract

Mental health issues have become a significant global concern which was affecting millions of people and influencing societies at multiple levels. This chapter explores the key mental health issues, including the rise in stress anxiety and depression-related (SAD) disorders and identifies underlying factors, such as socio-economic pressures, stigma, and limited access to quality care. The concerns surrounding mental health, particularly the inadequacies of current healthcare systems, underscores the urgent need for comprehensive reforms. This research examines potential solutions to address these concerns, such as increasing mental health literacy, incorporating the mental health services into the primary healthcare, promoting early intervention programs, and increasing the usage of digital mental health platforms. By investigating the relationship between mental well-being and societal factors, the chapter presents a holistic approach to improving mental health support, aiming to create sustainable, accessible, and effective solutions for individuals across diverse communities.

**Corresponding author*: narasimharaja.y@presidencyuniversity.in;
ORCID: 0009-0005-7127-787X
Suvendu Narayan Mishra: ORCID: 0000-0002-0309-1310
Shweta Bajaj: ORCID: 0000-0001-6646-5298
M. N. Nachappa: ORCID: 0000-0002-4007-5504

Sudesh Yadav, Pethuru Raj, Satya Prakash Yadav and Victor Hugo C. de Albuquerque (eds.) Natural Language Processing in Mental Health Care: Methodologies and Clinical Practice, (15–26) © 2026 Scrivener Publishing LLC

Keywords: Mental health, stress, Quality of Life (QoL), concerns, intervention programs

2.1 Introduction

Mental Health (MH) is a leading factor of the well-being of societies, people and countries. MH encompasses overall physical, social and mental well-being. A person's Quality of Life (QoL) and ability to reach their full potential depend heavily on their MH [1]. MH is a comprehensive term that incorporates a variety of mental, social, emotional, and behavioral functions. MH like physical health exists on a scale from good MH to bad MH and differs over the period of time, various situations, and various ages. Children with good MH demonstrate timely accomplishment of developing indicators, emotional growth, healthy social and excellent regulation, and coping abilities; mentally strong children operate effectively in a variety of situations, including the home, community, and school. Poor mental health and severe, ongoing symptoms can result in mental illnesses (MI) [2]. Positive MH is defined not only as the absence of the Mental Disorders (MD), it also as the existence of positive characteristics. It is divided into three fields, such as psychological, social and emotional well-being, to capture an individual's positive MH; it has been thought necessary to conduct a thorough evaluation of well-being that encompasses both hedonic, subjective wellbeing, eudaimonic well-being consists of psychological well-being and social well-being [3]. The ability to address some of the limitations connected with receiving in-person services has made MH a prominent component of the digitization of healthcare. Although it is incorporated into digital health strategies, MH has not been given a position. MH frequently occupies an uncooperative place in the larger digital health space due to the delicate nature of data in the MH settings and the stigma that can follow MI [4].

The field of sports medicine is paying more attention to athlete MH. The sheer essence of competition can cause, exacerbate, or reveal psychological problems in athletes, despite the fact that sports involvement has numerous advantages. While some personality qualities might help people succeed in sports, they can also be linked to MH issues. The sports culture can affect pre-existing personality characteristics and MH conditions, which can affect psychological health and performance [5]. The implementation of substantial physical and social limitations, such as social separation and mass quarantine measures, has led to decreased access to traditional sources of support and improved psychological stress. It is a crucial but

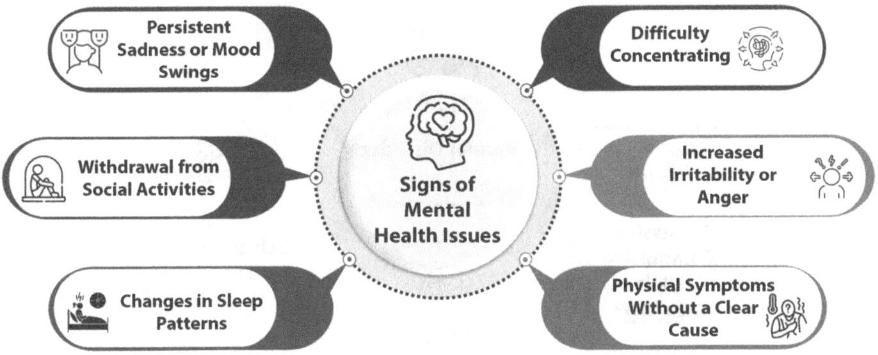

Figure 2.1 Signs of the MH issues. Source: Own elaboration.

extremely delicate situation: the present conditions place persons without pre-existing MH difficulties at danger of getting them, while the situations of those who currently have MH care concerns are predicted to worsen. At the similar time, availability and traditional methods of offering MH treatment are severely affected [6].

Students encounter increasingly stressful circumstances as they advance in their education, including a more challenging curriculum, challenging work assignments and projects, and living in dorms. Teachers have a duty to help their students to manage these demands so they can keep a healthy MH [7]. Figure 2.1 represents the signs of the MH issues.

The urgent need for substantial reforms is highlighted by the issues surrounding MH, especially the shortcomings of the present healthcare systems. This chapter looks at ways to solve these issues, including raising MH awareness, incorporating MH services into primary care, encouraging early intervention initiatives, and utilizing digital MH platforms more widely.

2.2 Psychological and Psychiatric Types

Various researches conducted in various industrialized and emerging countries over the past decade have found that students have a greater prevalence of SAD compared to the overall population. It is widely known that SAD, as a multifactorial condition, produces personal, physical, social, and occupational difficulties that can both directly and indirectly impact QoL. Life quality and wellbeing are negatively connected with the amount of stress stated in self-reported tests and surveys. Untreated MH issues can lead to students experiencing distress, which can have a detrimental effect

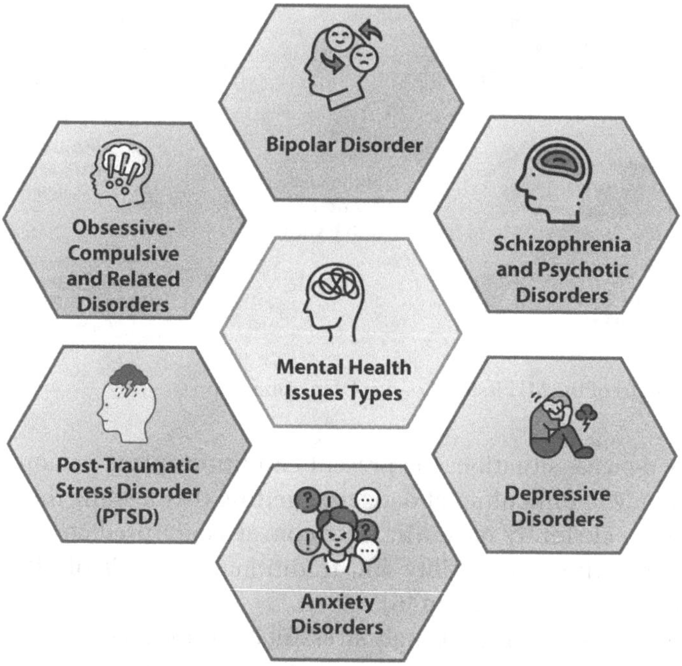

Figure 2.2 Types of MH issues. Source: Own elaboration.

on their QoL and academic performance. Poorer academic integrity, substance and alcohol abuse, diminished empathy, low self-esteem, unstable relationships, and suicidal thoughts are a few of these problems [8]. Figure 2.2 depicts the different types of MH issues.

2.2.1 Depression

Depression is characterized as an emotional disease that manifests as mood swings, sadness, and frustrated feelings. It is presently regarded as one of the common MDs in the world and postures a serious risk to public health. Changes in appetite, mood, and sleep patterns, lethargy, anhedonia, poor self-esteem and guilt emotions, difficulties in focusing, agitation, and suicidal thoughts are some of the primary symptoms of depression [9].

2.2.2 Anxiety Disorders

Anxiety Disorders (ADs) are one of the most frequent types of MD globally. Anxiety is clinically classified into five subtypes: Generalized Anxiety

Disorder (GAD), social ADs, panic disorder, particular phobias and agoraphobia. However, there is a sign for commonality amongst ADs at both the genetic and phenotypic levels [10]. ADs are biopsychosocial problems characterized by generic or situation-specific reactions to perceived dangers. Anxiety has always sparked significant interest historically. Ads are among the most prevalent MI. They often begin early in childhood and like other MDs have an intentionally protracted course and a significant functional influence. A growth in worldwide anxiety prevalence poses a substantial danger to the population's health and QoL [11].

2.2.3 Posttraumatic Stress Disorder (PTSD)

PTSD is a prevalent MH illness categorized by considerable discomfort and reduced functioning. This offers unique preventative chances that are not available for other illnesses [12]. This condition is characterized by uncomfortable sensations and thoughts, hyper arousal, avoiding signs that remind the people of the trauma, and repeating memories of the incident [13].

2.2.4 Stigma

Stigma is a negative barrier to MH care, especially for schizophrenia, which is one of the most stigmatized MDs. Schizophrenia, is one of the most stigmatized disorders, making it an important target for anti-stigma programs. Stigma reduction relies heavily on public awareness and education, with social media serving as an effective tool for fostering MH literacy. Social media allows people to share their experiences and influence public attitudes, but rigorous monitoring is required to avoid disinformation. It has investigated stigma associated with numerous MDs, but tracking stigma on social media is difficult, owing to the large volume of data. Psycholinguistic analysis, utilizing methods such as LIWC, can automatically detect stigmatizing utterances providing understanding on language patterns [14].

2.3 Mental Health Concerns

A major contributing factor to the disability is MH concerns. MH disorders affect behaviors, emotions and mental procedures, and their severity varies. It includes mood disorders, ADs, borderline personality disorder, PTSD and schizophrenia. Substance Use and Suicidal ideation (SI) disorders typically coexist with the MH problems [15]. To recognize young attitudes about getting treatment for MH difficulties, indices of social well-being and psychological health are considered as vital factors of health at a separate level. The evidence generally indicates that children experiencing poor MH are less inclined to seek treatment compared to children reporting excellent MH. Additionally, social well-being metrics like feeling connected to family and friends are thought to substitute a positive logic of self-worth, confidence, self-efficacy and belonging can be linked to constructive help-seeking behaviors [16].

MH issues are frequently highlighted in both conventional and internet media, adding to stigma and misunderstandings. Many people rely on the media for information regarding MH, and those with MI are usually portrayed as dangerous, criminal, or socially alienated. Individuals with MD are frequently portrayed as victims in the entertainment industry, reinforcing stereotypes. Such unfavorable portrayals breed prejudice, discrimination, and social distance. However, evidence suggests that people with MH issues are substantially less probable to conduct violent crimes compared with general population and they are actually more probable to be losses of violence.

Because of stigma, many are searching for knowledge and support through online forums. Research finds that people favor digital spaces for MH talks when some form of judgment in arenas available for discussion is evident. Online peer support, blogs, and social media are the places where people tell their stories, make connections, and heal together. Although online tools could serve as potential means of social capital growth, there is a distinct need to fine-tune the digital psychological interventions. In addressing misinformation to eliminate stigma, these issues necessitate accountability from media, a further enhanced digital MH tool, and elaborate support networks. Extended inquiries into online peer support provide a much more flexible approach towards a relaxed depiction of MH, leading to far-reaching and enmeshed ways for treatment delivery [17].

2.4 Potential Solutions for Mental Health

Addressing MH issues involves a multifaceted strategy that prioritizes early identification, rapid intervention, and greater access to care. Existing gaps in MH services could be overcome by improving preventative methods, healthcare infrastructure, and digital solutions. This section investigates critical solutions, such as early intervention, greater access to care, and novel approaches to increasing MH service availability.

Early Detection and Intervention in Mental Health

Early intervention and detection have been recognized as daring components for mitigating the influence of any theoretically substantial health problem. Even though the field of juvenile health has seen remarkable advancements, early intervention is indeed an unfulfilled target. This is particularly true of youth MH. The goal of MH care has always been to aid adult populations in times of crisis and major emergencies. Theoretical ideas concerning the possibility to interfere in MH with this definite age window are based on the research.

First, MH plays a significant role in a person's capability to function effectively in both their social and personal lives and to create coping mechanisms for life's challenges. Early infancy is crucial in this regard because of the sharp vulnerability and sensitivity of early brain growth, which could have long-term properties on the adult's behavioral, social, intellectual achievements and emotions. Second, the transition from childhood to early adulthood is when most MIs occur, with up to one in five people experiencing clinically serious MH problems before 25 years old and half of these individuals exhibiting signs before 14 years. MH issues, specifically mood disorders and ADs, accounts for 45% of the worldwide illness burden and are the primary reason for the Disability Adjusted Life Years (DALYs) in those under the age of 25. Problematic drug usage, including illicit and alcohol substances, is the core risk factor for the incident DALYs (9%). Finally, most MH programs, as previously designed, have proven ineffectual in delivering healthcare in this critical era, with poor utilization because of the greater prevalence of MH problems among the young people.

Furthermore, people aged 0 to 25 experiences the greatest delay in seeking early treatment when symptoms occur. This is mostly attributable to two aspects. In one scenario, young people, mainly those who are male, ethnic minorities, and low-income are less expected to seek MH care for the first time, and stigma is a substantial barrier. When they act, they exhibit high degrees of disengagement. In contrast, considerable delays in receiving care can be linked to services' poor ability to promptly provide professional MH care to children in need following an initial basic care appointment. When treatments become accessible, the majority of treatments are not evidence-based. Based on the findings, there is an imperative requirement to create or enhance the existing adolescent care models that incorporate preventive and early intervention methods.

Although there has been growth in treating psychotic diseases, such as the successful utilization of the idea of at-risk mental state, it is basically not examined in the common MDs including eating disorders, depression, anxiety and drug abuse. It is vital to concurrently rethink early intervention and detection services for the young inhabitants by encouraging multidisciplinary associations among several specialized healthcare providers in an improved and combined the prolonged primary care service to address the requirement for early intervention into the young adult and childhood MH difficulties [18].

Access to Mental Health Care

Integrating the MH services into the primary health care is an effective method of decreasing the MH treatment gap in Low- and Middle-Income Countries (LMICs), mostly in the rural areas. This integration in LMICs revealed better attitudes of the healthcare specialists regarding MHDs and the value of linking healthcare employees with the MH service consumers. Non-medical physicians such as old healers play a vital role in the paths of care in the LMICs because of their availability, cost, and belief in their services.

Somatization of psychological problems as physical complaints can be noticed and diagnosed in many ethnic groups with proper training at the primary care and secondary care levels. Similarly, studying teenager's perceptions of their MD could help guide culturally acceptable therapies. There is a therapy gap for MHDs even in high-income nations for individuals with high levels of education and employment and associated physical diseases. Regulations recognizing the psychological risks of occupational risk and focused interventions in business and educational environments are therefore required [19].

Solutions to Increase Access to MH Services

Primary and community care programs have demonstrated efficacy in enhancing access and providing early interventions, as well as producing financial gains. Crucially, they also hold promise for enhancing the provision of MH care to priority inhabitants, such as youth and children, by stepped care models. Community based MH distribution and tiered care models can enhance access to the MH services and reduce wait times by coordinating treatment. Early interventions might be provided by allied health, community and primary care providers through incorporating related services of health professionals into policies of the health insurance and ensuring primary care consultants receive proper training.

Early therapies, as opposed to primary care and preventive care, can reduce care delays and, thus, offer significant returns on investment since the majority of mental health disorders and illnesses begin in adolescence. In fact, it has been determined that increasing early interventions and MH promotion is essential to lowering the burden of illness and keeping public expenses under control. The evidence-based strategy to remove barriers to the MH services is to increase access to psychotherapy, which has been shown to improve QoL, as demonstrated by the successful implementation of the grantbased Improving Access to Psychological Therapies (IAPT) program.

Clients who participated in the IAPT's stepped care route reported substantial improvements in their MH for both common and severe illnesses. E-mental health inventiveness is growing and showing capable outcomes in extending access to MH care. The Stepped Care 2.0 program was found to be efficient in mixing personal care therapy with distance technology to provide MH treatments with a wider geographic reach. The method combines a stepped-care approach with e-MH courses [20].

2.5 Conclusion

MH challenges have been described as a global concern affecting individuals and communal aspects on various fronts. The chapter focused on major MH issues from anxiety, depression, and stress-related illnesses, with socioeconomic constraints, stigma, and inadequacy of access to healthcare being singled out as the underlying causes. Increasing mental health awareness, incorporating services into primary care, encouraging early intervention, and utilizing digital platforms are some of the options presented. Through the association between societal conditions and mental well-being, this research allowed a more holistic approach to enhancing MH assistance to find more sustainable, accessible, and effective solutions. It was limited by a lack of conformity in various locales in terms of MH knowledge, access to treatment, and the rapidly changing nature of digital MH interventions. Future analyses can highlight areas, such as AI-powered MH diagnostics, personalized care options, and legislation frameworks for the consideration of MH in global healthcare systems.

AI disclosure statement: The author confirms that no artificial intelligence (AI)-generated content or AI-assisted writing tools were used in the preparation of this chapter (including summaries and the abstract). All text, analysis, and conclusions are the result of the author's original work.

References

1. Chiao, J.Y., *et al.*, Cultural neuroscience and the research domain criteria: Implications for global mental health. *Neurosci. Biobehav. Rev.*, 116, 109–119, 2020, https://doi.org/ 10.1016/j.neubiorev. 2020.06.005.
2. Bitsko, R.H., Mental health surveillance among children—United States, 2013–2019. *MMWR Suppl.*, 71, 1–42, 2022, http://dx.doi.org/10.15585/mmwr.su7102a1.
3. Capone, V. and Petrillo, G., Mental health in teachers: Relationships with job satisfaction, efficacy beliefs, burnout and depression. *Curr. Psychol.*, 39, 5, 1757–1766, 2020, https://doi.org/10.1007/s12144-018-9878-7.
4. Marshall, J.M., Dunstan, D.A., Bartik, W., Clinical or gimmickal: The use and effectiveness of mobile mental health apps for treating anxiety and depression. *Aust. New Z. J. Psychiatry*, 54, 1, 20–28, 2020, https://doi.org/10.1177/0004867419876700.
5. Chang, C.J., *et al.*, Mental health issues and psychological factors in athletes: Detection, management, effect on performance, and prevention: American medical society for sports medicine position statement. *Clin. J. Sport Med.*, 30, 2, e61–e87, 2020, https://doi.org/10.1136/ bjsports-2019-101583.
6. Feijt, M., *et al.*, Mental health care goes online: Practitioners' experiences of providing mental health care during the COVID-19 pandemic. *Cyberpsychol. Behav. Soc. Netw.*, 23, 12, 860–864, 2020, https://doi.org/10.1089/cyber.2020.0370.
7. Asif, S., *et al.*, Frequency of depression, anxiety and stress among university students. *Pak. J. Med. Sci.*, 36, 5, 971, 2020, https://doi.org/10.12669/pjms.36.5.1873.
8. Mofatteh, M., Risk factors associated with stress, anxiety, and depression among university undergraduate students. *AIMS Public Health*, 8, 1, 36, 2020, https://doi.org/10.3934/publichealth. 2020057.
9. Farfán-Latorre, M., *et al.*, Mental health in the post-pandemic period: Depression, anxiety, and stress in Peruvian university students upon return to face-to-face classes. *Sustainability*, 15, 15, 11924, 2023, https://doi.org/10.3390/su151511924.
10. Purves, K.L., *et al.*, A major role for common genetic variation in anxiety disorders. *Mol. Psychiatry*, 25, 12, 3292–3303, 2020, https://doi.org/10.1038/s41380-019-0559-1.
11. Javaid, S.F., *et al.*, Epidemiology of anxiety disorders: Global burden and sociodemographic associations. *Middle East Curr. Psychiatry*, 30, 1, 44, 2023, https://doi.org/10.1186/s43045-023-00315-3.
12. Bisson, J.I., *et al.*, Preventing the onset of post traumatic stress disorder. *Clin. Psychol. Rev.*, 86, 102004, 2021, https://doi.org/10.1016/j.cpr.2021.102004.
13. Ressler, K.J., *et al.*, Post-traumatic stress disorder: Clinical and translational neuroscience from cells to circuits. *Nat. Rev. Neurol.*, 18, 5, 273–288, 2022, https://doi.org/ 10.1038/s41582-022-00635-8.

14. Li, A., *et al.*, A comparison of the psycholinguistic styles of schizophrenia-related stigma and depression-related stigma on social media: Content analysis. *J. Med. Internet Res.*, 22, 4, e16470, 2020, https://doi.org/10.2196/16470.
15. Navas, C., *et al.*, Patient and provider perspectives on emergency department care experiences among people with mental health concerns. *Healthcare*, 10, 7, MDPI, 1297, 2022, https://doi.org/10.3390/healthcare10071297.
16. Doan, N., *et al.*, Reluctancy towards help-seeking for mental health concerns at secondary school among students in the COMPASS study. *Int. J. Environ. Res. Public Health*, 17, 19, 7128, 2020, https://doi.org/10.3390/ijerph17197128.
17. Smith-Frigerio, S., "You are not alone": Linking peer support to information and resources for mental health concerns in advocacy groups' social media messaging. *Health Commun.*, 36, 14, 1980–1989, 2021, https://doi.org/10.1080/10410236.2020.1808415.
18. Colizzi, M., Lasalvia, A., Ruggeri, M., Prevention and early intervention in youth mental health: Is it time for a multidisciplinary and trans-diagnostic model for care? *Int. J. Mental Health Syst.*, 14, 1–14, 2020, https://doi.org/10.1186/s13033-020-00356-9.
19. Javed, A., *et al.*, Reducing the stigma of mental health disorders with a focus on low-and middle-income countries. *Asian J. Psychiatry*, 58, 102601, 2021, https://doi.org/10.1016/j.ajp.2021.102601.
20. Moroz, N., Moroz, I., D'Angelo, M.S., Mental health services in Canada: Barriers and cost-effective solutions to increase access. *Healthcare Manage. Forum*, vol. 33, 6, pp. 282–287, Sage Publications, Sage CA, Los Angeles, CA, 2020, https://doi.org/10.1177/0840470420933911.

3

AI Technologies, Tools, and Industrial Use Cases

Kalpana K. Harish[1]*, Sasanka Choudhury[2], Awakash Mishra[3] and Haripriya V.[4]

[1]*Department of Computer Science & Engineering, Presidency University, Bengaluru, Karnataka, India*
[2]*Department of Mechanical Engineering, Siksha 'O' Anusandhan (Deemed to be University), Bhubaneswar, Odisha, India*
[3]*Maharishi School of Engineering and Technology, Maharishi University of Information Technology, Uttar Pradesh, India*
[4]*Department of CSIT, Jain (Deemed-to-be University), Bangalore, Karnataka, India*

Abstract

Artificial intelligence (AI) is transforming industries by boosting productivity, enhancing decision-making, and fostering innovation across various sectors. The chapter delves into key AI technologies, including machine learning (ML), natural language processing (NLP), computer vision, and robotics, while highlighting the significant impact on various industrial applications. It also examines the tools that facilitate AI adoption, such as deep learning (DL) frameworks, AI platforms, and cloud computing services, all of which streamline the development and deployment of AI solutions. Industrial use cases in manufacturing, healthcare, finance, and transportation demonstrate how AI is optimizing processes, improving safety, and driving operational efficiency. The chapter also discusses issues like data privacy, integration with legacy systems, and the need for a skilled workforce while emphasizing AI's potential to promote sustainable growth. AI tools and technologies are being used by businesses more and more to improve customer

**Corresponding author*: kalpana.k@presidencyuniversity.in: ORCID: 0009-0004-5741-8210
Sasanka Choudhury: ORCID: 0000-0002-9195-084X
Awakash Mishra: ORCID: 0009-0002-5447-7499
Haripriya V.: ORCID: 0000-0003-2035-2452

Sudesh Yadav, Pethuru Raj, Satya Prakash Yadav and Victor Hugo C. de Albuquerque (eds.) Natural Language Processing in Mental Health Care: Methodologies and Clinical Practice, (27–38) © 2026 Scrivener Publishing LLC

experience, increase productivity, automate processes, scale operations, and offer individualized services and suggestions.

Keywords: Natural language processing, computer vision, artificial intelligence, robotics

3.1 Introduction

Artificial intelligence (AI) is a dynamic game-changer that has revolutionized all industries from automation to wipeout, improved decision-making, and increased process efficiencies. These days, several AI technologies, including machine learning (ML), natural language processing (NLP), computer vision, and robotics, have a big influence on corporate operations [1–3]. Organizations become ready for the development of revolutionary novel products and services and also a significant update of corporate processes at lower prices. Although these industries use AI to improve customer satisfaction, productivity, and data-driven decision-making, implementing highly intelligent AI systems requires human intervention [4]. Even though its significance is constantly emphasized, AI continues to perform poorly and faces several obstacles in various industries regarding the use of AI solutions. Other urgent problems enterprises face include integrating AI with legacy systems, managing large volumes of data while maintaining security and safety, and, most importantly, a shortage of workers with the necessary skills to create and implement AI-driven applications [5]. Addressing ethical concerns like AI model algorithmic bias and its effects on the environment computing is necessary for a sustainable AI deployment. It is essential to comprehend the main AI tools, technologies, and industrial applicationsto resolve these problems and permit the unfettered use of AI's capabilities [6]. The purpose of the chapter is to analyze various AI tools and technologies in the future by outlining their characteristics, capabilities, and real-world applications. How many firms are employing AI is explained in depth *via* the lens of its efficacy, value, and innovative features. Investigating how AI is changing sectors, determining the main factors that facilitate and impede its adoption in businesses, and examining the most effective implementation strategies are some of the goals of the research.

3.2 Key AI Technologies

Automation, efficiency, and intelligent decision-making are made possible by AI, which is reliant on a set of fundamental technologies to spread throughout several sectors. ML enables computers to learn from data to make judgments or predict events without explicit programming; it stands out among other technologies in the web of technologies. Large volumes of data are examined using ML algorithms to identify trends that support applications, such as automated decision making in the medical field or logistics, fraud detection in financial transactions, predictive maintenance in the manufacturing industry, and personalized recommendations. Thus, as algorithms continuously improve from new data input, the potential for increased accuracy and flexibility in the field of AI applications grows. Figure 3.1 shows the core components of AI technology.

It is used in chatbots, virtual assistants such as Siri and Alexa, real-time language translation, and sentiment analysis tools to evaluate customer feedback and market trends. Businesses use NLP to automate customer support, process documents, and improve user interaction through intelligent, conversational AI systems. DL has greatly improved NLP's ability to recognize contextual implications, tonal variations, and user intent, which smooths human–computer interaction. The technology is widely employed in many different applications, including autonomous cars for object detection and navigation, medical imaging for illness diagnosis, quality control

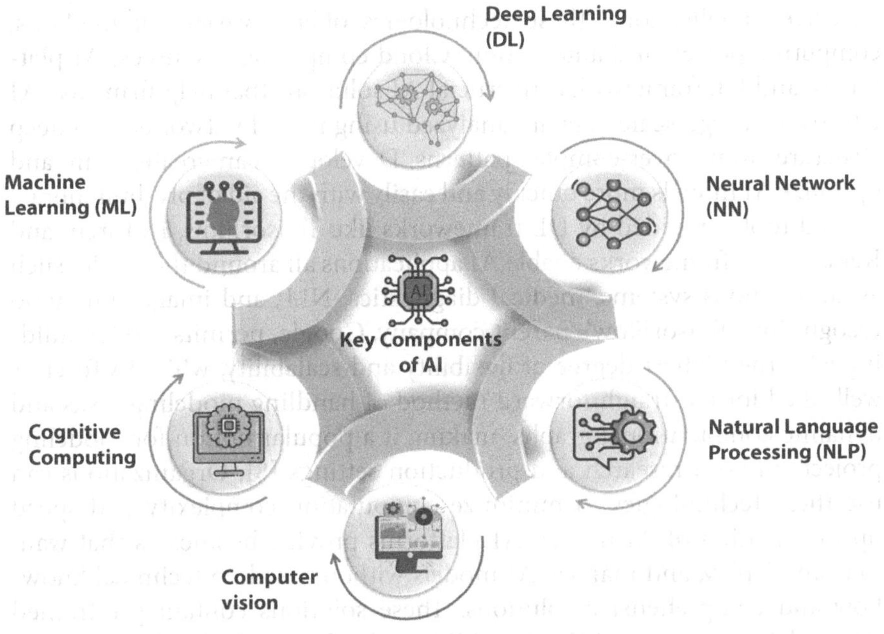

Figure 3.1 Core components of artificial intelligence technology. Source: https://medium.com/@hello_44141/key-technologies-behind-generative-ai-a-beginners-guide-e37ba5c38b6f.

in manufacturing facilities, and facial recognition for security authentication. AI-powered computer vision systems can perform automated inspections, increase security, and enhance diagnostic accuracy in healthcare by imitating human vision. Robotics builds intelligent machines that can do tasks on their own by combining AI with other mechanical systems. AI-driven robotic systems automate repetitive operations, improve operational efficiency, and increase accuracy, thereby continuously changing industries. Robots assist with product assembly and quality assurance in manufacturing. While robotic systems in healthcare help with surgery and patient care, logistics businesses are introducing AI-based robotic systems for storage automation and delivery services. Autonomous vehicles, in which AI assists self-driving automobiles in interpreting their environment and making decisions in real-time, are also based on the science of robotics.

3.3 AI Tools and Platforms

Strong tools and platforms support the endurance and maintenance stages of the AI solution life cycle and are crucial for the variables impacting the effective adoption of AI across sectors and its deployment [7]. To improve AI-driven applications, these technologies offer a variety of methods, computing power, and automation. Cloud computing resources, AI platforms, and DL frameworks are crucial AI solutions that help firms use AI effectively. Large-scale data are analyzed using neural networks with deep structures to uncover complex patterns. Developers can create, train, and optimize AI models more quickly and easily with the aid of pre-built libraries and tools provided by DL frameworks like TensorFlow, PyTorch, and Keras. These frameworks enable AI applications all around the world, such as autonomous systems, medical diagnostics, NLP, and image and audio recognition. TensorFlow's parent company, Google, permits model building with the highest degree of flexibility and scalability, while PyTorch is well-liked for its straightforward method of handling modeling tasks and dynamic computational graphs, making it a popular option for modeling projects in both research and production settings [8]. Organizations can use these technologies to minimize computation complexity and speed up the creation of AI models.AI platforms provide businesses that want to train, deploy, and manage AI models without needing technical know-how and comprehensive solutions. These solutions contain pre-trained AI models, automated ML (AutoML), and other tools for data processing, model evaluation, and deployment [9]. Some of the market's main AI platforms include Google AI Platform, Amazon SageMaker, IBM Watson, and Microsoft Azure AI.Amazon SageMaker also automates model training and tuning, making the deployment of AI solutions scalable and without the hassle of learning to program or use complex software. For its research solutions, IBM Watson is well known for its NLP and analytics capabilities for applications in the healthcare, finance, and customer service sectors. AI platforms have been said to lower development costs and also improve operational efficiency by providing scalable, cloud-based AI solutions. Google AI platform is said to have complete compliance with TensorFlow and BigQuery for a holistic environment when developing AI.Cloud computing plays a crucial role in AI implementation because it offers the high-performance computing power, storage, and infrastructure required to analyze massive data sets and run AI models effectively. Real-time applications like virtual assistants, fraud detection, predictive analytics, and automated decision-making are supported by cloud-based AI technologies. Another advantage of cloud services is that it can speed up deployment and improve accessibility while enabling large-scale AI model training. Cloud computing has made it possible for companies to reduce operational complexity and infrastructure expenses while advancing AI innovation.

3.4 Industrial Applications of AI

The AI is transforming industries through the optimization of standards, procedures, and operational effectiveness. AI technologies are used by businesses across many industries to improve decision-making, streamline operations, and foster innovation [10]. Through its most notable uses and advantages, the part would demonstrate how AI has affected manufacturing, healthcare, finance, and transportation. All machines are always on, and the thought of AI-vision autonomous-predictable existence in present and future possibilities understandings has made industrial operations different. Predictive maintenance powered by AI enables the manufacturer to address machine failures far in advance of their occurrence, allowing repair to be performed during scheduled production halts. According to load analysis, AI models can forecast equipment wear and tear based on sensor data and past performance, allowing for prompt replacement and repair. Similar to this, AI vision systems improve quality checks and are more accurate than humans in identifying product flaws during manual quality inspection. These automated inspection devices help minimize production waste while achieving consistency. Intelligent workflow optimization and process automation using AI-powered robotic devices also increase productivity while lowering the need for human intervention [11]. By automating repetitive processes like inventory management, assembly line labor, and logistics, robotic process automation (RPA) is leading the way in increasing operational efficiency and reducing costs. Customizing medication design and diagnosis through treatment is a key component of modernizing the healthcare system. AI-powered medical imaging evaluation gives radiologists additional patient-centered choices for precisely identifying illnesses, including cancer, neurological problems, and cardiovascular ailments. Even before the current AI revolution started, images like x-rays, MRIs, and CT scans were being examined for quick anomaly identification using DL techniques. AI is also embraced by personalized medicine, which compiles all patient data into a treatment plan supported by lifestyle data, medical history, and genetic configuration. A plan lowers unpleasant responses and increases the efficacy of medication. By analyzing large datasets, AI also guarantees very quick selection and identification of potential drug candidates in drug design, which guarantees a significant reduction in time and costs for any new drug development [12]. AI predictive analytics can maximize hospitals' administrative efficiency in patient scheduling, resource management, and health services demand forecasting. Figure 3.2 on health care and drug discovery shows the various applications of AI in health care, including personalized

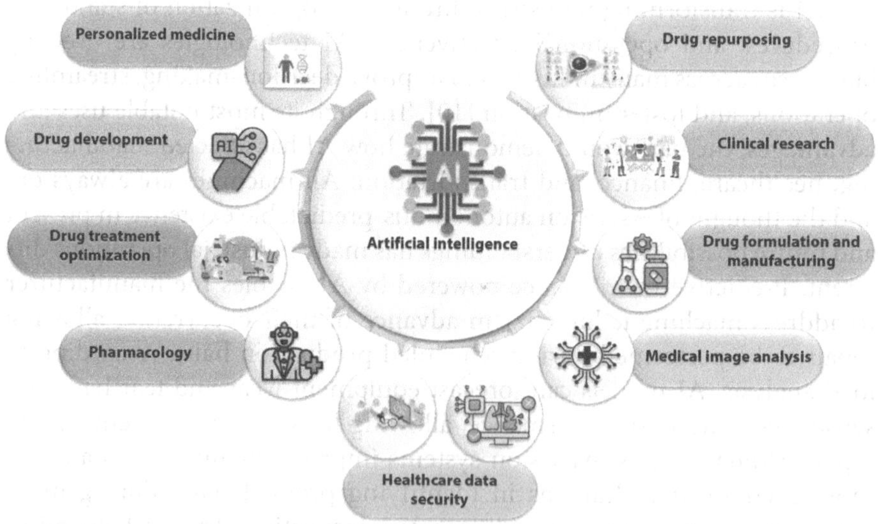

Figure 3.2 AI transforming healthcare and drug development. Source: [12].

medicine, drug discovery, clinical research, medical imaging, pharmacology, and security of health data. It increases the capabilities for treatment precision, expedites drug development, and enhances care.

➢ **Finance: AI-Driven Security, Risk Management, and Customer Service**

AI-powered applications are mostly utilized in banks for automated trading systems, risk analysis, and fraud detection. To assist banks and other financial institutions in identifying and stopping fraud and cybercrime, these fraud detection systems also examine transactional patterns and assist in real-time anomaly identification. AI-enabled risk assessment algorithms examine past financial data and concurrent market data to forecast future market movements, providing firms with an informed investment perspective that might lead to future profits. AI creates buy or sell signals in algorithmic trading, which are applied to the deal in milliseconds to maximize profit without involving human mistakes. AI chatbots and virtual assistants, which quickly answer consumer questions and automate loan approval procedures to provide a fully personalized banking experience, are examples of new features that are gradually improving customer service. These cutting-edge AI technologies improve operational efficiency, which in turn raises consumer engagement with the provided financial services. The advancements in automation, traffic management, and logistics efficiency have resulted in a sophisticated transformation of the transportation sector that appears comprehensive. To reduce human error and improve road safety, autonomous vehicles, such as trucks and self-driving cars, use intelligent algorithms on their computers to simulate human navigation and road conditions. These algorithms make decisions in real time. The trafficresearch recommends the optimal routes to save time and fuel, minimizing commuter congestion, using AI-driven optimization paths. Public transit, supply operations, and ride-sharing businesses are all effectively utilizing the technology. With AI-enabled predictive system maintenance, fleet managers can track the globe in real-time and keep their fleet operating with no disruption. Urban Planning: AI-enabled traffic analysis for city planners, infrastructure optimization, pollution reduction, and general mobility enhancement are all examples of AI in urban planning.

3.5 Challenges in AI Adoption

Crucial technological safeguards like encryption, anonymization, and verified data governance regulations should be added to the confidence in AI applications. Integrating AI with legacy systems is another major obstacle. Many industries suffer from outdated IT infrastructure, and traditional processes do not support the newest AI technology, particularly manufacturing, healthcare, and finance [13]. To integrate AI into these infrastructures, upgrades, cloud migrations, and interoperability solutions might be necessary. The adoption of AI is also hampered by resistance to change and the difficulty of switching from manual or semi-automated operations to AI-driven automation. When integrating AI, organizations need to have a well-thought-out strategic plan that emphasizes cooperation and gradual integration of AI with current business processes. Therefore, trust in AI applications should be supplemented with some important technical measures like encryption, anonymization, and validated data governance policies. One more significant challenge is legacy systems integration with AI. Quite a few sectors, especially manufacturing, health care, and finance, suffer from antiquated infrastructure and conventional workflows do not offer any support for the latest AI technologies. Upgrades, cloud migrations, and interoperability solutions can be required to incorporate AI into these environments. Resistance to change and complexity in transitioning from manual/semi-automated processes into AI driving automation-aspect also pose a problem of AI adoption. Organizations must have a proper strategic roadmap for implementing AI, focusing more on the incremental integration and collaboration between AI and existing business processes. The lack of skilled workers who can use AI is another significant obstacle to its deployment. For example, businesses require ML engineers, data scientists, and AI ethicists; the demand for these professionals outpaces the supply. In the fields of algorithm optimization, data analytics, and AI model building, many businesses are struggling to find qualified workers [14]. Therefore, businesses have to encourage and fund training initiatives, AI education, and partnerships with academic institutions. To close the talent gap and prepare a workforce that can exhibit AI advances, there must be a convergence of AI with transdisciplinary learning and applied training. The benefits generated would be those that enable companies to fully reap the rewards of using AI in a way that is efficient, safe, and moral.

3.6 AI's Role in Sustainable Growth

One of the primary factors propelling the adoption of sustainable development is AI environmental concerns thatcontinue to hound those who aspire to grow sustainably. AI technologies enable firms in the struggle against their environmental impact to remain lucrative and productive by increasing resource utilization, decreasing waste production, and even improving operational efficiency [15]. AI's significance for sustainability affects many sectors of the economy, from waste management to energy efficiency to responsible AI development. AI's major contributions are energy efficiency and AI. AI models employ data analysis to improve cities, homes, and companies' energy use. Smart grids prevent losses while maintaining power supply stability by monitoring energy demand and supply in real time. AI is also being used in smart buildings, where the lighting, heating, and cooling systems are intelligently adjusted according to the presence of occupants and environmental conditions to avoid unnecessary energy use [16]. AI-based predictive maintenance for industrial and manufacturing machinery aims to reduce energy loss by making sure the machinery runs as efficiently as possible. AI is revolutionizing the way renewable energy is produced. For example, it is possible to enhance the power efficiency of solar and wind energy through analytical prediction and real-time adjustments, making clean energy more affordable and reliable.AI-driven technologies play a key role in reducing waste in a variety of industries, particularly supply chain and retail, from consumer behavior and consumption patterns to preference-based purchasing trends. AI-powered inventory management systems predict demand to optimize stock levels and avoid overproduction and unimportant waste [17]. It is significant in the food industry as AI prevents food from spoiling by predicting consumption patterns and modifying orders appropriately. Similarly, AI-assisted manufacturing quality control can spot any faulty goods early in the production process. It prevents a great deal of material from being wasted in that way. Robotics and computer vision increase the accuracy of garbage categorization, ensuring that recyclable materials can be recycled and that objects are categorized correctly. Although AI designs are energy-intensive, due to the designs of the future, rely not only on a reduction in processing power but also on a significant reduction in carbon emissions. Large, expensive hardware is not necessary for AI algorithms that use less energy [18]. In addition, ethical AI principles aim to guarantee that algorithms, including digital ones, provide accountability, transparency, and fairness in decision-making to eradicate the associated problems of prejudice and discrimination in the systems. Sustainable data practices are also supported by responsible AI frameworks, reducing adverse environmental effects. Organizations that prioritize green computing and have sustainable AI infrastructure can profit from AI's technology advancements while adhering to international ethical and environmental norms.

3.7 Conclusion

The responsible deployment of AI requires that organizations adopt transparent, fair, and unbiased AI models aligned with regulatory guidelines to ensure user data and privacy protections; additionally, the organization must invest in upskilling the workforce to address the talent gap and have innovations nurtured under AI. AI is revolutionizing manufacturing, healthcare, finance, transportation, and many other industries by simply enabling businesses to optimize processes and performance through automation, forecasting, and smart decision-making. The other way businesses stay competitive is by effectively improving customer experiences and scaling the business with an AI context. Beyond the potential economic and environmental benefits, there is no doubt that AI applications and technology offer far-reaching advantages, particularly in terms of enabling future developments. Though AI offers many benefits, it also presents challenges that need answers in several areas, including ethics, private data, and the workforce itself. AI's integration with sustainable growth guarantees energy efficiency, waste reduction, and resource optimization, therefore, promoting both economic and environmental sustainability.

AI disclosure statement: The author confirms that no artificial intelligence (AI)-generated content or AI-assisted writing tools were used in the preparation of this chapter (including summaries and the abstract). All text, analysis, and conclusions are the result of the author's original work.

References

1. Devagiri, J.S., *et al.*, Augmented Reality and Artificial Intelligence in industry: Trends, tools, and future challenges. *Expert Syst. Appl.*, 207, 118002, 2022, https://doi.org/10.1016/j.eswa.2022.118002.
2. Raj, R., *et al.*, Analyzing the potential benefits and use cases of ChatGPT as a tool for improving the efficiency and effectiveness of business operations. *BenchCouncil Trans. Benchmarks Stand. Eval.*, 3, 3, 100140, 2023, https://doi.org/10.1016/j.tbench.2023.100140.
3. Bécue, A., Praça, I., Gama, J., Artificial intelligence, cyber-threats and Industry 4.0: Challenges and opportunities. *Artif. Intell. Rev.*, 54, 5, 3849–3886, 2021, https://doi.org/10.1007/s10462-020-09942-2.
4. Ebert, C. and Louridas, P., Generative AI for software practitioners. *IEEE Software*, 40, 4, 30–38, 2023, https://doi.org/10.1109/MS.2023.3265877.
5. Rožanec, J.M., *et al.*, Human-centric artificial intelligence architecture for industry 5.0 applications. *Int. J. Prod. Res.*, 61, 20, 6847–6872, 2023, https://doi.org/10.1080/00207543.2022.2138611.

6. Sjödin, D., *et al.*, How AI capabilities enable business model innovation: Scaling AI through co-evolutionary processes and feedback loops. *J. Bus. Res.*, 134, 574–587, 2021, https://doi.org/10.1016/j.jbusres.2021.05.009.
7. Fitria, T.N., Artificial intelligence (AI) in education: Using AI tools for teaching and learning process. *Prosiding Seminar Nasional & Call for Paper STIE AAS*, 2021, https://doi.org/10.1016/j.cmpb.2021.106541.
8. Ashok, M., *et al.*, Ethical framework for artificial intelligence and digital technologies. *Int. J. Inf. Manage.*, 62, 102433, 2022, https://doi.org/10.1016/j.ijinfomgt.2021.102433.
9. Gao, P., Li, J., Liu, S., An introduction to key technology in artificial intelligence and big data driven e-learning and e-education. *Mobile Netw. Appl.*, 26, 5, 2123–2126, 2021, https://doi.org/10.1007/s11036-021-01777-7.
10. Nahavandi, D., *et al.*, Application of artificial intelligence in wearable devices: Opportunities and challenges. *Comput. Methods Programs Biomed.*, 213, 106541, 2022, https://doi.org/10.1016/j.cmpb.2021.106541.
11. Rehman, A.U., *et al.*, Role of artificial intelligence in revolutionizing drug discovery. *Fundam. Res.*, 5, 3, 1273–1287, 2024, https://doi.org/10.1016/j.fmre.2024.04.021.
12. Yadav, S., *et al.*, Revolutionizing drug discovery: The impact of artificial intelligence on advancements in pharmacology and the pharmaceutical industry. *Intell. Pharm.*, 2, 3, 367–380, 2024, https://doi.org/10.1016/j.ipha.2024.02.009.
13. Nam, K., *et al.*, The adoption of artificial intelligence and robotics in the hotel industry: Prospects and challenges. *Electron. Mark.*, 31, 553–574, 2021, https://doi.org/10.1007/s12525-020-00442-3.
14. Wang, K., *et al.*, Analyzing the adoption challenges of the Internet of Things (IoT) and artificial intelligence (AI) for smart cities in china. *Sustainability*, 13, 19, 10983, 2021, https://doi.org/10.3390/su131910983.
15. Balsalobre-Lorente, D., *et al.*, Tourism, urbanization and natural resources rents matter for environmental sustainability: The leading role of AI and ICT on sustainable development goals in the digital era. *Resour. Policy*, 82, 103445, 2023, https://doi.org/10.1016/j.resourpol.2023.103445.
16. Mhlanga, D., Artificial intelligence in the industry 4.0, and its impact on poverty, innovation, infrastructure development, and the sustainable development goals: Lessons from emerging economies? *Sustainability*, 13, 11, 5788, 2021, https://doi.org/10.3390/su13115788.
17. Maiurova, A., *et al.*, Promoting digital transformation in waste collection service and waste recycling in Moscow (Russia): Applying a circular economy paradigm to mitigate climate change impacts on the environment. *J. Clean. Prod.*, 354, 131604, 2022, https://doi.org/10.1016/j.jclepro.2022.131604.
18. Yigitcanlar, T., Mehmood, R., Corchado, J.M., Green artificial intelligence: Towards an efficient, sustainable and equitable technology for smart cities and futures. *Sustainability*, 13, 16, 8952, 2021, https://doi.org/10.3390/su13168952.

4

NLP Techniques, Tools, and Use Cases of Speech Tagging

Kuppala Saritha[1]*, Prabhat Kumar Sahu[2], Trapty Agarwal[3] and Ganesh D.[4]

[1]*Department of Computer Science & Engineering, Presidency University, Bengaluru, Karnataka, India*
[2]*Department of Computer Science and Information Technology, Siksha 'O' Anusandhan (Deemed to be University), Bhubaneswar, Odisha, India*
[3]*Maharishi School of Engineering and Technology, Maharishi University of Information Technology, Uttar Pradesh, India*
[4]*Department of CSIT, Jain (Deemed-to-be University), Bangalore, Karnataka, India*

Abstract

Natural language processing (NLP) techniques, particularly part of speech (POS) tagging, are essential for understanding and processing natural languages. POS tagging involves classifying words, such as nouns, verbs, and adjectives, based on their contextual usage within a sentence. Despite significant advancements, challenges remain in improving accuracy, reducing false positives, and handling unknown words. Additionally, ambiguity in word meanings, influenced by sentence context, continues to be a major obstacle. Recent advancements in deep learning (DL) and machine learning (ML) have shown promise in addressing these challenges, resulting in more efficient and accurate POS taggers. This chapter analyzes various DL and ML-based techniques and tools employed in POS tagging, emphasizing the strengths and limitations of current methods. It also discusses the latest advancements in these approaches, focusing on their performance valuation metrics. Furthermore, the practical use cases of POS tagging in applications, such as information retrieval, sentiment analysis, and machine translation are explored.

**Corresponding author*: kuppala.saritha@presidencyuniversity.in; ORCID: 0000-0002-5799-2325
Prabhat Kumar Sahu: ORCID: 0000-0002-0460-9783
Trapty Agarwal: ORCID: 0009-0007-4081-4999
Ganesh D.: ORCID: 0000-0002-4220-3821

Sudesh Yadav, Pethuru Raj, Satya Prakash Yadav and Victor Hugo C. de Albuquerque (eds.) Natural Language Processing in Mental Health Care: Methodologies and Clinical Practice, (39–52) © 2026 Scrivener Publishing LLC

Finally, the chapter identifies existing research gaps and recommends further enhancing ML- and DL-based POS tagging tools.

Keywords: Natural language processing, part of speech tagging, deep learning, machine learning

4.1 Introduction

Artificial intelligence (AI) implements NLP as a subfield, enabling computers to interpret and generate human language with understanding. The discipline applies computational linguistics with ML and DL methods to process large volumes of data in its natural language form. The different NLP applications run on machine translation and sentiment analysis together with chatbots and speech recognition. The main objective of NLP is to connect human communication methods with machine computational abilities, which results in both more convenient and faster interactions [1]. POS tagging is an essential NLP operation because it tags words within texts with grammatical classifications. POS tagging enables machines to conduct successful syntactic analysis by providing structural understanding through the classification of words into grammatical categories. Multiple modern NLP systems use this approach for text-to-speech conversion, information retrieval and language translations. A key application of NLP is shown in Figure 4.1.

The process of POS tagging requires one of three principal execution approaches. It is a rule-based system, statistical systems, and DL-based systems. The language foundation consists of POS, which establishes word categories, according to sentence functions. The basic words that constitute the English language consist of eight main categories, which include nouns, pronouns, verbs, adjectives, adverbs, and prepositions, in addition to conjunctions and interjections. The term noun designates objects, locations, and individuals while pronouns function to take the place of those items. The expression of actions or states belongs to verbs and adjectives that describe the nature of nouns [2].

Several types of words known as adverbs modify verbs adjectives or other adverbs providing information about timing extent or method. The relationship between words becomes clear through prepositions, whereas conjunctions serve to link words or phrases together along with clauses. Interjections represent emotions that appear independently in sentences throughout a text [3]. Acquiring knowledge about POS helps learners achieve better grammar skills that enable them to construct clear sentences

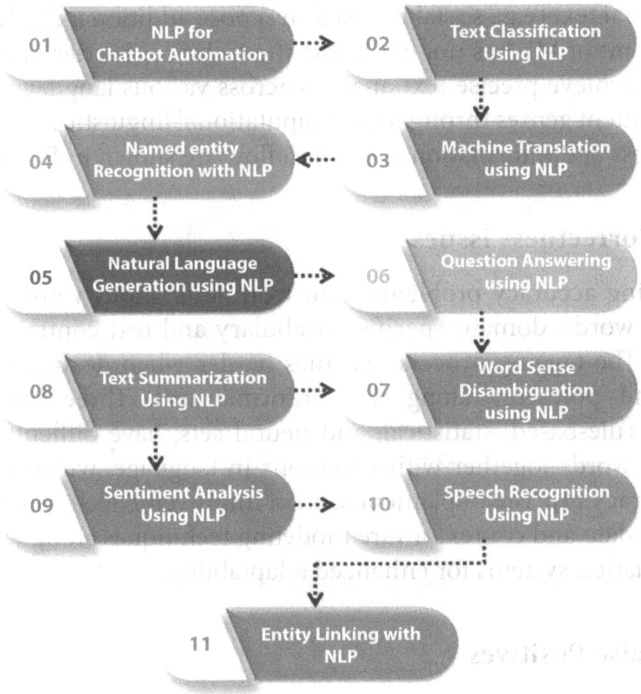

Figure 4.1 Key applications of NLP. Source: Own elaboration.

for effective communication. The mastery of POS enables writers to enhance their documents while it improves their reading capabilities and accelerates language development to establish essential communication skills.

4.2 Challenges in POS Tagging

The processing technique of POS tagging encounters multiple obstacles because of linguistic complexities combined with ambiguous situations. The tagging system faces significant issues because the same word can belong to different parts of speech depending on its context. For example, 'book' is a noun in 'Read the book' but the verb in 'Book a ticket'. The tagging of new or rare words lacking previously tagged information constitutes the main out-of-vocabulary (OOV) challenge. Multiple forms of inflected words in languages create problems for determining proper tags. The task of tagging becomes harder due to context sensitivity since the meaning of single word changes, according to surrounding words. Domain-specific language and informal text (e.g., social media slang) pose additional challenges. The advancement of ML has not overcome the technical barrier, which makes it hard to achieve precise text analysis across various language types and written content genres throughout computational linguistics. The POS tagging process and information extraction flow are shown in Figure 4.2.

4.2.1 Correctness Issues

POS tagging accuracy problems stem from ambiguous words as well as unknown words, domain-specific vocabulary and text contextual understanding. The tagging process becomes harder when dealing with homonyms and polysemy along with informal text. Three model types, including rule-based, statistical, and neural sets, have difficulties identifying rare words together with variations in language, which diminishes their accuracy [4]. The implementation of improvements depends on large annotated data and context-aware modeling techniques along with hybrid disambiguation systems for enhanced adaptability.

4.2.2 False Positives

A POS tagging error occurs when a system accidentally assigns an incorrect POS tag to one or more words. The main causes for wrong assignments

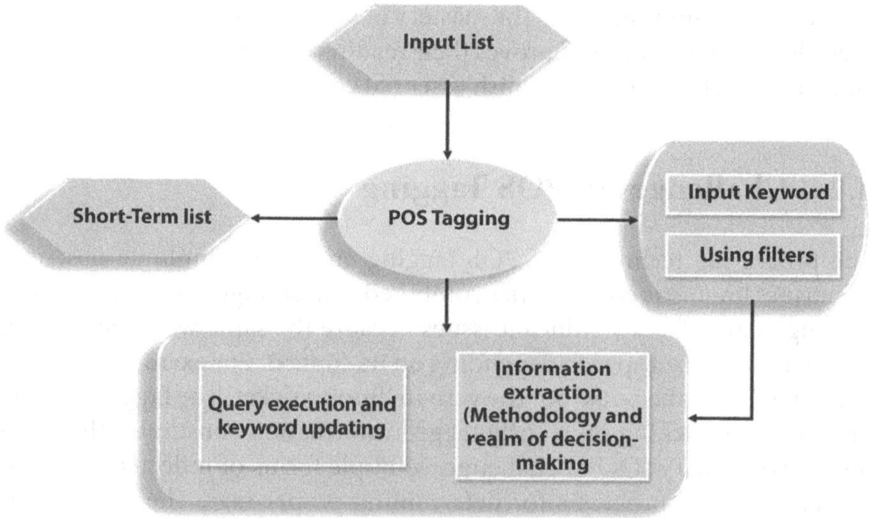

Figure 4.2 POS tagging process and information extraction flow. Source: Own elaboration.

include unpredictable words and uncertain contextual meanings as well as confusing word meanings. Three common obstacles for POS tagging systems include homonyms, such as 'run' being used as a noun and verb, domain-specific vocabulary and the inconsistent manner in which text is annotated [5]. The errors caused by ML models incorrectly interpreting syntax result in mistakes when processing NLP tasks, such as parsing and sentiment analysis.

4.2.3 Handling Unknown Words

The task of tagging unknown words presents difficulties in POS tagging since there is no available lexical information. Unknown words pose problems for rule-based and statistical models because they may be rare instances of specialized terminology or new technical terms. Three tagging strategies, which include morphological analysis and suffix-based tagging and the usage of neural models, function together to predict tags [6]. Accurate POS tagging benefits from contextual information and large data collections yet faces challenges from ambiguous words and limited word occurrences.

4.2.4 Ambiguity in Word Meanings

Word meaning ambiguity creates a substantial difficulty in tagging POS tags. Numerous words require multiple POS annotations based on contextual understanding since this affects the correct tagging process. The sentence "They can fish" contains dual possible interpretations for "can" as either a verb or a modal auxiliary verb and "fish" as either a noun or verb. In the sentence "Read the book" book takes the noun position, while in "Book a flight" it acts as a verb [7]. Statistical and rule-based taggers experience substantial problems with ambiguous word contexts, particularly when these contexts produce subtle indications. The challenges in POS tagging are shown in Table 4.1.

4.3 Advancement in ML and DL for POS Tagging

Advanced tools from ML and DL allow complex linguistic pattern recognition, which enhances both the accuracy and operational speed of POS tagging systems. A shift in POS tagging methodology occurred when explorers began replacing and improving previous rule-based and statistical methods, incorporating neural network-based approaches. The sequence-dependent

Table 4.1 Key challenges in POS tagging and their impact.

Challenge	Description
Unknown or Out-of-Vocabulary (OOV) Words	Some words, slang terms and domain-specific terms that should be tagged might not exist in the training data, therefore resulting in mistaken tagging.
Morphological Variations	The transformation of words based on tense and plural forms together with derivation patterns ("run" to "running") makes tagging more complicated.
Contextual Dependencies	The interpretation and application of words by rule-based systems become difficult because words need context from surrounding words to acquire meaning.
Multilingual and Code-Switching Issues	The utilization of multiple languages in one document alongside language intermixing during code-switching becomes a challenge for classic part-of-speech taggers.
Domain-Specific Variations	Organizations working in medical, legal, and technical domains need tagging models that specialize in their unique linguistic patterns.

Source: Own elaboration.

text processing requires Recurrent Neural Networks (RNNs) specifically long Short-Term Memory (LSTM) networks, to produce context-sensitive tagging results. The extended tagging performance of bidirectional long short-term memory Networks (BiLSTMs) operates by utilizing word sequences that extend from before to after the current sentence.

The transformer-based (bidirectional encoder representations from transformers) BERT model, along with other transformer models, transformed POS tagging through its self-attention functionality, which facilitates the analysis of entire sentences to extract profound contextual information [8]. Multiple pre-trained language models, including BERT, generative pre-trained transformer (GPT), and text-to-text transfer transformer (T5) received fine-tuning for POS tagging, thus their application requires less extensive labeled datasets, while they exhibit better accuracy in low-resource language settings. The combination of DL methods with linguistic characteristics and ordinary ML systems shows evidence of strengthening system performance, specifically when dealing with unidentified words and complex situations. Transfer learning procedures combined with large corporate training have improved practical model execution through model adaptation for specific languages and domains. Modern ML and DL approaches have effectively reduced traditional methodology challenges to create precise and flexible POS taggers, which boost numerous NLP programs, such as information retrieval and machine translation as well as sentiment analysis [9].

4.4 Various ML and DL Tools are Used for POS Tagging

Different ML and DL tools have been created to enhance POS tagging systems both in their accuracy and processing speed. The tools use statistical modeling together with contextual information and linguistic patterns to perform grammatical category identification of words.

ML-Based Tools

Conventional ML models are based on hand-designed features and statistical methods:

Hidden Markov Model (HMM): A statistical model that predicts POS tags from word sequences. It takes into account the likelihood of a word belonging to a particular tag given the preceding tags.

Conditional Random Fields (CRF): A sequence model that extends the HMM approach by examine the entire sequence instead of transitions independently.

Support Vector Machines (SVM): The POS tagging method that utilizes SVM applies supervised learning to tag words based on their contextual features for achieving precise part-of-speech labeling of sentence words.

Decision Trees and Random Forests: The POS tag classification process by Decision trees and Random Forests depends on learning word patterns from annotated text samples, which subsequently enhances accuracy through ensemble learning in Random Forests [10].

DL-Based Tools

With the evolution of Neural Networks, DL-based techniques have superseded classical ML methods:

Recurrent Neural Networks (RNN): Text sequences become better analyzed by RNNs for part of speech tagging because it handles sequential dependencies between words, which enhances accuracy rates within the text context.

LSTM: A sophisticated RNN variant that eliminates the vanishing gradient problem, achieving improved performance on long sequences.

Bidirectional LSTM (BiLSTM): The POS tagging accuracy benefits from BiLSTM because it processes sequences with past and future contexts to analyze nearby words.

Transformer-Based Models (BERT, GPT): Use attention mechanisms to capture word meanings in terms of sentence context, reaching state-of-the-art accuracy [11].

4.5 Performance Evaluation

The performance evaluation of POS tagging models relies on four main metrics, which include accuracy, precision, recall along with f1-score for assessment. Accuracy measures the correct tag identification of words, while precision and recall evaluate word-tagging correctness and word-tagging completeness separately. The analysis of misclassified tags becomes possible through the use of confusion matrices. Perplexity along with sequence labeling scores complements the performance analysis of sequence models. DL models, like BiLSTM and transformer-based approaches (e.g., BERT) outperform traditional methods due to better contextual understanding. Different organizations compare tagging performance [12]. Three main factors that affect overall evaluation include system speed and computational efficiency as well as the ability to handle ambiguous input and work across multiple language systems.

4.6 Application of POS Tagging

The applications of POS tagging include phonetic translation, where it supports grammatical framework analysis and sentiment evaluation through emotional adjective and verbal detection and information retrieval that enhances search results. The processing of natural language receives enhancement from POS tagging for its ability to refine linguistic operations in speech recognition and Chatbots as well as text-to-speech systems. Named Entity Recognition (NER) along with grammar-checking tools heavily depends on the implementation of POS tagging. The application of POS tagging in NLP is shown in Table 4.2.

Machine Translation

For machine translation (MT) software POS tagging functions as a tool for learning sentence arrangements, which leads to precise word match-ups and proper grammatical accuracy. The technology allows better translation handling through ambiguity solutions, which combined with noun and verb identification as well as adjective recognition leads to contextually precise translations of languages whose grammatical rules are sophisticated [13].

Table 4.2 Applications of POS tagging in NLP.

Application	Description
Speech Recognition	The system executes better speech-to-text recognition by interpreting word syntactic functions in spoken communications.
Text-to-Speech (TTS) Systems	The correct pronunciation and intonation emerge through identifying words through their Part-of-Speech (POS) tags such as "read" used as a noun or verb.
Chatbots & Virtual Assistants	The system improves ordinary conversation through its capability to correctly understand words and generate proper responses.
Grammar Checking & Text Correction	The program detects grammatical errors through its analysis of word categories together with sentence structures that ensure proper syntax.
Named Entity Recognition (NER)	The method enables NER by distinguishing proper and common nouns alongside other word categories to recognize entities consisting of names and locations together with organizations.

Source: own elaboration.

Sentiment Analysis

The sentiment analysis application of POS tagging uses word identification to recognize sentiment-bearing words, which can be adjectives (happy, sad) and verbs (love, hate) to identify text emotions. POS tagging improves the analysis of opinions in customer reviews alongside social media content and user feedback [14]. POS tagging analysis helps understand text context, which leads to better detection accuracy of text sentiment expression and emotion classification.

Information Retrieval

The information retrieval field benefits from POS tagging through search engines when it needs to improve understanding of search queries and document indexing processes. The application of POS tagging supports search result enhancement through the identification of essential search terms and verbs and nouns in texts [15]. POS tagging analyzes word categories to improve search accuracy, enhancing document ranking in Chatbots and recommendation systems and search platforms, like Google and Bing.

4.7 Recommendations for Enhancing ML and DL Based Tool for POS Tagging

Several enhancements should be applied to DL and ML-based tools. The use of extensive, diverse datasets enables models to establish generalizations between different languages, dialects, and content domains. The use of multilingual training together with cross-lingual embeddings produces improved tagging results for languages with limited resources. Detective models that use combination methods from statistical, rule-based, and DL approaches generate improved accuracy by assigning linguistic rules and information-driven techniques [16]. The tagging system based on Bidirectional Long Short-Term Memory with Conditional Random Fields (BiLSTM-CRF) or Transformer-based structures helps dissolve interpretation issues and boost sequence guesswork accuracy. Self-supervised learning models achieve better results when their parameters are optimized through POS tagging tasks, although labeling data remains minimal.

The application of knowledge distillation generates lightweight yet powerful models for real-time usage because it reduces computational expenses. Adversarial training improves robustness through its ability to show models' inconsistent or confusing inputs during training.

Training strategies become more effective through error analysis and augmentation techniques, which help discover routine misclassifications [17]. Devices working with AI-driven POS taggers will gain more trust when deployment systems include built-in clarity and interpretability features. Specialized domain tuning enables better accuracy when annotating medical or legal texts, among others. Accurate POS tagging tool development benefits from better evaluation standards and standardized analysis frameworks, which enable reliable assessment and development of efficient tools [18]. Humans can achieve increased accuracy and robustness in different NLP tasks through the application of the proposed recommendations.

4.8 Conclusion

A significant problem exists regarding ambiguous word analysis because words display multiple meanings that depend on the context. Given their ability to understand contextual meaning BERT along with GPT demonstrates limited performance when encountering unusual special words. Multilingual POS tagging poses issues because models educated in a single language struggle to learn different linguistic structures in various languages. The majority of POS tagging models experience difficulties with low-resource languages because their training takes place mainly in high-resource languages such as English.

Using syntactic and semantic rules from external sources together with DL architectures would produce better performance. The main challenge with DL-based POS taggers is their lack of clarity along with interpretability because neural network models operate as unexplainable black boxes. Further exploration needs to analyze and find ways to enhance the transparency of these models. Additional work needs to be performed on POS tagging solutions for informal text, including social media posts and conversational AI, because of their inconsistent grammar and slang terminology. The implementation of solutions to these gaps will boost the accuracy together with the adaptability and efficiency of POS taggers.

AI disclosure statement: The author confirms that no artificial intelligence (AI)-generated content or AI-assisted writing tools were used in the preparation of this chapter (including summaries and the abstract). All text, analysis, and conclusions are the result of the author's original work.

References

1. Pathak, D., *et al.*, Part-of-speech tagger for Bodo language using deep learning approach. *Nat. Lang. Process.*, 31, 2, 1–15, 2024, https://doi.org/10.1017/nlp.2024.15.
2. Zhou, H., *et al.*, Bridging pre-trained language models and hand-crafted features for unsupervised POS tagging. *arXiv preprint arXiv: 2203.10315*, 2022, https://doi.org/10.48550/arXiv.2203.10315.
3. Safitri, D., Students' Grammatical Errors in Essay Writing: A Pedagogical Grammar Reflection. *Int. J. Lang. Educ.*, 5, 2, 74–88, 2021.
4. Cing, D.L. and Soe, K.M., Improving accuracy of part-of-speech (POS) tagging using hidden markov model and morphological analysis for Myanmar Language. *Int. J. Electr. Comput. Eng.*, 10, 2, 2023, 2020, https://doi.org/10.11591/ijece.v10i2.pp2023-2030.
5. Sulaiman, N.R. and Siraj, M.M., South China Sea Conflicts Classification Using Named Entity Recognition (NER) and Part-of-Speech (POS) Tagging. *Int. J. Innov. Comput.*, 10, 1, 41–48, 2020, https://doi.org/10.11113/ijic.v10n1.255.
6. Ullah, S., *et al.*, Part-of-Speech Tagging for Balochi Language: A Data driven application of Conditional Random Fields. *Asian Bull. Big Data Manag.*, 4, 229–236, 2024.
7. AlMousa, M., Benlamri, R., Khoury, R., A novel word sense disambiguation approach using WordNet knowledge graph. *Comput. Speech Lang.*, 74, 1013375, 2022, https://doi.org/10.1016/j.csl.2021.101337.
8. Bani, R., *et al.*, Deep neural networks for part-of-speech tagging in under-resourced Amazigh. *Rev. Intell. Artif.*, 37, 3, 611, 2023, https://doi.org/10.18280/ria.370310.
9. Neerudu, P.K.R., *et al.*, On robustness of finetuned transformer-based nlp models, *arXiv preprint arXiv: 2305.14453*, 2023, https://doi.org/10.48550/arXiv.2305.14453.
10. Ali, M., Khan, M., Alharbi, Y., A conditional random field based approach for high-accuracy part-of-speech tagging using language-independent features. *PeerJ Comput. Sci.*, 10, e25775, 2024, https://doi.org/10.7717/peerj-cs.2577.
11. Fetahi, E., *et al.*, Neural Network and Transformer-Based PoS Tagger for Low Resource Languages. *2024 International Conference on Information Technologies (InfoTech)*, IEEE, 2024, https://doi.org/10.1109/InfoTech63258.2024.10701401.
12. Bonilla, J.E., Spoken Spanish PoS tagging: gold standard dataset. *Lang. Resour. Eval.*, 59, 2, 1–30, 2024, https://doi.org/10.1007/s10579-024-09751-x.
13. Perera, R., *et al.*, Improving english to sinhala neural machine translation using part-of-speech tag, *arXiv preprint arXiv:2202.08882*, 2022, https://doi.org/10.48550/arXiv.2202.08882.

14. Kanakkahewa, K.H.S.L., Mohotti, W.A., Subhashini, L.D.C.S., PoS tag-based Attention for Feature Selection in Sentiment Analysis, 2023, https://doi.org/10.21203/rs.3.rs-3151544/v1.
15. Altuncu, E., *et al.*, Improving Performance of Automatic Keyword Extraction (AKE) Methods Using PoS-Tagging and Enhanced Semantic-Awareness, *arXiv preprint arXiv: 2211.05031*, 2022, https://doi.org/10.48550/arXiv.2211.05031.
16. Imani, A., *et al.*, Graph-based multilingual label propagation for low-resource part-of-speech tagging, *arXiv preprint arXiv: 2210.09840*, 2022, https://doi.org/10.48550/arXiv.2210.09840.
17. Hoojon, R. and Nath, A., BiLSTM with CRF Part-of-Speech Tagging for Khasi language. *2023 4th International Conference on Computing and Communication Systems (I3CS)*, IEEE, 2023, https://doi.org/10.1109/I3CS58314.2023.10127278.
18. Imran, H. and Sani, M., Natural Language Understanding in Big Data: AI-Driven Approaches for Automated Insights, 2025.

Part 2

AI AND MACHINE LEARNING FOR BEHAVIORAL UNDERSTANDING

5

Classification and Regression Algorithms in Behavioral NLP

Selvaraj Poornima[1]*, Manoranjan Parhi[2], Smita Mishra[3] and Raghavendra R.[4]

[1]*Department of Computer Science & Engineering, Presidency University, Bengaluru, Karnataka, India*
[2]*Centre for Data Science, Siksha 'O' Anusandhan (Deemed to be University), Bhubaneswar, Odisha, India*
[3]*Maharishi School of Business Management, Maharishi University of Information Technology, Uttar Pradesh, India*
[4]*Department of CSIT, Jain (Deemed-to-be University), Bangalore, Karnataka, India*

Abstract

Behavioral natural language processing (NLP) leverages machine learning (ML) to analyze human language and extract psychological, emotional, and cognitive elements. This technology plays a pivotal role in behavioral NLP by enabling sentiment analysis, mental health detection, personality predictions, and behavior forecasting. Classification and regression algorithms are at the core of behavioral NLP, facilitating the analysis of textual data and the prediction of human behavioral outcomes. These algorithms categorize text into predefined classes, detect emotional states, and predict continuous emotional measures, such as distress or trait probabilities. Support vector machine (SVM), Logistic regression (LR), and Naïve Bayes (NB) were assessed for the classification and regression algorithm. Applications in areas like sentiment and emotion analysis have been proven useful for detecting stress and improving mental health through the analysis of social media and online interactions. Additionally, behavioral NLP models utilize regression techniques to quantify emotional intensity and evaluate mental health

**Corresponding author*: poornima.s@presidencyuniversity.in; ORCID: 0000-0002-9348-5371
Manoranjan Parhi: ORCID: 0000-0002-1625-6022
Smita Mishra: ORCID: 0000-0003-1199-9342
Raghavendra R.: ORCID: 0000-0003-3538-2339

Sudesh Yadav, Pethuru Raj, Satya Prakash Yadav and Victor Hugo C. de Albuquerque (eds.) Natural Language Processing in Mental Health Care: Methodologies and Clinical Practice, (55–68) © 2026 Scrivener Publishing LLC

through linguistic indicators. Despite the advancements, it also addresses the nuances of emotions and expands model sensitivity for better cross-cultural and multilingual emotional analysis. GBM has attained higher values in the dataset features of anger and fear, and SVM has observed higher values in the dataset feature of joy. The integration of classification and regression algorithms into behavioral NLP offers new possibilities for enhancing human–computer interaction, social media engagement, and mental health tracking.

***Keywords*:** Natural language processing, machine learning, human language, classification and regression algorithms

5.1 Introduction

The vital importance of natural language processing (NLP) technology allows machine learning (ML) to adopt text processing abilities, which enable its analysis of human language. Text analytics that extract psychological data together with emotional and cognitive elements constitute the core subfield of NLP called behavioral NLP. Behavioral NLP analyzes linguistic cues to conduct basic sentiment analysis operations, and it enables both mental health detection and personality predictions as well as conducts behavior forecasting [1]. Behavioral NLP's core techniques include classification and regression algorithms, which are used to anticipate human behavioral outcomes using textual data-based analysis [2]. Using algorithms as a basic framework enables scientific and professional users to group linguistic design elements for analyzing structured and unstructured data [3]. Behavioral NLP functions with various supportive categories of classification and regression algorithms that it needs for its operations. The purpose of classification models lies in the ability to assign text content into established categories, which proves effective in detecting sentiments, identifying purposes, and monitoring mental health scenarios [4, 5]. An algorithm using classification techniques detects whether a social media post shows either positive or negative expressions or a neutral tone. A regression model predicts continuous measurements, which include emotional distress strength and psychological trait probabilities [6, 7]. The predictive features enable Behavioral NLP to achieve precise measurement of human emotional responses and behavioral patterns. Behavioral NLP depends on regression algorithms to determine values continuously that behavioral variables can reach. These quantification models evaluate behavior through linguistic signs to compute engagement ratings together with stress evaluation and mental health condition strength [8, 9]. Various challenges exist despite the proven success of classification and regression algorithms in Behavioral NLP implementations [10]. The ability to develop quality Behavioral NLP to assign correct annotations faces resistance from behavior-related data as expert labeling requirements and privacy consent limitations exist. The use of classification along with regression algorithms in Behavioral NLP has become necessary to recognize human conduct through language interpretation and prediction [11, 12]. The objective of this chapter is to classify and evaluate the appearance of various regression of NLP behavior, as this includes comparing the effectiveness of fear, anger, and joy.

The remaining of this chapter was articulated as follows: Section 5.2 highlights literature reviews, Section 5.3 shows materials and methods, Section 5.4 depicts results and discussion, and Section 5.5 provides the conclusion.

5.2 Methodology

Through the assessment of linguistic patterns, Behavioral NLP delivers information about human emotional responses and cognitive processes as well as decision formation. Algorithms for classification and regression create frameworks for analysis to carry out the identification of sentiment along with mental health assessment and personality prediction tasks. ML models benefit from the merger between explainable artificial intelligence (AI) systems, which improve both understanding and ethical transparency of behavioral analysis. Figure 5.1 illustrates the flow of the methodology.

5.2.1 Data Collection

The Emotion Dataset Raw [13] is a labeled dataset created for NLP activities including sentiment analysis and emotion recognition. There are two columns in it: Text: Phrases or sentences that convey a range of ideas and situations. Emotion: Labels for the main emotion that is conveyed in the text, such as fear, anger, sadness, and joy. This dataset can be utilized in chatbots, recommendation systems, and mental health monitoring applications, and it offers a basis for training and assessing algorithms for emotion categorization. It works well for improving NLP models for emotion recognition and supervised learning techniques.

5.2.2 Classification and Regression Algorithm

This chapter investigates comprehensive behavioral NLP classification and regression models to detect emotions consisting of fear together with joy

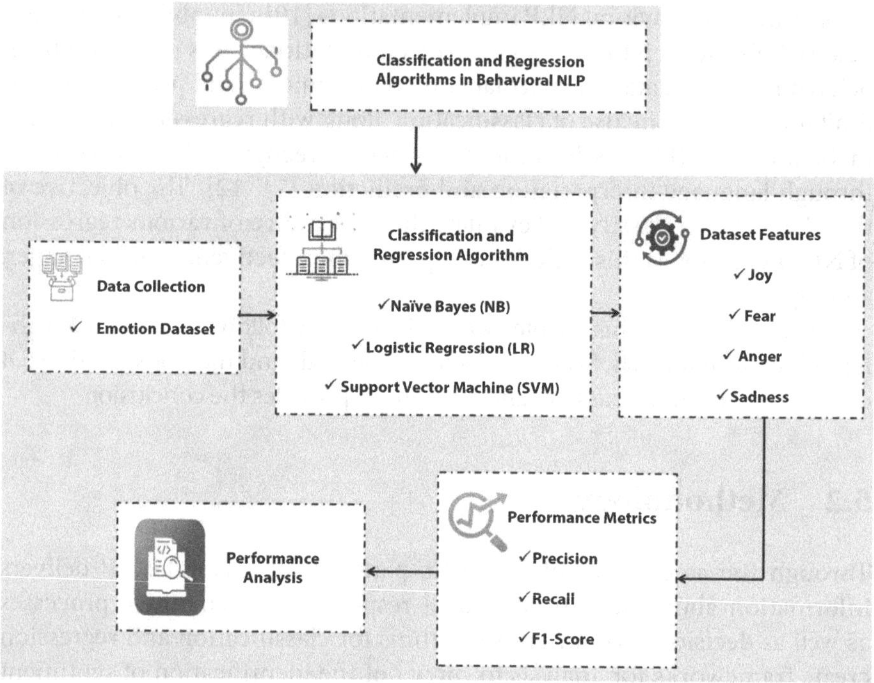

Figure 5.1 Flow of methodology. Source: Own elaboration.

and anger during this section. Such frameworks enhance sentiment analysis methods together with emotion detection capabilities, thus improving user interactions with technology-based systems. ML algorithms with complex methods evaluate behavioral data to detect and sort emotional states. The method achieves better human-system interaction through its exact detection and processing of emotional cues. High-dimensional data management with real-world use case-dependent performance requires the system to integrate multiple models that address the overfitting problems. The main goal is to establish an advanced emotion detection solution that can optimize human communication, specifically with sentiments and behavioral analysis systems.

5.2.3 Naïve Bayes (NB)

This chapter uses NB classification and regression algorithms in Behavioral NLP to predict behavioral labels assigned class indicators and binary feature indicators, with the assumption of conditional independence among features within categories. Prior probabilities for class membership and feature presence are represented to estimate *via* prior distributions. Non-informative priors are applied to class hyper parameters, while feature hyper parameters, influenced by feature density in the emotion data, play a critical role in model flexibility and accuracy in Behavioral NLP. Despite assuming feature independence, the algorithms show strong performance, especially for smaller categories. NB shows that well-tuned feature hyper parameters improve performance, while excessively high values reduce accuracy. The NB feature model assumes that, for each class, the features are independently distributed, as shown in the Equations (5.1) and (5.2).

$$O(D = d, W = w|\Psi = \varphi, \Theta = \vartheta\theta) = \prod_{j=1}^{m} O(D_j = d_j|\Psi = \varphi)$$
$$\prod_{i=1}^{n} O(W_{j,i}, w_{j,i}|D_j = d_j, \Theta_i = \theta_i) \quad (5.1)$$

$$O(D_m = l|W = w, D_{obs} = d_{obs})\alpha(\alpha_l - m_l')\prod_{i=1}^{n}(\beta_s - m_{ilk}') \quad (5.2)$$

5.2.4 Support Vector Machine (SVM)

The SVM functions as a vital component in Behavioral NLP to execute classification and regression operations. The SVM system performs text or behavioral pattern classification efficiently to identify emotional states or to analyze sentiments and social behavior from linguistic input. The mathematically optimal hyperplane created by an SVM efficiently classifies data between different groups to successfully identify positive versus negative content. SVM functions as a regression model besides classification because it engages in the prediction of variable behavioral outcomes like forecasting user engagement or stress identification through linguistic signs. This technique proves beneficial for Behavioral NLP due to its ability to process high-dimensional spaces and handle non-linear data through kernel tricks, as shown in Equation (5.3), which illustrates the SVM classifier.

$$\min_{x,a,\zeta} \frac{1}{2}||x||^2 + D\sum_{j=1}^{m}\zeta_j$$

Where,

$$z_j(x^S w_j + a) \geq 1 - \zeta_j, \zeta_j \geq 0, \forall j \quad (5.3)$$

5.2.5 Logistic Tegression (LR)

The LR model has been widely used to develop efficient Behavioral NLP classification and regression models that detect emotions consisting of anger and joy, in addition to fear. ML techniques enable this chapter to develop enhanced sentiment analysis methods and emotion recognition capabilities, thus improving human-computer communication. Classifying data items is the goal of the LR algorithm. In LR, the target variable is binary, meaning it includes data categorized as 1 or 0, which in this case denotes an efficient Behavioral NLP classification and regression model. ALR model provided in Equation (5.4) below serves as the foundation for the logistic regression procedure. Figure 5.2 presents the architecture of LR.

$$O(z=1|\omega)=\frac{1}{1+f^{-(\sum_{j=0}^{n}\omega_j w_j)}} \tag{5.4}$$

This chapter assesses the detection of emotional states between anger and fear and joy by classification and regression algorithms in Behavioral NLP systems. This solution utilizes SVM together with LR and NB to enhance its sentiment analysis and emotion detection capabilities. This chapter aims to improve human-computer interaction systems by the accurate detection of emotional cues that are present in text-based data.

5.3 Result

In the context of behavioral NLP, this chapter focuses on categorizing and evaluating the effectiveness of various regression methods; this includes

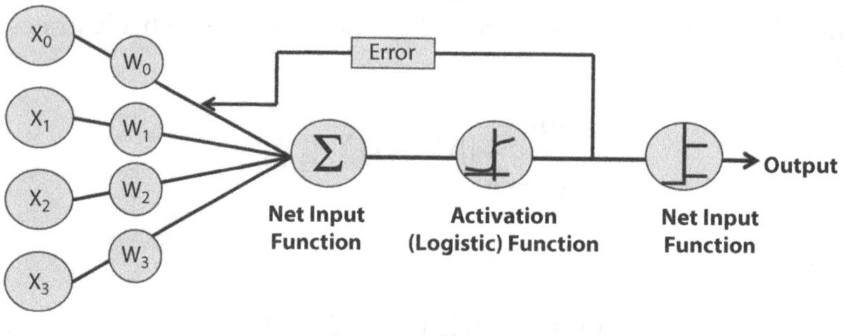

Figure 5.2 Architecture of LR. Source: https://sebastianraschka.com/faq/docs/softmax_regression.html.

comparing the effectiveness of fear, anger, joy and sadness. Precision, recall, and F1-score are crucial for assessing NLP models in behavioral analysis. Precision ensures accurate emotion detection by reducing false positives, while recall minimizes missed emotional instances. The F1-score combines both metrics, providing a balanced performance measure, especially for imbalanced emotional data, and ensuring reliable and sensitive emotional analysis.

5.3.1 Emotional Analysis in Behavioral NLP: Anger, Fear, Joy and Sadness

Behavioral NLP analyzes emotions, such as fear, anger, joy and sadness, to identify emotional states by processing word decisions, syntactic structureclassification and regression algorithms. Analyzing anger through NLP depends on finding strong language patterns and identifying negative emotions, but fear detection relies on emotional verbal indicators and strength measurements. Joy operates as a positive emotion to evaluate emotional messages in social relationships, mental health platforms, and digital communities. The analysis of emotions supports applications that include customer response evaluation as well as mental health tracking and improvements to AI systems. Table 5.1 shows the values of emotional analysis in behavioral NLP: anger, fear, joy, and sadness.

5.3.1.1 Anger

The domain of NLP in this chapter examines anger as an emotion that emerges from text-based datasets. Language patterns that indicate anger contain forceful words together with negative emotions and phrases that display aggressive or frustrated behavior. The main goal of Behavioral NLP is to analyze written communication's emotional indicators, which help to detect both anger presence and measure its strength and effect on message content. Emotional responses, which include anger, affect both the linguistic content and tonal delivery of messages by causing authors to use stronger, forceful language that becomes hostile. Emotional behavior analysis through this chapter of these linguistic indicators helps NLP models understand the formation patterns of human anger in communication. Such language analysis serves numerous applications, which include measuring consumer opinions and examining mental health practices through angry communication interpretation for more appropriate therapeutic interventions. Figure 5.3 presents the values of performance metrics in the feature of anger.

Table 5.1 Emotional analysis in behavioral NLP: anger, fear, joy, and sadness.

Methods	Anger			Joy			Fear			Sadness		
	P	R	F1	P	R	F1	P	R	F1	P	R	F1
NB [14]	0.80	-	-	0.83	-	-	0.33	-	-	0.50	-	-
SVM [15]	0.94	0.87	0.90	0.92	0.87	0.89	0.83	0.81	0.82	0.84	0.87	0.85
LR [16]	0.63	0.55	0.59	0.62	0.76	0.68	0.74	0.65	0.69	0.59	0.57	0.58

Note: Precision as P, Recall as R, F1-Score as F1

Source: Own elaboration

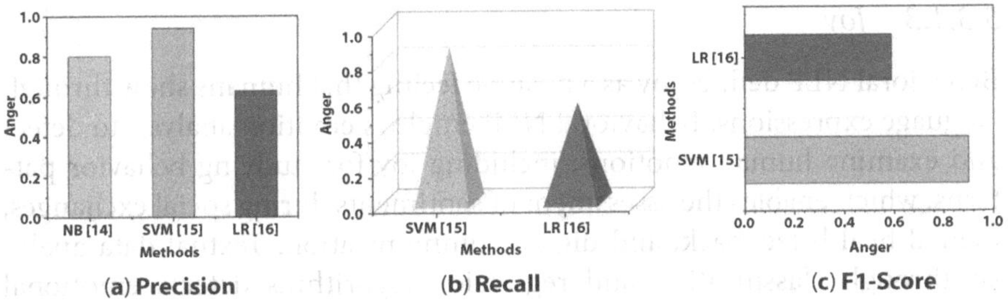

Figure 5.3 Graphical representation of anger in performance metrics. Source: Own elaboration.

5.3.1.2 *Fear*

Behavioral NLP analyzes fear together with several basic emotions that can be identified from text-based indicators. NLP fear analysis depends on identifying verbal indicators that exist with written language by word selection as well as voice and syntax patterns. Textual data classification and regression algorithms require these patterns to analyze and predict behavioral states through textual information. Text classification operates through the process of applying labels to distinct text examples to differentiate fear expressions from other emotions, such as joy or sadness. The prediction of emotional intensity levels requires using regression algorithms to produce continuous fear measurement results. Social media activities and forums as well as transcribed communication can be accessed through Behavioral NLP combined with these algorithms to reveal how emotions influence interchanges. The analysis of fear-based interactions enhances multiple fields through behavioral monitoring of mental health along with security functions, customer service, and marketing implementation, which measure the impact of fear on human behavioral choices and strategic communication plans. Figure 5.4 presents the values of performance metrics in the feature of fear.

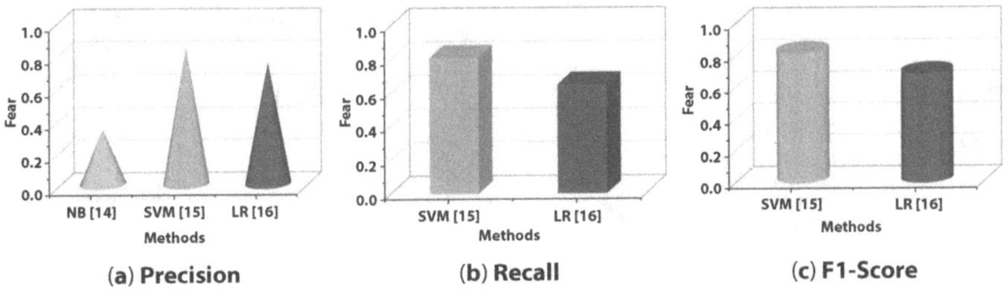

Figure 5.4 Graphical representation of fear in performance metrics. Source: Own elaboration.

5.3.1.3 Joy

Behavioral NLP defines joy as a positive feeling that humans show through language expressions. Behavioral NLP employs emotion analysis to detect and examine human emotions, including joy for studying behavior patterns, which enables the assessment of sentiments during social exchanges, mental health feedback, and digital communication. Textual data analysis through classification and regression algorithms detects emotional expressions of joy that assign proper classifications and create predictions about these emotional states. Text classification algorithms evaluate text to identify emotions from a set of defined categories through word selection combined with textual meaning and syntactic construction. Through regression algorithms, users can gain detailed emotional insights because these models determine the number and strength of emotions present in textual content. Behavioral NLP utilizes these algorithms to both the existence of joy and how it relates to human connections and the sources that trigger it. The analysis generates benefits for customer feedback evaluation as well as mental health tracking and AI-based system enhancement when employed to detect and measure joy in text communication. Figure 5.5 presents the values of performance metrics in the feature of joy.

5.3.1.4 Sadness

Behavioral NLP analyzes sadness by pinpointing linguistic markers for negative emotions, such as sorrow, loss, or hopelessness. The markers are typically evident in word selection, tone, and syntax that express a feeling of loss or despondency. NLP models use classification and regression techniques to identify and measure melancholy in text according to its presence and intensity. This affective analysis becomes important in diverse

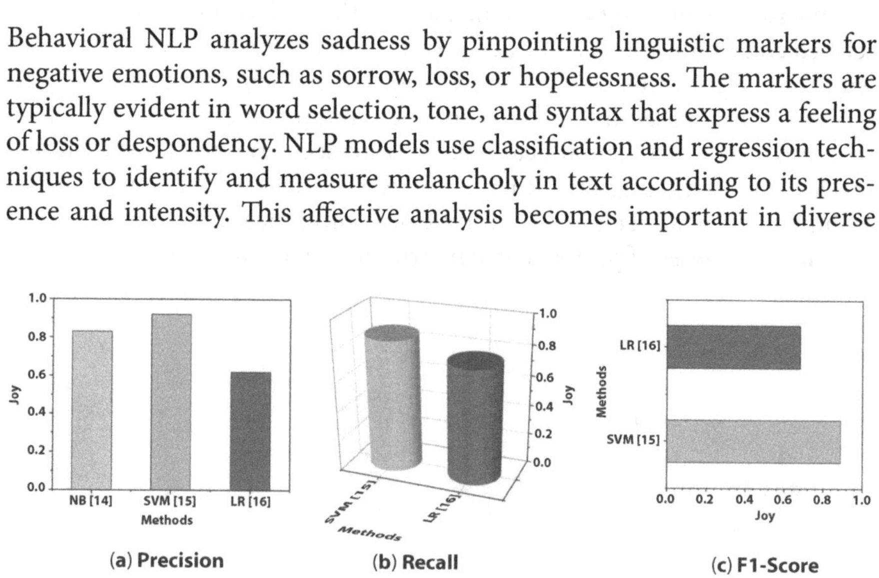

Figure 5.5 Graphical representation of joy in performance metrics. Source: Own elaboration.

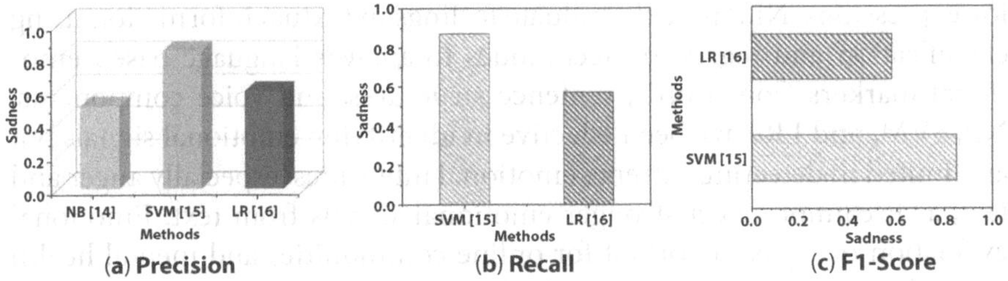

Figure 5.6 Graphical representation of sadness in performance metrics. Source: Own elaboration.

applications, including mental health counseling, customer complaint analysis, and content filtering, where the analysis of sadness can improve interventions, reactions, and communication strategies as a whole. Figure 5.6 presents the values of performance metrics in the feature of sadness.

5.3.1.5 Discussion

Behavioral NLP is essential for understanding emotional dynamics. By examining linguistic patterns, word selections, syntactic structures, and vocal tonality, classification and regression techniques allow NLP models to identify emotional states. To quantify the intensity of hostile language and the emotional impact of conversations, it is necessary to identify language that produces force to detect rage. To evaluate behavior patterns in the areas of marketing, security, and mental health, linguistic signals, and intensity ratings are essential in identifying fear. Increased emotional intensities in detecting anger and fear are plagued by the inability of SVM, LR, and NB to identify strong emotional signals from text documents. These approaches have lower efficiency in detecting extreme levels of emotions, which leads to lower performance in terms of accuracy, precision, recall, and F1-score. LR and SVM also illustrate the limited ability to measure the level of strength in intense emotions. NB, despite its simplification assumptions, also performs comparatively well in emotional state detection but finds it difficult to detect extreme expressions of emotions, especially in the case of high intensity.

5.4 Conclusion

Behavioral NLP gathers vital information regarding human emotions using text-based communication measurement, which identifies anger, fear, and joy expressions. NLP models evaluate feelings in textual information using classification and regression techniques to analyze language-based emotional markers from words, sentence structures, and voice components. NB, SVM, and LR have been effective in identifying emotional signals but are limited in detecting extreme emotional intensities, especially anger and fear, as it cannot detect stronger emotional signals from text. Emotional evaluation of joy is important for online communities and mental health use, aiding in the analysis of social relationship dynamics. Emotion analysis is important in customer feedback systems, mental health monitoring platforms, and AI system design. Nonetheless, emotion detection is hindered by the complexity of emotions and differences in language, which can lead to misinterpretations or elementary mistakes. Improvements in the future should aim to increase NLP model sensitivity to subtle emotional cues while extending capabilities for multilingual and cross-cultural settings to enable more extensive emotional analysis.

AI disclosure statement: The author confirms that no artificial intelligence (AI)-generated content or AI-assisted writing tools were used in the preparation of this chapter (including summaries and the abstract). All text, analysis, and conclusions are the result of the author's original work.

References

1. Naithani, K. and Raiwani, Y.P., Realization of natural language processing and machine learning approaches for text-based sentiment analysis. *Expert Syst.*, 40, 5, e13114, 2023, https://doi.org/10.1111/exsy.13114.
2. Zhen, Y., Luo, J.-D., Chen, H., Prediction of academic performance of students in online live classroom interactions—an analysis using natural language processing and deep learning methods. *J. Soc. Comput.*, 4, 1, 12–29, 2023, https://doi.org/10.23919/JSC.2023.0007.
3. Tanana, M.J., *et al.*, How do you feel? Using natural language processing to automatically rate emotion in psychotherapy. *Behav. Res. Methods*, 53, 5, 1–14, 2021, https://doi.org/10.3758/s13428-020-01531-z.
4. Dikmen, I., *et al.*, Automated construction contract analysis for risk and responsibility assessment using natural language processing and machine learning. *Comput. Ind.*, 166, 1042515, 2025, https://doi.org/10.1016/j.compind.2025.104251.
5. Mah, P.M., Analysis of artificial intelligence and natural language processing significance as expert systems support for e-health using pre-train deep learning models. *Acadlore Trans. AI Mach. Learn.*, 1, 2, 68–80, 2022, https://doi.org/10.56578/ataiml010201.

6. Pruneski, J.A., *et al.*, Natural language processing: using artificial intelligence to understand human language in orthopedics. *Knee Surg. Sports Traumatol. Arthrosc.*, 31, 4, 1203–1211, 2023, https://doi.org/10.1007/s00167-022-07272-0.
7. Sen, O., *et al.*, Bangla natural language processing: A comprehensive analysis of classical, machine learning, and deep learning-based methods. *IEEE Access*, 10, 38999–390445, 2022, https://doi.org/10.1109/ACCESS.2022.3165563.
8. Ullah, W., *et al.*, Identification of depressing tweets using natural language processing and machine learning: Application of grey relational grades. *J. Radiat. Res. Appl. Sci.*, 18, 1, 101299, 2025, https://doi.org/10.1016/j.jrras.2025.101299.
9. Kumar, A., *et al.*, An evolutionary study on technologies for polyethylene terephthalate waste recycling using natural language processing. *Comput. Chem. Eng.*, 95, 109011, 2025, https://doi.org/10.1016/j.compchemeng.2025.109011.
10. Ma, L., Ou, W., Lee, C.S., Investigating consumers' cognitive, emotional, and behavioral engagement in social media brand pages: A natural language processing approach. *Electron. Commer. Res. Appl.*, 54, 1011795, 2022, https://doi.org/10.1016/j.elerap.2022.101179.
11. Nijhawan, T., Attigeri, G., Ananthakrishna, T., Stress detection using natural language processing and machine learning over social interactions. *J. Big Data*, 9, 1, 33, 2022, https://doi.org/10.1186/s40537-022-00575-6.
12. Bhatt, P., *et al.*, Machine learning for cognitive behavioral analysis: datasets, methods, paradigms, and research directions. *Brain Inf.*, *10*, 1, 18, 2023, https://doi.org/10.1186/s40708-023-00196-6.
13. Dataset, https://www.kaggle.com/datasets/rikinzala/emotion-dataset-raw.
14. Machová, K., *et al.*, Detection of emotion by text analysis using machine learning. *Front. Psychol.*, 14, 11903265, 2023, https://doi.org/10.3389/fpsyg.2023.1190326.
15. Albu, I.-A. and Spînu, S., Emotion detection from tweets using a BERT and SVM ensemble model, *arXiv preprint arXiv:2208.04547*, 2022, https://doi.org/10.48550/arXiv.2208.04547.
16. Moulya, S. and Pragathi, T.R., Mental health assist and diagnosis conversational interface using logistic regression model for emotion and sentiment analysis. *J. Phys. Conf. Ser.*, 2161, 1, 012039, IOP Publishing, 2022, https://doi.org/10.1088/1742-6596/2161/1/012039.

6

Deep Learning Algorithms for Behavioral Understanding of Mental Health

Balamurugan S.[1]*, M. Chandra Sekhar[2], Jitendriya Biswal[3], Savita[4] and Sarbeswar Hota[5]

[1]Department of CSIT, Jain (Deemed-to-be University), Bangalore, Karnataka, India
[2]Department of Computer Science & Engineering, Presidency University, Bengaluru, Karnataka, India
[3]Department of Psychiatry, IMS and SUM Hospital, Siksha 'O' Anusandhan (Deemed to be University), Bhubaneswar, Odisha, India
[4]Maharishi School of Engineering and Technology, Maharishi University of Information Technology, Uttar Pradesh, India
[5]Department of Computer Applications, Siksha 'O' Anusandhan (Deemed to be University), Bhubaneswar, Odisha, India

Abstract

Deep learning (DL), which provides insights into diagnostic and intervention options, has become a potent tool for comprehending behavioral patterns linked to mental health disorders. However, challenges, such as data scarcity, moral concerns, and interpretability of DL models limit their widespread application in mental health work. This chapter aims to develop an effective DL-based framework for analyzing mental health conditions and predicting psychological outcomes. Mental health datasets sourced from Kaggle were utilized, providing structured and unstructured data on psychological conditions. Various DL methods, including autoencoder, generative adversarial networks (GAN), convolutional neural networks (CNN), long short-term memory (LSTM), gated recurrent unit (GRU),

**Corresponding author*: balamurugan.s@jainuniversity.ac.in; ORCID 0000-0002-9437-3662
M. Chandra Sekhar: ORCID 0009-0009-9983-9976
Jitendriya Biswal: ORCID 0000-0003-4343-4880
Savita: ORCID 0000-0002-4826-4721
Sarbeswar Hota: ORCID 0009-0006-0921-8323

Sudesh Yadav, Pethuru Raj, Satya Prakash Yadav and Victor Hugo C. de Albuquerque (eds.) Natural Language Processing in Mental Health Care: Methodologies and Clinical Practice, (69–84) © 2026 Scrivener Publishing LLC

and bidirectional LSTM (Bi-LSTM), were analyzed to assess their effectiveness in predicting mental health outcomes. The results demonstrated that DL models effectively captured behavioral patterns, with some methods exhibiting higher accuracy and robustness than others. These results demonstrate the possibilities of DL for mental health analysis, but they also emphasize the necessity to resolve issues with data and enhance model interpretability for real-world applications.

Keywords: Deep learning, mental health, long short-term memory (LSTM), gated recurrent unit, convolutional neural network, generative adversarial networks

6.1 Introduction

Deep learning (DL) algorithms have received much interest for their applicability in identifying behavioral causes associated with different mental health disorders. These models use data from speech, facial expressions, social media, and other physiological signs and symptoms to identify products of depression, anxiety, and stress among other mental conditions [1]. Through the use of large data samples, these algorithms can identify other hidden behavioral patterns that could not be easily identified using conventional status and state assessments, which can be useful in monitoring the mental health status of a patient in real time to conduct an early intervention [2]. Through its modern wearable devices, it became possible to monitor vital signs in a continuous manner, which allows DL algorithms to evaluate heart rate variability, sleep and movement patterns, as well as others to evaluate the mental health status [3]. Moreover, machine learning using sourced data, such as text, voice, or physiological data, improves the rate of prediction, hence improving the understanding of mental health conditions [4]. However, several challenges prevent the increased application of DL for mental health analysis. An important issue that could be encountered is data quality and availability. Most of the datasets concerning mental health are small, contain private information, and are skewed in distribution, making it challenging to train a model without imposing bias. This privacy and consent can also be regarded as ethical dilemmas when collecting and manipulating personal and behavioral data [5]. Another limitation is model interpretability; DL algorithms are opacity and their workings cannot be easily described, thus making it hard when making clinical decisions. Also, the problem of generalization persists, as the models are developed on particular datasets, and can behave differently on others due to cultural, linguistic, and behavioral differences [6]. Moreover, some of the DL methods are computationally intensive, especially in real-time applications under limited computational resources [7].

Objective: To develop a psychological outcome prediction framework through DL-based mental health condition analysis. Different DL models receive evaluation to determine their ability in detecting behavioral patterns and enhancing mental health assessment methods.

6.2 Methodology

Research used datasets related to mental health from the Kaggle platform that include both structured and unstructured data on psychological disorders. Various DL models, such as convolutional neural networks (CNN), Autoencoder, generative adversarial networks (GAN), gated recurrent unit (GRU), bidirectional long short-term memory (Bi-LSTM), and long short-term memory (LSTM), were used for behavioral pattern identification and mental health prognosis.

6.2.1 Dataset

For this research, three datasets were assessed: the mental health dataset [8], which was obtained from Kaggle and includes a variety of variables about demographics, survey responses, and mental health disorders. The sentiment analysis for the mental health dataset [9], which includes textual data intended to comprehend sentiment variances in mental health conversations, was also used. Additionally included was the depression and mental health data analysis dataset [10], which included important metrics related to stress, depression, and mental health. These datasets facilitate DL applications for mental health evaluation by offering insightful information about emotional states and behavioral patterns.

6.2.2 DL Techniques for Mental Health Behavior Analysis

Machine learning (ML) develops the algorithms to find the patterns in the improved features of data but the traditional approach to the preparation involves a lot of feature engineering. DL is a branch of ML that encompasses the capability of succeeding through end-to-end training by mapping the inputs with a set of outputs through multi-layers. These are increasingly used in the behavioral understanding of mental health.

6.2.3 Convolutional Neural Network (CNN)

The CNN uses the extracted features (*EF*) as inputs. The pooling, convolutional, and entirely linked layers make up the well-liked DL model.

By employing several modules to examine multiple mapping features, the convolutional layer enables the identification of behavioral patterns associated with mental health. Through the feature map, each neuron is connected to its neighbors. Figure 6.1(a) depicts the CNN architecture. The feature values in the e_k layer for a given location e_a, e_b are computed as follows in Equation (6.1).

$$H_{e_a,e_b,e_c}^{e_k} = w_{e_c}^{e_k{}^T} * EF + F_{e_c}^{e_k} \tag{6.1}$$

In any case, $w_{e_c}^{e_k{}^T}$ is the weight during training, and $e_k{}^T$ is the weight. $F_{e_c}^{e_k}$ represents the bias term. By introducing non-linearity, the activation function makes it possible to quickly identify complicated mental health indicators. Equation (6.2) illustrates the activation value calculation process.

$$\alpha_{e_a,e_b,e_c}^{e_k} = \phi(H_{e_a,e_b,e_c}^{e_k}) \tag{6.2}$$

Pooling layer: By lowering dimensionality, the pooling layer refines behavioral features by down sampling. To extract the most pertinent information, the pooling function @(.) works with the activation values shown in Equation (6.3).

$$\lambda_{e_a,e_b,e_c}^{e_k} = @(\alpha_{e_a,e_b,e_c}^{e_k}), \forall(e_p,e_q) \in \Omega_{e_p,e_q} \tag{6.3}$$

The difference between expected and actual behavioral patterns is represented by the CNN loss function, which is calculated by Equation (6.4).

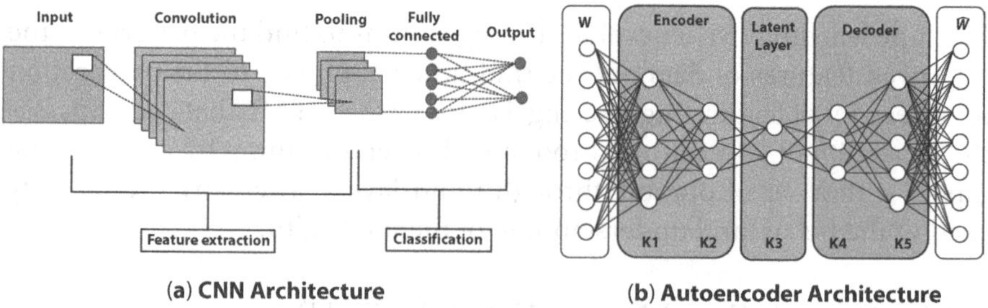

Figure 6.1 Schematic Structure of (a) CNN & (b) autoencoder. Source: (a) https://www.upgrad.com/blog/basic-cnn-architecture/(b) https://cendikiaishmatuka.medium.com/autoencoder-anomaly-detection-for-vibration-data-6c1dff82fd43

$$Loss = \frac{1}{D_e} \sum_{e_q=1}^{C_e} l(\theta, \lambda_{e_q}, OT_{e_q}) \tag{6.4}$$

Where θ contains parameters about $w_{e_c}^{e_k^T}$ in addition to $F_{e_c}^{e_k}$ whereas the amount of input-output relations is represented by D_e. The CNN outputs, target labels, and input features are provided by F_{e_q}, as well as OT_{e_q}, in turn. The CNN result helps with a mental health assessment by offering insights into behavioral patterns.

6.2.4 Autoencoder

An autoencoder is referred to as a feed-forward artificial neural network that has the same target output and input. An information bottleneck due to a very small hidden layer in an autoencoder network forces the network to reduce the data into a low-dimensional form. This modeling approach can be used to analyze behavioral trends and mental disorders by extracting key latent features from raw psychological or physiological data. Figure 6.1 (b) depicts the autoencoder architecture. The vector of the hidden unit activity g, for a basic autoencoder with a single hidden layer is provided by Equation (6.5).

$$g = e(X_f.b + bias_f) \tag{6.5}$$

where X_f is a parameter matrix, $bias_f$ is a vector of bias parameters, and e is the activation function (this approach utilizes the logistic sigmoid function). The decoding function is then used to translate the hidden representation of behavioral data back into the space of $\hat{b}$ are shown in Equation (6.6).

$$\hat{b} = e(X_c.g + bias_c) \tag{6.6}$$

The bias factors are expressed by $bias_c$, while the data decoding matrix is represented by X_c. Equation (6.7) illustrates how the autoencoder's parameters are learned using stochastic gradient descent to minimize the reconstruction error, which is represented as the Mean Squared Error (MSE) among b and $\hat{b}$.

$$MSE(b,\hat{b}) = || b,\hat{b} ||_2^2 = || b - (X_c.g + bias_c) ||_2^2 \tag{6.7}$$

The autoencoder discovers a compressed description of mental health-related behavioral tendencies when the hidden layer has less dimension than b. Through learning to map the data onto its first l principal components, an autoencoder with l linear hidden units will produce a structured description of the leading behavioral inclinations. The most salient behavioral contrasts are retained when the decoded data matrix is the same as the matrix. More latent layers enhance the ability of the autoencoder to represent complex behavioral and cognitive trends, whereas non-linear hidden units enable it to recognize more complex mental states.

6.2.5 Long Short-Term Memory

It is used to learn patterns in psych states by breaking down time series data, i.e., speech patterns, mood changes, and physiologic signs. Every LSTM unit has a memory cell and three gates are involved, which are the output gate, forget gate, and input gate; these entrances assist in controlling data flowing in and out of the unit. The cell state is a memory of the position it passed through and its value is calculated by the point-wise multiplication and sigmoid activation to decide what should be forgotten or remembered. With this method, knowledge concerning behavior gets retained while irrelevant information gets forgotten to enhance the mental health evaluations. The use of the forget gate allowed the LSTM unit to determine which behavioral data should be erased from memory. It comprises of the previous cell state D_{s-1}, the current input w_s, and the prior hidden state g_{s-1}. For each of the elements of g_{s-1} it produces a number lying in the range [0, 1], with 0 suggestive of forgetting, and 1 of recalling. This is a calculation of the forget gate as presented in Equation (6.8).

$$e_s = \sigma(X_e.[g_{s-1}, w_s] + a_e) \tag{6.8}$$

A sigmoid layer, also known as the entrance gate layer, selects which values should be updated in the state, while a tangent hyperbolic layer generates a candidate value D_s. The input gate is an essential component of the LSTM unit because it determines what new data should be kept in the cell state. This is because no new data enters the memory cell when the input entrance is closed, preserving important behavioral characteristics until the values need to be updated. The input gate uses the following equations to update the cell state by merging new and retained data, as illustrated in Equations (6.9–6.11).

$$j_s = \sigma(X_j.[g_{s-1}, w_s] + a_j) \tag{6.9}$$

$$\ddot{D}_s = \tanh(X_D.[g_{s-1}, w_s] + a_D) \tag{6.10}$$

$$D_J = e_s * g_{s-1} + j_s * \ddot{D}_s \tag{6.11}$$

Finally, the behavioral information that has been processed and should be sent as output is decided by the output gate. The sigmoidal layer controls which slice of the cell state is pertinent for output, and the output gate activation and the *tanh* transformed cell state are multiplied element-wise to produce the final hidden state g_s. This guarantees the dissemination of only significant behavioral knowledge. The definition of the output gate is shown in Equations (6.12–6.13).

$$P_s = \sigma(W_{jP}.[g_{s-1}, w_s] + a_O) \tag{6.12}$$

$$g_s = P_s * \tanh(D_s) \tag{6.13}$$

Because it can capture enduring patterns of behavior in consecutive data, such as mood changes, sleep cycles, or mental responses over time, LSTM networks are very valuable in mental health work. By the use of this feature, LSTMs give a strong tool for the prediction and understanding of patterns of mental health based on previous behavior.

6.2.6 Generative Adversarial Networks

GAN is a neural network model that imitates specific distributions in the adversarial setting to generate new data. Its two main components are a discriminator (H) and a generator (C). Where the discriminator is trained to identify whether a sample is constructed artificially or is present in the actual data distribution, the generator maps a sample of a specified data distribution. Using acquired distributions of data to produce accurate approximations of psychological state and symptoms, this adversarial process allows GANs to imitate complex patterns of behavior in mental illness. To mislead H, a sample from random noise y is generated with $C.H$ classifies real samples and samples generated with C. The discriminator gets a reward for identifying data correctly, and the generator gets a reward for generating samples that can fool H. Until Nash equilibrium is reached, C and H cannot improve further; this loop continues. Here, let $C(t)$ stand for the likelihood that a sample comes from actual behavioral data rather than the generator. Both C and H use a minimax game to maximize their performance, which is stated as follows in Equation (6.14).

$$\underset{H}{min}\,\underset{C}{\min}\,U(C,G) = F_{t\sim O_{data}}(t)[\log C(t)] + F_{y\sim O_y}(Y)\left[\log\left(1 - C\left(H(y)\right)\right)\right] \tag{6.14}$$

This allows for their behavioral assessment and analysis by virtue of GANs ability to generate fake mental illness data such as voice intonation, affect display, or physiological characteristics.

6.2.7 Gated Recurrent Unit

It consists of the current value of memory content of the flip-flop, a reset signal and an update signal. These elements allow the GRU unit to selectively pass or store information that is crucial in determining a pattern, especially in applications involving mental related behavior. This is the update gate denoted by y_s which regulates the quantity of the past data that is to be stored. The weight matrix, X_y is then obtained from the input value, w_s, and the previous hidden state, g_{s-1}, for each step. The data is computed with a sigmoidal activation function, which gives an output ranging from 0 to 1. It decreases the influence of the vanishing gradient problem by prescribing how much of the old data has to be retained with this gate. Working similarly, the reset gate, represented as q_s, determines how much of the previous data will be forgotten. The current contents of the memory, represented by g_s are calculated by performing a Hadamard product operation between q_s and g_{s-1}, making sure that only pertinent historical data is retained. Following that, the summation is subjected to a tanh activation function. The last memory representation in the GRU unit, represented by the symbol g_s, combines data from the current and previous states. Current input is prioritized if y_s is close to 1, while historical information is highlighted if y_s is close to 0. These operations are defined by the following Equation (6.15).

$$y_s = \sigma(X_y.[g_{s-1}, w_s])$$

$$q_s = \sigma(X_q.[g_{s-1}, w_s])$$

$$\tilde{g}_s = \tanh(X.[q_s g_{s-1}, w_s])$$

$$g_s = (1 - y_s)g_{s-1} + y_s.g_s \tag{6.15}$$

The vanishing gradient problem has been solved by both LSTM and GRU models in a way that they can emulate long-distance dependencies in behavioral data. GRU, in contrast, is computationally cheaper and possesses fewer parameters, and hence it can be applied to real-time monitoring of mental well-being. GRUs is capable of detecting abnormal speech behaviors, and emotional fluctuations, and enhance person-oriented mental health assessment by finding temporal relationships in behavioral data.

6.2.8 Bidirectional LSTM

Sequential behavioral data can be analyzed by RNNs, however because of memory constraints and the vanishing gradient issues, RNNs have trouble handling long-term dependencies. These problems are addressed by LSTM networks, which use memory cells controlled by three gates: output forget f_t, and input i_t. The historical behavioral patterns that should be kept or discarded are decided by the forget gate, as shown in Equation (6.16).

$$f_t = \sigma(W_t[g_{t-1}, y_t] + c_i) \tag{6.16}$$

The input gate modifies pertinent data are illustrated in Equation (6.17).

$$i_t = \sigma(W_t[g_{t-1}, y_t] + c_i) \tag{6.17}$$

The following is used to update the original cell state D_t is depicted in Equation (6.18).

$$D_t = f_t \odot D_{t-1} + i_t \odot tanh(W_d[g_{t-1}, y_t] + c_d) \tag{6.18}$$

Lastly, the next concealed state is determined by the output gate are shown in Equation (6.19).

$$g_t = o_t \odot \tanh(D_t) \tag{6.19}$$

By processing behavioral data both forward and backward, Bi-LSTM enhances LSTM and captures trends in mental health from the past and future are illustrated in Equation (6.20).

$$g_t = \overrightarrow{g_t} \oplus \overleftarrow{g_t} \tag{6.20}$$

Bi-LSTM is more useful for mental health analysis since it improves knowledge of emotional states, stress levels, and cognitive health.

6.3 Results

The results proved that it is possible to train DL models that are capable of detecting behavioral characteristics related to mental diseases. Variations in accuracy and robustness among the models could be observed, meaning that certain models performed better than the others. These results show that framework recognition is crucial for improved performance and that DL can be used to investigate mental disorders.

Experimental Setup: The experiment is conducted on a high-performance computing system equipped with an NVIDIA RTX 3090 GPU, 64GB RAM, and 2TB SSD storage to ensure efficient DL model training and testing. The framework employs TensorFlow/PyTorch, leveraging optimized batch processing and real-time data augmentation techniques.

6.3.1 Comparative Analysis of DL-Based Approaches

To assess the effectiveness of DL-based methods in behavioral analysis of psychological health to recognize and classify mental health trends. The measures such as F1 score, accuracy, recall, and precision account for each method's specific characteristics. Table 6.1 displays the results of the accurate, precise, recall and f1 score assessment. Figure 6.2 indicates the accuracy level and the F1 score.

Table 6.1 Performance comparison of DL methods for behavioral understanding of mental health.

Methods	Accuracy (%)	F1- Score (%)	Precision (%)	Recall (%)
GAN [11]	91.6	92.1	-	-
Autoencoder [12]	96.3	92.9	95.9	95.6
BiLSTM [13]	78	79	-	-
CNN [13]	64	65	-	-
GRU [14]	62	64	-	-
LSTM [14]	76	77	-	-

Source: Own elaboration

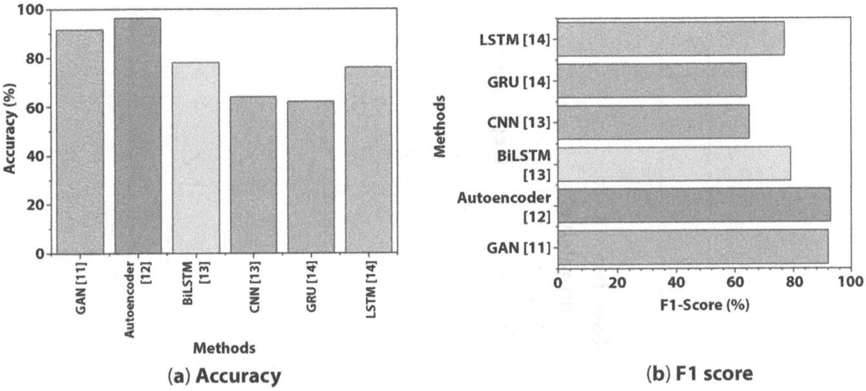

Figure 6.2 Comparative outcome of DL-based models for mental health behavior recognition. (a) Accuracy. (b) F1 score. Source: Own elaboration.

Accuracy: The behavioral understanding of mental health describes a model's ability to properly identify and classify psychological health-linked behavioral patterns. The accuracy ratio derives from dividing observed cases by the correct predictions of mental health statuses. The autoencoder model attained the highest accuracy at 96.3%, demonstrating its superior ability to classify mental health statuses effectively.

Precision: The percentage of true positives out of all the expected positive samples is the degree of correctness in the behavioral assessment of mental health. This addresses the points that it is able to identify such behaviors while minimizing false positives. The autoencoder model exhibited the highest precision at 95.9%, ensuring that most identified cases were indeed positive instances.

Recall: The percentage of accurately detected cases among all actual mental health disorders is measured by recall in behavioral comprehension of mental health. It shows how effectively the model can identify certain behaviors while having a small number of false negatives. With the maximum recall of 95.6%, the autoencoder model proved to be effective in detecting activities linked to mental health with little misclassification.

F1 Score: By computing the harmonic mean of precision and recall, it assesses a model's total performance and guarantees a fair evaluation of predictive capacity. The model successfully reduces false positives and false negatives when the F1 score is high. With the greatest F1 score of 92.9%,

Table 6.2 Behavioral pattern analysis in mental health using DL-based methods.

References	Methods	Patterns of behavior in mental health					
		Schizophrenia	Bipolar disorder	Anxiety	Post-Traumatic Stress Disorder (PTSD)	Obsessive-Compulsive Disorder (OCD)	Depression
[17]	CNN	✓	✓	✓	–	✓	✓
[18]	Autoencoder	✓	–	–	–	–	✓
[19]	LSTM	–	–	–	–	–	
[20]	GAN	✓	–	–	✓	✓	
[21]	GRU	✓	✓	✓	✓	–	✓
[22]	BiLSTM	✓	✓	–	✓	–	✓

Source: Own elaboration

the autoencoder model proved to be highly effective in correctly identifying behavioral patterns associated with mental health.

6.3.2 DL-Based Methods for Analyzing Behavioral Patterns in Mental Health Disorders

It emphasizes the application of DL-based methods in investigating behavioral patterns with mental health diseases [15]. Table 6.2 depicts the analyzing outcome of behavioral patterns in mental health. CNN has been largely employed to mine spatial features from behavior data to identify depression, anxiety, bipolar disorder, OCD, schizophrenia, and PTSD. Autoencoders have targeted mainly schizophrenia and depression using unsupervised learning. While GANs enhance recognition by generating synthetic data for depression, schizophrenia, and PTSD, LSTM models effectively learn sequential dependencies to recognize anxiety and depression. GRU models work effectively on sequential data and can recognize a range of diseases, including PTSD and bipolar disorder. Using BiLSTM increases the capacity to recognize PTSD, schizophrenia, bipolar disorder, and depression. These methods emphasize how critical DL is in enhancing behavioral analysis-based mental health evaluation [16].

6.3.3 Discussion

The comparative analysis emphasizes the efficacy and limitations of various DL-based methods in modeling behavioral patterns associated with mental disorders. Autoencoders [18] are extremely accurate, especially in the classification of depression and schizophrenia. The synthesis of new data by GANs [20] has proven to be efficient in the diagnosis of PTSD and schizophrenia. LSTM [19] and GRU [21] models are effective in handling sequential data with capturing dependencies among behavioral patterns associated with anxiety, bipolar disorder, and PTSD. CNN [17] is best in capturing spatial features and is hence efficient in detecting various disorders, such as OCD and schizophrenia. BiLSTM [22], with its bidirectional learning, enhances the accuracy of detection for PTSD and bipolar disorder. These results highlight the importance of choosing suitable DL models to maximize mental health evaluation using behavioral analysis, enhancing early detection and intervention plans [23].

6.4 Conclusion

This chapter highlighted the importance of DL as incapable of analyzing mental health conditions and psychological results and could help in determining these patterns through structured and unstructured structures. Comparing methods like CNN, autoencoder, GAN, GRU, Bi-LSTM, and LSTM, it was found that their accuracy and robustness are different and some work better for psychological trends. The analysis proves that DL can play an important role in the psychological health field with significant contributions to analysis and diagnosis as well as to the intervention process. It is evident that by adopting various DL methodologies, mental health work strategies can be enhanced by advancing the methods of pattern recognition and prediction. However, incorporating these models with domain knowledge can enhance the diagnostic type and the intervention models, and hence, DL can be a beneficiary tool for more development in the case of mental health.

AI disclosure statement: The author confirms that no artificial intelligence (AI)-generated content or AI-assisted writing tools were used in the preparation of this chapter (including summaries and the abstract). All text, analysis, and conclusions are the result of the author's original work.

References

1. Ahmed, U., *et al.*, Attention-based deep entropy active learning using lexical algorithm for mental health treatment. *Front. Psychol.*, 12, 6423475, 2021. https://doi.org/10.3389/fpsyg.2021.642347.
2. Chung, J. and Teo, J., Mental health prediction using machine learning: taxonomy, applications, and challenges. *Appl. Comput. Intell. Soft Comput.*, 1, 2022, 9970363, 2022. https://doi.org/10.1155/2022/9970363.
3. Nouman, M., *et al.*, Recent advances in contactless sensing technologies for mental health monitoring. *IEEE Internet Things J.*, 9, 274–297, 2021. https://doi.org/10.1109/JIOT.2021.3097801.
4. Dogan, G. and Patlar Akbulut, F., Multi-modal fusion learning through biosignal, audio, and visual content for detection of mental stress. *Neural Comput. Appl.*, 35.34, 24435–24454, 2023. https://doi.org/10.1007/s00521-023-09036-4.
5. Timmons, A.C., *et al.*, A call to action on assessing and mitigating bias in artificial intelligence applications for mental health. *Perspect. Psychol. Sci.*, 18.5, 1062–1096, 2023. https://doi.org/10.1177/17456916221134490.

6. Dadi, K., *et al.*, Population modeling with machine learning can enhance measures of mental health. *GigaScience*, 10.10, giab071, 2021. https://doi.org/10.1093/gigascience/giab071.
7. Kannan, K.D., *et al.*, Advancements in machine learning and deep learning for early detection and management of mental health disorder. *arXiv preprint arXiv:2412.06147*, 2024. https://doi.org/10.48550/arXiv.2412.06147.
8. Mental Health Dataset: https://www.kaggle.com/datasets/bhavikjikadara/mental-health-dataset/data.
9. Sentiment Analysis for Mental Health Dataset: https://www.kaggle.com/datasets/suchintikasarkar/sentiment-analysis-for-mental-health/data.
10. Depression and Mental Health Data Analysis Dataset: https://www.kaggle.com/datasets/shashwatwork/depression-and-mental-health-data-analysis/data.
11. Liu, M., An IoT-Enabled Mental Health Monitoring System for English Language Students Using Generative Adversarial Network Algorithm. *Mob. Netw. Appl.*, 1–22, 2024. https://doi.org/10.1007/s11036-024-02408-7.
12. Dubey, S., Sharma, R., Malik, A., Autoencoder-Driven Framework for Mental Health Disorder Prediction in Online Social Networks. *GK Int. J. Adv. Work Eng. Technol.*, 1.2, 31–39, 2024. https://doi.org/10.34293/gkijaret.v1i2.2024.14.
13. Fudholi, D.H., Mental health prediction model on social media data using CNN-BILSTM. *Kinetik Game Technol. Inf. Sys. Comput. Netw. Computing Electronics Control*, 9, 1, 29–44, 2024. https://kinetik.umm.ac.id/index.php/kinetik/article/view/1849.
14. Ameer, I., *et al.*, Mental illness classification on social media texts using deep learning and transfer learning. *arXiv preprint arXiv:2207.01012*, 2022. https://doi.org/10.48550/arXiv.2207.01012.
15. Arif, M., *et al.*, Mental illness classification on social media texts using deep learning and transfer learning. *Computación y Sistemas*, 28.2, 451-464, 2024, https://doi.org/10.13053/cys-28-2-487328.
16. Srivastava, S., Arora, N., Gupta, V., An Efficient Deep Learning Model using Harris-Hawk Optimizer for Prognostication of Mental Health Disorders. *International Work Journal of Multidisciplinary Technovation*, vol. 6.4, pp. 106–123, 2024, https://orcid.org/0000-0002-9317-0660.
17. He, L., Cheung-Wai Chan, J., Wang, Z., Automatic depression recognition using CNN with attention mechanism from videos. *Neurocomputing*, 422, 165–1755, 2021, doi: 10.1016/j.neucom.2020.10.015.
18. Sharma, V., Rup Prakash, N., Kalra, P., Depression status identification using autoencoder neural network. *Biomed. Sig. Process. Control*, 75, 1035685, 2022. https://doi.org/10.1016/j.bspc.2022.103568.
19. Saeedi, A., *et al.*, Major depressive disorder diagnosis based on effective connectivity in EEG signals: A convolutional neural network and long short-term memory approach. *Cognit. Neurodyn.*, 15.2, 239–252, 2021. https://doi.org/10.1007/s11571-020-09619-0.

20. Zhao, J., *et al.*, Functional network connectivity (FNC)-based generative adversarial network (GAN) and its applications in classification of mental disorders. *J. Neurosci. Methods*, 341, 1087565, 2020. https://doi.org/10.1016/j.jneumeth.2020.108756.
21. Pushpa, G., *et al.*, An Advanced AI Framework for Mental Health Diagnostics Using Bidirectional Encoder Representations from Transformers with Gated Recurrent Units and Convolutional Neural Networks. *Ingenierie Des. Systemesd'Information*, 30.1, 213, 2025. DOI:10.18280/isi.300118.
22. Xin, C. and Qadri Zakaria, L., Integrating Bert with CNN and Bilstm for Explainable Detection of Depression in Social Media Contents. *IEEE Access*, 12, 161203–161212, 2024. https://doi.org/10.1109/ACCESS.2024.3488081.
23. Misgar, M.M. and Bhatia, M.P.S., Unveiling psychotic disorder patterns: A deep learning model analysing motor activity time-series data with explainable AI. *Biomed. Sig. Process. Control*, 91, 1060005, 2024. https://doi.org/10.1016/j.bspc.2024.106000.

7

Mental Health Detection Using Natural Language Processing

Murugan R.[1*], Syed Siraj Ahmed[2], Snehanshu Dey[3], Shweta Bajaj[4] and Bichitrananda Patra[5]

[1]*Department of CSIT, Jain (Deemed-to-be University), Bangalore, Karnataka, India*
[2]*Department of Computer Science & Engineering, Presidency University, Bengaluru, Karnataka, India*
[3]*Department of Psychiatry, IMS and SUM Hospital, Siksha 'O' Anusandhan (Deemed to be University), Bhubaneswar, Odisha, India*
[4]*Maharishi School of Pharmaceuticals, Maharishi University of Information Technology, Uttar Pradesh, India*
[5]*Department of Computer Applications, Siksha 'O' Anusandhan (Deemed to be University), Bhubaneswar, Odisha, India*

Abstract
Mental health detection using text data is the center of attention with the introduction of AI. The chapter utilizes a dataset of user-psychologist conversations and social media discussions to analyze the mental health conditions. Text preprocessing techniques are utilized to normalize and refine the textual data for better classification. Word embedding techniques enhance contextual understanding in natural language processing (NLP) by representing words as numerical vectors that capture their semantic relationships and usage patterns within a given language model. The context and sequential patterns within this text are applied through different models, both machine learning (ML) and deep learning (DL) models, to be able to classify a mental health condition. Performance evaluation is conducted using various parameters to assess classification effectiveness.

**Corresponding author*: murugan@jainuniversity.ac.in; ORCID: 0000-0003-0903-5982
Syed Siraj Ahmed: ORCID: 0000-0003-3943-604X
Snehanshu Dey: ORCID: 0000-0002-7937-4093
Shweta Bajaj: ORCID: 0000-0001-6646-5298
Bichitrananda Patra: ORCID: 0000-0001-6414-5389

Sudesh Yadav, Pethuru Raj, Satya Prakash Yadav and Victor Hugo C. de Albuquerque (eds.) Natural Language Processing in Mental Health Care: Methodologies and Clinical Practice, (85–102) © 2026 Scrivener Publishing LLC

In a recent round of experiments, it was found that using AI for mental health assessments would aid in the early identification of the pathology and early interventions. The results also reinforce the significance of computational methods in mental health: scalable and automated solutions for psychological evaluation.

Keywords: Mental health detection, natural language processing, word embedding, machine learning, deep learning

7.1 Introduction

Mental health disorders impact both individuals experiencing them and the broader society, influencing social interactions, productivity, and overall well-being. Those disorders have emotional, social, and productive consequences [1]. Depression, anxiety, and stress are on the rise; therefore, development methods should be timely and scalable. Mental health has been assessed by clinical evaluation, self-reported surveys, and psychological tests. Although these processes provide a solid understanding, they are generally tedious, inaccessible, or subjective [2]. Communication over various digital platforms has created a great wealth of textual data that allows one to examine the wider perspective of mental health trends [3]. Natural language processing (NLP) is growing into powerful, yet theoretical, tool in the analysis of human language, thus laying the groundwork for automated mental health identification through the analysis of textual data. An array of techniques makes use of linguistic and semantic features to identify any features characterizing psychological distress in both speech and writing [4]. Such features, including language markers, like sentiment shifts, emotional expressions, and syntactic structures, appear in social media posts, online forums, and conversational texts, thereby serving as indicators of mental health conditions [5]. These advancements allow for passive, continuous, and scalable monitoring of mental health. The fusion of AI with NLP has allowed more precise identification of elaborate language hints regarding mental health [6]. Deep learning-based models have allowed substantial improvements in processing complex linguistic structures but it kept the context and nuance of changes in tone, sentiment, and choice of words [7]. There are challenges of ethical considerations, data privacy, and misinterpretation risks associated with understanding inherently complex and variable human language [8]. Tackling these challenges would require an interdisciplinary approach involving AI ethics, psychology, and linguistics to create responsible and accurate systems for detecting mental health issues. With a global rush to emphasize mental health awareness, NLP-based solutions show immense promise in complementing conventional psychological assessments for early detection and uncovering of mental health trends at both the individual and societal levels [9]. The aim of using NLP, ML, and DL models are to develop an AI-based framework for diagnosing mental disorders from text data, thereby complementing early diagnosis, improving classification accuracy, and making psychological testing scalable.

7.2 Methodology

The methodology includes processing a user-psychologist conversation dataset from Kaggle and social media tagged with mental illness labels. Preprocessing techniques, for instance, text preparation, noise reduction, and feature extraction, are used to enhance the input quality. Classification is facilitated using two types of NLP techniques to recognize contextual meaning and linguistic features. Different ML and DL models are used to evaluate patterns in mental health and consider the objective of AI-based diagnostics and personalized intervention plans.

Dataset

The dataset consists of anonymous exchanges between users and psychologists, which could be very useful in training NLP models meant for mental health analysis. It supports AI-driven applications in mental health, such as chatbot-based interventions and automated counselling [10]. The dataset was integrated from several Kaggle sources and included statements tagged with mental health status labels like normal, depression, anxiety, stress, suicidal tendencies, bipolar disorder, and personality disorders. Sentiment analysis and predictive modeling towards mental health detection are enabled through data from Reddit and Twitter. Furthermore, a second dataset with 120 records of patients involved stipulates 17 important symptoms related to mania, bipolar disorder, depression and major depressive disorder [11]. It offers an AI-enabled mental health evaluation cipher as the unique identification species, statements with relationship explicit mental health labels. Among other things, they include sadness, exhaustion, sleep disturbances, suicidal thoughts, anxiety, and mood fluctuations. This dataset refines NLP-rich psychiatric analyses, aiding in AI-assisted mental health diagnostics, predictive analytics, and personalized treatment recommendations [12]. Integrating social media data with clinical records in the dataset allows for holistic mental health modeling using NLP methodologies, an improvement for early detection and intervention strategies. It acts as a stepping-stone for unleashing AI-driven tools aimed explicitly at improving mental health monitoring and support systems.

Data Preprocessing

The dataset has been refined through text standardization, unnecessary elements removal, and irrelevant content filtering. The conversational data structuring maintains a linguistic style that allows for accurate analysis. Class distribution correction helps in handling data imbalance, increasing the reliability of predictions. Key features are pulled from the data to keep the essential information while converting the structured records into one standardized numerical format. Data scaling aligns the records from multiple sources into a more usable input for the model. Noise reduction cleans up the text, and changes in dimensionality lead to quicker computations. These preprocessing steps ensure the dataset is well-structured for NLP-based mental health analysis, supporting accurate sentimentality classification and predictive diagnostics.

Word Embedding Techniques in Natural Language Processing

Word embedding techniques in NLP map words into dense vector spaces, capturing semantic and syntactic relationships. Embeddings improve context understanding in text data within ML and DL models, providing better sentiment analysis for mental health detection, and supporting the accurate classification of emotional states, leading to early diagnosis and personalized interventions.

Bidirectional Encoder Representations from Transformers

In mental health detection, bidirectional encoder representations from transformers (BERT) enhances sentiment analysis by capturing subtle emotional cues in user conversations. BERT [13] takes into consideration the meanings of words in the context of the whole sentence by building an understanding of the meanings of the preceding and succeeding words. It allows the differentiation between semantically similar words carrying varied emotional intensities, thereby improving chatbot response and AI-assisted psychological evaluations. BERT's very deep contextual understanding, identifying signs of distress, suicidal tendencies, or fluctuations in mood are done more efficiently. It has been found that fine-tuning BERT with datasets of mental health in depression and anxiety disorders resulted in an improved predictive performance. Its strength in the manipulation of complicated construction of sentences insists on its importance for NLP-oriented mental health applications.

Embeddings from Language Models

Embeddings from language models (ELMo) is a word representation algorithm built on language understanding of sentences as a whole rather than taking each word into account in isolation. Due to how word embeddings are dynamically changed according to surrounding contexts, ELMo is exceedingly effective in a variety of areas, such as mental health detection. ELMo [14] provides state-of-the-art performances in NLP models, dealing with dialogue around the treatment of depression, anxiety, and other disorders, by providing a better understanding of the nuances of emotional expression. By identifying subtle linguistic patterns in speech that could signal psychological distress, ELMo enhances chatbot-based counselling systems, enabling more accurate detection of emotional states and providing timely, context-aware mental health support Furthermore, ELMo aids in the sentimentality analysis and in the response given towards the context by classifying the changes in tone, allowing AI-driven models to define emotional poignancy and render corresponding mental health interventions.

Dependency Parsing

Dependency parsing (DP) examines the interrelations between the words of a sentence to create meaning depending on different relationships made by different words to different senses within them. In mental health detection, that is used to interpret hints of distress drawn from these sentence structures closely associated with psychological problems. For instance, the sentiment of negative combined with emotional stimuli could enrich the understanding of possible anxiety or depression of the user [15]. The AI model would better understand the user intent by recognizing those dependencies from the sentence, which allows to respond less generically and perform automated psychological assessment services in the case of chatbots. Such methods involve the improvement of mental health-related sentiment analyses by the ability to detect elements, such as negations or intensifiers. This would allow better accuracy in detecting emotional distress and enhance NLP-based mental health assessments.

Lexical Processing (LP)

LP standardizes and refines the language of the texts through normalized variants of words, spelling error corrections, and management of informal language use. For finding mental diseases, it sets standards in the analysis of user-generated content derived from social media, chatbots, and clinical records for their use in enhancing the accuracy of the NLP model [16]. This method eliminates insignificant elements caused by slang phrases, abbreviated symbols, and wrong spelling mistakes, thus quite substantively improving the trustworthiness of sentiment analysis. LP augments the application of AI in mental health with uniform language that allows deeper extraction of worthwhile features in such tasks and provides the classifiers a boost to polished performance. To improve psychological evaluations based on improved data quality, hence successfully enabling NLP models to ascertain practically all manifestations of emotional distress and any associated mental health condition with improved accuracy.

Mental Health Detection in Machine Learning (ML) and Deep Learning (DL)

ML and DL methods are used in NLP techniques to qualitatively and quantitatively analyze natural language conversations, systematically identifying emotional patterns resembling various psychological support problems. Here, machine-learning models can classify various features as radiological text-based, while deep-learning architectures further improve contextual understanding. Such a technique helps early diagnosis, automates the assessment, and delivers personalized support and intervention for empowerment through AI-driven analysis in terms of accessible mental healthcare.

Support Vector Machine (SVM)

An SVM algorithm is used to classify users, based on their linguistic expressions, into mental health conditions, while different linguistic features—including word embeddings [17] and sentiment scores—age processed into specific mental conditions, with depression, anxiety, and stress being among them. SVM seeks to find the best set of decision boundaries between different mental states by mapping the input text to a high-dimensional space. The essential capability of chatbot-based assessments with social media post analysis and distress signal detection within conversations makes up a crucial point [18]. The system uses multiple abilities to detect conditions early while delivering AI-enabled mental health applications for providing time-sensitive assistance to intervene in situations that many people cannot handle because of their intricate nature and high complexity. Text data analysis through the SVM technique classifies users into mental health categories using linguistic features found in their data. The function for classification operates, according to the following Equation (7.1).

$$f(x) = \omega^T x + b \tag{7.1}$$

where x represents the extracted feature vector from user text w is the weight vector learned during training, and b is the bias term that adjusts the decision boundary. The algorithm finds an optimal hyperplane by Equations (7.2–7.4).

$$\min_{\omega,b} \frac{1}{2} \| \omega \|^2 \tag{7.2}$$

$$y_i(\omega^T x_i + b) \geq 1, \forall i \tag{7.3}$$

$$K(x_i, x_j) = \varnothing(x_i)^T = \varnothing(x_i) \tag{7.4}$$

Random Forest

Random forest improves the recognition of mental health conditions by combining multiple decision trees, increasing the consistent accuracy within classification tasks. These models use the extracted features of linguistic patterns, emotional tones, and frequency of words in the text for psychological condition detection [19]. RF has been extensively adopted in predictive models aimed at evaluating risks regarding disorders, such as depression and suicidal tendencies. Learning from structured mental health datasets enables the classification of users, according to symptoms and behavioral patterns. In AI-driven therapy applications, RF helps to refine chatbot responses and personalize interventions according to the level of distress detected [20]. RF's resistance to overfitting, therefore, makes it a trustworthy method for analyzing large-scale text data in mental health. RF enhances classification by aggregating multiple decision trees, improving prediction robustness. The final classification probability is computed as Equation (7.5).

$$P(y|X) = \frac{1}{T} \Sigma_{t=1}^{T} h_t(X) \tag{7.5}$$

where $P(y|X)$ represents the probability of a mental health condition given user input X, T is the number of decision trees, and $h_t(X)$ is the prediction from each tree. Feature selection is based on information gain in Equations (7.6 and 7.7).

$$IG = H(Y) - \Sigma_i P(Y_i) H(Y_i) \tag{7.6}$$

$$Gini = 1 - \Sigma_{i=1}^{C} P_i^2 \tag{7.7}$$

Naïve Bayes

Sentiment analysis and psychological state classification utilize Naïve Bayes (NB) [21] in mental health detection. It analyzes word distributions to determine the probability of a user mentioning some specific mental health condition. NB is, useful in detecting verbal references to depressive thoughts, anxiety, and suicidal ideation. The algorithm is most commonly used for social media data, chat transcriptions, and therapy transcripts, considering its efficiency. Such AI-powered systems for mental health monitoring rely on NB to quickly assess the user's emotional state and provide immediate support [22], as well as risk alerts if they detect distress signals. In real-time screening of mental health, it becomes extremely important. NB classifies text based on probabilistic sentiment analysis, determining the likelihood of a mental health condition. The core probability function using Equation (7.8):

$$P(y|X) = \frac{P(X|y)o(y)}{o(x)} \tag{7.8}$$

where $P(y|X)$ is the probability of mental health condition y given the text input X, $P(y|X)$ is the likelihood of the observed words occurring in a specific condition, and P(y)P(y)P(y) is the prior probability of the condition. The likelihood is computed in Equations (7.9 and 7.10).

$$O(X|y) = \Pi_{i-1}^{N} O(x_i \mid y) \tag{7.9}$$

$$O(x_i|y) = \frac{1}{\sqrt{2\pi\sigma_y^2}} e^{\frac{(x_i-\mu_y)^2}{2\sigma_y^2}} \tag{7.10}$$

Logistic Regression

Logistic regression (LR) helps with classification problems in mental health detection, such as predicting whether or not a user is likely at risk for depression or anxiety [23]. It takes linguistic features, sentiment scores, and emotional cues from conversations with users to predict psychological distress. LR is often adopted in AI-based mental health assessment tools to decide if any intervention is needed. The method is used to interpret structured patient datasets, social media posts, and chatbot conversations [24]. Due to its simplicity and interpretability, LR is widely used in clinical decision support systems to gain insights into mental health trends and early risk prediction. LR predicts mental health conditions by modelling the probability of distress using the sigmoid function using Equations (7.11–7.13).

$$P\left(y = \frac{1}{X}\right) = \frac{1}{1 + e^{-(\beta_0 + \sum_{i=1}^{n} \beta_i x_i)}} \tag{7.11}$$

$$J(\beta) = -\frac{1}{m} \sum_{i=1}^{m} [y_i \log(h_\beta(x_i)) + (1 - y_i)\log(1 - h_\beta(x_i))] \tag{7.12}$$

$$\beta_j := \beta_j = -\alpha \frac{\partial J(\beta)}{\partial \beta_j} \tag{7.13}$$

where ∂J is the learning rate, ensuring accurate classification of users experiencing psychological distress.

Recurrent Neural Networks

Recurrent neural networks (RNNs) are utilized in mental health detection to analyze sequential dependencies in conversations. They generally process text in context, thereby letting AI models understand the gradual shifts in a user's emotional state over time [25]. Hence, RNNs can help inform in real time of distress signals picked out from the analysis of therapy sessions, chatbot interactions, and social media posts. Their skill in preserving the context of the past makes them possibly successful in detecting patterns of depression, anxiety, and tendencies to commit suicide. AI-driven mental health applications utilize RNNs [26] to generate chatbot replies in an empathetic way and assist in observing, by providing insights into long-term emotional trends in the patients' textual expressions, and therapists. RNNs process sequential user conversations to detect emotional distress patterns. The hidden state updates Equations (7.14–7.16).

$$h_t = \sigma(W_h h_{t-1} + W_x x_t + b) \tag{7.14}$$

Where h_t represents the hidden state at time t, W_h and W_x are weight matrices, and x_t is the current input text. The classification probability is determined as:

$$P(y_t | h_t) = sofmax(W_o h_t + b_o) \tag{7.15}$$

Where W_o and b_o are output layer parameters. Backpropagation through time updates gradients as:

$$\delta_t = \frac{\partial J}{\partial h_t} + W_h^T \delta_{t+1} \tag{7.16}$$

where J represents the loss function, this enables continuous monitoring of mental health trends over time.

Long Short-Term Memory

Long short-term memory (LSTM) improves mental health discovery by preserving long-range dependencies in conversations. Unlike standard RNNs, LSTMs retain pertinent past information, enabling accurate analysis of emotional shifts over lengthy dialogues [27]. This makes them useful for sensing prolonged depressive thoughts, anxiety episodes, and mood swings. AI-driven mental health chatbots use LSTMs to generate more contextually conscious responses, improving user engagement in digital therapy. LSTMs are also effective in analyzing therapy transcripts and predicting mental health deterioration over time [28]. Their aptitude to process long sequences of text makes them crucial for understanding complex psychological patterns in user connections. LSTM overcomes the vanishing gradient issue in RNNs, improving long-term emotional state prediction. The forget, input, and output gate functions using Equations (7.17–7.19).

$$f_t = \sigma(W_f x_t + U_{ft-1} + b_f) \tag{7.17}$$

$$i_t = \sigma(W_i x_t + U_i h_{t-1} + b_i) \tag{7.18}$$

$$o_t = \sigma(W_o x_t + U_o h_{t-1} + b_o) \tag{7.19}$$

where f_t, t_t, o_t determine memory retention, and h_t represents the current hidden state, enabling analysis of prolonged psychological distress.

Convolutional Neural Networks

Persons involved in mental health detection use convolutional neural networks (CNNs) to analyze text content by extracting advanced textual characteristics. CNN analyzes word embeddings through convolutional filters to find patterns that link to psychological distress [29].

Unlike sequential models, CNNs analyze entire text segments simultaneously, making them computationally efficient. Through CNN AI, mental health systems analyze social media posts, chatbot messages, and online therapy documents to assign different mental disease classifications. AI systems can detect essential emotional signs, which helps with early stress detection, depression analysis and desperate thoughts, consequently enabling AI [30] mental health applications to deliver swift solutions and personalized psychological interventions. CNNs extract high-level features from text, using convolutional operations using Equation (7.20):

$$h_i f(W.X_i + b) \tag{7.20}$$

where W is the convolutional filter and X_i is the input matrix. The pooling layer simplifies data using Equation (7.21).

$$p_i = \underset{j \epsilon R_i}{max} \tag{7.21}$$

This ensures efficient feature extraction from mental health-related text.

Transformer Networks (TN)

Transformer networks, including models like BERT and ELMo, enable AI-powered mental health detection by processing text in a context-aware manner. Unlike RNNs, transformers analyze entire sentences at once, capturing deep semantic relationships [31]. They enhance chatbot-based therapy by improving emotional understanding and sentiment classification. AI-driven mental health applications use transformers to analyze distress signals in online conversations, detect crises, and personalize mental health interventions. By leveraging self-attention mechanisms, transformers improve predictive modeling of mental disorders, ensuring accurate and empathetic AI-generated responses [32, 33]. Their ability to model long-range dependencies makes them highly effective for NLP-based psychological assessments using Equations (7.22–7.24).

$$Z = softmax\left(\frac{OK^T}{\sqrt{d_k}}\right)V \tag{7.22}$$

$$PE_{(pos,2i)} = sin\left(\frac{pos}{10000^{2i/d}}\right) \tag{7.23}$$

$$PE_{(pos,2i+1)} = cos\left(\frac{pos}{10000^{\frac{2i}{d}}}\right) \tag{7.24}$$

7.3 Result

The experimental setup utilizes a high-performance computing system with an Intel Core i9 processor, 32GB RAM, and an NVIDIA RTX 3090 GPU. The models are implemented using Python, TensorFlow, and PyTorch. The ability of ML and DL models to unveil mental health conditions through textual data ranges from classifiers that adequately uncover psychological patterns to transformer-based models that assist in improving the understanding of those patterns based on context. Sentence DP and the lexical aspect analysis add to classifying capacities by parsing mother structures and enhancing the disbursement of certain words. Such findings open the promise for the potential of AI-based methods in the assessment of mental health, augmenting automated counseling programs, chatbot interventions, and scalable foresight into early detection and psychological support.

Performance Comparison of NLP Embedding Methods and Classifiers
In Table 7.1, LP-based classification enhances the detection of mental illness based on word analysis. LR provides stable binary classification while SVM works toward optimizing the detection of various disorders through textual analysis. RNN allows the sequential processing of user conversation, enabling classification for early intervention. These models refine AI-driven diagnostics through the combination of lexical structures to ensure precise predictions.

BERT [13] and ELMo [14] based classifications enhance psychological pattern recognition by capturing contextual meanings in user conversations. SVM and RF balance classification accuracy, while LSTM and RNN improve sequential text analysis for emotional understanding. CNN extracts high-level textual features, refining sentiment classification. TN leverages deep contextual representations for chatbot-based interventions. Collectively, these models advance AI-driven mental health assessments, enabling precise diagnostics and personalized support through NLP-based predictive analytics, as shown in Table 7.1 and Figure 7.1.

Table 7.1 Comparative analysis of NLP embeddings and classifier performance metrics.

Embedding method in NLP	Classifier	Accuracy	F1 score	Recall	Precision
BERT	SVM	80	82	79	81
	LSTM	83	85	83	84
	TN	86	88	86	87
ELMo	RF	77	79	76	78
	RNN	81	83	81	82
	CNN	79	81	78	80
DP	NB	73	75	72	74
	LSTM	78	80	78	79
	CNN	76	78	76	77
Lexical Processing (LP)	LR	70	72	70	71
	SVM	75	77	74	76
	RNN	77	79	76	78

Source: own elaboration

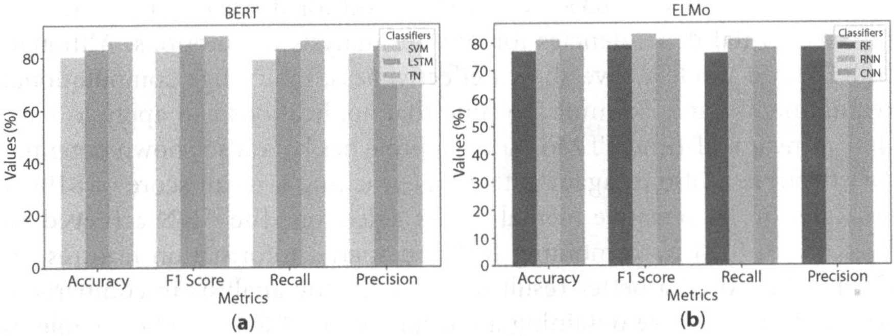

Figure 7.1 Classifiers for mental health (a) BERT, (b) ELMo. Source: own elaboration.

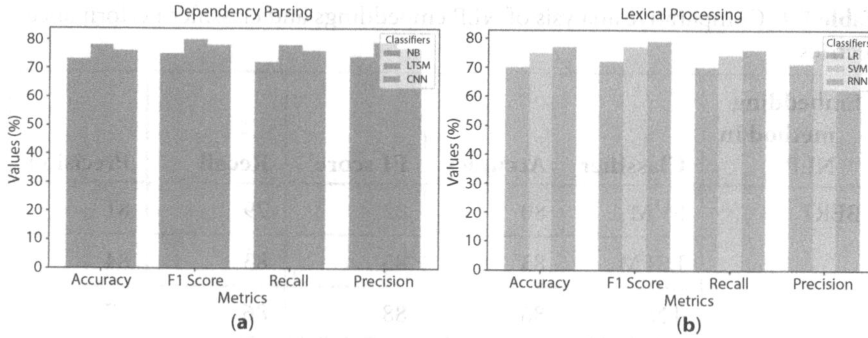

Figure 7.2 Classifiers using various metrics for mental health detection (a) dependency parsing, (b) lexical processing. Source: Own elaboration.

Table 7.1 and Figure 7.2 highlight DP [15] and LP [16] classifications in AI-assisted mental health assessments. NB offers moderate classification, while LSTM improves sequential text analysis, enhancing emotion detection. CNN strengthens feature extraction from structured texts. LR ensures stable classification, SVM optimizes disorder detection, and RNN processes sequential user conversations for early intervention. These models refine AI-driven diagnostics, integrating syntactic and lexical structures for precise predictions.

7.4 Discussion

Different NLP techniques applied for the detection of mental healthiness have been reported to work differently on the various models. The BERT-based classifiers were best with the transformer networks, which worked by 86% and proved contextualized embedding to be important. LSTM came next with 83%, which was good for it because it could capture sequential dependencies for further analysis of emotions. Although BERT-based models have shown effectiveness, their huge computational requirements can also limit the time that applications can apply to real-time or near real-time. ELMo-based approaches have also shown potential for effective solutions, again with RNN reaching a recall score of 81%, a critical score in sensitive mental illness detection. The CNN achieved an F1-score of 81% by combining text and spatial information features. In DP, LSTM scored a better result on the syntactic analysis in comparison with NB, in this case obtaining an accuracy of 78%, hence being able to model word dependencies. The LP approach was moderately successful with SVM and RNN achieving accuracies of 75% and 77%, respectively. Logistic regression secured an F1-score of 72% but struggled with nuanced text interpretation. Extra improvements could involve real-time application and multimodal data synthesis for improved mental health detection.

7.5 Conclusion

The findings highlight the importance of deep contextual designs and sequential modeling in mental health detection. Models based on BERT, specifically transformer networks, achieved an overall effectiveness of 86%, which establishes their ability to comprehend complex mental health-related texts. With an 83% accuracy, the LSTM was successful in capturing the sequential dependencies and beneficial in terms of emotional state analysis. However, the high computational intensity was an issue, preventing real-time implementation. In contrast to Lexicon and dependency-based methods, this approach mostly focused on syntactic analysis; however, it did grapple with nimble language variants that chronic mental illness discursions ordinarily adopt. Future improvements shall focus on optimizing computational efficiency and incorporating real-time processing for AI-driven psychological assessments. The predictive accuracy would be enhanced through the integration of multimodal data, voice and facial expressions included. In addition, interpretability and ethical considerations are just as essential in any AI application, as its implementation should be carried out responsibly. Incorporating linguistic diversity can enhance the research of a user-friendly smart mental health checker ensuring it is ubiquitous, accessible, and generalizable across diverse populations.

AI disclosure statement: The author confirms that no artificial intelligence (AI)-generated content or AI-assisted writing tools were used in the preparation of this chapter (including summaries and the abstract). All text, analysis, and conclusions are the result of the author's original work.

References

1. Swaminathan, A., *et al.*, Natural language processing system for rapid detection and intervention of mental health crisis chat messages. *npj Digit. Med.*, 6.1, 213, 2023.

2. Saha, T., *et al.*, Mental health disorder identification from motivational conversations. *IEEE Trans. Comput. Soc. Syst.*, 10.3, 1130–1139, 2022, https://doi.org/10.1109/TCSS.2022.3143763.
3. Inamdar, S., *et al.*, Machine learning driven mental stress detection on Reddit posts using natural language processing. *Hum.-Centric Intell. Syst.*, 3.2, 80–91, 2023, https://doi.org/10.1007/s44230-023-00020-8.
4. Ríssola, E., Aliannejadi, M., Crestani, F., Mental disorders on online social media through the lens of language and behaviour: Analysis and visualisation. *Inf. Process. Manage.*, 59, 3, 102890, 2022, https://doi.org/10.1016/j.ipm.2022.102890.
5. Dai, S., *et al.*, Deep learning-based natural language processing for screening psychiatric patients. *Front. Psychiatry*, 11, 5339495, 2021, https://doi.org/10.3389/fpsyt.2020.533949.
6. Kodati, D. and Tene, R., Advancing mental health detection in texts *via* multi-task learning with soft-parameter sharing transformers. *Neural Comput. Appl.*, 37.5, 3077–3110, 2025, https://doi.org/10.1007/978-981-19-3679-1_16.
7. Chen, L., Immersive artificial intelligence technology based on entertainment game experience in simulation of psychological health testing for university students. *Entertain. Comput.*, 52, 100839, 2025. https://doi.org/10.70589/JRTCSE.2022.2.3.
8. Kerz, E., *et al.*, Toward explainable AI (XAI) for mental health detection based on language behavior. *Front. Psychiatry*, 14, 12194795, 2023, doi: 10.3389/fpsyt.2023.1219479.
9. Kishimoto, T., *et al.*, Understanding psychiatric illness through natural language processing (UNDERPIN): Rationale, design, and methodology. *Front. Psychiatry*, 13, 9547035, 2022, https://doi.org/10.3389/fpsyt.2022.954703.
10. Ji, S., *et al.*, Suicidal ideation and mental disorder detection with attentive relation networks. *Neural Comput. Appl.*, 34.13, 10309–10319, 2022, https://doi.org/10.1007/s00521-021-06208-y.
11. https://www.kaggle.com/datasets/suchintikasarkar/sentiment-analysis-for-mental-health
12. https://www.kaggle.com/datasets/cid007/mental-disorder-classification
13. https://www.kaggle.com/datasets/thedevastator/nlp-mental-health-conversations.
14. Hossain, MM., *et al.*, Multi task opinion enhanced hybrid BERT model for mental health analysis. *Sci. Rep.*, 15.1, 3332, 2025, https://doi.org/10.1007/978-3-030-85251-1_15.
15. Syaputra, R.A. and Ali, R., Improving mental health surveillance over Twitter text classification using word embedding techniques. *Artificial Intelligence, Machine Learning, and Mental Health in Pandemics*, pp. 235–258, Academic Press, 2022, https://doi.org/10.1016/B978-0-323-91196-2.00014-4.

16. Xu, Z., *et al.*, Developing and validating a parser-based suicidality detection model in text-based mental health services. *J. Affect. Disord.*, 335, 228–2325, 2023, https://doi.org/10.1016/j.jad.2023.04.128.
17. Spruit, M., *et al.*, Exploring language markers of mental health in psychiatric stories. *Appl. Sci.*, 12.4, 2179, 2022, https://doi.org/10.3390/app12042179.
18. Sharma, C.M., Yin Min Thein, K., M. Chariar, V., Optimized Support Vector Machines for Detection of Mental Disorders, in: *Artificial Intelligence in Healthcare*, pp. 190–219, CRC Press, 2024, https://doi.org/10.1201/9781003522096-10.
19. Kodipalli, A. and Devi, S., Prediction of PCOS and mental health using fuzzy inference and SVM. *Front. Public Health*, 9, 7895695, 2021, https://doi.org/10.3389/fpubh.2021.789569.
20. Mohamed, E.S., *et al.*, A hybrid mental health prediction model using Support Vector Machine, Multilayer Perceptron, and Random Forest algorithms. *Healthc. Anal.*, 3, 1001855, 2023, https://doi.org/10.1016/j.health.2023.100185.
21. Adeniji, O.D., Adeyemi, S.O., Ajagbe, S.A., An improved bagging ensemble in predicting mental disorder using hybridized random forest-artificial neural network model. *Informatica*, 46, 4, 2022, https://doi.org/10.31449/inf.v46i4.3916.
22. Kabir, M.K., *et al.*, Detection of depression severity using Bengali social media posts on mental health: a study using natural language processing techniques. *JMIR Formative Res.*, 6.9, e36118, 2022, https://doi.org/10.2196/36118.
23. Raj, S. and Masood, S., Analysis and detection of autism spectrum disorder using machine learning techniques. *Procedia Comput. Sci.*, 167, 994–10045, 2020, https://doi.org/10.1016/j.procs.2020.03.399.
24. Wijaya, V. and Rachmat, N., Comparison of SVM, Random Forest, and Logistic Regression Performance n Student Mental Health Screening. *JEECS (J. Electr. Eng. Comput. Sci.)*, 9.2, 173–184, 2024, https://doi.org/10.54732/jeecs.v9i2.9.
25. Hendra, H., Mat Deris, M., Safitri Windiarti, I., Mental Health Classification Using Machine Learning with PCA and Logistics Regression Approaches for Decision Making. *Eng. Proc.*, 84.1, 47, 2025, https://doi.org/10.3390/engproc2025084047.
26. Kanaparthi, S.D., Patle, A., Jairam Naik, K., Prediction and detection of emotional tone in online social media mental disorder groups using regression and recurrent neural networks. *Multimed. Tools Appl.*, 82.28, 43819–43839, 2023, https://doi.org/10.1007/s11042-023-15316-x.
27. Kamra, V., Kumar, P., Mohammadian, M., An intelligent disease prediction system for psychological diseases by implementing hybrid Hopfield recurrent neural network approach. *Intell. Syst. Appl.*, 18, 2002085, 2023, https://doi.org/10.1016/j.iswa.2023.200208.

28. Zhu, L., Hou, S., Cheng, T., Mental Health Status Detection Model Based on LSTM Neural Network. *Procedia Comput. Sci.*, 243, 842–8495, 2024, https://doi.org/10.1016/j.procs.2024.09.101.
29. Tate, A.E., *et al.*, Predicting mental health problems in adolescence using machine learning techniques. *PLoS One*, 15.4, e0230389, 2020, https://doi.org/10.1371/journal.pone.0230389.
30. Fei, Z., *et al.*, Deep convolution network based emotion analysis towards mental health care. *Neurocomputing*, 388, 212–2275, 2020, https://doi.org/10.1016/j.neucom.2020.01.034.
31. Shafiei, S.B., *et al.*, Identifying mental health status using a deep neural network trained by visual metrics. *Transl. Psychiatry*, 10.1, 430, 2020, https://doi.org/10.1038/s41398-020-01117-5.
32. Kerasiotis, M., Ilias, L., Askounis, D., Depression detection in social media posts using transformer-based models and auxiliary features. *Soc. Netw. Anal. Min.*, 14.1, 196, 2024, https://doi.org/10.1007/s13278-024-01360-4.
33. Abbas, M.A., *et al.*, Novel transformer based contextualized embedding and probabilistic features for depression detection from social media. *IEEE Access*, *12*, 54087–54100, 2024, https://doi.org/10.1109/ACCESS.2024.3387695.

8

Behavioral Signal Processing

Rengarajan A.[1*], Raghavendra T. S.[2], Praveen Priyaranjan Nayak[3] and Trapty Agarwal[4]

[1]*Department of CSIT, Jain (Deemed-to-be University), Bangalore, Karnataka, India*
[2]*Department of Computer Science & Engineering, Presidency University, Bengaluru, Karnataka, India*
[3]*Department of Electronics and Communication Engineering, Siksha 'O' Anusandhan (Deemed to be University), Bhubaneswar, Odisha, India*
[4]*Maharishi School of Engineering and Technology, Maharishi University of Information Technology, Uttar Pradesh, India*

Abstract

The emerging field of behavioral signal processing examines human-generated signals as an interdisciplinary area of diversified behavioral signals. This research addresses the challenge of analyzing multimodal signals using advanced machine learning (ML) and deep learning (DL) techniques. The aim is to develop an integrated framework that leverages EEG signals for physiological insights and speech signals for precise recognition. Data was gathered from high-resolution EEG recordings and speech samples, forming a comprehensive dataset representing diverse behavioral cues. Various ML and DL methodologies were implemented to process and classify these signals. Key performance indicators, including precision, accuracy, F1 score, and recall, were used to assess their performance. Comparative analysis reveals significant differences between ML and DL methods, highlighting the superior potential of DL models to improve performance in behavioral signal processing. These promising results pave the way for robust applications in neurotechnology and human–computer interaction.

Keywords: Behavioral signal processing, physiological signals, speech signals, human behavior analysis, EEG signal

**Corresponding author*: a.rengarajan@jainuniveristy.ac.in; ORCID: 0000-0002-4168-3333
Raghavendra T. S.: ORCID: 0009-0008-5982-1352
Praveen Priyaranjan Nayak: ORCID: 0000-0003-1726-1605
Trapty Agarwal: ORCID: 0009-0007-4081-4999

Sudesh Yadav, Pethuru Raj, Satya Prakash Yadav and Victor Hugo C. de Albuquerque (eds.) Natural Language Processing in Mental Health Care: Methodologies and Clinical Practice, (103–118) © 2026 Scrivener Publishing LLC

8.1 Introduction

The crossroads between technology and human behavior has gained much prominence and resulted in behavioral signal processing (BSP) as an interdisciplinary field. The BSP organization deeply engages with behavioral modeling and human analytics through speech monitoring along with facial expression detection, physiological signal processing and body movement analysis [1]. The process of BSP identifies and interprets faint behavioral indications to gain knowledge about human emotional states and communication processes. The increasing need for objective, machine-based evaluation of human behavior across a broad spectrum of applications has motivated the development of BSP, a standard feature of human-centered technology [2].

Human behavior is naturally multidimensional, driven by cognitive, emotional, and social factors. Traditional techniques of observing behavior are likely to be based on descriptive quantifiers and self-referential data that is unreliable and subject-dependent [3]. BSP sidesteps such pitfalls with the help of data-driven approaches for obtaining valuable conclusions from multimodal signals of human behavior. By observing nonverbal expressions and oral speech, BSP boasts an impeccable and quantifiable description of human behavior that offers space for previously unimaginable areas for personalized and tailored systems [4].

BSP drives innovation through healthcare advancements, which particularly benefit mental health care and wellness functions [5]. Automated behavioral analysis demonstrates valuable potential within medical diagnostics and treatment evaluation and therapeutic applications, which help diagnose depression, anxiety, autism spectrum disorder, and posttraumatic stress disorder [6]. Medical professionals can receive important patient mental state assessments through their capacity to notice delicate changes in various speech and facial expressions and physiological signs [7].

Besides healthcare, BSP has been applied in other sectors, such as education, human–computer interaction, customer service, and security. Education can use BSP to enable students' personalized learning experiences by finding levels of engagement and emotional states of the students during interactions [8]. Customer service behavior cues can be used to improve automatic sentiment analysis to better serve customers and deliver quality services. Security is also another area, where BSP can help surveillance systems identify suspicious activity through body movement and facial features [9]. One of the central interests of BSP is to ensure automatic readings of human behavior are accurate and reliable. Individual variability in expression, cultural diversities, and richness of affective states all enhance signal analysis complexity. Additionally, the issues regarding privacy, protection of data, and possible biases of the systems need to be addressed for the responsible utilization of BSP.

Objective: The aim of behavioral signal processing (BSP) assessment is to enhance accuracy through the integration of multibehavioral signals like speech, and physiological signals. With sophisticated machine learning algorithms as well as broad, representative data sets, bias can be circumvented.

8.2 Methodology

The study examined datasets related to signal processing, including speech and physiological signals, such as speech emotion recognition and EEG. Different types of AI approaches, like harmony search algorithm-long short-term memory (HAS-LSTM), ResNet152, DenseNet, and random forest for physiological signal and speech signal use extreme gradient boosting (XGBoost), deep neural networks (DNNs), regularized convolutional neural networks (RCNN), and one-dimensional deep convolutional neural networks (1-D DCNN) were utilized for behavior signal processing.

8.2.1 Data Collection

The physiologic signal data EEG available in Kaggle web: https://www.kaggle.com/datasets/samnikolas/eeg-dataset.The EEG dataset includes genuine multichannel EEG information that researchers obtained from participants in different cognitive experiments. The dataset contains both time series information and metadata tags, which prove advantageous for neural signal studies and brain–computer interface system development.

The speech signal data available in Kaggle web https://www.kaggle.com/datasets/uwrfkaggler/ravdess-emotional-speech-audio. RAVDESS emotional speech audio dataset includes professional actors performing emotional spoken sentences in its recordings. The dataset includes 24 emotional categories, each containing male and female recordings, making it suitable for research on speech emotion recognition.

8.2.2 AI Methods for Behavior Signal Processing

8.2.3 Physiological Signal Using EEG

The classification of EEG signals depends on processing methods, including HAS-LSTM, ResNet152, DenseNet, and random forest. The integration between HAS-LSTM systems helps improve temporal feature extraction. Through skip connections, ResNet152 functions as a deep residual network design, which enables the learning of complex features. The application of densely connected layers within DenseNet enables improved information transfer, which results in higher performance when analyzing EEG data. EEG data are classified using random forest (RF), which efficiently extracts characteristics and patterns.

8.2.4 Harmony Search Algorithm-Long Short-Term Memory

Raw EEG signals are preprocessed for the elimination of noise and unnecessary objects in a manner that only appropriate brain activity signals remain. It removes unwanted noise, cleans the data, and offers better-quality signals, as well as greater accuracy for further analysis.

HAS—A metaheuristic optimization method called Harmony Search Algorithm (HSA) selects important features from EEG data. The optimization process in HSA duplicates musical harmony techniques to find ideal feature combinations while also decreasing data dimensions for more efficient computation. The present study's purpose is to improve classification accuracy through optimization. The function of fitness is defined by Equation 8.1:

$$E = Maximize\left[feature\ (E_l)\right] \tag{8.1}$$

Fitness is characterized as an expression of *the feature* (E_l).

LSTM—LSTM deep neural networks utilize the chosen feature set because they demonstrate superior capability in detecting temporal patterns that exist in sequential EEG signals. By analyzing the time-based characteristics in brain signals, the LSTM neural network develops highly efficient task classification abilities. It consists of 4 levels with distinct communication mechanisms. By increasing the number of contacts in each module, the long short-term memory, an RNN advancement, addresses the current RNN drawbacks. One kind of RNN that can process input for extended periods and develop long-term dependencies is called an LSTM. A network structure serves as the foundation for the LSTM model. While LSTM consists of four layers with distinct communication mechanisms, RNN repeats the same structure. The architecture of the LSTM neural network is shown in Figure 8.1.

Applications using EEG-based brain–computer interfaces benefit greatly from the model's high classification accuracy, which is made possible by the hybrid of HAS-LSTM.

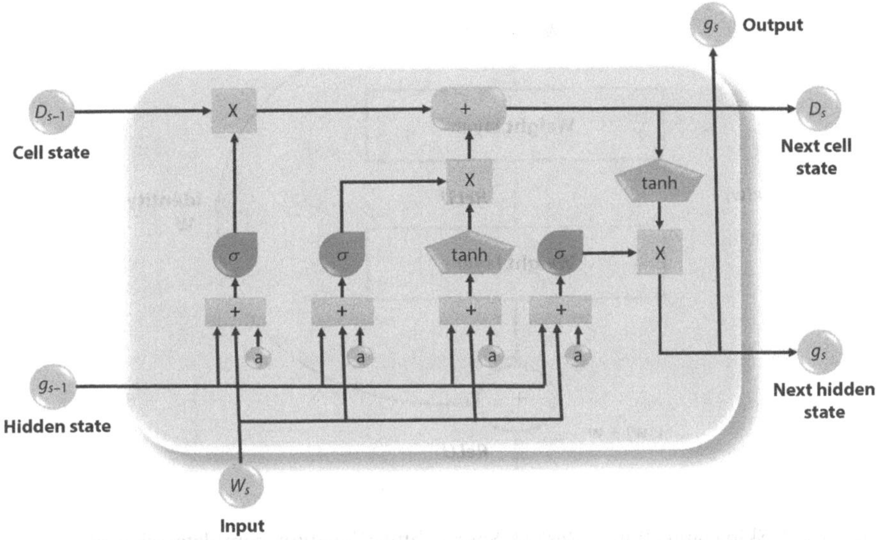

Figure 8.1 LSTM architecture. Source: https://medium.com/@parhamm/from-brain-cells-to-algorithms-4-algorithms-inspired-by-the-human-brain-a4644526bcdf.

8.2.5 ResNet

The ResNet architecture was developed to solve gradient vanishing issues, which normally affect deep neural network performance. The gradient deterioration becomes problematic during backpropagation because it operates at such high speeds that it hinders convergence. ResNet benefits from skip connections, which enable gradients to bypass layers to promote information flow better through the neural network. The model input spectrograms of size 224x224 pixels went through the network, which was followed by a custom two-way Softmax layer for final classification to achieve accurate detection. Figure 8.2 depicts a visual summary of Skip Connections.

8.2.6 DenseNet

The standard convolutional network with 'K' layers contains exactly the 'K' amount of connections. DenseNet applies $K(K+1)/2$ connections to facilitate the processing of physiological signals, such as EEG data effectively. DenseNet passes the combination of outputs generated by prior layers to successive layers so that subsequent layers receive information from all preceding layers as input. The EEG signal processing utilized a 121-layer architecture, which included Softmax output training for the analysis of various brain activity patterns. Figure 8.3 depicts the dense block structure, which applies to EEG data processing.

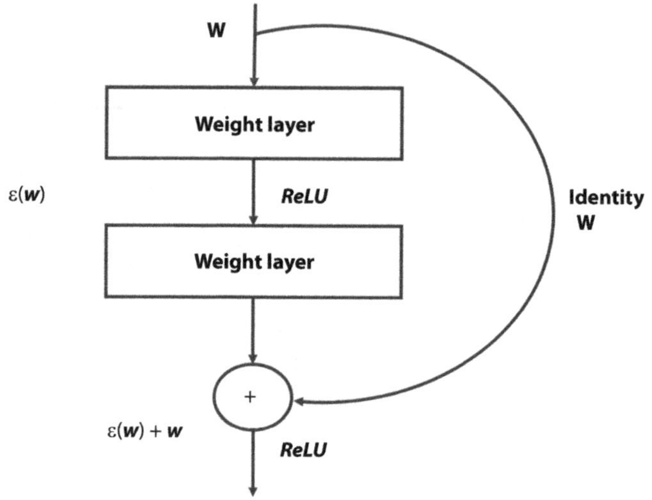

Figure 8.2 Skip connection of ResNet. Source: https://medium.com/data-science/an-overview-of-image-classification-networks-3fb4ff6fa61b.

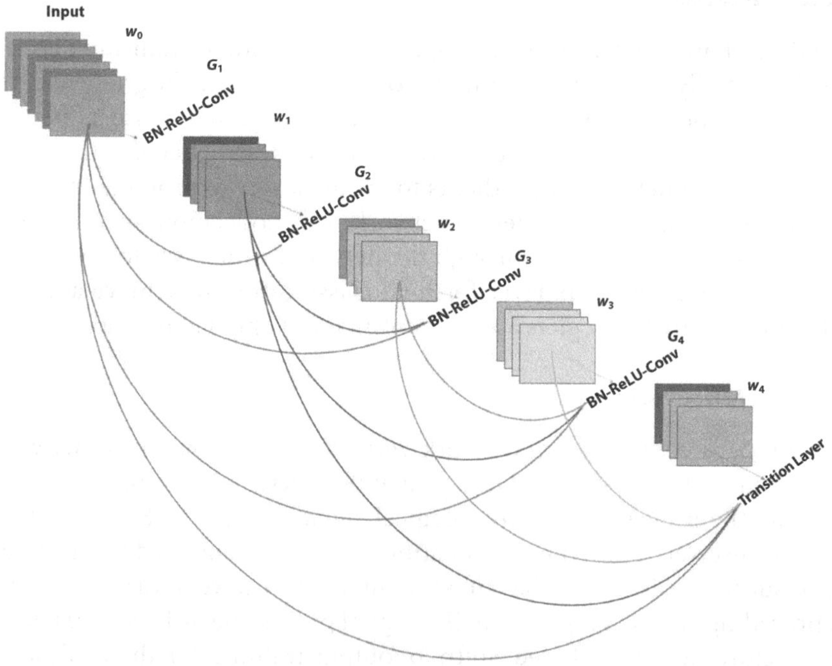

Figure 8.3 Dens block structure. Source: https://blog.chatbotslife.com/resnets-highwaynets-and-densenets-oh-my-9bb15918ee32.

8.2.7 Random Forest

RF serves as an ensemble learning model for making highly precise predictions by combining results generated from numerous decision trees. The use of RF in EEG-based physiological signal processing depends on bagging with bootstrap samples to create multiple decision trees, which leads to improved robustness performance. The accuracy optimization and overfitting reduction function of the RF algorithm is achieved through the n-estimator parameter that determines the number of trees, while max-depth limits the tree complexity. Reproducibility during training is achieved through the random state.

8.2.8 Speech Emotion Recognition (SER) Using Speech Signal

The collection of advanced machine learning and deep learning methods for Speech Emotion Recognition, includes XGBoost, DNNs, RCNN, and 1-D DCNN. The models break down speech signals into features, which they process for emotion classification using temporal and spectral pattern detection. This strengthens error rate control in speech-focused human–computer interaction systems.

8.2.9 XGBoost

Machine learning technique boosting strengthens inadequate classifiers to achieve higher performance results. Signal processing of speech emotions through SER becomes more exact by using boosting to eliminate classification distortions together with random errors. The SER system uses weak learners as classification algorithms that succeed above random interpretation, but strong learners excel at detecting emotions from speech characteristics. The optimized gradient boosting algorithm XGBoost implements decision trees as fundamental base classifiers for its operation. The rapid performance together with scalability advantages and maximized efficiency makes this system popular for SER applications. The training makes new trees successively improve upon the errors found in previous trees. XGBoost's objective function Equation (8.2) follows:

$$L(\Theta) = \Sigma_{j=1}^{m} k(z_j,\ \hat{z}_j) + \Sigma_{l=1}^{l} \Omega(e_l) \tag{8.2}$$

The loss function $k(z_j,\ \hat{z}_j)$ determines the variance among real and forecast emotion labels. The regularized term $\Omega(e_l)$ determines the complexity of the built model. XGBoost allows SER models to reach higher accuracy levels, thus establishing as an effective alternative for voice-based emotion detection.

8.2.10 DNN

The practice of Speech Emotion Recognition (SER) through speech signals employs deep learning (DL) techniques prominently using Deep Neural Networks (DNNs). The model architecture consists of three stages that serve to discover connections between speech characteristics and emotional conditions: DNNs combine an input layer with multiple hidden layers and an output stage. The input layer in SER systems receives audio features that capture speech tone, pitch, and intensity characteristics. The hidden layers serve to teach the model how emotional cues are hierarchically arranged within the speech signal. The classification of emotional state occurs at the output layer by referencing the features that the model learned. The training process for DNNs in SER employs backpropagation to minimize error through weight updates between predicted and actual emotion labels. The algorithm for weight update during backpropagation follows this mathematical Equation (8.3):

$$x = x - \eta \cdot \frac{\partial \mathrm{K}}{\partial \mathrm{x}} \tag{8.3}$$

In this case, x stands for weight, η for learning rate, K for function of loss, and $\frac{\partial \mathrm{K}}{\partial \mathrm{x}}$ for the gradient of the loss relative to weight. By repeating this procedure iteratively, the model's accuracy in classifying emotions from voice signals is improved.

8.2.11 RCNN

The RCNN performs SER tasks from voice signals. The model design include four successive 1D convolutional layers. The model begins with two layers that contain 256 units followed by layers with 128 units then layers with 64 units which activate through *ReLU* functions. The passage of each convolutional layer depends on a *MaxPooling* operation which extracts significant speech characteristics. The initial layer uses Dropout together with L_1 and L_2 regularization to minimize overfitting and achieve better-generalized results. The fully connected layer with a *softmax* activation performs emotional state classification. The following is the expression for the RCNN optimal Equation (8.4) with L_1 and L_2 regularization:

$$L(\theta) = L_0(\theta) + \lambda_1 \,\|\theta\|_1 + \lambda_2 \,\|\theta\|_2^2 \tag{8.4}$$

Where $L_0(\theta)$ is the initial loss function, $\|\theta\|_1$ promotes sparsity by eliminating unnecessary weights. Large weights are penalized by $\|\theta\|_2$ to avoid overfitting. λ_1 and λ_2 determine the effect of regularization.

8.2.12 1-D DCNN

The acoustic characteristics that are taken from speech signals are used by the 1-D DCNN. A network design incorporates three convolutional layers with filters that increase from 32–64–128 as well as compact 1 × 3 filters, which enable efficient local and global feature extraction. The combined usage of zero-padding maintains feature dimensions and *ReLU* activation stops gradient vanishing during processing. The definition of the convolution operation is as follows in Equation (8.5):

$$y(m) = feat(m) \times x(m) = \sum_{m-0}^{j=1} feat(n) \times x(m-n) \tag{8.5}$$

The mathematical expression indicates how $Feat(m)$ represents speech features from inputs with the filter kernel designated as $x(m)$. The progressive generation of high-level characteristics in speech emotions happens through each convolutional layer that creates feature maps. The processed information enters two fully connected layers that transform the features into discriminative space.

$$z_{il}(w) = e\left(\sum_{j=1}^{mG} X_{il} w_j + xj_0\right) \tag{8.6}$$

The system includes an input feature vector w together with weights X and an activation function e, in Equation (8.6). The *softmax* classifier chooses emotion labels through the maximum probability values.

$$\hat{z} = \arg\max_i Q_i \tag{8.7}$$

Equation (8.7) Q denotes the probabilities of class. The 1-D DCNN efficiently applies its capabilities to identify short-term and long-term dependencies in speech signals to perform optimally for SER operations.

8.3 Result

The results proved that it is possible to train ML and DL models that are capable of identifying behavioral characteristics related to signal processing.

There were differences in the models' accuracy and adaptability, indicating that several of them outperformed others. These findings demonstrate that ML and DL can be used to signal-processing experiments and that framework recognition is essential for enhanced performance.

8.3.1 Comparison Evaluation of ML and DL-Based Methods

To assess the effectiveness of ML and DL-based methods in behavioral signal analysis for speech and EEG signal recognition. Measures, like F1 score, recall, accuracy, and precision account for the unique features of each approach.

8.3.1.1 Accuracy

The overall correct identification rate of speech or EEG signals by a model represents its accuracy measurement. The accuracy ratio determines the integer of accurate instances against the total integer of instances. The accuracy metric becomes unreliable in unbalanced datasets, so organizations need to implement supplementary assessment methods to gauge model performance correctly.

8.3.1.2 Precision

The reliability of positive predictions in speech and EEG classification systems is evaluated by precision measure. This measurement enables the detection of correct signals in their intended category while omitting erroneous detection results. Speech emotion recognition and medical EEG diagnosis depend on precision levels to minimize wrong class assignments.

8.3.1.3 Recall

Assessing the model's capability to detect all relevant speech and EEG signals constitutes the recall evaluation. The identification performance of correct instances determines how well the system avoids missing valid instances while processing data. Recall requires high priority in EEG-based emotion detection to prevent missing important emotional states, especially in cases of stress.

8.3.1.4 F1 Score

The F1 score represents an optimal metric for speech and EEG signal classification, since it provides harmonious control between precision and recall performance measurements. F1 score provides an essential assessment of detection systems specifically in healthcare because it finds application particularly in unbalanced data scenarios that require high recognition rates while minimizing false positive results.

8.3.1.5 *EEG Signal*

Evaluation of different EEG-based methods for behavioral signal processing demonstrates differences in achieved performance metrics as shown in Figure 8.4 and Table 8.1. The accuracy of ResNet152 reaches 91.30% but

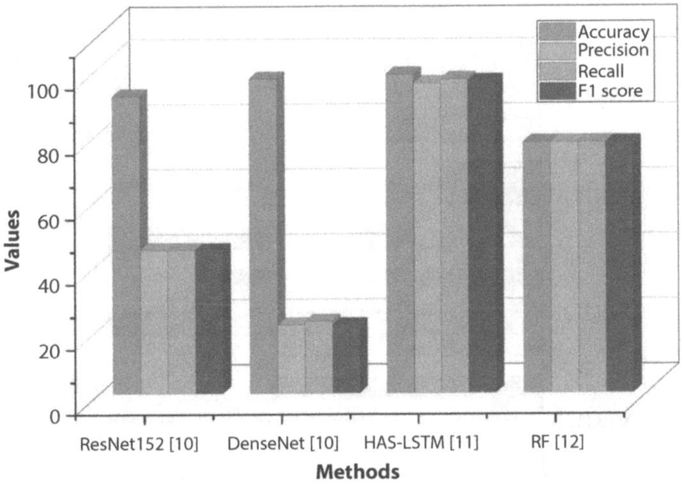

Figure 8.4 Performance analysis of different EEG-based methods for BSP. Source: Own elaboration.

Table 8.1 Comparison of EEG-based methods for BSP.

Methods	Accuracy (%)	Precision (%)	Recall (%)	F1 score (%)
ResNet152 [10]	91.30	44	44	44
DenseNet [10]	96.67	21	22	21
HAS-LSTM [11]	97.92	95.24	96.43	95.83
RF [12]	77	77	77	77

Source: Own elaboration.

its low precision of 44%, recall 44% along with F1 score of 44% demonstrate inadequate true positive detection efficiency. The 96.67% accuracy achieved by DenseNet reductions is short because its precision of 21%, recall of 22%, and F1 score of 2% measurements reveal inadequate detection of positive cases. The HAS-LSTM method demonstrates superior performance through its highest accuracy level of 97.92%, precision of 95.24%, recall of 96.43%, and an F1 score of 95.83%, which makes it an ideal solution for EEG-based behavioral signal processing. RF achieves moderate classification performance while maintaining stable scores across all metrics that amount to 77.

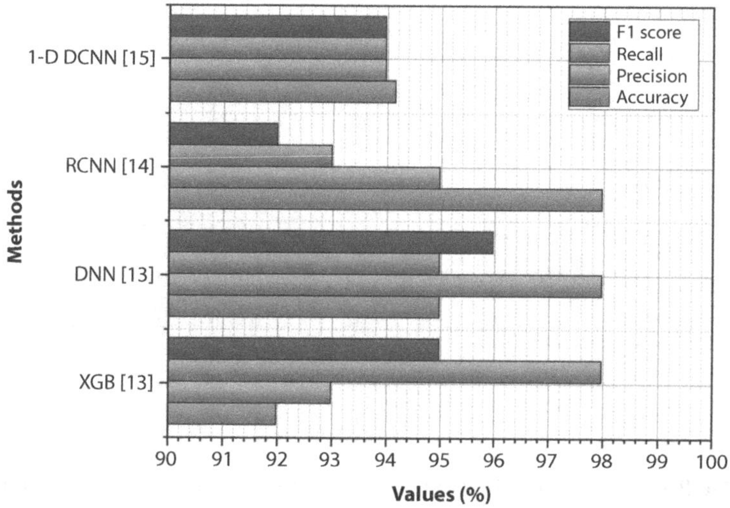

Figure 8.5 Performance analysis of different speech signal-based methods for BSP. Source: Own elaboration.

Table 8.2 Comparison of speech signal-based methods for BSP.

Methods	Accuracy (%)	Precision (%)	Recall (%)	F1 score (%)
XGB [13]	92	93	98	95
DNN [13]	95	98	95	96
RCNN [14]	98	95	93	92
1-D DCNN [15]	94.18	94	94	94

Source: Own elaboration.

8.3.1.6 Speech Signal

The key evaluation metric for BSP models shows accuracy as a measure of model precision in speech emotion recognition, as shown in Figure 8.5 and Table 8.2. With an accuracy of 98%, the RCNN implementation is the most accurate classification model, followed by XGB at 92%, DNN at 95%, and 1-D DCNN at 94.18%. Precision indicates the accurate identification rate of positive cases among all predicted instances. The precision level of DNN is the highest at 98%, while XGB follows with 93%, RCNN maintains 95% and 1-D DCNN achieves 94%. This indicates that DNN detects the fewest incorrect predictions. Recall identifies how well the model detects all applicable situations. The recall rate of 98% belongs to XGB, making the model that detects positive cases most effectively among the others, including DNN (95%), 1-D DCNN (94%), and RCNN (93%).

The F1 score combines precision and recall to measure complete performance effectiveness. The research establishes that DNN delivers top results with F1 score of 96% above XGB's score of 95% while 1-D DCNN stands at 94% and RCNN ends at 92%. This proves that DNN has the optimal precision-recall ratio. The implementation of RCNN delivers the highest accuracy levels, but XGB produces the strongest recall performance and DNN reaches optimal precision and F1 score points which demonstrates different applications' strength for speech emotion recognition in BSP contexts.

8.3.2 Discussion

The combination of physiological and speech signals in multibehavioral signal processing makes use of AI through ML and DL techniques for analysis. The methods demonstrate improved capabilities for recognizing and interpreting data and making decisions in clinical settings and human–machine interfaces as well as systems that detect emotions. The experimentation reveals that HAS-LSTM [11] surpasses all other techniques in EEG-based BSP, while attaining superior accuracy metrics. The model's capability to detect patterns within time-related EEG signal data increases its performance in both extraction and classification steps. ResNet152 [10] alongside DenseNet [10] demonstrates high accuracy, yet their precision and recall performance are decreased, which results from difficulties detecting refined EEG manifestations. RF [12] demonstrates the lowest performance, since the algorithm fails to recognize the complex nonlinear patterns in EEG signals. The analysis of physiological EEG data for behavioral signal processing demonstrates that deep learning models show higher effectiveness, especially through the HAS-LSTM model implementation.

Multiple speech-based behavioral signal processing helps to achieve better performance in speech emotion recognition tasks. The ensemble model XGB [13] uses tree-based structures to improve decision trees for reliable classification. Several hidden layers in DNN [13] models extract complex speech patterns, because it create powerful feature learning capabilities. RCNN [14] uses convolutional layers together with recurrent structures to acquire spatial and temporal attributes in speech signals. However, 1-D DCNN [15] functions efficiently on speech signals through frequency-based feature detection while preserving computational effectiveness. These methods provide beneficial features for BSP applications through their different learning capabilities and computational efficiency and capacity for speech variation processing.

8.4 Conclusion

The evaluation involved creating an integrated framework to analyze multidimensional signals obtained from both physiological and speech signal data. Researchers used high-resolution EEG recordings and speech samples together with multiple ML and DL approaches for signal processing and classification activities. Multiple evaluative metrics, including precision, recall, accuracy, and F1 score measured the operational success of these processing techniques. The analysis showed ML approaches produce less effective results than DL methods in terms of performance outcomes. The developed framework showed potential in enhancing signal processing methods according to examination results, which should enable new applications in neuroethology fields alongside human–computer interfaces.

Limitation and future scope: The examination had several limitations because of its small sample size along with signal noise forms and a restricted scope of generalizability to real-world situations. Larger datasets, sophisticated noise reduction methods, and real-time applications should be explored in future directions. Increased multimodal integration and improved model designs further enriched behavioral signal processing, and increasingly powerful neurotechnology and adaptive human–computer interaction systems. Close collaboration and ongoing validation continue to be crucial.

AI disclosure statement: The author confirms that no artificial intelligence (AI)-generated content or AI-assisted writing tools were used in the preparation of this chapter (including summaries and the abstract). All text, analysis, and conclusions are the result of the author's original work.

References

1. Yang, K., *et al.*, Behavioral and physiological signals-based deep multimodal approach for mobile emotion recognition. *IEEE Trans. Affective Comput.*, 14.2, 1082–1097, 2021, https://doi.org/10.1109/TAFFC.2021.3100868.
2. Luo, J.-F., *et al.*, Human-Centered Financial Signal Analysis Based on Visual Patterns in Stock Charts. *IEEE Trans. Multimed.*, 27, 4193–4205, 2025, https://doi.org/10.1109/TMM.2025.3535278.
3. Kumar, D., *et al.*, Highly efficient back-end-of-line compatible flexible Si-based optical memristive crossbar array for edge neuromorphic physiological signal processing and bionic machine vision. *Nano Micro Lett.*, 16.1, 238, 2024, https://doi.org/10.1007/s40820-024-01456-8.
4. Samayamantri, L.S., *et al.*, AI-Driven Multimodal Approaches to Human Behavior Analysis, in: *Advancing Intelligent Networks Through Distributed Optimization*, pp. 485–506, IGI Global, USA, 2024, doi: 10.4018/979-8-3693-3739-4.ch025.
5. Thirupathi, L., *et al.*, AI and IoT in Mental Health Care: From Digital Diagnostics to Personalized, Continuous Support, in: *Intelligent Systems and IoT Applications in Clinical Health*, pp. 271–294, IGI Global, India, 2025, https://doi.org/10.4018/979-8-3693-8990-4.ch012.
6. Mercado-Diaz, L.R., *et al.*, EDA-Graph: Graph Signal Processing of Electrodermal Activity for Emotional States Detection. *IEEE J. Biomed. Health. Inf.*, 28, 4599–4612, 2024, https://doi.org/10.1109/JBHI.2024.3405491.
7. Li, X., Research on Intelligent Analysis Algorithm for Student Learning Behavior Based on Multi-Source Sensor Data Fusion. *Int. J. High Speed Electron. Syst.*, 2540198, 2025, https://doi.org/10.1142/S0129156425401986.
8. Chintala, S., Emotion AI in Business Intelligence: Under-standing Customer Sentiments and Behaviors. *Cent. Asian J. Math. Theory Comput. Sci.*, 5.3, 205–212, 2024.
9. Haleem, A. and Javaid, M., Role of cognitive computing in enhancing innovative healthcare solutions. *Adv. Biomarker Sci. Technol.*, 6, 152–165, 2024, https://doi.org/10.1016/j.abst.2024.08.002.
10. Radhakrishnan, M., *et al.*, Performance analysis of deep learning models for detection of autism spectrum disorder from EEG signals. *Traitement du Signal*, 38.3, 853–863, 2021, https://doi.org/10.18280/ts.380332.
11. Nakra, A. and Duhan, M., Deep neural network with harmony search based optimal feature selection of EEG signals for motor imagery classification. *Int. J. Inf. Technol.*, 15.2, 611–625, 2023, https://doi.org/10.1007/s41870-021-00857-x.
12. Daghriri, T., *et al.*, Electroencephalogram signals for detecting confused students in online education platforms with probability-based features. *Electronics*, 11.18, 2855, 2022, https://doi.org/10.3390/electronics11182855.

13. Rahman, S., *et al.*, Classification of Parkinson's disease using speech signal with machine learning and deep learning approaches. *Eur. J. Electr. Eng. Comput. Sci.*, 7.2, 20–27, 2023. http://dx.doi.org/10.24018/ejece.2023.7.2.488.
14. Olatinwo, D.D., *et al.*, IoT-enabled WBAN and machine learning for speech emotion recognition in patients. *Sensors*, 23.6, 2948, 2023, https://doi.org/10.3390/s23062948.
15. Bhangale, K. and Kothandaraman, M., Speech emotion recognition based on multiple acoustic features and deep convolutional neural network. *Electronics*, 12.4, 839, 2023, https://doi.org/10.3390/electronics12040839.

9

Prediction of Suicidal Thoughts and Pychiatric Symptoms

Manju Bargavi S. K.[1]*, Y. Narasimha Raja[2], Surjeet Sahoo[3] and Trapty Agarwal[4]

[1]*Department of CSIT, Jain (Deemed-to-be University), Bangalore, Karnataka, India*
[2]*Department of Management, Presidency University, Bengaluru, Karnataka, India*
[3]*Department of Psychiatry, IMS and SUM Hospital, Siksha 'O' Anusandhan (Deemed to be University), Bhubaneswar, Odisha, India*
[4]*Maharishi School of Engineering and Technology, Maharishi University of Information Technology, Uttar Pradesh, India*

Abstract

Suicidal thoughts and psychiatric symptoms are significant mental health issues, often influenced by complex psychological, social, and biological factors. However, conventional assessment methods rely on self-reporting and clinical evaluations, which cannot always capture underlying distress accurately. This chapter aims to enhance the prediction of suicidal thoughts and psychiatric symptoms using advanced text and image analysis techniques. Natural language processing (NLP) is applied to textual data from social media posts, comments, likes, and shares, while deep learning (DL) and machine learning (ML) models analyze facial expressions and visual cues from images to identify distress indicators. The experimental results demonstrate high predictive accuracy in detecting suicidal ideation and psychiatric symptoms, with the model outperforming traditional assessment techniques. These findings highlight the potential of artificial intelligence (AI)-driven approaches in mental health screening, emphasizing the need for further research to improve interpretability, ethical considerations, and real-world clinical integration.

**Corresponding author*: b.manju@jainuniversity.ac.in; ORCID: 0000-0001-7112-5810
Y. Narasimha Raja: ORCID: 0009-0005-7127-787X
Surjeet Sahoo: ORCID: 0000-0003-2445-9994
Trapty Agarwal: ORCID: 0009-0007-4081-4999

Sudesh Yadav, Pethuru Raj, Satya Prakash Yadav and Victor Hugo C. de Albuquerque (eds.) Natural Language Processing in Mental Health Care: Methodologies and Clinical Practice, (119–134) © 2026 Scrivener Publishing LLC

***Keywords*:** Suicidal thoughts, psychiatric symptoms, deep learning, natural language processing, artificial intelligence, machine learning

9.1 Introduction

Suicidal thoughts and psychiatric symptoms are crucial topics in mental health, and self-harm and suicidal behaviors have relevance to general human health and medical practice [1]. Major depression, anxiety, bipolar disorders, and schizophrenia are some of the psychopathological conditions for which individuals are more at risk of developing suicidal thoughts [2]. Assessing predictive factors for suicidal thoughts and psychic symptoms is a difficult task because mental disorder is influenced by genetic, neurobiological, psychological, as well as environmental factors [3]. Modern approaches to assessment use questionnaires and clinical evaluations. Although these methods are useful, they rely on self-reported and therefore subject to over and underestimation. Among the most significant technologies that have proven to be rather informative in the analysis of the mentioned types of data, there are Machine Learning (ML), Deep Learning (DL), and Natural Language Processing (NLP) [4]. However, the following is a list of some of the challenges that affect the validity of current predictive models: A weakness of the study is the small volume of high-quality datasets available to be used more frequently because mental health data are often limited due to privacy and prejudice. Furthermore, most of the developed models have a serious problem with generalization because of demographic and cultural differences, making it difficult to develop universal prediction systems [5]. Moral issues, such as data privacy and consent also pose a challenge for implementation due to concerns about the misuse of the predictive models. However, real-time prediction remains an issue as suicidal ideation and psychiatric symptoms are constantly changing and should be assessed more frequently rather than periodically [6]. Many studies also fail to account for individual differences, such as coping mechanisms and personal resilience, which can influence mental health trajectories. The interpretability of machine learning models in psychiatry is another challenge, as black-box algorithms often lack transparency, making it difficult for clinicians to trust and apply their findings in practice [7]. Hence, this chapter proposes the use of text and image analysis to enhance the prediction of suicidal ideation and psychiatric symptoms. Its application is to create a more effective and efficient screening model for mental health with comparisons to the more conventional method of self-assessment.

9.2 Methodology

It employs NLP for the text analysis of the data gathered from social media and DL/ML for the analysis of expressions and movements from videos. The integration of text and image-based analysis with visual analysis helps in the improvement of suicidal ideation and psychiatric symptom identification.

9.2.1 Datasets

The dataset required for model implementation is available on the open-source platform. The data compilation includes Twitter and Reddit posts that feature mental health-related text-based content with accompanying comments and responses. The textual information is saved in .csv files that consist of user-created posts along with metadata timestamps alongside likes shares and comments. Another source of data includes images of facial expressions from public databases that are sad, neutral, and happy. These are pictures labeled with self-assessment data or observed behavioral signs related to mental conditions. The file is transferred to Google Drive to edit, as the next step toward model integration or for further data processing using Python packages.

9.2.2 Data Preparation for the Classification Model

Data preparation and feature extraction is the process of preparing data for a classification model for data type, including text, image, and video. Text data is preprocessed by removing the stop words, stemming or lemmatizing the documents, and the features are extracted through Term Frequency-Inverse Document Frequency (TF-IDF) or Word to Vector (Word2Vec). The image data are normalized, resized, and enhanced by principal component analysis (PCA) or convolutional neural network (CNN) or the Histogram of oriented gradients (HOG) feature extraction models. The treatment of videos involves frame extraction, conversion to grayscale, and feature extraction through 3D CNN or optical flow. Categorical data is a normalized or standardized format for structured numerical data. That data is further archived for use in subsequent model integration and analysis.

9.2.3 Text Analysis Method

Textual insights are derived through processing methods, including NLP, and sentiment analysis, as well as topic modeling, which analyze data through specific techniques. It examines comments by evaluating their

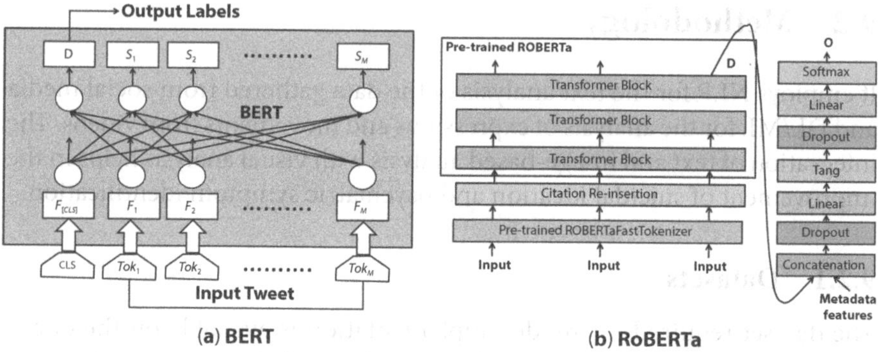

Figure 9.1 Schematic structure of (a) BERT, & (b) RoBERTa. Source: (a) https://www.genspark.ai/spark/bert-step-by-step-tutorial-hugging-face-for-text-classification/6629b755-d1ba-4921-98b1-63da5b4845a8, (b) https://www.comet.com/site/blog/roberta-a-modified-bert-model-for-nlp/

sentiments while identifying important keywords as well as taking into account their context for realizing emotional responses and level of participation. Figure 9.1 depicts the structural diagram of BERT, and RoBERTa.

9.2.4 Bidirectional Encoder Representation from Transformer

Google's bidirectional encoder representation from transformer (BERT) model applied in NLP identifies the psychiatric symptoms and suicidal thoughts by employing the large data set and labeled data approach. It consists of six bidirectional transformer layers with a multihead self-attention mechanism, feed-forward, residual connections, and layer normalizations. In BERT [8], self-attention is described in Equation (9.1).

$$Attention(R,L,U) = softmax\left(\frac{RL^S}{\sqrt{c_L}}\right)U \tag{9.1}$$

where R *and* L stand for the dimension c_l of the query and key matrices. R, L, *and* U, stand for the query, key, and value matrix structures, respectively. Equation (9.2) illustrates how multihead attention extends this method.

$$MultiHead(R,L,U) = Concat(head1,\ldots,headg)X^0 \tag{9.2}$$

Self-attention is applied independently by each head before concatenation. The model can capture a variety of contextual relationships. It is assumed to be a bidirectional model that can simultaneously receive context from both the left and the right sides which is useful for deciphering mental health symptoms or looking for suicidal ideas in textual data. To that effect, the self-attention mechanisms adopted in BERT improve overall language cues related to common mental health conditions, hence enhancing prognosis and treatment patterns.

9.2.5 Robustly Optimized BERT Pretraining Approach (RoBERTa)

It seeks to build on improvements of the BERT model to give more accurate predictions on psychiatric symptoms and suicidal tendencies [9]. Robustly optimized BERT pretraining approach (RoBERTa) makes changes in the schedule of the pretraining isolation, mini-batch size, and complete sentence learning without next sentence prediction (NSP) loss, and a higher Byte-Level Byte Pair Encoding (BPE). In RoBERTa, the self-attention mechanism is the same as in BERT. In particular, in the process of pre-training, RoBERTa employs the denoising autoencoder objective, since the denoising autoencoder $Loss\ (K_{denoise})$ is expressed as Equation (9.3).

$$K_{denoise} = \sum_{(s=j)}^{S} LogO(w_s \,|\, Corrupt(w_s);\theta) \tag{9.3}$$

If W_s is an input token, Corrupt w_s is its corrupted variant, and θ stands for model parameters. The denoising autoencoder loss and task-specific losses are combined to form the overall training loss, as shown in Equation (9.4).

$$K_{total}(\theta) = \lambda K_{total}(\theta) + \sum_j K_{task_j}(\theta) \tag{9.4}$$

Where K_{task_j} the loss for a specific prediction is task, and λ is a hyperparameter that balances the denoising objective with task-specific objectives. These improvements allow RoBERTa to identify better syntactic and other patterns in the text and therefore its assessment of psychiatric symptoms.

9.2.6 Logistic Regression

Logistic regression (LR) [10] is a pertinent method for determining whether suicidal thoughts is present or absent because it is developed from the linear model and is especially well suited for binary classification problems. In a linear function, the log-odds of the probability in an LR model with k features are modeled from features $W = w_1, w_2, \ldots, w_k$ using the Equations (9.5 and 9.6).

$$\log\left(\frac{o}{1-0}\right) = \Sigma_{i=1}^{l} \beta_i z_i \leftrightarrow 0 = \frac{1}{1 + f^{-\Sigma_i \beta_i z_i}} \tag{9.5}$$

$$k\beta \, \Sigma_{j=1}^{m}[w_j z_j \beta - \log(1 + f^{y_j \beta})] \tag{9.6}$$

The parameters β shrank as a result of penalization, and Lasso allowed selection by setting specific β values to zero and it is illustrated in Equation (9.7).

$$k\beta \, \Sigma_{j=1}^{m}[w_j z_j \beta - \log(1 + f^{z_j \beta})] \tag{9.7}$$

The likelihood ratio test was used to compare nested models to choose variables. Main effects were retained in the first phase only if their corresponding P values were less than 0.05. In the second stage, all previously maintained main effects were incorporated in models that were methodically fitted to evaluate all second-order interactions. For interaction testing, P values less than 0.10 were taken into account. Only the interactions with P values less than 0.10 were kept after a model was built that included the retained main effects and significant second-order interactions. Using comparable methods, third-order and fourth-order interaction terms were chosen from this model. Lasso and ridge penalization were used to improve the predictive accuracy of evaluating psychiatric symptoms and suicidal thoughts. At that time, the function to maximize was shown in Equation (9.8).

$$k_\lambda^\omega = \Sigma_{j=1}^{m}[x_j y_j \beta - \log(1 + f^{y_j \beta})] - \lambda \Sigma_{i=1}^{l} |\beta_i|^\omega \tag{9.8}$$

A fundamental method for determining the probability of suicidal thoughts based on a variety of clinical and psychological signs was made possible by this LR framework.

9.2.7 Long Short-Term Memory (LSTM)

It is designed for diagnosing and prognoising the psychiatric symptoms and risk of suicidal thoughts from time series data patterns. An LSTM [11] unit includes a memory cell and three control gates, which include the input, forget, and output gates. The cell state is at the center of the model as a mechanism for passing information between clusters in a controlled manner. The forget gate mechanism controls the amount of data from the previous concealed state and inputs the hidden state at the current time step that is to be erased or remembered. The input coupling controls the incoming information through a sigmoid and hyperbolic tangent *tang* function to control the memory cell. Afterward, the output gate corresponds to the relevant information to create a final output so that only relevant features contribute to the prediction. Mathematically, these gates function as follows in Equations (9.9–9.11).

Forget gate

$$e_s = \sigma(X_e[g_{s-1}, w_s] + a_e) \tag{9.9}$$

Input gate

$$j_s = \sigma(X_j[g_{s-1}, w_s] + a_j)$$

$$\tilde{D}_s = tang(X_D[g_{s-1}, w_s] + a_d) \tag{9.10}$$

$$D_s = e_s * D_{s-1} + j_s * \tilde{D}_s$$

Output gate

$$p_s = \sigma(X_p[g_{s-1}, w_s] + a_p) \tag{9.11}$$

$$g_s = p_s * tang(D_s)$$

LSTM networks are particularly useful for identifying attributes of psychiatric symptoms and suicidal thinking due to their ability to learn about dependencies within time series data, which are highly useful in the monitoring and early risk assessment of a patient.

9.2.8 Image Analysis Methods

Image processing techniques are techniques for analyzing images and some examples include filtering, edge detection, and DL feature extraction.

These techniques facilitate object recognition, classification, segmentation, and pattern detection to be used in different applications.

9.2.9 Convolutional Neural Networks (CNN)

It is employed in DL models for feature extraction and classification to predict suicidal thoughts and mental symptoms. The CNN's [12] convolutional, pooling, and fully connected layers use the features Ξ_{EF} as inputs. Each neuron in the convolution layer links to neighboring neurons inside the feature map, and the convolution layer uses numerous kernels to analyze feature maps. The feature values of the $\tilde{d}^{th}$ feature map in the $\tilde{l}^{th}$ layer at a specific location $(\tilde{b}, \tilde{a})$ are computed in Equation (9.12).

$$H^{\tilde{l}}_{\tilde{b},\tilde{a},\tilde{d}} = \tilde{X}^{\tilde{l}^S}_{\tilde{d}} \Xi_{EF} + F^{\tilde{l}}_{\tilde{d}} \tag{9.12}$$

where $\tilde{X}^{\tilde{l}}_{\tilde{d}}$ symbolizes the weight used for training, and $F^{\tilde{l}}_{\tilde{d}}$ is the phrase used for bias. By enhancing nonlinearity, the activation function makes it easier to recognize intricate patterns in the dataset. The activation value is calculated by Equation (9.13).

$$\mathfrak{R}^{\tilde{l}}_{\tilde{b},\tilde{a},\tilde{d}} = \mathfrak{R}\left(H^{\tilde{l}}_{\tilde{b},\tilde{a},\tilde{d}}\right) \tag{9.13}$$

Pooling Layer: To decrease spatial dimensions while keeping important information, the pooling layers down sample. The process of pooling is defined as Equation (9.14).

$$\lambda^{\tilde{l}}_{\tilde{b},\tilde{a},\tilde{d}} = M\left(\mathfrak{R}^{\tilde{l}}_{\tilde{o},\tilde{r},\tilde{d}}\right), \forall(\tilde{o},\tilde{r}) \in \Xi_{\tilde{o},\tilde{r}} \tag{9.14}$$

In this case, the pooling function applied to activation values is indicated by $M(.)$.

Loss Function: It calculates the differences between expected and actual results, as illustrated in Equation (9.15).

$$Loss = \frac{1}{\tilde{D}} \Sigma^{\tilde{d}}_{\tilde{r}=1} \tilde{l}(\theta; \lambda^{(\tilde{r})}, PS^{(\tilde{r})}) \tag{9.15}$$

The total parameters are represented by θ, and $\lambda^{(\tilde{r})}$ indicates the features that were extracted, and $PS^{(\tilde{r})}$ is the CNN output that corresponds to the first input feature $\tilde{r}^{th}$. Early identification and intervention are made easier by the CNN output, which acts as the ultimate prediction for suicidal thoughts and mental health symptoms.

9.2.10 Support Vector Machine (SVM)

The best hyperplane for classifying fresh data is found through structural risk reduction in this supervised learning classifier. SVM simultaneously minimizes training error and generalization errors to find the optimal hyperplane. To determine the link between the Vapnik–Chervonenkis (VC) dimension and the best hyperplane, the margin between the hyperplane and the closest data point is maximized. The structure that maintains a balanced training error and has the lowest VC dimension is the ideal hyperplane [13]. Figure 9.2 shows the architecture of SVM. The following Equation (9.16) provides the splitting hyperplane constraint.

$$a \leq min\left[\frac{R^2}{f^2}\right], C+1 \tag{9.16}$$

Where R is the lowest sphere diameter that includes all input features Ξ_{EF} and C is the dimensionality of the input space. SVM efficiently lowers the VC dimension by raising the margin, improving classification performance. It assigns risk categories that reflect the probability of suicidal ideation by classifying people based on extracted data to predict suicidal

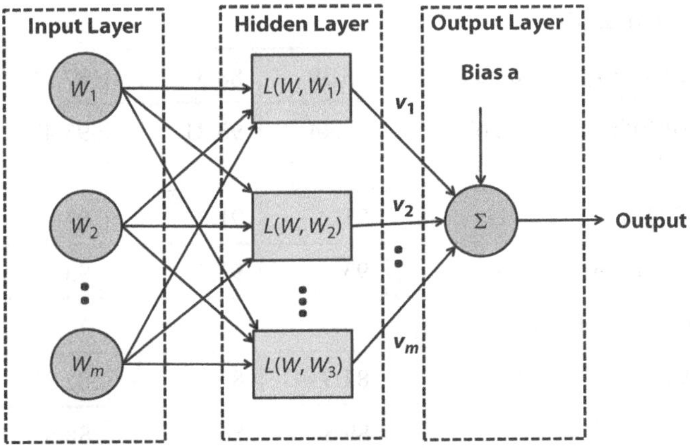

Figure 9.2 SVM architecture. Source: https://www.bdifk.store/?ggcid=2775375.

thoughts and mental symptoms. The model's output is an essential part of a larger prediction framework that might include other ML models for improved accuracy.

9.3 Result

Suicidal thoughts and mental illnesses can be accurately forecast with a high degree of effectiveness. The use of the proposed AI-driven tactic is even more effective than traditional approaches as demonstrated in the assessment technique, hence showing promising signs for early intervention. The experimental setup includes a powerful computing system equipped with an Intel Core i9 processor, 32GB RAM, and an NVIDIA RTX 3090 GPU, optimized for DL tasks. A 2TB SSD is utilized for efficient storage and management of large-scale text and image datasets.

The comparison research assesses how well different text and image-based models predict mental health symptoms and suicidal ideation. Performance measurements that show the advantages and disadvantages of each approach in identifying distress indicators include recall, precision, accuracy, and F1 score. Table 9.1 represents the accuracy results acquired by proposed and existing models.

Table 9.1 Evaluation of different methods for predicting suicidal thoughts and psychiatric symptoms.

Methods	Precision (%)	Recall (%)	Accuracy (%)	F1 score (%)
Text analysis				
BERT [14]	83.04	93.39	88.3	87.91
RoBERTa [14]	92.67	98.44	95.21	95.47
LR [15]	91	91	91.2	91
LSTM [15]	93	93	93.5	93
Image analysis				
SVM [16]	81.1	84.5	82.5	82.8
CNN [16]	87.8	89.8	86.6	88.8

Source: Own elaboration

Accuracy: The percentage of accurately detected cases (both positive and negative) out of all the predictions the model made is known as the accuracy in predicting suicidal thoughts and psychiatric symptoms. It demonstrates the model's overall effectiveness in correctly detecting distress cues in both textual and visual data. Figure 9.3 and Table 9.1 show the accuracy results. Overall, the findings demonstrated that RoBERTa outperformed the other model forecasting mental symptoms and suicidal thoughts with the best accuracy (95.21%).

Precision: It is the proportion of true positive forecasts (correctly diagnosed cases of distress) among all cases that the model predicts as positive. In detecting people who have psychiatric symptoms or suicidal thoughts, it assesses the model's capacity to prevent false positives. Table 9.1 and Figure 9.4 depict the precision result. The ability of LSTM to correctly identify people at risk while reducing false positives is demonstrated by its highest precision of 93%.

Recall: It is the percentage of real positive instances that are accurately detected out of all real cases of distress in the prediction of suicidal thoughts and mental symptoms. It assesses how well the model can identify people exhibiting psychiatric symptoms or suicidal thoughts without overlooking pertinent cases. Table 9.1 and Figure 9.5 depict the recall evaluation. RoBERTa had the highest recall (98.44%), indicating that it is capable of identifying real-world instances of psychiatric symptoms and suicidal thoughts.

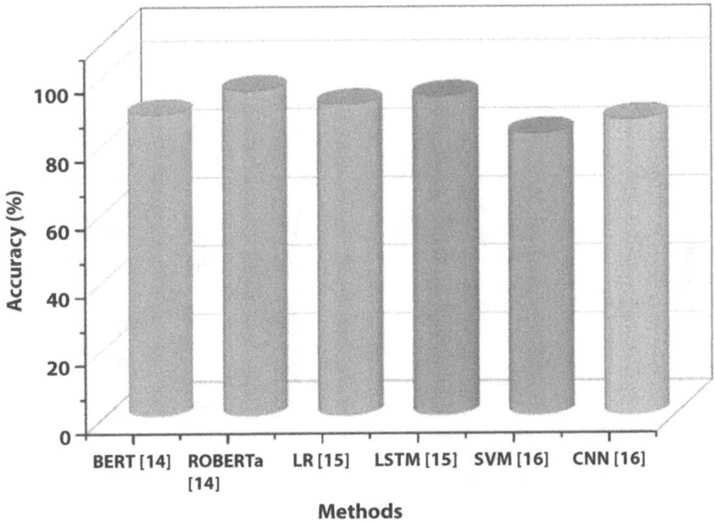

Figure 9.3 Accuracy distribution across text and image-based models. Source: Own elaboration.

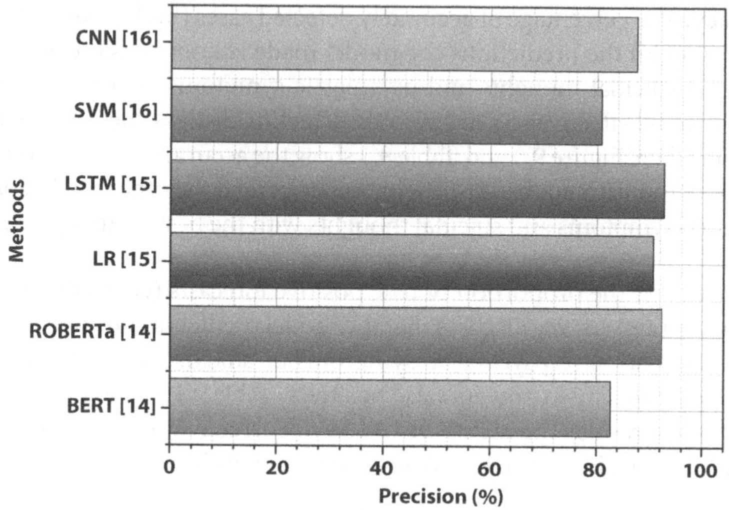

Figure 9.4 Precision analysis of prediction models. Source: Own elaboration.

F1 Score: The average of precision and recall is used to evaluate the balance between false positives and false negatives in the prediction of suicidal thoughts and mental symptoms. This statistic provides a thorough assessment of the model's precision in identifying distress while

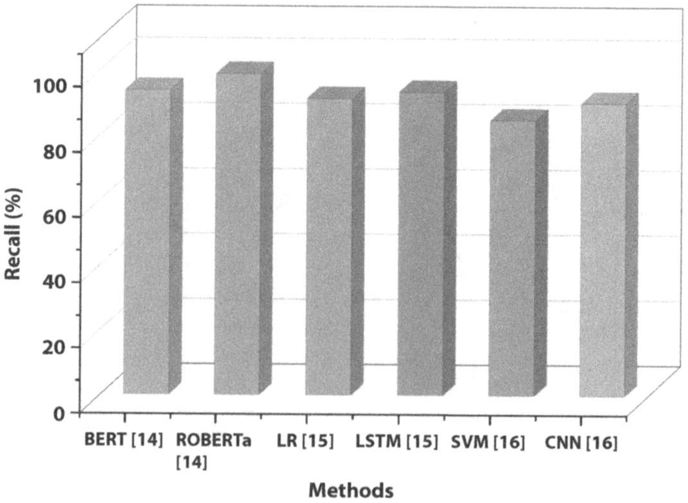

Figure 9.5 Recall performance in detecting suicidal thoughts and psychiatric symptoms. Source: Own elaboration.

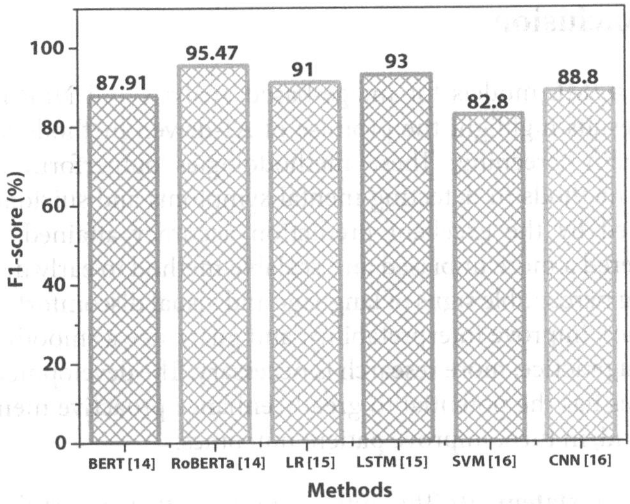

Figure 9.6 F1 score comparison of different methods. Source: Own elaboration.

reducing mistakes. The F1 Score results are shown in Table 9.1 and Figure 9.6. RoBERTa achieved the highest F1 score (95.47%), demonstrating its balanced recall and precision in identifying mental health issues.

9.3.1 Discussion

The comparison analysis demonstrates how well AI-driven solutions outperform conventional techniques in predicting psychiatric symptoms and suicidal thoughts. With the highest recall (98.44%), accuracy (95.21%), and F1 score (95.47%) among the models tested, RoBERTa [8] continuously outperformed the others, demonstrating its potent capacity to detect distress instances with few false negatives. With the highest precision (93%), LSTM [9] successfully reduced false positives while preserving dependable detection capabilities. With CNN attaining an accuracy of 86.6%, image-based models, like CNN and SVM fared worse than text-based models, indicating that textual data offers more trustworthy prediction insights. These results highlight how sophisticated NLP approaches can be used for early intervention in mental health assessments. It also highlights how crucial it is to use high-performance AI models to increase detection accuracy and ensure prompt support [11].

9.4 Conclusion

By using DL/ML models for image-based analysis and NLP for textual data, the results highlight the promise of AI-driven methods to improve mental health screening. These methodologies outperform traditional evaluation methods in detecting mental symptoms and suicidal ideation, as evidenced by the excellent prediction accuracy attained. AI-driven models offered a more unbiased and scalable method to early detection by recognizing perceptible signs of language and visual discomfort. To resolve ethical issues, improve interpretability, and guarantee a smooth transition into clinical practice, more research is necessary. The development of these technologies has the potential to greatly enhance proactive mental health therapies and, in turn, improve patient outcomes.

AI disclosure statement: The author confirms that no artificial intelligence (AI)-generated content or AI-assisted writing tools were used in the preparation of this chapter (including summaries and the abstract). All text, analysis, and conclusions are the result of the author's original work.

References

1. Zortea, T.C., *et al.*, The impact of infectious disease-related public health emergencies on suicide, suicidal behavior, and suicidal thoughts. *Crisis*, 42, 6, 474–487, 2021, https://doi.org/10.1027/0227-5910/a000753.
2. Zhu, H., *et al.*, Prevalence and risk factors of suicidal ideation in adult inpatients with five different types of mental disorders. *J. Affect. Disord.*, 291, 344–3515, 2021, https://doi.org/10.1016/j.jad.2021.05.033.
3. DiBlasi, E., Kang, J., R. Docherty, A., Genetic contributions to suicidal thoughts and behaviors. *Psychol. Med.*, 51.13, 2148–2155, 2021, https://doi.org/10.1017/S0033291721001720.
4. Yang, X. and Li, G., Psychological and Behavioral Insights From Social Media Users: Natural Language Processing–Based Quantitative Study on Mental Well-Being. *JMIR Formative Res.*, 9, e602865, 2025, https://doi.org/10.2196/60286.
5. Ghanadian, H., Nejadgholi, I., Al Osman, H., Socially aware synthetic data generation for suicidal ideation detection using large language models. *IEEE Access*, 12, 14350–143635, 2024, https://doi.org/10.1109/ACCESS.2024.3358206.
6. Czyz, E.K., *et al.*, Ecological momentary assessments and passive sensing in the prediction of short-term suicidal ideation in young adults. *JAMA Netw. Open*, 6.8, e2328005–e2328005, 2023. doi:10.1001/jamanetworkopen.2023.28005.

7. Sheu, Y.-., Illuminating the black box: interpreting deep neural network models for psychiatric research. *Front. Psychiatry*, 11, 551299, 2020, https://doi.org/10.3389/fpsyt.2020.551299.
8. Gorai, J. and Kumar Shaw, D., A BERT-encoded ensembled CNN model for suicide risk identification in social media posts. *Neural Comput. Appl.*, 36.18, 10955–10970, 2024, https://doi.org/10.1007/s00521-024-09642-w.
9. Tank, C., *et al.*, Su-RoBERTa: A Semi-supervised Approach to Predicting Suicide Risk through Social Media using Base Language Models. *arXiv preprint arXiv:2412.01353*, 2024, https://doi.org/10.48550/arXiv.2412.01353.
10. Velzen, V., S., L., *et al.*, Classification of suicidal thoughts and behaviour in children: Results from penalised logistic regression analyses in the Adolescent Brain Cognitive Development study. *Br. J. Psych.*, 220.4, 210–218, 2022, https://doi.org/10.1192/bjp.2022.7.
11. Feng, Y., *et al.*, Construction of a mental health risk model for college students with long and short-term memory networks and early warning indicators. *J. Intell. Syst.*, 33.1, 20230318, 2024, https://doi.org/10.1515/jisys-2023-0318.
12. Priyamvada, B., *et al.*, Stacked CNN-LSTM approach for prediction of suicidal ideation on social media. *Multimed. Tools Appl.*, 82.18, 27883–27904, 2023, https://doi.org/10.1007/s11042-023-14431-z.
13. Mohamed, E.S., *et al.*, A hybrid mental health prediction model using Support Vector Machine, Multilayer Perceptron, and Random Forest algorithms. *Healthc. Anal.*, 3, 1001855, 2023, https://doi.org/10.1016/j.health.2023.100185.
14. Haque, F., *et al.*, A transformer based approach to detect suicidal ideation using pre-trained language models. *2020 23rd International Conference on Computer and Information Technology (ICCIT)*, IEEE, 2020, http://dx.doi.org/10.1109/ICCIT51783.2020.9392692.
15. Haque, R., *et al.*, A comparative analysis on suicidal ideation detection using NLP, machine, and deep learning. *Technologies*, 10.3, 57, 2022, https://doi.org/10.3390/technologies10030057.
16. Renjith, S., *et al.*, An ensemble deep learning technique for detecting suicidal ideation from posts in social media platforms. *J. King Saud Univ. Comput. Inf. Sci.*, 34.10, 9564–9575, 2022, https://doi.org/10.1016/j.jksuci.2021.11.010.

Part 3

ADVANCED METHODS AND EVALUATION TECHNIQUES

10

Evaluation of Model Performance—Confusion Matrices, Sensitivity, Specificity, Kappa Statistics, Precision, Recall F-Measure, ROC Curve, Etc.

Kamalraj R.[1]*, Akkamahadevi C.[2], Duryodhan Jena[3] and Aditya Yadav[4]

[1]*Department of CSIT, Jain (Deemed-to-be University), Bangalore, Karnataka, India*
[2]*Department of Computer Science & Engineering, Presidency University, Bengaluru, Karnataka, India*
[3]*Department of Management, Siksha 'O' Anusandhan (Deemed to be University), Bhubaneswar, Odisha, India*
[4]*Maharishi School of Business Management, Maharishi University of Information Technology, Uttar Pradesh, India*

Abstract

Evaluating model performance is crucial for ensuring the reliability and effectiveness of machine learning (ML) and deep learning (DL) models in mental health applications, particularly in natural language processing (NLP)-based assessments. Key evaluation metrics provide insights into classification accuracy, error distribution, and predictive capabilities in detecting and assessing mental health conditions. This chapter aims to evaluate the performance of ML and DL models in mental health assessment using NLP by analyzing various evaluation techniques, ensuring accurate classification and predictive reliability. A confusion matrix enables a detailed examination of model predictions, forming the basis for calculating recall, sensitivity, precision, specificity, and the F measure. Sensitivity measures the ability to correctly identify individuals with mental health

**Corresponding author*: r.kamalraj@jainuniversity.ac.in; ORCID: 0000-0003-0489-6062
Akkamahadevi C.: ORCID: 0009-0007-2069-5857
Duryodhan Jena: ORCID: 0000-0002-9025-0905
Aditya Yadav: ORCID: 0000-0002-3986-0775

Sudesh Yadav, Pethuru Raj, Satya Prakash Yadav and Victor Hugo C. de Albuquerque (eds.) Natural Language Processing in Mental Health Care: Methodologies and Clinical Practice, (137–150) © 2026 Scrivener Publishing LLC

conditions, while specificity quantifies the accuracy of classifying those without. The kappa statistic assesses agreement between observed and predicted values beyond chance. The receiver operating characteristic (ROC) curve and area under the curve (AUC) offer a comprehensive view of model performance across different classification thresholds. A thorough assessment of these metrics ensures the robustness of ML and DL models, optimizing their accuracy in mental health diagnostics and contributing to more effective and personalized interventions.

Keywords: Deep learning, area under the curve, natural language processing, machine learning, receiver operating characteristic

10.1 Introduction

To ensure the dependability and efficacy of deep learning (DL) and machine learning (ML) in the examination of emotional disorders and communicative qualities, it is critical to evaluate the psychological and expressive natural language processing (NLP) models in the treatment of mental health issues [1]. Many statistical and computational techniques are used to examine these models, enabling their incorporation into future mental health diagnostic and treatment procedures [2]. Sensitivity, specificity, accuracy, and recall can be calculated using the confusion matrix, which compares expected and actual classifications [3]. The model's ability to accurately identify individuals with mental diseases is indicated by its sensitivity or true positive rate (TPR), whereas its specificity demonstrates its ability to accurately classify individuals who are not affected by such illnesses. While recall measures a model's ability to detect actual positives among all real positive cases, precision evaluates the proportion of predicted positive samples that are truly positive [4]. Recall and precision are combined into a single metric called the F-measure, which makes it easier to calculate the relative costs of missing cases and false positive detections. While statistical chance agreement is taken into account when assessing the reliability of data influenced by opinion, the kappa statistic calculates the frequency of agreement between observers on classification [5]. Receiver operating characteristic (ROC) curves represent the TPR against the false positive rate (FPR), across different classification thresholds and area under the curve (AUC) provides a measure of how well the models separate the conditions from nonconditions. A higher AUC also means better classifying performance and it is more helpful when it comes to clinical decisions [6]. These metrics are important to estimate by ML and DL models to enhance the accuracy of the classification. These evaluation metrics are critical for further enhancing psychological and expressive NLP models, fine-tuning algorithms aimed at sentiment and emotion estimation, and risk classification [7]. The multi-information evaluation utilizing multiple efficiency criteria confirms the validity of the suggested model, identifies potential development issues, and increases resistance to interference in various communicative and psychologic datasets. The improvement of psychological and expressive NLP models through the combinations of ML and DL with these evaluation techniques can increase the effectiveness and the probability density of the mental health assessment [8]. This chapter aims at evaluating the usefulness of the proposed ML and DL models in mental health assessment through NLP by comparing different assessment techniques, such as accuracy, sensitivity, specificity, precision, F-measure, kappa statistic, ROC curve, and AUC as an index of classification accuracy and reliability of the models.

10.2 Evaluation Metrics

Effective model performance evaluation enables NLP-based mental health assessments to accurately identify and categorize mental health disorders. Kappa statistics together with sensitivity, accuracy, specificity, and recall share importance with confusion matrices, precision, AUC, F-measure and the ROC curve as evaluation measures. ML and DL models achieve better precision and efficiency in mental health diagnosis through these assessment methods, which reveal details about classification performance while showing the distribution of errors and predictive outcomes.

Accuracy

Accuracy describes the efficiency of a mental health classification model in terms of the rate of correct identification of both the cases at risk and the stable cases [9]. Equation (10.1) expresses the number of true negatives (TN) and true positives (TP) relative to the total number of predictions, which also include false positives (FP) and false negatives (FN). High accuracy means that most of the classifications made are correct; however, using accuracy as a metric can be problematic where the dataset is imbalanced. In mental health applications, a model may appear accurate, but it must also effectively identify at-risk individuals. It shows a modest number of FP in addition to accuracy in detecting people at risk of the disease. Two ellipses that show how accuracy is calculated, as shown in Figure 10.1.

$$Accuracy = \frac{TP + TN}{TP + TN + FP + FN} \tag{10.1}$$

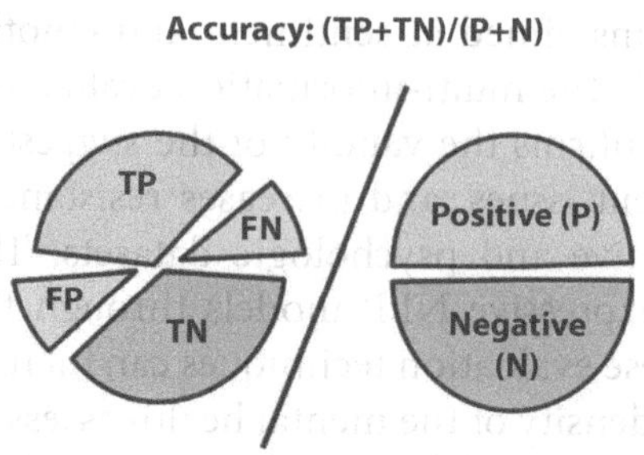

Figure 10.1 Visualization of accuracy calculation using ellipses. Source: https://moredvikas.wordpress.com/2017/09/12/what-is-true-positive-and-true-negative-confusion-matrix/.

Precision

Precision measures the percentage of the population of the target group that is considered at-risk through classification. Equation (10.2) is defined as true positives divided by total positive prediction, including false positives. A high precision [10] rate produces accurate predictions of at-risk individuals, which decreases overall false alarms and reduces unnecessary concern. In mental health classification, it is essential to ensure that individuals classified as at-risk require care. Optimizing precision rates directly influences recall performance to the point, where at-risk cases can be missed. A proper risk assessment model needs to maintain an equilibrium between precise predictions and thorough assessments for making accurate determinations. Figure 10.2 depicts the precision calculation using ellipses. A model that operates optimally produces minimal incorrect assessments to enable effective mental health condition detection without causing either excessive stress or medical oversight.

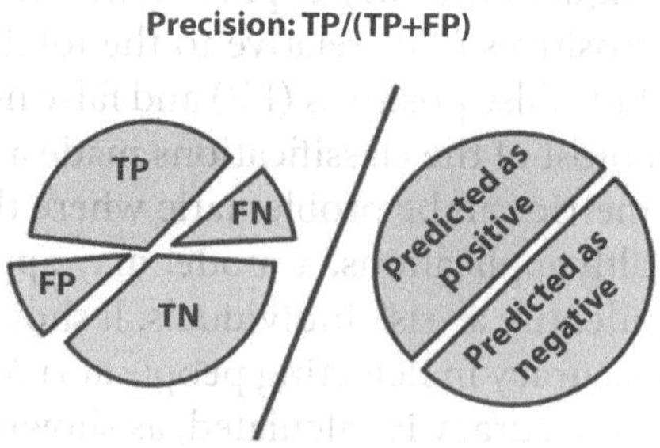

Figure 10.2 Precision calculation illustrated with elliptical representation. Source: https://moredvikas.wordpress.com/2017/09/12/what-is-true-positive-and-true-negative-confusion-matrix/.

$$Precision = \frac{TP}{TP + FP} \tag{10.2}$$

Recall

Recall measures the extent to which a model effectively captures suspects with one or multiple mental health conditions. Equation (10.3) is expressed as the ratio of TP cases identified by the model to the total actual positive cases inclusive of the negative cases incorrectly overlooked by the model. High recall means that the majority of high-risk individuals are captured by the models with very few of left behind. In mental health classification, it is used to identify those at risk, which could have disastrous effects. However, models optimized for recall tend to produce a high number of false positives, leading to more unnecessary interventions. This means that when developing the classification system, efforts should be made to achieve both high recall and high precision, ensuring that the system accurately and comprehensively identifies different mental health issues [11].

$$Recall = \frac{TP}{TP + FN} \tag{10.3}$$

Sensitivity

Sensitivity defines the capacity of a particular classification of mental health to differentiate the precursors of risks that exist in an individual. It is formulated by establishing a relationship between the correctly identified at-risk classes (TP) and the actual at-risk classes (P). Equation (10.4) illustrates the formula of sensitivity. A high TPR means that these are accurately identified by the system to need help with mental health issues, and the number of FN results is low. The maximum possible is 1.0, which implies that all patients at risk have been successfully identified. Conversely, the minimum possible TPR of 0.0 indicating that no at risk patient have been identified. Therefore, increasing TPR in mental health assessments is imperative to addressing worsening states in patients who need mental health services [12]. Figure 10.3 shows the elliptical representation of the sensitivity calculation.

$$Sensitivity = \frac{TP}{TP + FN} = \frac{TP}{P} \tag{10.4}$$

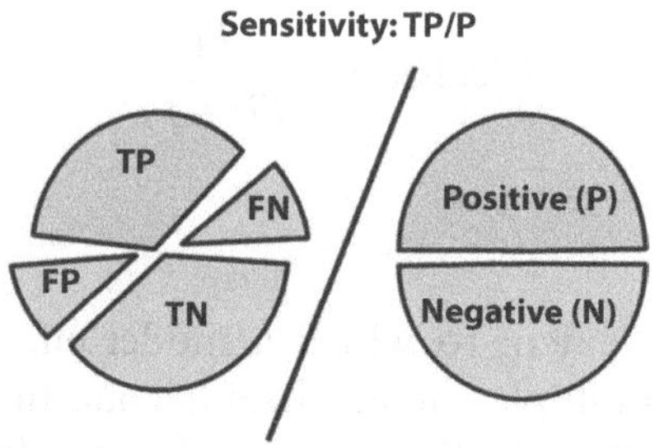

Figure 10.3 Graphical representation of sensitivity using two ellipses. Source: https://moredvikas.wordpress.com/2017/09/12/what-is-true-positive-and-true-negative-confusion-matrix/.

Specificity

Specificity evaluates the accuracy of a mental health classification model in correctly identifying individual with a stable mental state. It is defined as the number of negative cases that were correctly classified as such (true negative) divided by the total actual negative cases (N). The high value of TNR means that the model retains absence with the rates that do not need diagnosis, hence minimizing false alarms. Equation (10.5) demonstrates the specificity formula. The best possible specificity is 1.0, means that the stable individuals are correctly classified and to minimize needless stress or therapy, it is crucial in mental health screening to avoid incorrectly labeling healthy people as at-risk. It is the counterpart of sensitivity and is also proportionate for an excellent classification system [13]. Figure 10.4 depicts the specificity calculation through ellipses.

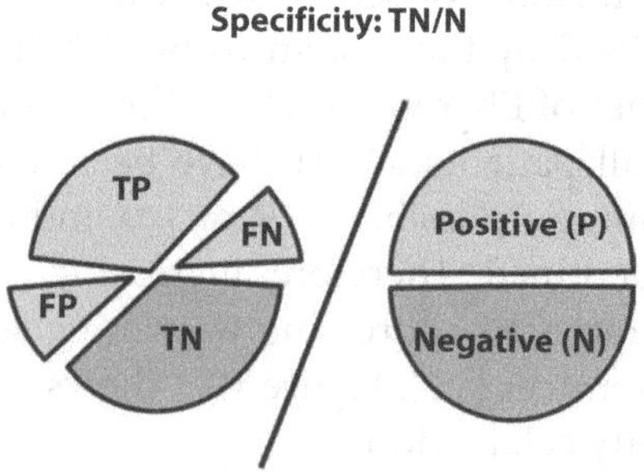

Figure 10.4 Ellipse-based visualization of specificity calculation. Source: https://moredvikas.wordpress.com/2017/09/12/what-is-true-positive-and-true-negative-confusion-matrix/.

$$Specificity = \frac{TN}{TN + FP} = \frac{TN}{N} \tag{10.5}$$
$$Specificity = 1 - FPRate$$

F-Measure

F-measure allows for assuring the quality of proposed mental health classification models by taking into consideration both FP and FN outcomes. It is especially useful when working with imbalanced datasets with distinct accuracy, which can be quite deceptive. Equation (10.6) depicts the F-measure formula. A higher F-measure has been provided, which shows that the model can find out the real at-risk people with almost large number of erroneous predictions. This metric aims to achieve a balance between recall and precision, preventing the classification model from having either high precision with low recall or high recall or with low precision. Because failing to identify an at-risk individual is dangerous, while labeling a stable individual as at-risk is extremely stressful for them, the F-Measure is an important outcome measure for diagnosing mental disorders. It is a normalized value that can take values from 0 to 1, where models with higher values improved [14].

$$F - Measure = \frac{Two \times (Precision \times Recall)}{(Precision + Recall)} \tag{10.6}$$

Confusion Matrix

Confusion Matrix is an essential metric for comparing the performance of the mental health classification models, as it shows the interaction between the classifications of the model and the actual status of the patients, separating those patients at risk and stable ones. This is particularly relevant for mental health screening, as precise classification assists in early identification and appropriate support for individuals in need. Every element of the confusion matrix [15] offers important information about the advantages and disadvantages of the categorization model:

- **TP** indicates situations in which a person is accurately classified as being at risk for mental health issues. This is an upright result, since it guarantees those who require intervention are appropriately identified.
- **FP** signifies the result of misclassifying someone as at risk when they are stable. This Type 1 Error could result in misdiagnosis, improper treatment, or needless concern.

- **FN** represents situations in which a person who is at risk is mistakenly categorized as stable. In applications related to mental health, this Type 2 Error is especially troubling, since it can postpone essential action, which could make a person's situation worse.
- **TN** occurs when a stable person is accurately identified as such, confirming the model's ability to recognize individual who are not at risk.

Binary Classification Confusion Matrix for Mental Health: It measures the efficiency of mental health screening models by distinguishing between correct and incorrect predictions. It assists in evaluating the possibility of misclassification of people as high-risk or as stable to provide the necessary attention. In mental health status, the people are categorized as 'At Risk (1) or Stable (0)'. From these classifications, the model can make its predictions and the results can be measured using the confusion matrix. Figures 10.5 (a & b) depicts the performance of binary classification analysis.

Confusion Matrix for Multi-Class Mental Health Classification: Multi-class confusion matrix is similar to the binary confusion matrix, aimed at comparing estimations of ML models that differentiate multiple classes, such as various levels of mental health risk. It assists in explaining the capacity of the model to recognize the differential levels of severity. Figure 10.6 represents a multi-class confusion matrix because it includes four different classes (A, B, C, and D). Multi-class confusion matrices are used to evaluate classification models that predict more than two categories.

In mental health classification, misclassifying could have severe impacts, as false positives will cause unnecessary stress, stigma, or medical treatment that the person does not require and FN means that the people who need attention will not be identified. Metrics, such as confusion matrices,

Class designation		Actual class	
		True (1)	False (0)
Predicted class	Positive (1)	TP	FP
	Negative (0)	TP	TN

(a)

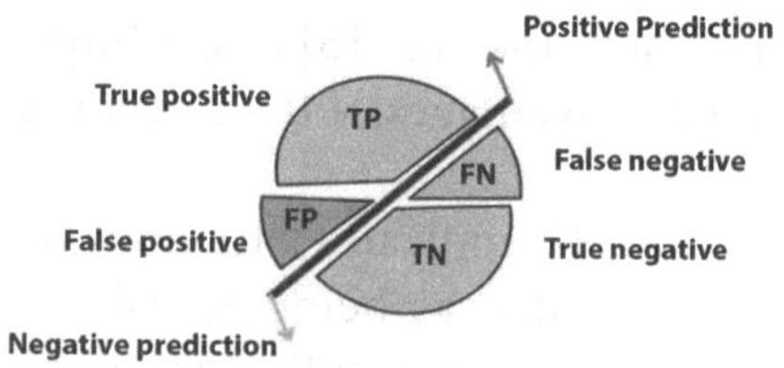

(b)

Figure 10.5 Binary classification performance representation: (a) confusion matrix, & (b) pie chart of classification outcomes. Source: (a) https://towardsdatascience.com/precision-and-recall-made-simple-afb5e098970f/, (b) https://moredvikas.wordpress.com/2017/09/12/what-is-true-positive-and-true-negative-confusion-matrix/.

Actual value →

Predicted value ↓

	A	B	C	D
A	100	0	0	0
B	80	9	1	1
C	10	0	8	0
D	10	1	1	9

Figure 10.6 Multiclass confusion matrix for four-class classification. Source: https://medium.com/@shubhanshi.shubh860/confusion-matrix-in-machine-learning-cd7333d72f5d.

allow the machine learning model to be adjusted for high sensitivity in identifying individuals at risk while minimizing incorrect classification. Moreover, the confusion matrix's assessment assists in uncovering biases within the models so that corrective action can be taken to enhance performance for different groups of people. In general, it is a form of performance confirmation tool that increases the effectiveness and applicability of the mental health classification model.

Kappa Statistics

Kappa Statistics computes the degree of mental health classifications supposing the degree of chance agreement between the predicted and actual classifications. Cohen's kappa coefficient κ is a statistic measure, where the interpretation analyses compare the extent of the identification given by the machine learning model with the actual mental health conditions excluding the possibility of haphazard chance. This helps to evaluate the model more than the simple accuracy of the model in its prediction [16]. Cohen's kappa result is depicted in Equation (10.7).

$$K = \frac{(p_0 - p_e)}{(1 - p_e)} \tag{10.7}$$

where:

- The overall accuracy of the mental health classification model is denoted by p_0.
- The expected agreement by chance, represented by p_e, is computed in Equation (10.8).

$$p_e = p_{e1} + p_{e2} \tag{10.8}$$

p_{e1} is the possibility that the model's predictions will coincide at random with the real occurrences of "healthy," and p_{e2} is the likelihood that the "at-risk" group will coincide at random. It is assumed that the actual and anticipated classifications are unrelated. The number of cases in each class is multiplied by the proportion of expected classifications in that class to arrive at these probabilities. By adopting the kappa statistic to assess mental health classification models, it becomes easier to compare whether the model's ability to predict which individuals are at risk is significantly high and not a mere chance occurrence.

Receiver Operating Characteristic Curve

ROC measures the performance of a classifier in distinguishing between various mental health disorders. It shows two measures, namely the TPR and the FPR. Initially, implemented initially in the context of radar signals, the ROC [17] curve is applied in various fields, such as medicine and ML including diagnostics of mental health status. The ROC curve shows the model's output to all classification steps by using FPR and TPR for all the threshold values. There are different cut-off points regarding the identification of mental disorders. By conducting this, the number of identified positive cases tends to be higher, thus the TPs, but also the FPs, are also high. An occasional increase in threshold leads to a significant decrease in the value of both FP and TP. This curve is useful in mental health assessments, especially because it takes into account all possible thresholds, while evaluation metrics work well at a single threshold. The ROC curve helps in choosing the threshold level that brings out maximum correct positive results while minimizing the number of FP. Ideally, the ROC curve is a plot that has a TPR score of 100% and an FP rate of zero, representing the perfect classification. Furthermore, because the proportion of individuals with psychological conditions is nearly equal to that of individuals without, the ROC curve is extremely useful in balanced samples. Figure 10.7 illustrates the sample ROC curve.

Since calculating multiple points on the curve can be unproductive, a distinct form of measurement known as AUC is used. AUC is a measure of discriminative ability that is important in determining the effectiveness of mental health classification models.

Area Under the Curve

Area under the curve (AUC) is a common metric for assessing the efficiency of any mental health classification model. It is particularly useful in binary classification problems, where potential clients with or without mental health conditions are differentiated. The AUC [18] characterizes

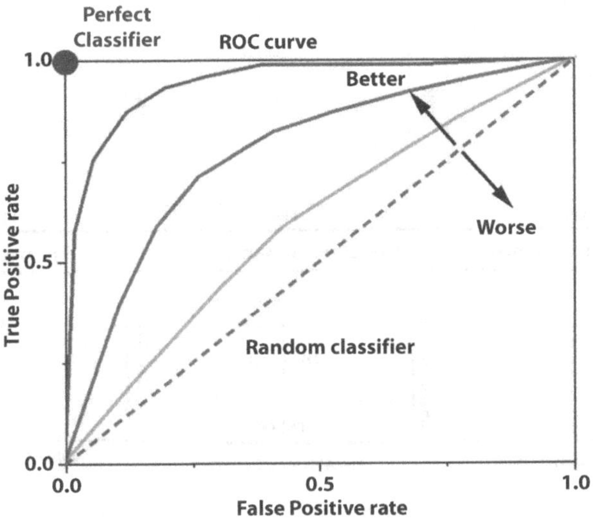

Figure 10.7 Model ROC performance curve. Source: Own elaboration.

the entirety of the ROC curve to be used for the unified evaluation of the model across all the classification thresholds. The ROC AUC can be calculated in different ways, including the simplest one, the trapezoidal rule. This approach winds the ROC curve into trapezoids using vertical lines at points of FPR and horizontal lines at TPR and approximates the whole area. Calculating the areas of these trapezoids and adding all their amounts produces the overall AUC approximation. Since AUC is a number from 0 to 1, classifiers with an AUC of 1 are flawless classifiers that accurately recognize every entity, whereas the most inaccurate classifiers that mistakenly classify every entity have an AUC of 0. A higher AUC means better model performance in differentiating between patients with and without a mental health condition. Another benefit of AUC is that it is scale-invariant and classification threshold-invariant, as it measures the performance of the model across different scales as well as thresholds. An AUC = 0.5 indicates that the model is operating at the rate of chance and is unable to discriminate between any two groups. Such models are called no-skill classifiers. However, AUC has certain drawbacks in mental health assessment, particularly when ignoring a certain type of classification error, such as either FP or FN. FN, or failing to identify people who need help, can be more detrimental than false positives in mental health diagnosis, for instance. In these situations, choosing an ideal classification threshold or striking a balance between recall and precision is a more improved plan of action than depending on AUC. Furthermore, AUC can provide false results in

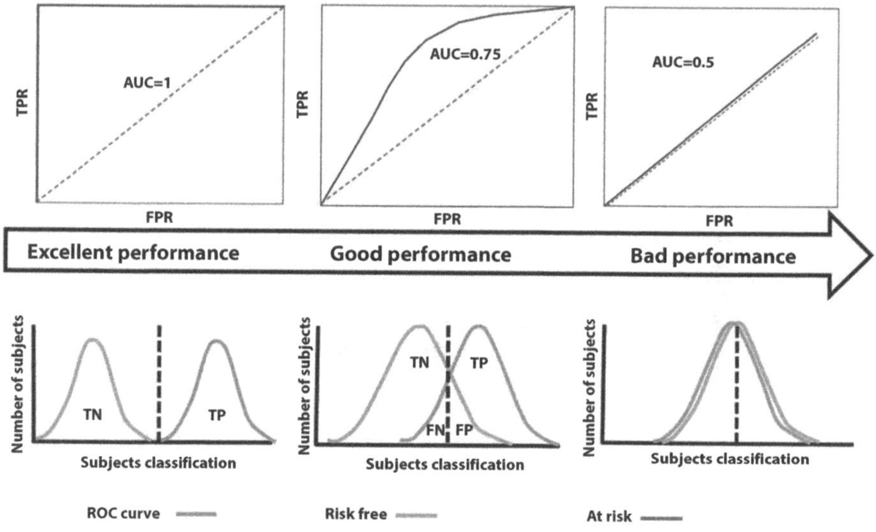

Figure 10.8 AUC performance metric. Source: Own elaboration.

circumstances of substantial class imbalance, such as a vast preponderance of undiagnosed cases relative to diagnosed cases. Figure 10.8 depicts the classification performance through AUC.

10.3 Conclusion

For ML and DL models to be reliable and successful, especially in NLP-based applications, their performance in mental health evaluation must be evaluated. A thorough grasp of model performance can be attained by employing important evaluation measures, such as the confusion matrix, sensitivity, specificity, accuracy, recall, and F-measure. By assessing agreement beyond chance, the kappa statistic improves this assessment. A model's performance across various classification thresholds becomes evaluable by using both ROC curve analysis and AUC values, allowing for better choices in model optimization decisions. The evaluation process of these model parameters leads to improved prediction reliability and classification accuracy, which creates valuable contributions for ML and DL approaches in mental health diagnosis. The improvement of mental health results occurs through the development of customized interventions because of these assessment tools.

AI disclosure statement: The author confirms that no artificial intelligence (AI)-generated content or AI-assisted writing tools were used in the preparation of this chapter (including summaries and the abstract). All text, analysis, and conclusions are the result of the author's original work.

References

1. Kasanneni, Y., *et al.*, Effective Analysis of Machine and Deep Learning Methods for Diagnosing Mental Health Using Social Media Conversations. *IEEE Trans. Comput. Soc. Syst.*, 12, 1, 274–294, 2024, https://doi.org/10.1109/TCSS.2024.3487168.
2. Tejavibulya, L., *et al.*, Predicting the future of neuroimaging predictive models in mental health. *Mol. Psychiatry*, 27, 8, 3129–3137, 2022, https://doi.org/10.1038/s41380-022-01635-2.
3. Bokolo, B.G. and Liu, Q., Deep learning-based depression detection from social media: Comparative evaluation of ML and transformer techniques. *Electronics*, 12, 21, 4396, 2023, https://doi.org/10.3390/electronics12214396.
4. Menon, V.A., *et al.*, Evaluating NLP Models for Mental Health: Performance and Accuracy in User-Psychologist Conversations, in: *Exploring Psychology, Social Innovation and Advanced Applications of Machine Learning*, pp. 67–86, IGI Global Scientific Publishing, India, 2025, https://doi.org/10.4018/979-8-3693-6910-4.ch004.
5. Powers, D.MW., Evaluation: from precision, recall and F-measure to ROC, informedness, markedness and correlation, *arXiv preprint arXiv:2010.16061*, 2020, https://doi.org/10.48550/arXiv.2010.16061.
6. Janssens, A., Cecile, J.W., Martens, F.K., Reflection on modern methods: Revisiting the area under the ROC Curve. *Int. J. Epidemiol.*, 49, 4, 1397–1403, 2020, https://doi.org/10.1093/ije/dyz274.
7. Haque, R., *et al.*, A comparative analysis on suicidal ideation detection using NLP, machine, and deep learning. *Technologies*, 10, 3, 57, 2022, https://doi.org/10.3390/technologies10030057.
8. Straw, I. and Callison-Burch, C., Artificial Intelligence in mental health and the biases of language based models. *PLoS One*, 15, 12, e0240376, 2020, https://doi.org/10.1371/journal.pone.0240376.
9. Kim, J., *et al.*, A deep learning model for detecting mental illness from user content on social media. *Sci. Rep.*, 10, 1, 11846, 2020, https://doi.org/10.1038/s41598-020-68764-y.
10. Wani, M.A., *et al.*, Depression screening in humans with AI and deep learning techniques. *IEEE Trans. Comput. Soc. Syst.*, 10, 4, 2074–2089, 2022, https://doi.org/10.1109/TCSS.2022.3200213.

11. Karamat, A., *et al.*, A Hybrid Transformer Architecture for Multiclass Mental Illness Prediction using Social Media Text. *IEEE Access*, 13, 12148–12167, 2024, https://doi.org/10.1109/ACCESS.2024.3519308.
12. Lin, D., *et al.*, Feasibility of a machine learning-based smartphone application in detecting depression and anxiety in a generally senior population. *Front. Psychol.*, 13, 811517, 2022, https://doi.org/10.3389/fpsyg.2022.811517.
13. Diniz, E.JS., *et al.*, Boamente: A natural language processing-based digital phenotyping tool for smart monitoring of suicidal ideation. *Healthcare*, 10, 4, 698, MDPI, 2022, https://doi.org/10.3390/healthcare10040698.
14. Chowdhury, S., *et al.*, Machine Learning and Deep Learning Models for Predicting Mental Health Disorders and Performance Analysis through Chatbot Interactions. *Eur. J. Comput. Sci. Inf. Technol.*, 12, 9, 38–60, 2024, https://doi.org/10.37745/ejcsit.2013/vol12n93860.
15. Bhavani, B.H., Sreenatha, M., Kundur, N.C., Diagnosis and Classification of Depressive Disorders using ML and DL Models. *Eng. Technol. Appl. Sci. Res.*, 15, 2, 21383–21389, 2025, https://doi.org/10.48084/etasr.10017.
16. Cliffe, C., *et al.*, Using natural language processing to extract self-harm and suicidality data from a clinical sample of patients with eating disorders: A retrospective cohort study. *BMJ Open*, 11, 12, e053808, 2021, https://doi.org/10.1136/bmjopen-2021-053808.
17. Alkahtani, H., Aldhyani, T.HH., Alqarni, A.A., Artificial intelligence models to predict disability for mental health disorders. *J. Disabil. Res.*, 3, 3, 20240022, 2024, DOI: 10.57197/JDR-2024-0022.
18. Ding, Z., *et al.*, Efficient or Powerful? Trade-offs Between Machine Learning and Deep Learning for Mental Illness Detection on Social Media, *arXiv preprint arXiv:2503.01082*, 2025, https://doi.org/10.48550/arXiv.2503.01082.

11

Methods of Pruning and Tagging

Awakash Mishra[1]*, Gobi N.[2], Pallavi M.[3] and Avinash Samantra[4]

[1]*Maharishi School of Engineering and Technology, Maharishi University of Information Technology, Uttar Pradesh, India*
[2]*Department of CSIT, Jain (Deemed-to-be University), Bangalore, Karnataka, India*
[3]*Department of Computer Science & Engineering, Presidency University, Bengaluru, Karnataka, India*
[4]*Centre for Data Science, Siksha 'O' Anusandhan (Deemed to be University), Bhubaneswar, Odisha, India*

Abstract

Pruning and tagging procedures in natural language processing (NLP) for mental healthcare are examined in this chapter with a focus on their role in preparing text data for clinical analysis. Pruning strategies improve the accuracy and efficacy of NLP models, lower computing complexity, and improve data quality by eliminating superfluous information. To assist applications like sentiment analysis, psychological profiling, and cognitive evaluation, tagging systems; capacity to organize and categorize text makes it possible to extract important linguistic patterns, sentiment shifts, and cognitive indicators. Advanced pruning techniques like stop word removal and dimensionality reduction are covered in this chapter, along with tagging strategies. It also explores that these methods are used in practical mental health applications, including the early identification of mood disorders, the prediction of suicide risk, and tailored therapeutic interventions. Pruning and tagging improve textual data, which helps with predictive modeling, patient monitoring, and sentiment tracking in mental health treatment. These techniques improve overall mental health management, treatment planning, and diagnostic accuracy when included into clinical decision-support systems.

**Corresponding author*: awakash.mishra@muit.in; ORCID: 0009-0002-5447-7499
Gobi N.: ORCID: 0000-0003-3913-7744
Pallavi M.: ORCID: 0000-0003-1145-9389
Avinash Samantra: ORCID: 0000-0001-9913-3003

Sudesh Yadav, Pethuru Raj, Satya Prakash Yadav and Victor Hugo C. de Albuquerque (eds.) Natural Language Processing in Mental Health Care: Methodologies and Clinical Practice, (151–164) © 2026 Scrivener Publishing LLC

Keywords: Natural language processing, pruning and tagging, sentiment analysis, cognitive evaluation, mental health diagnosis

11.1 Introduction

The global increase in mental health illnesses led to an increased demand for digitally delivered interventions (DHIs) where chatbots use artificial intelligence (AI) and web-based therapy platforms and mobile applications. These interventions reach their goal through remedies that confront stigma and geographical borders, as well as practical shortages of registered practitioners to supply inexpensive, accessible solutions for mental health care. Users generate substantial textual data through their interactions with digital human interaction systems together with recorded therapy transcripts, self-reports and community-based text exchanges. Efficient evaluation of this material serves three crucial purposes, including patient development tracking and intervention outcome analysis to enhance treatment strategies [1]. The processing of text data related to mental health presents specific challenges for digestion purposes. The large volume of gathered information becomes difficult to convert into beneficial insights because a significant portion consists of repetitious and unimportant data. The procedure requires pruning strategies to refine text information by removing useless content while retaining relevant text fragments. Among the elements those pruning methods eliminate during data cleaning are stop-words and duplicate entries as well as pointless conversations alongside content that is too informal or unimportant analytically [2]. The application of pruning techniques enhances NLP model processing in mental healthcare through data refinement and target information selection, which results in accurate and pertinent outcomes.

Tagging proves essential for mental health content organization while serving as a method to establish classes for mental health data. The system of labeling textual data through established categories with tags leads to improved structural organization and analytical capability [3]. Tagging tools in mental health practice enable the detection of emotions along with mental states and cognitive misinterpretations alongside therapy development indicators and dangerous signals that include mental health distress triggers and attempted suicide indicators. Mental health forum discussions can be themed into categories including anxiety or depression and user-therapy chat logs can undergo annotation processes to watch for mood shifts. The annotation process and classification accuracy are enhanced through the use of machine learning combined with rule-based linguistic models [4].

NLP applications achieve better mental wellness through the integration of pruning and tagging methods. Text analysis effectiveness rises when the information management system removes additional materials to maintain only beneficial data inputs. The system helps physicians and AI-powered systems identify customized patterns for which it adjusts appropriate treatment recommendations to provide individualized care. Proprietary labeled data helps swift mental health intervention through its ability to detect warning signs, like elevated negativity and self-harm thoughts as well as social withdrawal [5]. Pruning operations together with tagging do present limitations in addition to their advantages. The main concern about editing sentences stems from potential over-trimming because it could result in eliminating vital contextual information unexpectedly. Specific linguistic details together with implicit distress indications could decrease the effectiveness of mental health evaluation when these elements are unintentionally removed from analysis. Developing well-defined taxonomies with annotated datasets for tagging requires substantial time and many resources [6]. Mental health data interpretation suffers from mistakes caused by improper classification, thus requiring thorough inspection of tagging model quality. Research of mental health-related texts should incorporate assessments of privacy concerns and ethical matters. The protective measures for data security, along with specific anonymization techniques and strict ethical guidelines, must be established to safeguard patient privacy when handling sensitive user data. The erroneous assessments created by biased processing of training data in algorithms coincide with the perpetuation of mental healthcare stigmas, so it becomes necessary to establish openness and fairness within NLP models. The development of data-driven mental health analysis needs enhanced pruning and tagging techniques because digital mental health interventions continue to expand [7]. NLP pruning and tagging procedures for mental health programs constitute the core objective of this chapter. It proposes to remove unnecessary text material from processing while preserving key information units. This chapter investigates various tagging methods to classify textual data more effectively as part of organizational processes. Sentiment analysis, along with cognitive evaluation and early mental health risk identification functions, benefits from these methods, according to the analysis.

11.2 Purpose of Pruning in Mental Healthcare NLP

Pruning is a technique used in mental healthcare NLP to improve huge, unstructured text collections by eliminating duplicate, noisy, or unnecessary material while maintaining clinically meaningful insights. Removing slang, stop-words, and irrelevant conversations from therapy sessions, self-reports, and mental health forums enhances the quality of the data. By lowering computational complexity, pruning improves model accuracy and efficiency, increasing the effectiveness of NLP algorithms in identifying patterns in mental health. For sentiment analysis, emotion recognition, and risk assessment, it ensures that only significant and contextually pertinent data is retained. Pruning helps therapists focus on important distress signals, cognitive distortions, and therapy progress by removing extraneous data, which also promotes improved patient monitoring [8]. The effectiveness of pruning in NLP can be assessed using a variety of metrics and benchmarks. Several domain-specific benchmarks are used to assess the effectiveness of pruning approaches in cognitive and behavioral NLP for mental health. These benchmarks function as common tasks or datasets for evaluating pruning techniques' efficacy in various NLP applications about mental health. In this regard, the following benchmarks are frequently used:

Mental Health Text Classification

The main purpose of pruning strategies in mental health text categorization is to improve model efficiency without compromising essential language patterns related to psychological illnesses [9]. The difficult task consists of maintaining model sensitivity to detect minor behavioral symptoms together with cognitive impairment and mental discomfort while performing compression. Clinical and digital health applications demand dependability testing of trimmed models, which must achieve appropriate levels of interpretability combined with robustness alongside accurate diagnostics.

Analysis of Emotion and Sentiment in Psychology

The method of pruning requires developers to maintain critical emotional indicators and achieve peak computational speed for mental wellness sentiment analysis tasks. Psychological emotion identification differs from standard sentiment analysis, since it relies on subtle language-related, tonal, and intensity-based contextual cues [10]. The efficiency of behavioral analysis remains strong because proper pruning techniques protect emotional warning signs that relate to mental health difficulties or anxiety and mood disorders.

Risk of Suicide and Identification of Self-Harm

The model pruning process needs to be sensitive to suicide risks and self-harm indicators so risk-based language remains detectable during compression. The main challenge exists in compressing the model system while maintaining its ability to recognize both dependent crisis expressions together with ambiguous verbalizations and hidden mental health warnings. Evaluation of pruned models requires examining their ability to detect at-risk people effectively with accurate recall and precise identification capabilities.

Mental Health Named Entity Recognition

The goal of pruning in mental health named entity recognition (NER) is to maximize entity extraction while preserving important behavioral, clinical, or psychiatric terms. The purpose is to simplify models while maintaining precise identification of important things, including symptoms, ailments, drugs, and therapies [11]. For mental health applications, a well-pruned NER model should retain high precision and recall, guaranteeing that crucial diagnostic and treatment data is preserved.

Comparative Analysis of Pruning Methods

In NLP, various pruning strategies aim to minimize the size and scope of neural network models. The pruning strategies covered in the research are summed up in Figure 11.1.

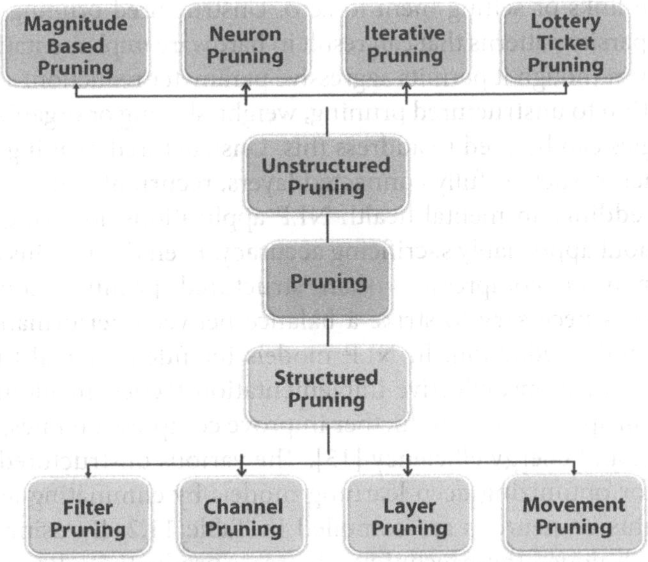

Figure 11.1 Structure of pruning methods. Source: Own elaboration.

Structured Pruning in NLP for Mental Health

In structured pruning, entire neural network components, like attention heads, neurons, or layers are eliminated while maintaining the network's general structure. This method maximizes models' efficiency in cognitive and behavioral NLP for mental health without compromising their capacity to identify linguistic patterns linked to psychological disorders. Structured pruning helps lower computing overhead while preserving the interpretability and sensitivity needed for mental health applications, which are crucial given the complexity of transformer-based and recurrent models used in sentiment analysis, risk assessment, and clinical text processing [12]. This guarantees that models continue to be successful in detecting important linguistic indicators associated with mental health symptoms, emotional distress, and cognitive deficits. Table 11.1 gives a summary of structured pruning.

Unstructured Pruning in NLP for Mental Health Applications

An NN optimization method called unstructured pruning eliminates specific weights or parameters, according to their magnitude or relevance scores. This method helps preserve performance while lowering computing needs, increasing efficiency, and simplifying mental health NLP models. Two crucial processes are involved in the process: identification, where weights are assessed based on standards, such as sensitivity analysis or magnitude-based ranking, and removal, where less important weights are trimmed, either by deleting all links or setting them to zero. Unstructured pruning generates irregular sparsity patterns that can result in hardware implementation inefficiencies, even though it permits aggressive parameter reduction.

In addition to unstructured pruning, weight-sharing or organized pruning strategies can be used to address this. Unstructured pruning can optimize elements, such as fully connected layers, recurrent connections, and word embeddings in mental health NLP applications, lowering memory needs without appreciably sacrificing accuracy. Even though this approach allows for more compression than structured pruning, considerable fine-tuning is necessary to strike a balance between performance retention and model reduction. In NLP models intended for real-time mental health evaluations, effective implementation tactics, including weight permutation approaches, can further improve compression rates, boosting throughput and energy efficiency [13]. The various unstructured pruning methods for optimizing deep learning models by eliminating less significant weights or neurons are compiled in Table 11.2. By using selective pruning techniques, these techniques increase productivity, lower memory consumption, and preserve model performance.

Table 11.1 Structured pruning methods for improving NLP models for mental health.

Structured pruning types	Description	Pruning criteria	Relevance in mental health NLP
Filter pruning	Reduces complexity in CNN-based models by eliminating less important filters.	Uses activation values to assess filter relevance. To improve efficiency, unnecessary filters are eliminated.	Utilized in CNN-based sentiment analysis to identify depression; assists in real-time chatbots for mental health by maximizing reaction speed.
Channel pruning	Reduces the computational load of convolutional models by removing entire channels.	Selection of the least helpful channels based on magnitude. Analysis of sensitivity for channel ranking.	Makes transformer-based models more efficient for digesting clinical text more quickly. Cuts down on inference time for tasks involving emotion recognition.
Layer pruning	Eliminates whole layers that make very little contribution to the model's decision-making.	Greedy selection at the layer level. Evaluation of layer relevance based on mutual information.	Used to reduce model complexity while preserving interpretability in transformer-based NLP. Improves clinical decision support systems' real-time inference.
Weight pruning	Prunes weights in an organized way without changing the design of the network.	Weight trimming based on magnitude. Weight trimming with sensitivity awareness.	Utilized models for assessing suicide risk that rely on deep learning. Enhances the deployment of the model on devices with minimal resources (e.g., mobile mental health apps).
Movement pruning	Prunes weights selectively according to that change during training iterations.	Use the pruning criterion of the least absolute movement. Refines the model after it has been pruned.	Increases the effectiveness of transformer models for identifying anxiety and PTSD in text from social media. Maintains performance in datasets related to mental health that have limited resources.

Source: Own elaboration

Table 11.2 Different unstructured pruning methods for optimizing neural networks.

Unstructured pruning types	Description	Key methods	Advantages
Neuron	Increases efficiency by getting rid of neurons that don't add much to the network's output.	Removing low-activation neurons, Regularization-based pruning Score-based reduction of importance.	Speeds up inference, uses less memory, and uses selective pruning to maintain accuracy.
Magnitude based	Eliminates weights with the lowest magnitudes, presuming that don't significantly affect the model's functionality.	Magnitude thresholding at the layer level, layer-based trimming that is adaptive, pruning with multi-objective latency awareness, Pruning in stages for organized sparsity.	Increases the effectiveness of NLP tasks, and decreases the size and complexity of models, Retraining can be used in conjunction with it to restore performance.
Iterative	Gradually reduces weights or neurons over several iterations, fine-tuning each time to bring accuracy back.	Pruning in multiple rounds with retraining and the systematic elimination of unnecessary elements.	Maintains accuracy while cutting parameters and increases model efficiency without experiencing sharp declines in performance.
Lottery ticket	Implies that there could be a sparse subnetwork (often known as a "winning ticket") within a dense model that can perform comparably or better.	Finding and restarting subnetworks with high performance and fine-tuning trimmed models to maximize effectiveness.	Identifies small, effective subnetworks and lessens redundancy in lengthy NLP models.

Source: Own elaboration

11.3 Tagging's Significance in Mental Healthcare NLP

Mental health NLP tagging systems help process textual data found in digital therapeutic recordings alongside patient reports and therapy transcripts. Language understanding benefits from the identification of key speech elements together with essential entities, which include mental health conditions as well as symptoms and medications. The function of sentiment tagging detects emotional changes to help diagnose mental health patterns alongside mood changes [14]. For focused intervention, thematic tagging group's conversations into pertinent categories like stress, anxiety, or sadness. The identification of crisis indicators, including thoughts about suicide and actions of self-harm, requires risk-level tagging for delivering timely help. Tagging systems help applications dedicated to mental health achieve better tracking and reaction while improving overall understanding.

Part-of-Speech (POS) Tagging's Purpose in Mental Healthcare NLP: NLP's POS tagging in mental health aids in the analysis of sentence structure in clinical notes, self-reports, and therapy interactions. By classifying words into nouns, verbs, adjectives, and other grammatical components, it improves language comprehension. This improves contextual understanding of patient narratives, sentiment analysis, and cognitive assessment. Additionally, POS tagging facilitates semantic analysis by assisting in the differentiation of various word usage in psychological situations. Better accuracy in NLP-based diagnosis models and mental health monitoring is ensured by organizing text data. Figure 11.2 represents the overview of POS tagging.

The process of giving a lexical class or part-of-speech label to every word in a collection. It can make a lot of different distinctions, which could result in big tag sets. It has to select a standard set of tags for POS tagging. A very coarse tag sets, such as noun, verb, adjective, and adverb could be chosen. A component of software that assigns parts of speech to each word it reads in a language is known as a POS Tagger. Three types of POS tagging techniques can be distinguished: hybrid, rule-based, and statistical tagging [15]. In addition to applying a set of handwritten rules, the rule-based POS uses contextual information to assign POS tags to words. This system's inability to function when the text is unknown is a drawback. Its inability to predict the relevant content is the issue. Thus, a comprehensive set of hand-coded rules should be implemented to increase the system's efficiency and accuracy.

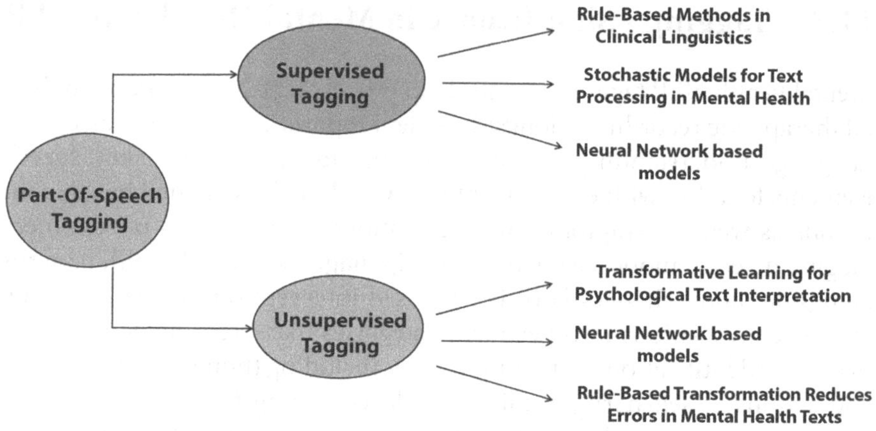

Figure 11.2 Different category of POS tagging. Source: Own elaboration.

Supervised POS Tagging in Mental Healthcare with NLP

POS tagging under supervision functions as a core process in mental healthcare NLP systems for clinical note analysis therapy sessions study and psychiatric evaluation assessment. Medical text clarification through statistical models depends on word frequency and probability measurements as inputs. System algorithms improve both linguistic structure understanding and symptom detection because they learn through pre-tagged dataset analysis. These programs help medical staff identify key linguistic elements while tracking emotional shifts and mental health indications that appear in (patient) verbal communication. Clinical NLP models require these models because their accuracy directly correlates with the number of annotated datasets.

Approaches in Clinical Linguistics Based on Principles

The tagging mechanism in rule-based POS systems proves beneficial for analytical tasks on structured medical documents because it follows predetermined linguistic rules during its tagging process. The system supports researchers in retrieving psychological indicators together with emotional symptom definitions and mental health terminology useful for natural language applications in psychology [16]. The established guidelines and clinical research documents lead to many of the required regulations. Manual interventions and expert knowledge requirements exist for the improvement of rule-based systems. The system faces limitations when trying to use informal patient language in practical applications.

Stochastic Models for Text Processing in Mental Health

The statistical probabilities of POS tags get assigned through stochastic approaches, which include conditional random fields (CRF), maximum likelihood estimation (MLE), and Hidden Markov Models (HMM). The algorithms demonstrate effectiveness in identifying patient psychological indications along with pattern recognition and sentiment monitoring. N-gram model types, including Unigram, Bigram, and Trigram, benefit from utilizing context found in preceding language segments to enhance their accuracy level. Additional adjustments are required to minimize cases of incorrect tag sequences that the system occasionally produces [17]. The Viterbi algorithm optimizes POS tagging along with reducing errors by finding the most likely successive word tags. The system enhances mental health NLP through the detection of early symptoms while performing mood analysis and emotional categorization operations. Psychiatric evaluations perform more accurately when the algorithm removes excessive linguistic patterns from psychiatric interviews. Live patient speech monitoring through the algorithm enables contextually correct language processing in real time.

NLP for Unsupervised POS Tagging in Mental Health

Unsupervised POS tagging operates with great flexibility in mental health narratives because it functions without pre-labeled corpora, which supervised models require. Baum–Welch algorithm and similar sophisticated algorithms allow this method to determine tag sets and transformation rules. The technique demonstrates effective application for studying therapy dialogues and patient self-description and also unorganized clinical notes. The processing of extensive mental health datasets that lack labels works optimally through unsupervised methods, albeit supervised approaches continue to improve accuracy interests.

Transformative Learning for Psychological Text Interpretation

By learning correction rules, Brill's Transformation-Based Learning (TBL) improves POS tagging. This enhances language-based symptom tracking, mood analysis, and cognitive distortion identification in mental health NLP [18]. Adaptive mental health applications can benefit from the model's iterative mistake correction rather than reliance on manually created linguistic rules. Psychological assessments are more efficient because TBL eliminates the need for manual intervention by automating linguistic improvements.

Rule-Based Transformation Reduces Errors in Mental Health Texts
Both TBL and rule-based systems rely on pre-established tagging rules are comparable. First, stochastic approaches use context and word frequency to assign likely tags. To reduce tagging errors in literature about mental health, correction methods are implemented iteratively. By ensuring context-aware labeling, this technique enhances the interpretability of psychiatric narratives. Because TBL is adaptive, language models could be gradually improved, which makes it perfect for sentiment analysis during treatment sessions.

Unsupervised Learning for Expandable Mental Health Applications
For processing massive amounts of text about mental health, unsupervised POS tagging offers a scalable alternative. It makes it possible to track emotional expressions in real-time, identify linguistic biomarkers, and automatically organize mental health records. This approach proves superior for continuous patient narrative surveillance because its annotation requirements are lower than those of supervised methods. The method functions effectively to develop predictive analytics along with AI-driven mental health diagnoses.

11.4 Conclusion

To optimize text processing for improved clinical insights, this chapter examined trimming and tagging strategies in NLP for mental healthcare. The refinement of linguistic data for improved sentiment analysis, cognitive evaluation, and mental health risk identification was the aim of the chapter. While tagging classifies and annotates content for appropriate interpretation, pruning eliminates noise and redundancy to ensure concise and pertinent information. By efficiently organizing unstructured data, these techniques improve automated mental health assessments and diagnosis accuracy. More accurate and significant analysis is made possible by their incorporation into NLP-driven mental health care systems, which promotes better patient care and decision-making.

AI disclosure statement: The author confirms that no artificial intelligence (AI)-generated content or AI-assisted writing tools were used in the preparation of this chapter (including summaries and the abstract). All text, analysis, and conclusions are the result of the author's original work.

References

1. Berge, G.T., *et al.*, Combining unsupervised, supervised and rule-based learning: the case of detecting patient allergies in electronic health records. *BMC Med. Inf. Decis. Making*, 23.1, 188, 2023, https://doi.org/10.1186/s12911-023-02271-8.
2. Nanehkaran, Y.A., *et al.*, Diagnosis of chronic diseases based on patients' health records in IoT healthcare using the recommender system. *Wirel. Commun. Mob. Comput.*, 2022.1, 5663001, 2022, https://doi.org/10.1155/2022/5663001.
3. Chung, H.-Y., *et al.*, Microglia mediate neurocognitive deficits by eliminating C1q-tagged synapses in sepsis-associated encephalopathy. *Sci. Adv.*, 9.21, eabq7806, 2023, https://doi.org/10.1126/sciadv.abq7806.
4. Shafqat, S., *et al.*, NER sequence embedding of unified medical corpora to incorporate semantic intelligence in big data healthcare diagnostics, 2024, https://doi.org/10.21203/rs.3.rs-3148503/v2.
5. Abdullayeva, F.J., Internet of Things-based healthcare system on patient demographic data in Health 4.0. *CAAI Trans. Intell. Technol.*, 7.4, 644–657, 2022, https://doi.org/10.1049/cit2.12128.
6. Alfian, G., *et al.*, Utilizing random Forest with iForest-based outlier detection and SMOTE to detect movement and direction of RFID tags. *Future Internet*, 15.3, 103, 2023, https://doi.org/10.3390/fi15030103.
7. Banerjee, S., *et al.*, Pruning coherent integrated photonic neural networks. *IEEE J. Sel. Top. Quantum Electron.*, 29.2, Optical Computing, 1–13, 2023, https://doi.org/10.1109/JSTQE.2023.3242992.
8. Pandey, A. and Kumar, S., Mental Health and Stress Prediction Using NLP and Transformer-Based Techniques. *2024 IEEE Symposium on Wireless Technology & Applications (ISWTA)*, IEEE, 2024, https://doi.org/10.1109/ISWTA62130.2024.10651843.
9. Ahmed, U., *et al.*, EANDC: An explainable attention network-based deep adaptive clustering model for mental health treatment. *Future Gener. Comput. Syst.*, 130, 106–1135, 2022, doi: 10.1016/j.future.2021.12.008.
10. Tang, W., *et al.*, A Syntactic Information–Based Classification Model for Medical Literature: Algorithm Development and Validation Study. *JMIR Med. Inf.*, 10.8, e37817, 2022, https://doi.org/10.2196/37817.
11. Volkmer, S., Meyer-Lindenberg, A., Schwarz, E., Large language models in psychiatry: Opportunities and challenges. *Psychiatry Res.*, 339, 116026, 2024, https://doi.org/10.1016/j.psychres.2024.116026.
12. Yadav, G. and Ubaidullah Bokhari, M., Hybrid classifier for optimizing mental health prediction: Feature engineering and fusion technique. *Int. J. Mental Health Addict.*, 1–41, 2024, https://doi.org/10.1007/s11469-024-01343-8.
13. Nijhawan, T., Attigeri, G., Ananthakrishna, T., Stress detection using natural language processing and machine learning over social interactions. *J. Big Data*, 9.1, 33, 2022, https://doi.org/10.1186/s40537-022-00575-6.

14. Drougkas, G., M. Bakker, E., Spruit, M., Multimodal machine learning for language and speech markers identification in mental health. *BMC Med. Inf. Decis. Making*, 24.1, 354, 2024, https://doi.org/10.1186/s12911-024-02772-0.
15. Madan, S., *et al.*, Deep learning-based detection of psychiatric attributes from German mental health records. *Int. J. Med. Inf.*, 161, 1047245, 2022, https://doi.org/10.1016/j.ijmedinf.2022.104724.
16. Ismail, L., *et al.*, ML-NLPEmot: Machine Learning-Natural Language Processing Event-Based Emotion Detection Proactive Framework Addressing Mental Health. *IEEE Access*, 11, 144126–1441495, 2023, https://doi.org/10.1109/ACCESS.2023.3343121.
17. Diaa, N.M., *et al.*, Statistical Challenges in Social Media Data Analysis Sentiment Tracking and Beyond. *J. Ecohumanism*, 3.5, 365–384, 2024, https://doi.org/10.62754/joe.v3i5.3912.
18. Dutta, R., *et al.*, Identifying features of risk periods for suicide attempts using document frequency and language use in electronic health records. *Front. Psychiatry*, 14, 12176495, 2023, https://doi.org/10.3389/fpsyt.2023.1217649.

12

Social Media for Depression Detection in Mental Health

Smita Mishra[1]*, Febin Prakash[2], Rosan Basha[3] and Chinmaya Kumar Mohapatra[4]

[1]*Maharishi School of Business Management, Maharishi University of Information Technology, Uttar Pradesh, India*
[2]*Department of CSIT, Jain (Deemed-to-be University), Bangalore, Karnataka, India*
[3]*Department of Management, Presidency University, Bengaluru, Karnataka, India*
[4]*Department of Legal Studies, Siksha 'O' Anusandhan (Deemed to be University), Bhubaneswar, Odisha, India*

Abstract

Social media has become an influential medium for communication and self-expression, providing meaningful insights into individuals' mental well-being based on their shared content. However, using social media for depression detection presents significant limitations, including unreliable self-reported data, language complexities, privacy concerns, regulatory issues, and algorithmic biases that may lead to misclassification. This chapter aims to explore the potential of social media in detecting depression by addressing these challenges and improving detection accuracy. The data are available on the open-source platform Kaggle, containing social media posts labeled for depression-related content. Machine learning (ML) and deep learning (DL) techniques, including natural language processing (NLP) and sentiment analysis, are applied to classify and predict depression-related content. Experimental results demonstrate that advanced ML and DL models enhance prediction accuracy, though challenges, like false positives and negatives remain. The results underscore the potential of utilizing social media for detecting depression as a complementary approach to mental health assessment,

**Corresponding author*: smita.mishra@muit.in; ORCID: 0000-0003-1199-9342
Febin Prakash: ORCID ID: 0000-0003-4974-568X
Rosan Basha: ORCID ID: 0009-0007-2234-6757
Chinmaya Kumar Mohapatra: ORCID ID: 0000-0002-6243-3974

Sudesh Yadav, Pethuru Raj, Satya Prakash Yadav and Victor Hugo C. de Albuquerque (eds.) Natural Language Processing in Mental Health Care: Methodologies and Clinical Practice, (165–180) © 2026 Scrivener Publishing LLC

stressing the importance of regulatory frameworks and their integration with clinical evaluations.

Keywords: Social media, machine learning, mental health, deep learning, natural language processing

12.1 Introduction

Nowadays, the use of social media has become the norm, allowing people to express themselves, engage with others, and stay updated with the latest information. Social media content has gained popularity as millions of users express their thoughts, feelings, and experiences and it can be used to identify patterns in mental health [1]. Scholars and psychologists have also paid much attention to the potential use of social web data for the early detection of depression. Machine learning (ML) and natural language processing (NLP) algorithms have thus been used to recognize linguistic patterns, sentiment, and behavior, which indicate users who are at high risk of depression [2]. Twitter, Reddit, and Facebook provide vast amounts of data that could be used to underpin bio-surveillance for the timely identification of individuals who can require intervention and support in terms of mental health [3]. While it carries the possibility of high accuracy, there are several issues using digital platforms for identifying depression. One major issue is sampling and data validity, as individuals can express emotions on social media that do not accurately reflect their actual experiences. For this reason, self-reported mental health status can be overestimated or not reported, which distorts the model [4]. Furthermore, human language has more subtle components, such as sarcasm, complex expressions, and cultural differences that make it challenging for the model to accurately determine the sentiment and emotional intent. It will be important examine at other moral issues, such as the privacy of the user's data, their consent, and data security. The processing and mining of personal information and knowledge without the subject's consent is a legal and moral issue [5]. The other drawback is related to algorithmic bias because most datasets are not always inclusive of different populations. The predictions on at-risk persons or groups are skewed, and decisions based on these predictions can perpetuate or exclude those at risk to protect existing models trained on biased data [6]. The use of social network analysis is limited in assessing an individual's mental health status, since the content people share on their social media platforms does not always mirror their true state. Moreover, the false negative (FN), where individuals who are depressed are not identified as such, can prevent healthcare professionals from diagnosing those in need of assistance at the right time [7]. This chapter explores the feasibility of using social media to detect depression while addressing challenges, such as data credibility, privacy issues, and algorithm bias. It also examines how ML and DL, in conjunction with NLP and sentiment analysis, enhance detection accuracy.

12.2 Methodology

For this work, a socially related dataset is available in Kaggle to assess the posts reported as containing depression details. Some of the ML and DL algorithms, including random forest (RF), gradient boosting decision tree algorithm (GBDT), logistic regression (LR), Naive Bayes (NB), decision tree (DT), and bidirectional long short-term memory (BiLSTM), were employed combined with NLP and sentiment analysis to increase the detection rate.

12.2.1 Dataset

In this study, three existing datasets were examined. The Reddit Cleaned Dataset [8], available on Kaggle, was employed to examine linguistic patterns through Reddit posts labeled for depression. Posts collected from mental health-related subreddits were included in the Depression Detection from Reddit Dataset [9], which was used for sentiment analysis and depression categorization. The Depression to Capture Emotional Expressions on Twitter Dataset [10] provided tagged tweets, which were utilized for sentiment analysis and depression identification. These datasets were used to gain a comprehensive understanding of user attitudes and behaviors affecting mental health, supporting deep learning (DL) applications in depression detection and mental health assessment.

12.2.2 Data Preparation

Preprocessing and feature extraction are text preprocessing techniques that enhance social media text for depression diagnosis. Preprocessing of data involves lemmatization, tokenization, and cleaning of the text to make the data consistent. Feature extraction transforms the textual data into numerical form and the most commonly used are Word to Vector (Word2Vec), Bidirectional Encoder Representations from Transformers (BERT) embeddings, and Term Frequency-Inverse Document Frequency (TF-IDF). Sentiment and topic analysis enhance the perception of emotional tones and informal and formal discussions concerning mental health.

12.2.3 Social Media Depression Detection Models

Social media information is analyzed for mental health indicators using a number of Machine Learning (ML) and Deep Learning (DL) techniques. The methods, such as GBDT, NB, RF, DT, LR, and Bi-LSTM, help in improving the classification as the features are able to detect patterns in text as well as sentiments.

12.2.4 Gradient Boosting Decision Tree

GBDT [11] is used to diagnose depression from social media information, utilizing a regression tree model based on classification and regression trees (CART), as indicated in Equation (12.1). The GBDT structure is depicted in Figure 12.1(c).

$$g\ (x) = \sum_{i=1}^{I} d_i\ .J\ (w \in S_i \tag{12.1}$$

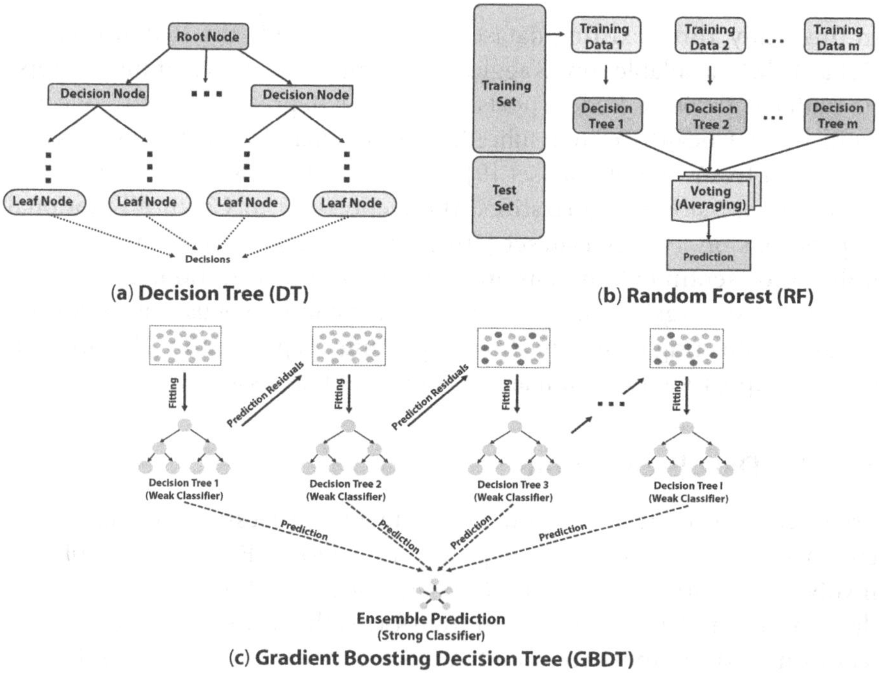

Figure 12.1 Schematic structure of (a) DT, (b) RF, and (c) GBDT. Source: (a) https://www.geeksforgeeks.org/machine-learning/decision-tree/. (b) https://www.simplilearn.com/tutorials/machine-learning-tutorial/random-forest-algorithm. (c) https://botpenguin.com/glossary/machine-learning-algorithms.

The data space is divided into I units (I leaf nodes) where the output value of each unit is denoted by d_i. Equation (12.1) indicates that GBDT effectively estimates the link between text elements in social media and depression classification using ML techniques. However, as a result of sampling operations, GBDT has the potential risk of overfitting the model; therefore, adding a learning rate (η) at each iteration can help mitigate this challenge. To enhance generalization, an approach to random subsampling was established. This reduces the variance of the model and makes the model more stable by randomly selecting a part of the training data for each boosting phase without replacement. To avoid the same feature selection in each case, a new feature vector is also randomized after each selection stage. Learning rate modification and random subsampling are employed in GBDT to enhance the classification process, minimize overfitting and identify patterns associated with depression on social media.

12.2.5 Naive Bayes

A probabilistic classification method called NB [12] uses Bayes' theorem to determine whether a particular social media post shows symptoms of depression. It is mathematically effective and useful for massive datasets since it assumes that characteristics (such as words, phrases, and sentiment ratings) are distinct from one another. Despite its ease of use, Naïve Bayes excels at challenging text analysis tasks, such as social network depression detection. The subsequent probability of a class (such as depressed or non-depressed) is determined using Equation (12.2).

$$Q(b / z) = Q(z / b), Q(b)) / Q(z) \tag{12.2}$$

Where:

- The posterior probability of depression based on the recorded social media post is $Q(b/z)$.
- The dataset's prior probability of depression is denoted by $Q(b)$.
- The probability of the observed characteristics given the depression class is represented by $Q(z/b)$.
- The prior probability of the observed characteristics over all postings is denoted by $Q(z)$.

The capacity of Naïve Bayes to handle features with high dimensions provides a great asset for text classification challenges and a useful tool for detecting mental health issues in social media conversation.

12.2.6 Random Forest

Multiple DTs are constructed using the RF [13] algorithm to categorize social media text information to detect depression. Because text data is highly dimensional, RF reduces noise while choosing the most useful characteristics. The RF architecture is depicted in Figure 12.1 (b). The steps in the RF model are as follows:

Sampling: To ensure variety in training data, the database is chosen at random with substitution to form different subsets $D_1, D_2, \ldots, D_L$.

Tree Construction: DT is constructed using an arbitrary collection of features (n-try features) for every subset D_L. To improve prediction accuracy, the optimum characteristic splits are identified using a probabilistic approach.

Leaf Node Decision: Each tree continues to grow until a stopping criterion is encountered, assigning classification labels based on feature probabilities derived from social media text patterns.

Ensemble Decision: To ensure a reliable forecast of depression signs in social media postings, the final classification decision is made by merging L unpruned trees, indicated as $h_1(X_1), h_2(X_2), \ldots\ldots$ in a majority vote method. The RF approach improves classification accuracy for identifying depression-related material in social media interactions by utilizing several DTs to capture complicated linkages within text data.

12.2.7 Decision Tree

A supervised learning technique used to categorize social media text data for depression diagnosis is the DT [14] algorithm. It is a hierarchical structure, where the leaf nodes contain the classification output, branches depict decision rules and nodes, and intermediate nodes represent text-based properties. Figure 12.1 (a) depicts the DT structure. It consists of:

- **Decision Nodes** comprise certain attributes extracted from social media postings and direct the categorization procedure across several branches.
- **Leaf Nodes** indicate the final categorization categories, such as non-depression content or possible depression indications, without further branching.

Information Gain and Entropy, which gauge each feature's efficacy and degree of uncertainty in text data classification, are used by the DT model to construct the tree. The information gain is computed by Equation (12.3).

$$Gain(T,B) = Entropy(T) - \sum_{j=1}^{d} |Tu/T| Entropy(Tu) \quad (12.3)$$

If B is the chosen text feature, Tu is the subset of data where B takes a certain value, and d is the number of classes (e.g., depressed vs. non-depressive postings). The DT efficiently categorizes social media postings about depression detection by examining trends in textual characteristics including mood, word frequency, and contextual clues.

12.2.8 Logistic Regression

LR is the first ML model used to identify depression in social media posts [15]. LR is a binary classification model that uses a variety of variables taken from social media language to represent the outcome variable (depression or non-depression). The log-odds of the probability p (i.e., the chances of depression) in an LR with l characteristics are represented as a linear function of the features $W = (w_1, w_2, \ldots, w_l)$ are illustrated in Equation (12.4).

$$\log\left(\frac{o}{1-0}\right) = \sum_{i=1}^{l} \beta_i z_i \leftrightarrow 0 = \frac{1}{1+f^{-\sum_i \beta_i z_i}} \quad (12.4)$$

In this case, the parameters calculated by maximizing the log probability function are represented by $\beta = (\beta_1, \beta_2, \ldots, \beta_k)$. The log-likelihood function for n observations, where z_j indicates the depression state and w_j is the characteristic vector for the jth observation, is provided by Equation (12.5).

$$k\beta \sum_{j=1}^{m} [w_j z_j \beta - \log(1 + f^{z_j \beta})] \quad (12.5)$$

The chance ratio test is used to compare nested models to choose variables. First, only if the corresponding p-values are less than 0.05 are the major effects (features) maintained. Then, starting with second-order interactions, higher-order interactions are investigated one at a time. Included are relationships with p-values below 0.10. With comparable inclusion criteria, the procedure moves on to more complex interactions (third and fourth-order). The Lasso and Ridge penalization techniques are used to reduce the parameters β and avoid overfitting. The purpose of penalization is to maximize, as illustrated in Equation (12.6).

$$k_{\lambda}^{\omega} = \sum_{j=1}^{m}[w_j z_j \beta - \log(1+f^{z_j\beta})] - \lambda \sum_{i=1}^{l} |\beta_i|^{\omega} \quad (12.6)$$

For Lasso, $\omega = 1$ (which permits β_i to be adjusted to 0 for parameter choosing) or Ridge, $\omega = 2$ (which shrinks β into 0), λ is the tuning parameter. Main effects and second- to fourth-order interactions are included in the model fitting, with λ set at 1. To classify depression in social media postings, LR models trained with up to j^{th} -order interactions are indicated.

12.2.9 Bidirectional Long Short-Term Memory

Recurrent Neural Networks (RNNs) are widely used for evaluating sequential data, making them ideal for processing social media material. However, RNNs have memory retention constraints, which make it difficult to understand long-term dependencies and lead to the issue of gradient vanishing. To overcome these issues, LSTM networks were developed [16]. The LSTM uses memory cells to store over time facts and a gating mechanism to control data flow. The three basic gates in an LSTM unit the input, forget, and output gate, determine how information is updated in the network. The forget gate uses the input text and the previous concealed state to control which data should be retained or discarded. Transition values between 0 and 1 are subjected to a sigmoid activation function, where values towards zero denote information that has been eliminated and values towards 1 represent data that has been retained by Equation (12.7).

$$e_s = \sigma(X_e[g_{s-1}, w_s] + a_e) \quad (12.7)$$

Additionally, the data is modified in the cell states is selected by the input gate and illustrated by Equation (12.8).

$$j_s = \sigma(X_j[g_{s-1}, w_s] + a_j) \quad (12.8)$$

To modify the new memory cell, a $\tan g$ activation function processes the new information and concealed state are shown in Equation (12.9).

$$\hat{D}_s = \tan g(X_d[g_{s-1}, w_s] + a_d)$$

$$D_s = D_s.D_{s-1} + j_s.\hat{D}_s \quad (12.9)$$

The output gate ascertains the model's subsequent concealed state determined by Equation (12.10).

$$p_s = \sigma(W_p[g_{s-1}, w_s] + a_p)$$

$$g_s = p_s.\tan g(D_s) \tag{12.10}$$

The capacity of a typical LSTM to understand contextual connections within textual input is limited since it analyzes information in a single forward direction. BiLSTM is made up of two LSTM layers, one of which processes data in a forward manner and the other in a backward way. This dual-layered design allows Bi-LSTM to extract both past and prospective context from social media posts. Equation (12.11) depicts the hidden state at time s, which includes both forward ($\tilde{g}_s$) and backward ($\leftarrow g_s$) outputs.

$$g_s = \tilde{g}_s \oplus \leftarrow g_s \tag{12.11}$$

Where $\oplus$ stands for summing by elements. BiLSTM outperforms regular LSTMs and RNNs in classification tasks, enhancing contextual knowledge and sentiment interpretation to improve depression identification from social media postings.

12.3 Result

The results of the experimental part showed that ML and DL methods could enhance the depression identification of accuracy from the posts. Nevertheless, some concerns, like false positives (FP) and FN persist, requiring further optimization.

Experimental setup: For effective data processing, the experimental setup made use of a machine with an Intel Core i7 CPU, 512GB SSD, and 16GB RAM. *Python, Tensor Flow,* and *NLP libraries* were used to create ML and DL models using Kaggle datasets.

12.3.1 Performance Analysis

To evaluate the performance of different ML and DL techniques, multiple methods were applied to the task of depression detection from social media. Performance was assessed using F1-score, precision, accuracy, and recall to discern the merits and demerits of the models. Table 12.1 depicts the results of ML and DL techniques.

Table 12.1 Evaluation metrics of different models for identifying depression through social media analysis.

Methods	F1-score (%)	Precision (%)	Accuracy (%)	Recall (%)
RF [17]	81	82	80	80
Bi-LSTM [17]	90	89	93	91
LR [18]	96.55	98.13	96.60	95.02
GBDT [18]	96.47	98.05	96.53	94.94
NB [19]	91	91.4	90.9	90.9
DT [20]	75.33	63.53	89.33	83.14

Source: Own elaboration

Accuracy indicates the proportion of correctly categorized depressive and non-depressive posts to the total number of posts examined. It represents the model's ability to recognize depression-related material in social media data. Figure 12.2 depicts the outcome of accuracy. The capacity of

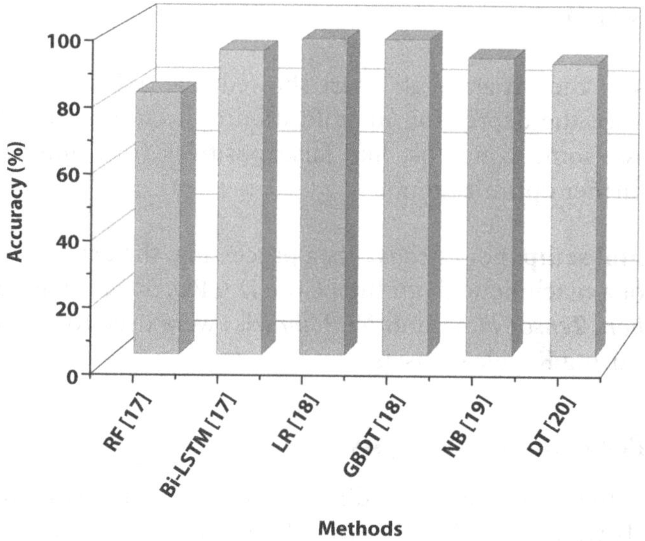

Figure 12.2 Accuracy trends across different models for depression detection. Source: Own elaboration.

LR to accurately categorize social media postings connected to depression is demonstrated by its greatest accuracy of 96.60%.

Precision calculates the fraction of accurately detected depression-related posts among all posts labeled as depressed. It demonstrates the model's capacity to reduce FPs in depression identification. Figure 12.3 shows the precision outcomes. LR achieves the best precision (98.13%) indicating that it effectively reduces FPs in the identification of depression.

Recall calculates the percentage of real depression-related postings accurately detected by the algorithm. It represents the model's ability to reduce FNs when recognizing depressing material. Figure 12.4 shows the recall results. LR also achieves the maximum recall (95.02%), indicating that it is successful in recognizing the majority of postings that are connected to depression.

F1-Score is the harmonic mean of accuracy and recall, which balances FPs and FNs. It offers a single metric for determining the model's performance in detecting depression-related postings. Figure 12.5 depicts the F1-score evaluation. LR attains the highest F1 score (96.55%), balancing precision and recall for optimal performance in depression detection.

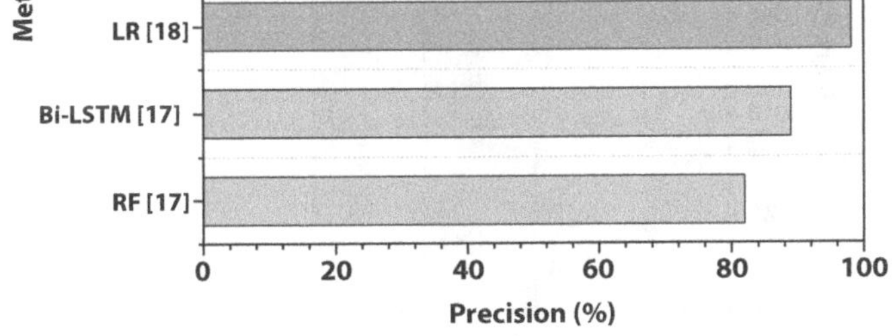

Figure 12.3 Precision analysis of machine learning models in depression classification. Source: Own elaboration.

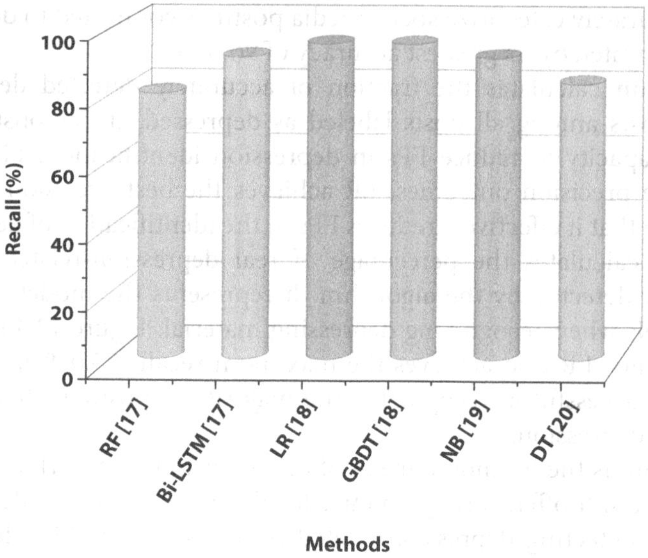

Figure 12.4 Recall performance of various algorithms in detecting depression. Source: Own elaboration.

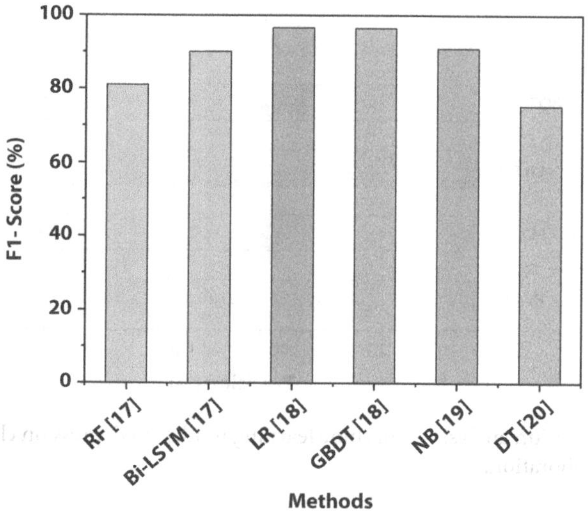

Figure 12.5 F1-score evaluation for depression identification models. Source: Own elaboration.

12.3.2 Discussion

The performance comparison of several ML and DL models in recognizing depression from social media posts shows variations in the ability of the models. LR [18] is the best performing model among all, with an overall F1 score of 96.55%, precision of 98.13%, recall of 95.02%, and accuracy of 96.60%. This demonstrates its high efficiency in accurately recognizing depression-related posts with minimal FP and FN results. GBDT [18] followed closely, making it a competitive alternative to LR. RF [17] and DT [20] performed slightly lower, with RF reaching 80% accuracy, while DT had a deprived precision of only 63.53%, indicating difficulty in reducing FP rates. Compared to the exact model LR, models, like Bi-LSTM [17] and NB [19] had higher recall but lower precision and F1 score. Based on FP and FN rates, LR was the most accurate model for depression detection from social media posts. This highlights that selecting the right model can significantly impact the performance of mental health detection.

12.4 Conclusion

Social media was used as a modality for identifying depressive content through ML and DL models to improve classification outcomes. This chapter also utilized data obtained from Kaggle, which contains publicly available text patterns of social media posts associated with depression using NLP and sentiment analysis. However, there were limitations, such as reliance on self-reported data, the subjective nature of language, privacy issues, and algorithmic bias in more developed models. Several factors, such as FPs and FNs, were identified, and highlighted the need for model improvement. Despite these constraints, the results demonstrated the potential of utilizing digital platform data for supplementary screening of depression. However, the utilization of emerging technologies raises several issues that require regulation and moral consideration. These methods must be combined with clinical assessments to enhance the reliability of the mental health monitoring process while relying on social media.

AI disclosure statement: The author confirms that no artificial intelligence (AI)-generated content or AI-assisted writing tools were used in the preparation of this chapter (including summaries and the abstract). All text, analysis, and conclusions are the result of the author's original work.

References

1. Bailey, E.R., *et al.*, Authentic self-expression on social media is associated with greater subjective well-being. *Nat. Commun.*, 11.1, 4889, 2020, https://doi.org/10.1038/s41467-020-18539-w.
2. Kim, J., *et al.*, A deep learning model for detecting mental illness from user content on social media. *Sci. Rep.*, 10.1, 11846, 2020, https://doi.org/10.1038/s41598-020-68764-y.
3. Torous, J., *et al.*, The growing field of digital psychiatry: current evidence and the future of apps, social media, chatbots, and virtual reality. *World Psychiatry*, 20.3, 318–335, 2021, https://doi.org/10.1002/wps.20883.
4. Safa, R., Edalatpanah, S.A., Sorourkhah, A., Predicting mental health using social media: A roadmap for future development, in: *Deep learning in personalized healthcare and decision support*, pp. 285–303, Academic Press, 2023, https://doi.org/10.1016/B978-0-443-19413-9.00014-X.
5. Olaniyan, D., *et al.*, Utilizing an attention-based LSTM model for detecting sarcasm and irony in social media. *Computers*, 12.11, 231, 2023, https://doi.org/10.3390/computers12110231.
6. Naslund, J.A., *et al.*, Social media and mental health: benefits, risks, and opportunities for research and practice. *J. Technol. Behav. Sci.*, 5.3, 245–257, 2020, https://doi.org/10.1007/s41347-020-00134-x.
7. Fleming, M.N., Considerations for the ethical implementation of psychological assessment through social media *via* machine learning. *Ethics Behav.*, 31.3, 181–192, 2021, https://doi.org/10.1080/10508422.2020.1817026.
8. Reddit Cleaned Dataset: https://www.kaggle.com/datasets/infamouscoder/depression-reddit-cleaned/data.
9. Depression Detection from Reddit Dataset: https://www.kaggle.com/datasets/deapdaru/depression-detection-from-reddit/data.
10. Twitter Dataset: https://www.kaggle.com/datasets/infamouscoder/mental-health-social-media/data.
11. Basyouni, A., *et al.*, A Suicidal Ideation Detection Framework on Social Media using Machine Learning and Genetic Algorithms. *IEEE Access*, 12, 124816–124833, 2024, https://doi.org/10.1109/ACCESS.2024.3454796.
12. Pande, S.D., *et al.*, Depression detection based on social networking sites using data mining. *Multimed. Tools Appl.*, 83.9, 25951–25967, 2024, https://doi.org/10.1007/s11042-023-16564-7.
13. Liu, J. and Shi, M., A hybrid feature selection and ensemble approach to identify depressed users in online social media. *Front. Psychol.*, 12, 8028215, 2022, https://doi.org/10.3389/fpsyg.2021.802821.
14. Hidayatullah, M.R. and Maharani, W., Depression detection on twitter social media using decision tree. *Jurnal RESTI (Rekayasa Sistem Dan Teknologi Informasi)*, 6.4, 677–683, 2022, https://doi.org/10.29207/resti.v6i4.4275.

15. Abbas, M.A., *et al.*, Novel transformer based contextualized embedding and probabilistic features for depression detection from social media. *IEEE Access*, 12, 54087–54100, 2024, https://doi.org/10.1109/ACCESS.2024.3387695.
16. Thekkekara, J.P., Yongchareon, S., Liesaputra, V., An attention-based CNN-BiLSTM model for depression detection on social media text. *Expert Syst. Appl.*, 249, 1238345, 2024, https://doi.org/10.1016/j.eswa.2024.123834.
17. Ahmad, H., *et al.*, Applying deep learning technique for depression classification in social media text. *J. Med. Imaging Health Inf.*, 10.10, 2446–2451, 2020, https://doi.org/10.1166/jmihi.2020.3169.
18. Wang, Y., *et al.*, Online social network individual depression detection using a multitask heterogenous modality fusion approach. *Inf. Sci.*, 609, 727–7495, 2022, doi: 10.1016/j.ins.2022.07.109.
19. Nusrat, M.O., Shahzad, W., Ahmed Jamal, S., Multi class depression detection through tweets using artificial intelligence. *arXiv preprint arXiv:2404.13104* 2024, https://doi.org/10.48550/arXiv.2404.13104.
20. Noor, F., *et al.*, Depression Detection In Social Media Using Bagging Classifier. *Depression*, 42.01, 2023, 2023, https://doi.org/10.17605/OSF.IO/EVXB7.

13

Creation of Cognitive Behavioral Chatbots for Mental Health

Monika Joshi[1]*, Pushpa J.[2], Sharon M.[3] and Manoranjan Dash[4]

[1]*Maharishi School of Pharmaceuticals, Maharishi University of Information Technology, Uttar Pradesh, India*
[2]*Department of CSIT, Jain (Deemed-to-be University), Bangalore, Karnataka, India*
[3]*Department of Computer Science & Engineering, Presidency University, Bengaluru, Karnataka, India*
[4]*Department of Management, Siksha 'O' Anusandhan (Deemed to be University), Bhubaneswar, Odisha, India*

Abstract

The creation of mental health service-oriented AI-powered chatbot psychologists uses methods from natural language processing (NLP), as this chapter demonstrates. The system contains essential components that enable successful cognitive behavioral therapy (CBT) implementations through entity extraction, sentiment analysis, intent recognition and semantic similarity processing methods. The chatbot system identifies user requests through cognitive restructuring before detecting emotional states and automatically modifies the emotional tone and content of its responses. Through confidence scores along with structured answer generation and reinforcement learning, the system achieves accurate responses that remain awareness-based throughout interactions. The analysis of practical therapeutic applications together with stress-lowering and emotional assistance strengthens user engagement and the mental health performance of chatbots.

**Corresponding author*: monika.joshi@muit.in; ORCID: 0000-0002-3708-9446
Pushpa J.: ORCID: 0009-0005-7321-4047
Sharon M.: ORCID: 0009-0008-0205-5757
Manoranjan Dash: ORCID: 0000-0003-3510-3299

Sudesh Yadav, Pethuru Raj, Satya Prakash Yadav and Victor Hugo C. de Albuquerque (eds.) Natural Language Processing in Mental Health Care: Methodologies and Clinical Practice, (181–194) © 2026 Scrivener Publishing LLC

***Keywords*:** AI-powered chatbot psychologists, cognitive behavioral therapy, natural language processing, sentiment analysis, therapeutic applications

13.1 Introduction

Mental health disorders rank as primary disability causes worldwide because the World Health Organization (WHO) states that four percent of people will face neurological or mental illness during their lives [1]. Progressive mental health problems affect a substantial number of people, yet many of these individuals cannot access mental health care because funding shortages, stigma and high costs create barriers to care. Modern mental health care needs alternative approaches that should be both affordable and conveniently accessible to fill the wide gaps in available mental healthcare. Current developments in natural language processing (NLP) and artificial intelligence (AI) allow systems to comprehend and react to human speech. AI-powered conversational agents known as chatbots have proven useful across multiple domains, which include education, healthcare and customer service support systems [2]. Chatbots allow the development of psychological support systems with direction features and intervention capabilities to assist users in distress for mental health purposes. People receiving therapy would gain extra support through AI-powered solutions that complement their standard treatment. Cognitive behavioral therapy, or CBT, is an evidence-based method that effectively helps people manage mental health issues like phobias, stress, anxiety, and depression [3]. The central principle of cognitive behavioral therapy emphasizes that distress develops from and sustains itself because of unhealthy thinking methods and problematic behaviors. People can improve their mental well-being through active identification and counteraction of problematic cognitive thoughts and by establishing more productive ways to think and respond to emotional situations. The implementation of CBT concepts together with its methods in the chatbot's database enables personal psychological therapy delivery [4]. The progress of an AI-powered mobile chatbot psychologist demands both essential CBT content and natural language processing (NLP) and generation combined in an extensive knowledge base. The adaptive system detects emotional states in users to provide personalized support necessary for achieving effective psychological intervention [5]. People can use the chatbot platform on their mobile devices because it has an easy-to-use interface. To assess the efficacy of the AI-enabled mobile chatbot psychologist, analysis is conducted with individuals experiencing varying degrees of psychological discomfort. Tests assess how well the chatbot delivers CBT treatments to users, maintains meaningful discussions and improves their mental health. The research creates essential fresh data about how this chatbot system functions as an accessible and scalable mental health care platform [6]. As an alternative to conventional therapy, the AI-enabled mobile chatbot psychologist satisfies the need for easily accessible and reasonably priced mental health solutions. Through its mobile platform, the chatbot helps reduce mental health provider caseloads while enabling individuals to gain personal psychological support, which it can manage autonomously. The innovative approach offers additional support to people in need while acting as a valuable addition to present mental health services [7]. The successful delivery of psychological wellbeing interventions with AI-powered conversational agents becomes possible through AIML integration with CBT principles in developing mobile chatbot psychologists. The application of AI is expanding throughout different areas, which include smart cities and homes, smart energy, NLP and various other operational fields.

To evaluate that the cognitive behavioral chatbots demonstrate effectiveness in managing stress, performing cognitive restructuring and delivering emotional support was the aim of the chapter. The analysis of chatbot success consists of evaluating user participation alongside mood changes and the correct identification of user intentions. Chatbots examine the emotional states of users to provide appropriate therapeutic responses. The evaluation tracks user communication patterns to establish the mental health influence of the chatbot system throughout time.

13.2 Methodology

This section presents methodologies for developing and improving an AI-guided chatbot psychologist that delivers CBT intervention services. The implementation of training and assessment relies on a Kaggle dataset that contains mental health-related interactions that have been tagged for analysis. User inputs are processed through NLP functions that include intent detection and entity extraction as well as sentiment analysis and semantic similarity methods to generate personalized responses. A combination of confidence scoring and reinforcement learning provides guaranteed accuracy and relevance in psychological support. Users follow better mental health pathways after using this chatbot because it provides emotional-based response customization and helps build cognitive skills alongside stress reduction practices.

Data Collection

The data for this chapter comes from an open source platform, which offers high-quality and varied mental health information. The dataset includes multiple categories, such as sentiment scores together with text-based chats and user interactions and psychological tests that pertain to chatbot-based interventions. The assessment and training of the chatbot for delivering CBT interventions use labeled data points that identify behavioral patterns, emotional states and cognitive distortion examples. An ML preprocessing method has formatted the data to resolve disparities and safeguard privacy while structuring it for ML applications. The specific dataset makes it possible for the chatbot to detect user emotions while delivering CBT-based advice and personalized responses that match psychological distress numbers for better mental health assistance.

The AI-Powered Chatbot Psychologist's Elements

The fundamental operation of AI-based mobile chatbots for psychological assistance will be explored alongside their capacity to understand user messages, analyze contextual information and deliver individualized mental health care. Through its operations, the chatbot demonstrates successful delivery of cognitive behavioral therapy methods while offering meaningful conversations. The process of an AI-powered chatbot intended to assist with mental health issues is depicted in Figure 13.1. To produce precise answers for emotional analysis, stress management, and anxiety evaluation, the system analyzes user interactions, extracts intent, and uses NLP techniques to classify data. Through data processing, storage, and training, the chatbot keeps getting better at improving therapeutic interventions.

Intent recognition and dialogue flow: The chatbot identifies user intentions through defined intent groups that understand user demands. The correct identification of user purposes remains fundamental for building

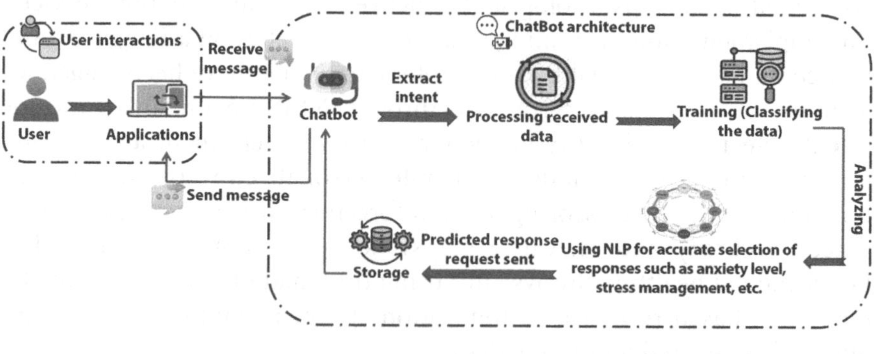

Figure 13.1 AI-powered chatbot architecture for mental support. Source: [15].

productive dialogue exchanges and offering proper psychological support. The system classifies all "stress management" related concerns from users, thus offering CBT-based coping solutions [8]. The system enhances its capability to understand user needs through intensive training that applies several example queries to each user intent. The chatbot transforms its responses between text messages and different multimedia formats like audio and video formats.

Entity extraction for personalized responses: This technology helps the chatbot enhance its responses through the utilization of extracted user input components known as entities. Software from a mental health standpoint includes individual conditions such as social anxiety and panic attacks together with appointment schedules as forthcoming appointments or depressive states such as anxiety, grief and dissatisfaction [9]. The chatbot delivers ideal therapeutic results because it detects entities precisely, which enables it to adapt interactions for individual users.

Utterances for enhanced understanding: End-users can express their messages through multiple strategies utilizing speech utterances. Such questions from someone searching for relaxation methods would include "Establishing Methods to Manage Stress." Users ask, "What are some methods to relax?" through their requests. The chatbot's training process includes multiple varieties of utterances for every purpose to build a better understanding of authentic language variances [10]. The system interprets user inquiries more accurately because it processes at least five to ten different statements for each possible intent.

Training and model optimization: The training for the chatbot occurs continuously through the use of mental health-focused talks that have been tagged. The application delivers precise results through NLP models for both things and intention classification. User input during reinforcement learning allows the chatbot to enhance the quality of its responses. The chatbot system ensures the progressive development of appropriate and encouraging psychological advice through time.

Confidence scoring for accurate response selection: The chatbot assigns confidence ratings to estimated purposes to pick the most relevant response. A high confidence score exists when users provide messages parallel to what the chatbot learned in its training data. To gain an understanding of user wants when the confidence score shows low performance, the chatbot could implement follow-up questions [11]. The methodology ensures patients access correct mental healthcare services while the system delivers valid replies.

Architecture of Chatbots for Cognitive-Behavioral Assistance
The chatbot psychologist uses cognitive behavioral strategies to support mental wellness. It converses with users, using sentiment analysis to determine their feelings, and then adjusts responses appropriately. While it uses cognitive restructuring through thought recording for negative emotions, it promotes journaling and content recommendations for happy emotions [12]. It indicates seeking professional assistance if there is no discernible improvement in emotional state. Sentiment models, structured response generation, and Python functions are used by the chatbot, which stores interactions for later analysis and modification.

NLP Methods for Chatbot Psychologist Analysis
A chatbot psychologist uses a variety of NLP strategies to improve its comprehension and responsiveness to user inputs. These techniques allow the chatbot to identify the user's intent, gather pertinent information, assess feelings, and produce suitable responses based on CBT.

Intent Recognition classifier determines user intentions between expressing discomfort, asking for coping strategies and seeking emotional support. The system uses phrase analysis together with keyword detection to categorize treatment demands from users. The answer system matches with precise mental health support needs of the users.

Entity Extraction enables the chatbot to identify crucial message elements, including stressors and feelings and particular issues [13]. Through analysis, the chatbot identifies that "exams" represent a cause of stress because it matches the emotional phrase "I feel anxious about my exams." Such focused CBT therapy interventions can be delivered by the chatbot when it identifies relevant components during user interactions.

Sentiment Analysis of the chatbot detects user communication to recognize positive, negative or neutral orientation. When anxiety about the exams arises, the chatbot tailors its response with emotional validation while presenting appropriate solutions such as gratitude writing and thought rephrase exercises. The system will direct users toward psychological counseling services when it identifies unmanageable negative emotions.

Named Entity Recognition (NER) enables the chatbot to identify certain names, conditions, and terms associated with therapy in user messages. When a user says terms like "social anxiety," "panic attacks," or "depression," the chatbot understands that these are significant mental health issues [14]. This makes it possible for it to offer pertinent self-help methods, learning materials, or recommendations for expert counseling as needed.

Part-of-Speech (POS) Tagging enables chatbots to evaluate user messages by identifying nouns, verbs and adjectives along with adverbs. The system identifies "feel" as a verbal term while understanding "hopeless" as an adjective that describes mental hardship in the statement "I feel extremely hopeless." The chatbot would provide better responses and accurately interpret user intentions and emotions by understanding phrase structure.

Semantic Similarity Analysis enables the chatbot to decipher user messages by interpreting their actual meanings above surface-level word matches. The chatbot uses this input as an indicator of stress after the user notes feeling "drained and overwhelmed" [15]. It enhances the chatbot's psychological support capabilities through its context-based response methodology.

By using these NLU strategies, the chatbot psychologist could identify emotional patterns, have contextually aware discussions, and provide tailored CBT interventions to help users properly manage their mental health.

13.3 Results and Discussion

User engagement, emotional support, and cognitive restructuring all significantly enhance when cognitive behavioral chatbots are used for mental health. Effectively recognizing user intents, extracting important entities, and processing responses using pre-established therapeutic approaches are all done by the chatbot. It correctly categorizes emotional states using sentiment analysis and modifies responses appropriately. While negative emotions set off cognitive restructuring activities, positive emotions lead to affirmations and guided writing. Chatbot interactions depending on various emotional circumstances are depicted in Figure 13.2 (a) Positive emotion shows a helpful dialogue in which the chatbot promotes introspection and affirms feelings of well-being. Figure 13.2 (b) Negative emotion illustrates the chatbot's sympathetic reaction to discomfort by providing coping mechanisms and pointing users in the direction of self-help resources. It emphasizes how the chatbot can identify emotions, modify its responses, and offer specialized mental health assistance.

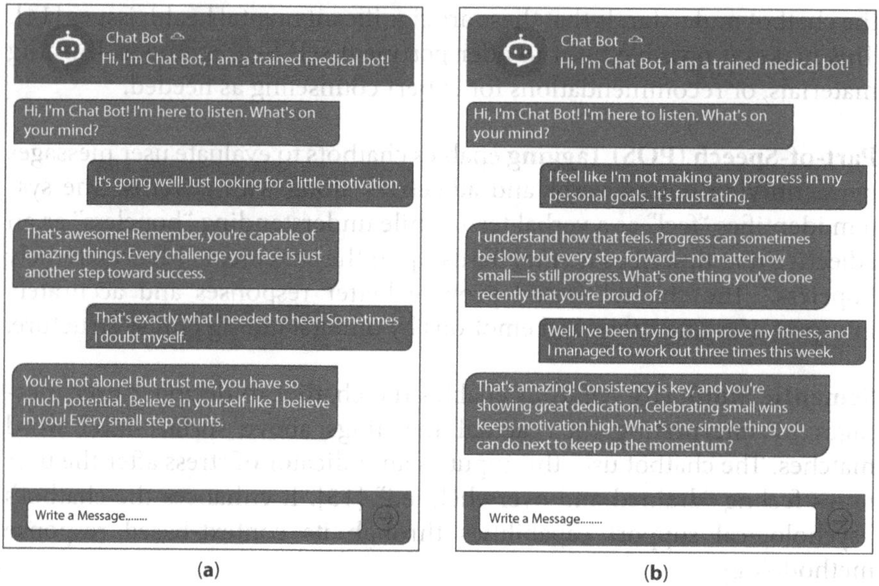

Figure 13.2 Chatbot conversation based on (a) positive and (b) negative emotional context. Source: Own elaboration.

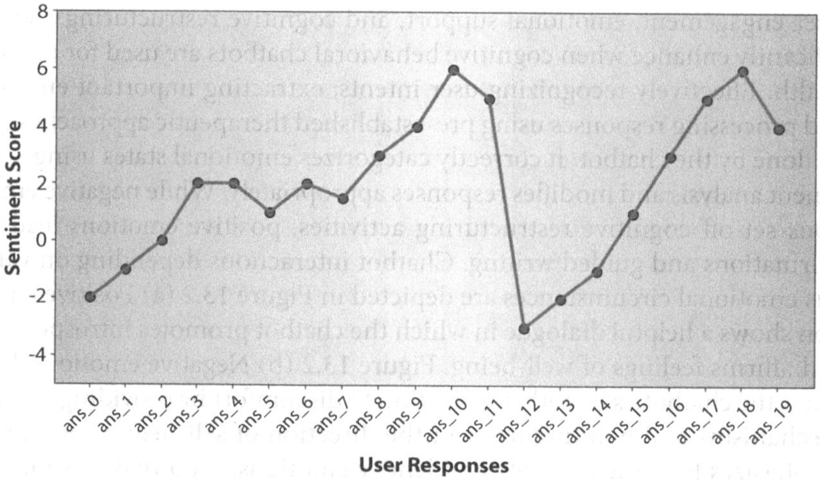

Figure 13.3 Sentiment progression during cognitive restructuring. Source: Own elaboration.

The sentiment progression of a user during a chatbot-guided cognitive restructuring session is depicted in Figure 13.3. It shows the sentiment polarity, which ranges from negative to positive feelings, and displays the user replies in chronological order. At first, sentiment varies, but following the chatbot's interventions, there is a noticeable improvement [16]. An upward trend indicates the user successfully recognized a constructive alternative concept, while a momentary dip indicates cognitive effort in challenging negative notions.

The distribution of user sentiments, such as Positive, Neutral, and Negative, based on chatbot interactions is depicted in Figure 13.4. The success of the chatbot in uplifting users is indicated by a larger percentage of positive sentiments. Negative feelings draw attention to areas that could require cognitive restructuring, whereas neutral sentiments imply mixed emotional states. This investigation aids in determining how the chatbot affects mental health.

The chatbot's ability to categorize user inquiries into the following intent categories: Emotional Support, Cognitive Restructuring, Stress Management, and General Queries, is shown by the intent recognition accuracy (Figure 13.5). A high accuracy rate indicates that the chatbot is correctly interpreting user demands and providing relevant answers. Additional optimization could be necessary for any category with lower accuracy.

Figure 13.6 displays engagement trends over a week and represents everyday chatbot conversations. A consistent rise in interactions indicates that users are sticking with the chatbot and that their trust in it is

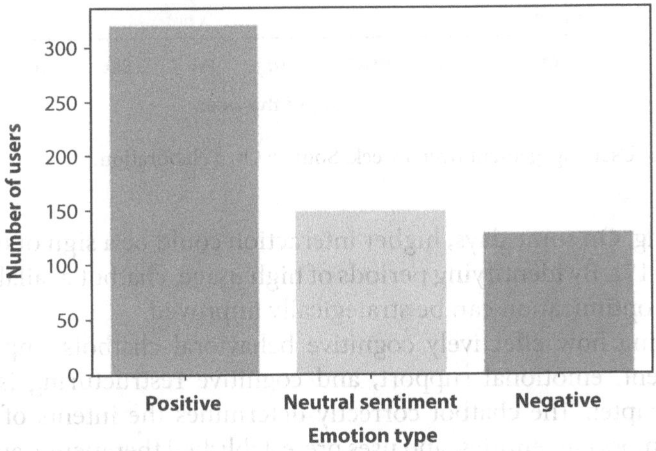

Figure 13.4 Sentiment analysis distribution. Source: Own elaboration.

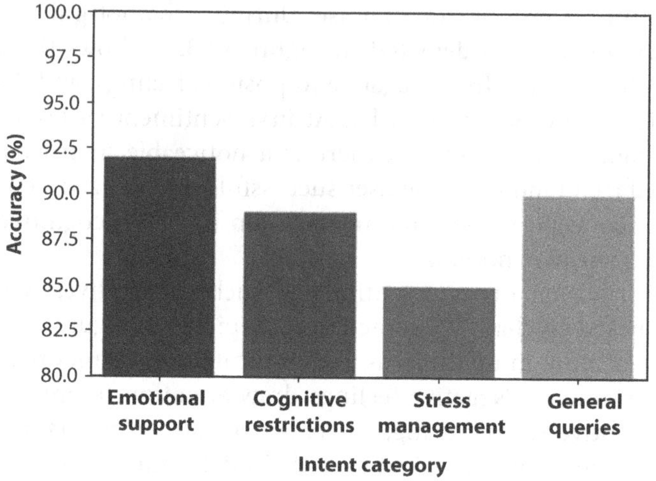

Figure 13.5 Intent recognition accuracy. Source: Own elaboration.

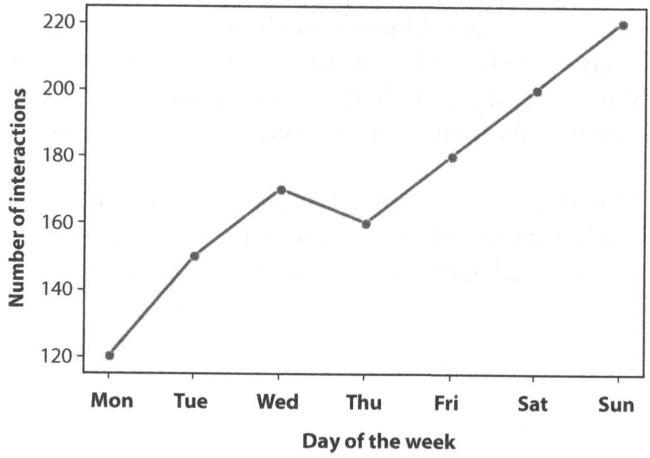

Figure 13.6 User engagement over a week. Source: Own elaboration.

developing. On some days, higher interaction could be a sign of user stress patterns [17]. By identifying periods of high usage, chatbot availability, and response optimization can be strategically improved.

Assessing how effectively cognitive behavioral chatbots improve user engagement, emotional support, and cognitive restructuring is the aim of this chapter. The chatbot correctly determines the intents of the user, extracts important entities, and uses pre-established therapeutic approaches to process responses. Sentiment analysis results show a clear transition from negative emotions to positive emotions, thus confirming the success of the cognitive intervention. Sentiment polarity from the chatbot helps users navigate through journaling or cognitive restructuring tasks, which enables the system to adapt its responses. The system shows strong success in understanding user questions through identifying categories like stress management combined with emotional feedback. Users experience elevated moods when the chatbot succeeds in its goals based on the majority of positive thoughts received but also face issues that require attention because of negative sentiments. Users demonstrate a greater ability to detect more constructive opinions as the sentiment levels rise over time. User participation trends during weekly cycles indicate progressively rising interaction data that indicate users dependably continue to trust and utilize the system. Increased periods of stress tend to convert peaks in chatbot activities because the platform plays an essential role in mental well-being promotion. The chapter findings demonstrate the chatbot achieves its objectives but also reveal the potential for improvements in multiple areas.

13.4 Conclusion

To determine which cognitive behavioral chatbots perform best in terms of user engagement, cognitive restructuring, and emotional support was the aim of this chapter. The sentiment analysis capabilities enabled the chatbot to identify user emotions and understand their requests so it could provide personalized care. The results showed the chatbot succeeded in assisting users through cognitive restructuring because participants demonstrated an essential transition from negative to positive emotional states. Users experienced better interactions because the high intent recognition accuracy produced suitable responses. The mental health support from the chatbot became possible because it could identify emotions and initiate appropriate treatment activities. Users spent more time engaging with the chatbot as their trust and emotional dependency on its services for health management increased. Sentiment progression occasionally declined due to the mental effort needed to change negative thoughts. The chapter pointed out specific areas that required improvement, which focused primarily on developing responsive options for varied feelings. The main design targets for forthcoming improvements should focus on real-time adaptive learning along with intent classification optimization and personalization features. This evaluation demonstrated both potential improvements for the chatbot and its value as a mental health care instrument.

AI disclosure statement: The author confirms that no artificial intelligence (AI)-generated content or AI-assisted writing tools were used in the preparation of this chapter (including summaries and the abstract). All text, analysis, and conclusions are the result of the author's original work.

References

1. Khawaja, Z. and Bélisle-Pipon, J.-C., Your robot therapist is not your therapist: understanding the role of AI-powered mental health chatbots. *Front. Digit. Health*, 5, 12781865, 2023, https://doi.org/10.3389/fdgth.2023.1278186.
2. Freitas, D., *et al.*, Chatbots and mental health: Insights into the safety of generative AI. *J. Consum. Psychol.*, 34.3, 481–491, 2024, https://doi.org/10.1002/jcpy.1393.
3. Balcombe, L., AI chatbots in digital mental health, in: *Informatics*, vol. 10, MDPI, Australia, 2023, https://doi.org/10.3390/informatics10040082.
4. Sabour, S., *et al.*, A chatbot for mental health support: exploring the impact of Emohaa on reducing mental distress in China. *Front. Digit. Health*, 5, 11339875, 2023, https://doi.org/10.3389/fdgth.2023.1133987.
5. Gupta, V., *et al.*, Chatbot for Mental health support using NLP. *2023 4th International Conference for Emerging Technology (INCET)*, IEEE, 2023, https://doi.org/10.1109/INCET57972.2023.10170573.
6. Schick, A., *et al.*, Validity of chatbot use for mental health assessment: experimental study. *JMIR mHealth uHealth*, 10.10, e28082, 2022, https://doi.org/10.2196/28082.
7. Moilanen, J., *et al.*, Supporting mental health self-care discovery through a chatbot. *Front. Digit. Health*, 5, 10347245, 2023, https://doi.org/10.3389/fdgth.2023.1034724.
8. Shah, J., *et al.*, Development and usability testing of a chatbot to promote mental health services use among individuals with eating disorders following screening. *Int. J. Eating Disord.*, 55.9, 1229–1244, 2022, https://doi.org/10.1002/eat.23798.
9. Potts, C., *et al.*, A multilingual digital mental health and well-being Chatbot (ChatPal): Pre-post multicenter intervention study. *J. Med. Internet Res.*, 25, e430515, 2023, https://doi.org/10.2196/43051.
10. Koulouri, T., D. Macredie, R., Olakitan, D., Chatbots to support young adults' mental health: An exploratory study of acceptability. *ACM Trans. Interact. Intell. Syst. (TiiS)*, 12.2, 1–39, 2022, https://doi.org/10.1145/3485874.
11. Trappey, A.JC., *et al.*, Development of an empathy-centric counseling chatbot system capable of sentimental dialogue analysis. *Processes*, 10.5, 930, 2022, https://doi.org/10.3390/pr10050930.

12. Ta-Johnson, V.P., *et al.*, Assessing the topics and motivating factors behind human-social chatbot interactions: Thematic analysis of user experiences. *JMIR Hum. Factors*, 9.4, e38876, 2022, https://doi.org/10.2196/38876.
13. Rathnayaka, P., *et al.*, A mental health chatbot with cognitive skills for personalized behavioral activation and remote health monitoring. *Sensors*, 22.10, 3653, 2022, https://doi.org/10.3390/s22103653.
14. Abubakar, A.M., Gupta, D., Parida, S., A reinforcement learning approach for intelligent conversational chatbot for enhancing mental health therapy. *Procedia Comput. Sci.*, 235, 916–9255, 2024, https://doi.org/10.1016/j.procs.2024.04.087.
15. Rizea, A., Deep Learning-based Solution for Mental Health Issues. *Database Syst. J.*, 13.1, 57–70, 2023.
16. Pandey, S., Sharma, S., Wazir, S., Mental healthcare chatbot based on natural language processing and deep learning approaches: Ted the therapist. *Int. J. Inf. Technol.*, 14.7, 3757–3766, 2022, https://doi.org/10.1007/s41870-022-00999-6.
17. Omarov, B., *et al.*, Artificial intelligence enabled mobile chatbot psychologist using AIML and cognitive behavioral therapy. *Int. J. Adv. Comput. Sci. Appl.*, 14, 6, 2023, https://doi.org/10.14569/IJACSA.2023.0140616.

Part 4

FUTURE DIRECTIONS IN BEHAVIORAL NLP

14

The Future of Behavioral Natural Language Processing in Healthcare

Monika Joshi[1]*, Nanthini K.[2], Devi S.[3] and Biswaranjan Swain[4]

[1]Maharishi School of Pharmaceuticals, Maharishi University of Information Technology, Uttar Pradesh, India
[2]Department of CSIT, Jain (Deemed-to-be University), Bangalore, Karnataka, India
[3]Department of Computer Science & Engineering, Presidency University, Bengaluru, Karnataka, India
[4]Centre for Internet of Things, Siksha 'O' Anusandhan (Deemed to be University), Bhubaneswar, Odisha, India

Abstract
The future of behavioral natural language processing (NLP) in healthcare is driven by advancements in AI-driven linguistic analysis, enabling the assessment of cognitive, emotional, and psychological states. Transformer-based models enhance mental health diagnostics, clinical decision-making, and patient engagement. Emerging innovations, including federated learning, real-time behavioral analytics, and multimodal processing, will shape the next generation of secure, adaptive, and personalized healthcare solutions. Addressing challenges, such as data privacy, bias, and model interpretability is crucial for achieving scalable and ethical deployment. Future research will focus on context-aware NLP models, AI-driven behavioral predictions, and seamless integration with Internet of Things (IoT) and wearable technologies. These advancements enable real-time monitoring, improved patient outcomes, and intelligent healthcare systems. This review provides a comprehensive analysis of technological progress, challenges, and future directions, ensuring NLP's role in transforming patient-centric, data-driven, and AI-powered healthcare solutions.

**Corresponding author*: monika.joshi@muit.in; ORCID: 0000-0002-3708-9446
Nanthini K.: ORCID: 0000-0002-6883-332X
Devi S.: ORCID: 0009-0007-6502-4205
Biswaranjan Swain: ORCID: 0000-0002-2560-8755

Sudesh Yadav, Pethuru Raj, Satya Prakash Yadav and Victor Hugo C. de Albuquerque (eds.) Natural Language Processing in Mental Health Care: Methodologies and Clinical Practice, (197–214) © 2026 Scrivener Publishing LLC

***Keywords*:** Behavioral natural language processing, healthcare, mental health diagnostics, real-time analytics, clinical decision making

14.1 Introduction

Artificial intelligence (AI) has advanced, natural language processing (NLP) [1] has changed dramatically, especially with transformer-based topologies that allow for more accurate language analysis and comprehension. By deriving cognitive, affective, and psychological knowledge from linguistic patterns, adaptive NLP expands this potential [2]. In healthcare, it is used to examine mental health, detect neurological disorders, and monitor cognitive decline. The integration of NLP with electronic health records (EHRs) [3] and telehealth has improved diagnosis accuracy, real-time patient assessment, and automated intervention options. Recent advances in multimodal NLP integrate audio, text, and physiological information to enhance the identification of behavioral patterns. These algorithms improve the identification of language biomarkers linked to neurodegenerative diseases, anxiety, and depression [4]. Additionally, NLP and virtual assistants are rapidly being used for mental health support, providing scalable, adaptive solutions. Nonetheless, significant obstacles exist, such as modelling comprehension, bias in algorithms, and information security. Compliance with laws and ethical adoption are still major concerns, especially when handling sensitive patient data [5]. Federated learning approaches are being investigated to improve security while maintaining data secrecy to overcome these constraints. Bias mitigation methods and fairness-driven optimization of models are also necessary for reliable and impartial behavioral analysis [6]. Subsequent investigations will concentrate on furthering real-time behavioral analytics, enhancing model generalization in a variety of demographics, and combining NLP with wearable biosensors for ongoing health monitoring [7]. The objective is to explore the applications and challenges of behavioral natural language processing (NLP) in healthcare, focusing on its potential to improve patient care, diagnosis, and mental health treatment. The research will also address ethical concerns and propose integration strategies for healthcare systems.

14.2 Natural Language Processing

Behavioral NLP is transforming healthcare through the ability to analyze linguistic patterns using AI and determine cognitive, emotional, and psychological states. Transformer-based model advancements, like bidirectional encoder representations from transformers (BERT) and generative pretrained transformer (GPT) [8], improve mental health diagnosis, patient sentiment analysis, and clinical decision making. NLP applications also include the detection of neurological disorders, enhancing telemedicine, and streamlining electronic health records. Although it has the potential to revolutionize, issues such as data privacy, bias, and model interpretability remain. Future developments will be centered on real-time behavioral analytics, federated learning for secure processing, and AI-based personalized interventions, making NLP a part of intelligent and ethical healthcare systems. Figure 14.1 illustrates a behavioral NLP-driven healthcare architecture, where data sources feed into real-time message ingestion and data storage systems. NLP modules leveraging cognitive services and HDInsight Spark process textual and behavioral data, storing insights in an analytical data store. The extracted information enhances analytics and reporting, enabling real-time behavioral analysis, mental health diagnostics, and clinical decision support, crucial for AI-driven healthcare advancements.

NLP is changing the game for the healthcare industry through the use of AI-based linguistic insights and multimodal learning involving text, speech, and physiological signals. Advanced deep learning models are increasing the accuracy of mental health assessments, neurological disorders, and patient sentiments. Explainable AI (XAI) [9] is becoming more popular to provide transparency and trust in clinical decision-making. Federated learning is becoming a favorable way to protect privacy in NLP and allows health data to be processed while the data is stored in a decentralized way without

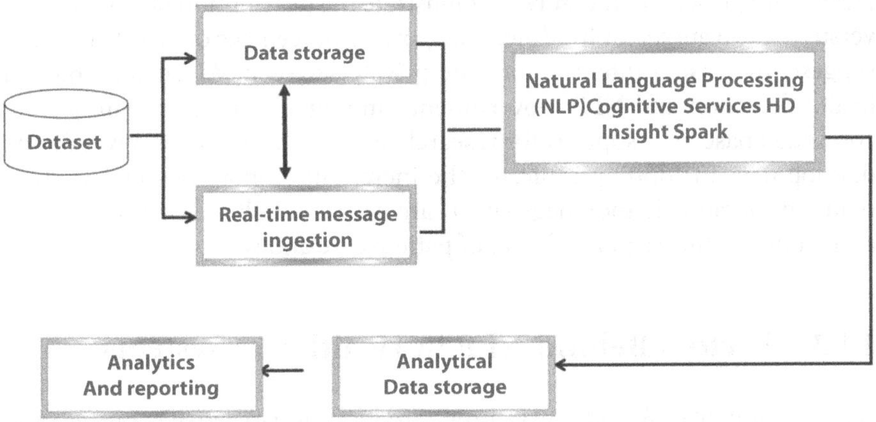

Figure 14.1 Flow of natural language processing. Source: Own elaboration.

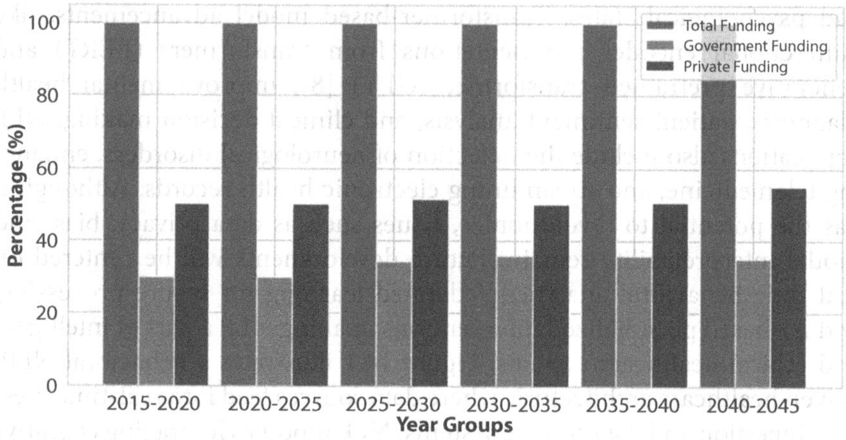

Figure 14.2 Projected funding trends for behavioral NLP. Source: Own elaboration.

compromising security. Also, NLP systems that are aware of emotions along with intelligent chatbots are changing virtual healthcare with real-time intervention for mental health disorders. Blockchain is being looked at for better and more secure ethical data management. It promises to help ensure the confidentiality of the patients and reduce biases in AI predictions [10]. Research will target the optimization of deep learning (DL) architectures for personalized healthcare, minimization of algorithmic biases, and integration of real-time behavior analytics for adaptive patient care. These all make behavioral NLP a key driver of next-generation smart healthcare systems through predictive diagnostics, clinical decision support, and patient-oriented therapies. The projected funding trends for Behavioral NLP in Healthcare presented in Figure 14.2 illustrate the distribution of government versus the private sector funding. The growing percentage of private funding suggests increasing interest from the private sector in AI-enabled mental health detection and NLP. Government funding appears stable, indicating continued base level support for research and policy initiatives. Overall, the development in funding indicates the increasing importance of DL, digitizing intracranial hemorrhage (ICH) archives, fetal ultrasound processing, and AI in healthcare to the future of patient care and safety.

14.3 Factors Behind NLP in Healthcare Systems

As a component of AI, NLP [11] aims to reduce the gap between human and machine capabilities. As it gains traction in the medical services industry, providers are focusing on developing systems that can understand, decode, and generate languages that people can understand. An additional need exists for voice recognition frameworks that can respond to patient and human services customer inquiries. Furthermore detailed below, there are numerous additional explanations for the use of NLP in healthcare. Figure 14.3, NLP has been integrated into healthcare communication systems. Data for NLP processing comes from various inputs, such as messages, social media, apps, etc., for mapping cognition, emotion, and psychographics. After processing the data, it is saved in a data storage system for analytics and interactions history while the knowledge base is fed insight relevant to the activity. This format helps in building various behavioral NLP applications, such as Sentiment Analysis, Mental health assessment, and Clinical decision support.

Managing the Increase in Clinical Information

The increased use of medical records in patient systems and drug advancements has led to an increase in the amount of data available to healthcare organizations. The desire to draw reliable information and make good use of this data turns out to be a significant motivator.

Support healthy population administration and quality care

The need for improved utilization of unorganized data has been driven by changes in strategies and desired outcomes. The goal of traditional health data systems has been to get insight from the 20% of information

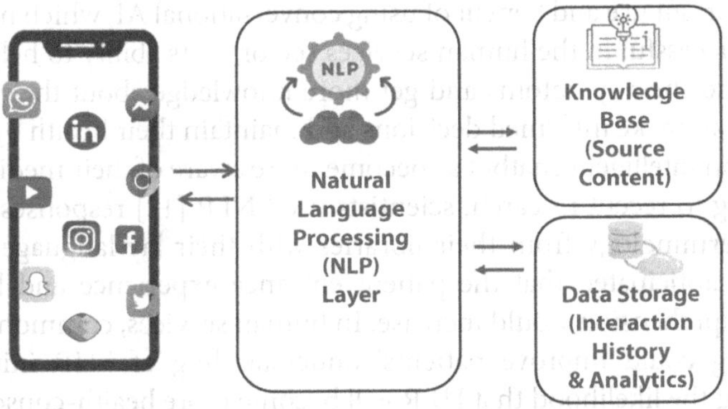

Figure 14.3 NLP in healthcare. Source: https://www.tech-sparks.com/branches-of-artificial-intelligence/.

about medical care that enters structured organizations *via* clinical channels. Utilizing the wealth of unorganized information that is currently being accumulated by healthcare organizations is imperative for advanced comprehension regarding medical record frameworks, managed care, Population Health Management (PHM) applications, and research and disclosure. Through a variety of application instances, NLP for health care could comprehend these challenges.

Enhance Communication between Patients and Providers with Electronic Health Records (EHR)

Patients today require the undivided attention of their human services professionals. Specialists are left feeling overburdened and exhausted as a result of managing complex documentation, such as charging governments, in addition to providing personalized services. Research has shown that a larger percentage of consideration specialists suffer from burnout in their workplaces. Integrating NLP with EHR systems will streamline research processes and reduce the workload for experts by enabling efficient data analysis, automated insights, and improved clinical decision-making. Remote assistants, such as Siri, Cortana, and Alexa, have successfully integrated into human services organizations by acting as authoritative mentors, helping with client administration tasks, and supporting work-related responsibilities. NLP for healthcare could lead administrative assistants to transition into the clinical component of the business as medical copyists or by asking collaborators.

Encourage Health Awareness among Clients

One important use and benefit of using conversational AI, which has already proven successful in the human services sector, is its ability to help patients understand their symptoms and get more knowledge about their ailments. Patients can make informed decisions and maintain their health by interacting with an intelligent chatbot as become more aware of their medical issues. According to recent research, scientists used NLP [12] responses to match clinical terminology from their libraries with their lay language partners. Research anticipated that the patient entrance experience and long-term EHR comprehension would increase. In human services, common language processing could improve patients' understanding of EHR initial steps, increasing the likelihood that HER will become more health-conscious.

Acknowledge the Need for Improved Quality of Healthcare

NLP can take the lead in assessing and enhancing quality of healthcare by identifying gaps for conveyance and evaluating physician performance.

Studies have shown that AI for healthcare can speed up the doctor evaluation process and automate tolerance finding, reducing the amount of energy and human effort needed to do repetitive tasks like silent conclusion. Additionally, NLP in healthcare helps identify and mitigate certain errors in consideration conveying. Analyses showed that NLP might be utilized for screening for compliance with clinical guidelines and estimating the type of personal services.

Identify Patients who Need Improved Care

The AI and NLP technologies will be able to identify people with complicated medical illnesses that require more attention and have a history of substance abuse or mental health issues. These patients could be persuaded to incur higher lifetime costs due to factors including food insecurity and unstable housing, which can deter treatment practices. Obtaining information about a patient's financial health and demographics might be challenging compared to clinical data due to its unstructured nature. This problem might be resolved with the use of NLP [13]. Additionally, NLP can be used to enhance care coordination for individuals with social health issues. Both ML and NLP can be used to explore patient data and find people who could potentially slip through any gaps in the healthcare system. Healthcare associations must refine both ordered and unorganized data produced by the medical services sector before implementing NLP in human services.

14.4 Technological Advancements in Behavioral NLP

Recent advancements in Behavioral NLP have significantly enhanced its capabilities in healthcare. Transformer-based tools such as BERT, GPT, and T5 [14] have made contextualization so effective that are capable of being used for sentiment and psychological state analysis. Multimodal learning combines insights from text, speech, and physiological signals to enhance the accuracy of behavioral assessments. Federated learning ensures privacy-preserving NLP by allowing decentralized data training without compromising patient confidentiality. XAI enhances transparency, making clinical NLP models more interpretable and reliable for healthcare professionals. Edge AI facilitates real-time behavioral monitoring through resource-efficient NLP models deployed on wearable devices [15]. Additionally, AI-powered chatbots and emotion-aware systems use cutting-edge NLP to deliver individualized mental health care and early intervention. Emerging research centres on bias prevention, ethical integration

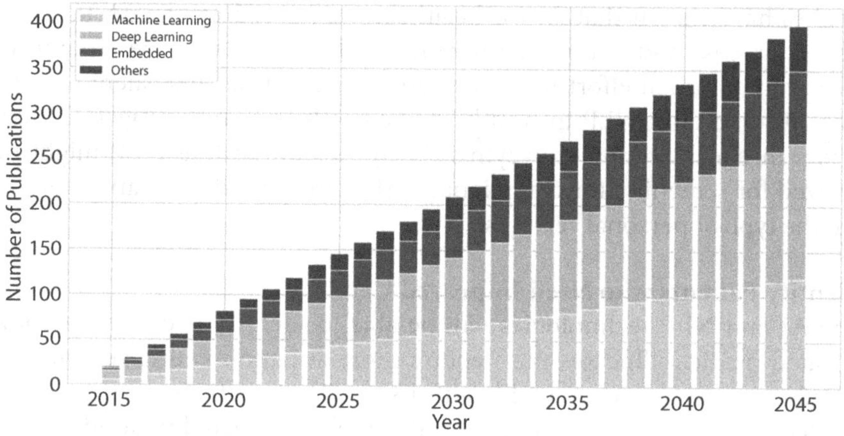

Figure 14.4 Projected growth of behavioral NLP in healthcare. Source: Own elaboration.

of AI, and adaptive learning platforms to enhance behavioral NLP applications in healthcare, making them more precise, secure, and ethical in decision-making for patient care. Figure 14.4 illustration shows the anticipated increases of BNLP in Healthcare, which presents higher usage of Machine Learning (ML), Deep Learning (DL), Embedded Systems, and other Techniques. ML and DL represent an important driver for detecting mental health, diagnosis through NLP, and AI solutions for healthcare. The increase in embedded systems is showing increases in the use of IoT and wearable systems, which better allow for monitoring in real-time and patient-centered care.

14.5 Applications of NLP in Healthcare

NLP contributes to healthcare through clinical text and structured data analysis, mental health assessment, and patient sentiment analysis/disease prediction. NLP allows for automated diagnostic support, EHR [16] improvements, telehealth/telemedicine applications, and AI-assisted chatbots for personalized care. NLP can also support the detection of neurological disorders and the real-time monitoring of patient behavior. Figure 14.5 illustrates key interventions associated with NLP, and how NLP can specifically improve Clinical Trial Management, Drug Discovery, Medical Coding & Billing, and Computational Phenotyping. Other applications associated with NLP include Clinical Documentation Management, Electronic Medical Records (EMR) -Implications, Sentiment Analysis,

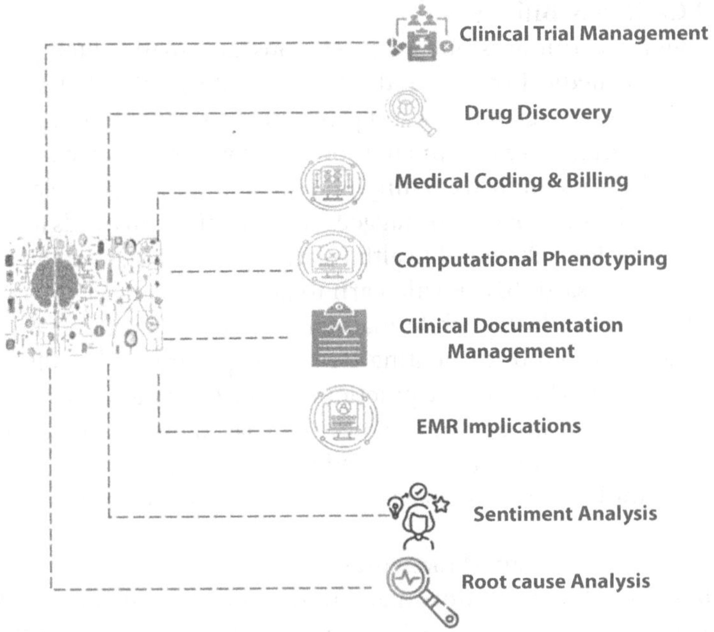

Figure 14.5 Application of the NLP. Source: https://savvycomsoftware.com/blog/natural-language-processing-trends/.

and Root Cause Analysis. Overall, the value of the different NLP applications presented illustrates NLP value to transform unstructured clinical data into organized and actionable insight, improve healthcare workflows, and ultimately improve patient care through more efficient use of accurate workflows.

Clinical Trial Management

Behavioral natural language processing (BNLP) plays a crucial role in advancing clinical trial management. BNLP collects behavioral extraction from medical records, study protocols, and the literature to enhance patient stratification and identification. BNLP explores behavior-established similar eligibility criteria as well as assists in identifying adverse behavioral patterns [17]. BNLP can also monitor compliance with regulatory standards, as well as closely track the behavior of patient outcomes throughout the trial process. BNLP creates a solution for safer and more efficient clinical trials, while also supporting data privacy and creating rational and additive efficacy for personalized behavioral health interventions to inform contemporary clinical research across studies.

Medical Coding & Billing

BNLP offers practitioners and organizations automatic intelligence and automation in medical coding and billing by interpreting behavioral signals encoded in physician notes and procedure documentation. Therefore, BNLP helps standardize documentation, improve coding accuracy, minimize manual errors, improve billing potential, and mitigate delays in billing. Behavioral indicators can be tagged if an organization needs to facilitate reimbursement for behavioral health treatments directly related to conditions being addressed. BNLP will learn to adjust to changing coding rules in the healthcare industry while maintaining compliance and documentation accuracy when documenting treatment progress and collaborative care. Ultimately, BNLP can give practices and organizations better revenue workflow while also streamlining behavioral-based billing processes based on insights derived from language used during administrative workflows, which allow for behavioral engagement with the fewest barriers possible.

Clinical Documentation Management

BNLP lightens clinicians' documentation load by transforming behavioral speech inputs into standardized entries. With voice recognition and speech-to-text capabilities, BNLP reduces the burden associated with EHRs, increasing the time physicians can spend on behavioral care. BNLP transfers emotional tone, stress patterns, and psychosocial stories *via* audio notes, thereby augmenting behavioral context in clinical notes. BNLP also identifies a patient's Social Determinants of Health (SDOH) and enhances Population Health Management (PHM) utilizing behavioral context, thus improving the future of documentation processes that value empathy and technology in the care environment.

Drug Discovery

BNLP expedites drug discovery through behavior-driven investigation of the scientific literature, clinical trials, and biomedical data, including identifying mechanistic psychological markers, behavioral symptoms/patterns, and patient response trends, among other aspects across which the literature can inform novel pharmacotherapeutic target selection. BNLP will augment the ability to formulate hypotheses based on language (verbal or written) indicative of lifestyle, mood, or cognitive patterns, when analyzed it will support increasingly personalized psychopharmacological options and development toward applying evidence-based personalized behavioral therapy. Research directed toward BNLP integration will promote better research focused on the accelerated identification of novel target therapeutics with better behavioral outcomes, optimizing behavioral treatment for complex conditions, and building a data-driven research effort or pipeline toward drug design in neuropsychiatric and mental health fields.

Electronic Medical Records (EMR) Implications

BNLP enhances EMRs by analyzing behavioral language patterns in physician notes, audio recordings, and diagnostic reports. Unstructured narratives with behavioral indicators—e.g., mood, stress signals, and behavioral habits get transcribed into structured EMR [18] documents. This enables one to conduct a more thorough analysis of patient behavior and support decision-making regarding diagnosis and treatment. As physicians move toward 'note-taking by voice' BNLP will seamlessly integrate the information and support holistic behavioral health records by ensuring that behavioral health records with subtle psychosocial contexts are not overlooked in care pathways.

Computational Phenotyping

BNLP transforms how computational phenotyping is done through the examination of behavioral language to categorize the mental and physical state of a patient. Rather than relying solely on biological biomarkers, BNLP relies on the presence of speech signals, tone variations, and emotional expressions to inform digital phenotyping. BNLP is capable of determining indications of disorders such as depression, Alzheimer's, and anxiety, based on behavioral language characteristics. Clinicians now have a deeper understanding of patients to develop more effective behavioral models, which can improve diagnostic and treatment decision-making for conditions affecting neurocognitive and psychiatric areas through intelligent and personalized behavioral language analysis and interpretation.

Sentiment Analysis

Behavioral sentiment analysis using NLP enhances sentiment analysis of a patient's emotional tone, intent, and psychological context for their feedback about care. Behavioral NLP interprets the emotional tone, intent, and psychological context of social media posts, customer reviews, and patient surveys, consistently informing satisfaction, distress, or behavioral health trends. Behavioral NLP identifies behavioral risk factors to monitor overall mental health, evaluates the quality of provider-patient relationships, and closely monitors care delivery in compliance with the Health Insurance Portability and Accountability Act (HIPAA) [19]. The information and insights from behavioral NLP equip and direct clinicians to provide improved services as well as clarify and enhance patient communication. Additionally, behavioral sentiment cues can provide a real-time feedback loop, impacting strategy concerning patient care and influencing decision-making for policies in behavioral health care delivery systems.

Root Cause Analysis
BNLP enhances root cause analysis by synthesizing behavioral expressions present in clinical narratives to the underlying health disparities. It processes a breadth of large datasets to describe socio-behavioral patterns across variables, such as demographics, geography, and race. BNLP reveals unseen behavioral triggers underlying chronic illnesses and health inequities. BNLP promotes strategies for prevention by illuminating lifestyle and mental health factors that contribute to health outcomes. This behavioral perspective enables holistic healthcare planning by identifying equitable functional solutions and personalized interventions that emerge from deep behavioral insight drawn from patient language.

14.6 Benefits of NLP in Healthcare

NLP is transforming healthcare by improving diagnostic accuracy, patient engagement, and the clinical decision-making process [20]. NLP aids in automating medical documentation and reducing human errors while also extracting insights from unstructured data. Figure 14.6 discussed the benefits of NLP on critical care identification, patient health awareness, and predictive analytics for personalized treatments and efficient resource allocation. NLP optimizes workflows and allows for real-time monitoring, whereas healthcare can deliver higher quality care, lower costs, and better patient outcomes in modern healthcare systems.

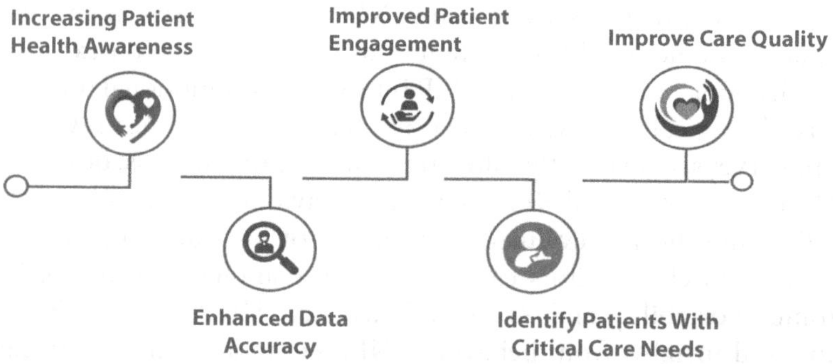

Figure 14.6 Outcomes of core benefits of NLP in enhancing healthcare efficiency. Source: https://appinventiv.com/blog/nlp-in-healthcare/.

Enhanced Data Accuracy

NLP improves accuracy in data within the healthcare space by unearthing actionable meaning from many disparate sources of regularly unstructured data, such as clinical notes, EHRs, and patient interactions with clinicians. AI-based NLP models effectively address manual data entry errors and support standardization of medical terminology and phrasing, which ultimately enhances consistency in clinical diagnostic processes. By automating and improving the data processing of patient information, NLP will support healthcare providers with accurate data and information that are both structured and synthesized, which ultimately supports better clinical decision-making and better outcomes for patients.

Identify Patients with Critical Care Needs

NLP assists in detecting patients who require urgent or specialized medical care; it makes use of clinical text, speech patterns, and real-time health data to identify those active patients. NLP allows for the recognition of early signs of clinical deterioration, predicts disease progression, and enables clinicians to prioritize patients who are in critical condition [21]. As a result, hospitals can allocate limited resources, monitor patients more effectively in high-acuity settings, and initiate relevant medical interventions more quickly, which will lower rates of mortality and better utilize health resources so patients and healthcare providers are better served.

Increasing Patient Health Awareness

Chatbots, virtual assistants, and recommendation systems driven by NLP give patients access to health information tailored to their specific needs. Using historical medical records, symptoms, and lifestyle habits, NLP provides insights and personalized information to support patients' understanding of their conditions, medication adherence, and wellness strategies in a way that supports patients being proactive in their health management, improves patient literacy, and supports preventive care ultimately resulting in a reduction in the burden on the health care system.

Improved Patient Engagement

Healthcare providers can increase patient involvement with the use of NLP or natural language processing, for applications like speech recognition, sentiment analysis, and automated health communication. NLP-based tools, such as AI-enabled virtual assistants [22], reminder messages, and personalized health recommendations, build better patient involvement and compliance with treatment plans. Also, NLP offers real-time patient feedback and tracking emotional sentiment, something that enhances the relationship between the doctor and the patient and leads to more overall satisfaction.

Improve Care Quality

NLP optimizes clinical workflows, automates documentation, and enhances decision-making, leading to improved care quality. It assists in accurate diagnostics, medical error reduction, and real-time health monitoring. Additionally, NLP-driven predictive analytics identifies high-risk patients, recommends personalized treatments, and optimizes resource management. By integrating AI-powered insights into healthcare, NLP ensures more precise, efficient, and patient-centric care delivery, improving outcomes and operational efficiency.

14.7 Future Behavioral Natural Language Processing in Healthcare

The fields of deep learning, machine learning, and embedded systems are advancing BNLP in healthcare in many different ways to improve communication with patients, identify mental health issues, and assist in clinical decisions. Trends in growth show a reduction in papers published every year, market siloing, and a growing list of capabilities powered by Artificial Intelligence in the health care market. As computational efficiency and real-time analytics improve, enhanced accuracy in clinical diagnosis, treatment

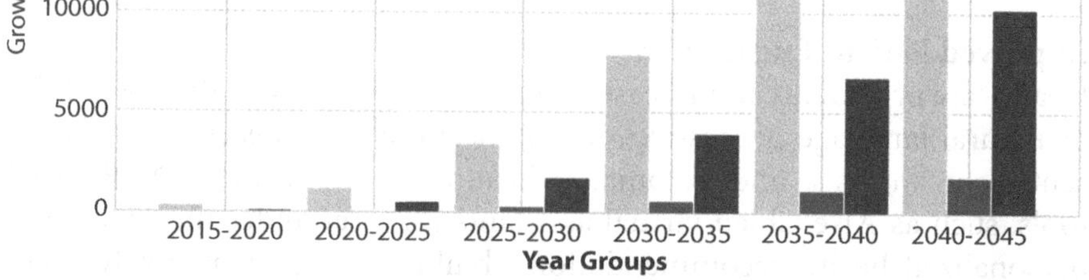

Figure 14.7 Projected growth trends of behavioral NLP in healthcare. Source: Own elaboration.

planning, and patient outcomes will follow. Due to increased scalability and accessibility, Behavioral NLP [23] is paving the way for personalized health care and intelligent medical data processing. Figure 14.7 shows the overall growth of Behavioral NLP in Healthcare across three growth metrics: research publications, market growth, and AI applications. Research publications suggest a growing interest in the Behavioral NLP field from the academic community. Market growth expands significantly, indicating increasing investments and commercial adoption. AI-driven applications grow exponentially, showcasing their integration into healthcare. These trends collectively reflect the advancing role of AI and NLP in transforming medical research and applications.

14.8 Discussion

The results of the research support the critical role BNLP plays in enhancing intelligent health systems. Transformer-based architectures such as BERT, GPT, and T5, have been found to considerably advance the extraction of latent behavior, emotion, and cognitive indicators from unstructured language data. In clinical settings, especially in areas such as mental health diagnostics, neuropsychological assessment, and affective computing, these models have promising potential. The context of multimodal learning frameworks that utilize textual, acoustic, and physiological signals has also improved the contextual representation and accuracy of behavioral analyses. The research highlights the need for privacy-preserving solutions. Federated learning allows for model training in a decentralized manner to secure sensitive health data while maintaining model performance. At the same time, this integration of explainable AI methods highlights the imperative push for transparency and explainability of clinical decision support systems. Advanced architectures offering real-time ingestion of messages, scalable data storage options, and approaches to distributed processing (e.g., using HDInsight Spark) [24] have demonstrated utility in processing high-throughput behavioral data analytics, but there are gaps. For example, challenges around data heterogeneity, algorithmic bias, and fairness in AI implementation remain underappreciated. Furthermore, the convergence of blockchain and edge AI paradigms presents a feasible path to strengthen data privacy and real-time behavior monitoring abilities. The increasing emergence of conversational agents powered by BNLP and emotion-aware systems offers disruptive opportunities for deploying proactive and personalized healthcare services [25]. To develop strong, morally sound, and practically useful BNLP uses, future research should concentrate on architecture optimizations, bias reduction techniques, and interdisciplinary frameworks.

14.9 Conclusion

The fundamental function of BNLP in accomplishing the goals of intelligent or smart healthcare in the future, with cutting-edge transformer-based architectures and multimodal learning frameworks, is that it can extract rich behavioral, emotional, and cognitive insights from unstructured clinical data. Federated learning models achieve decentralized model training while ensuring the confidentiality of data, which is vital in providing patient privacy in a sensitive situation. Moreover, explainable AI techniques are important in creating trustworthy clinical interpretations, which increases trust in machine-based clinical decisions. The use of scalable cloud-based architecture and real-time processing engines improves the responsiveness, adaptability, and robustness of healthcare systems. The combination of BNLP, distributed computing, and interpretable modeling research contributes to a strong foundation for developing personalized, adaptive, context-aware healthcare solutions. BNLP's transformational potential in providing more precise diagnoses, well-informed therapy treatments, and better patient outcomes across various clinical and mental healthcare settings is ultimately confirmed by the research.

AI disclosure statement: The author confirms that no artificial intelligence (AI)-generated content or AI-assisted writing tools were used in the preparation of this chapter (including summaries and the abstract). All text, analysis, and conclusions are the result of the author's original work.

References

1. Young, M., *et al.*, Natural language processing diagnosed behavioral disturbance phenotypes in the intensive care unit: characteristics, prevalence, trajectory, treatment, and outcomes. *Crit. Care*, 27.1, 425, 2023, https://doi.org/10.1186/s13054-023-04695-0.
2. Mihalcea, R., *et al.*, How developments in natural language processing help us in understanding human behavior. *Nat. Hum. Behav.*, 8.10, 1877–1889, 2024, https://doi.org/10.1038/s41562-024-01938-0.

3. West, R., *et al.*, Using machine learning to extract information and predict outcomes from reports of randomized trials of smoking cessation interventions in the Human Behaviour-Change Project. *Wellcome Open Res.*, 8, 4525, 2024, https://doi.org/10.12688/wellcomeopenres.20000.2.
4. Sedgwick, R., *et al.*, Investigating online activity in UK adolescent mental health patients: a feasibility study using a natural language processing approach for electronic health records. *BMJ Open*, 13.5, e061640, 2023, https://doi.org/10.1136/bmjopen-2022-061640.
5. Madan, M., Rishima, M., Thakur, P., Analysing the patient sentiments in healthcare domain using Machine learning. *Procedia Comput. Sci.*, 238, 683–6905, 2024, https://doi.org/10.1016/j.procs.2024.06.077.
6. Poniszewska-Marańda, A., ElinaVynogradnyk, and WitoldMarańda Medical data transformations in healthcare systems with the use of natural language processing algorithms. *Appl. Sci.*, 13.2, 682, 2023, https://doi.org/10.3390/app13020682.
7. Huang, G., *et al.*, From explainable to interpretable deep learning for natural language processing in healthcare: How far from reality? *Comput. Struct. Biotechnol. J.*, 24, 362–373, 2024, https://doi.org/10.1016/j.csbj.2024.05.004.
8. Solanki, P., Grundy, J., Hussain, W., Operationalising ethics in artificial intelligence for healthcare: a framework for AI developers. *AI Ethics*, 3.1, 223–240, 2023, https://doi.org/10.1007/s43681-022-00195-z.
9. Sreejith, R. and Sinimole, K.R., User-centric evaluation of EHR software through NLP-driven investigation: Implications for product development and user experience. *J. Open Innov. Technol. Mark. Complex.*, 10.1, 100206, 2024, https://doi.org/10.1016/j.joitmc.2023.100206.
10. Sarella, P.N.K. and Mangam, V.T., AI-driven natural language processing in healthcare: Transforming patient-provider communication. *Indian J. Pharm. Pract.*, 17, 1, 21–26, 2024, https://doi.org/10.5530/ijopp.17.1.4.
11. Silvestri, S., *et al.*, A machine learning approach for the NLP-based analysis of cyber threats and vulnerabilities of the healthcare ecosystem. *Sensors*, 23.2, 651, 2023, https://doi.org/10.3390/s23020651.
12. Baumgartner, C. and Baumgartner, D., A regulatory challenge for natural language processing (NLP)-based tools such as ChatGPT to be legally used for healthcare decisions. Where are we now? *Clin. Transl. Med.*, 13.8, e1362, 2023, https://doi.org/10.1002/ctm2.1362.
13. Singh, G.B., *et al.*, Transforming Healthcare Systems With AI: A Deep Dive Into NLP Applications, in: *Harnessing AI and Machine Learning for Precision Wellness*, pp. 111–130, IGI Global Scientific Publishing, India, 2025, https://doi.org/10.4018/979-8-3693-9521-9.ch004.
14. Pandian, A., *et al.*, Enhancing Trust and Collaboration Using Explainability in Natural Language Processing for AI-Driven Healthcare. *Explainable Artif. Intell. Healthc. Ind.*, 619–650, 2025, https://doi.org/10.1002/9781394249312.ch26.

15. Pashangpour, S. and Nejat, G., The Future of Intelligent Healthcare: A Systematic Analysis and Discussion on the Integration and Impact of Robots Using Large Language Models for Healthcare. *Robotics*, 13.8, 112, 2024, https://doi.org/10.1007/s11277-023-10312-8.
16. Das, A., *et al.*, The state of human-centered NLP technology for fact-checking. *Inf. Process. Manage.*, 60.2, 103219, 2023, https://doi.org/10.1016/j.ipm.2022.103219.
17. Dai, S., *et al.*, AI-based NLP section discusses the application and effect of bag-of-words models and TF-IDF in NLP tasks. *Artificial Intelligence General Science (JAIGS)*, vol. ISSN: 3006-4023 5.1, pp. 13–21, 2024, https://doi.org/10.60087/jaigs.v5i1.149.
18. Tyagi, N. and Bhushan, B., Demystifying the role of natural language processing (NLP) in smart city applications: background, motivation, recent advances, and future research directions. *Wirel. Pers. Commun.*, 130.2, 857–908, 2023, https://doi.org/10.1007/s11277-023-10312-8.
19. Vysotska, V., *et al.*, Intelligent analysis of Ukrainian-language tweets for public opinion research based on NLP methods and machine learning technology. *Int. J. Mod. Educ. Comput. Sci. (IJMECS)*, 15.3, 70–93, 2023, https://doi.org/10.5815/ijmecs.2023.03.06.
20. Yan, H., *et al.*, The application of natural language processing technology in the era of big data. *J. Ind. Eng. Appl. Sci.*, 2.3, 20–27, 2024, https://doi.org/10.5281/zenodo.11399706.
21. Shastry, K.A. and Shastry, A., An integrated deep learning and natural language processing approach for continuous remote monitoring in digital health. *Decis. Anal. J.*, 8, 1003015, 2023, https://doi.org/10.1016/j.dajour.2023.100301.
22. Denecke, K., *et al.*, Potential of large language models in health care: Delphi study. *J. Med. Internet Res.*, 26, e523995, 2024, https://doi.org/10.2196/52399.
23. Shooshtarian, S., Gurmu, A.T., Sadick, A.-M., Application of natural language processing in residential building defects analysis: Australian stakeholders' perceptions, causes, and types. *Eng. Appl. Artif. Intell.*, 126, 1071785, 2023, https://doi.org/10.1016/j.engappai.2023.107178.
24. Nagy, B., *et al.*, Privacy-preserving Federated Learning and its application to natural language processing. *Knowledge-Based Syst.*, 268, 1104755, 2023, https://doi.org/10.1016/j.knosys.2023.110475.
25. Pillai, A.S., Advancements in natural language processing for automotive virtual assistants enhancing user experience and safety. *J. Comput. Intell. Rob.*, 3.1, 27–36, 2023, https://orcid.org/0000-0001-7139-2804.

15

Medical Graph RAG: Toward Safe Medical Large Language Model *via* Graph Retrieval-Augmented Generation

Trapty Agarwal[1]*, Ramkumar Krishnamoorthy[2], Praveena K. N.[3], Adya Kinkar Panda[4] and Ayasa Kanta Mohanty[5]

[1]Maharishi School of Engineering and Technology, Maharishi University of Information Technology, Uttar Pradesh, India
[2]Department of CSIT, Jain (Deemed-to-be University), Bangalore, Karnataka, India
[3]Department of Computer Science & Engineering, Presidency University, Bengaluru, Karnataka, India
[4]Department of Radiology, IMS and SUM Hospital, Siksha 'O' Anusandhan (Deemed to be University), Bhubaneswar, Odisha, India
[5]Department of Management, Siksha 'O' Anusandhan (Deemed to be University), Bhubaneswar, Odisha, India

Abstract
Large language models (LLMs) offer promise for medical applications but are often hindered by inaccuracies, hallucinations, and limited interpretability, raising concerns about their safety and reliability. A major limitation is their reliance on unstructured data, which can lead to misinformation and errors in medical reasoning. To enhance the trustworthiness of medical LLMs, this chapter focuses on integrating structured Medical Knowledge through Graph-Based Retrieval-Augmented Generation (MedGraph RAG). The approach leverages a medical knowledge graph to refine information retrieval, ensuring that generated responses are contextually relevant and empirically accurate. By dynamically selecting and

**Corresponding author*: trapty@muit.in; ORCID: 0009-0007-4081-4999
Ramkumar Krishnamoorthy: ORCID: 0000-0003-1164-6504
Praveena K. N.: ORCID: 0000-0003-3047-8729
Adya Kinkar Panda: ORCID: 0000-0002-2104-5676
Ayasa Kanta Mohanty: ORCID: 0009-0003-5836-5395

Sudesh Yadav, Pethuru Raj, Satya Prakash Yadav and Victor Hugo C. de Albuquerque (eds.) Natural Language Processing in Mental Health Care: Methodologies and Clinical Practice, (215–232) © 2026 Scrivener Publishing LLC

incorporating graph-structured knowledge, medical graph RAG mitigates hallucinations, improves interpretability, and enhances response precision. Experimental evaluations demonstrate superior factual correctness and contextual reliability compared to traditional RAG and standalone LLMs. This framework advances the development of safer AI-assisted medical decision support systems, addressing key limitations of existing LLMs while improving their clinical applicability.

Keywords: Medical knowledge graph-based retrieval-augmented generation, medical knowledge graph, large language models, graph-structured knowledge

15.1 Introduction

The advancement of large language models (LLMs) has been disruptive with its contributions to the medical field and it has found application in clinical decision-making, answering medical questions, and supporting diagnostics [1]. Nevertheless, some limitations of conventional LLMs are evident, particularly when working with medical datasets where accuracy, reliability, and interpretability are crucial. Another issue and risk is the ability of LLMs to produce hallucinated or incorrect information, which is highly dangerous in medical applications. In contrast to structured medical knowledge databases, LLMs use pre-trained parameters and probabilistic text generation, which can lead to the provision of non-evidence-based answers [2]. However, these models have limitations with domain reasoning and struggle to update the latest knowledge about the medical field, often providing outdated or even conflicting conclusions [3]. To overcome these challenges, new methods such as Graph Retrieval-Augmented Generation (Graph RAG) have been introduced to help improve the safety and reliability of medical LLMs. By utilizing the structure of RAG, it incorporated information from credible medical sources, including biomedical literature, clinical guidelines, electronic health records, and verifiable information based on the context supplied [4]. Unlike other LLMs, which utilize training information to train the model and correspond with the inputs, the Graph RAG actively queries the related medical knowledge using graph-based representations, which enhances factual accuracy and reduces hallucinations. In addition, through the use of graph structures, reasoning over complex medical relationships can be accomplished; it makes the response more interpretable and less ambiguous [5]. Nonetheless, Graph RAG is not without drawbacks. The results furthermore show that the efficacy of the retrieval depends on the comprehensive and accurate underlying medical knowledge graph, and prejudicial or insufficient information in these sources can impact the model responses [6]. However, some of these techniques are based on graph processing, so the time required is more in this case, which hinders real-time clinical decision making. The constancy of updating and checking up the medical sources presents some problems, and creating solid ways of updating the newly emerging proof of the medical field. Further, the combination of such structured retrieval with generative models requires complex matching techniques to ensure the flow from retrieved knowledge to the generated text [7]. The goal of this research is to improve the security and dependability of medical LLMs by including structured Medical Knowledge using Graph-Based Retrieval-Augmented Generation (MedGraph RAG). Its main objectives are to increase interpretability, reduce hallucinations, and guarantee factually correct replies in AI-assisted medical decision support systems.

15.2 Methodology

This methodology builds on the use of a medical knowledge graph to boost up the pre-existing RAG while offering better clarity to the LLM models. Evaluation of different LLMs such as Gagan Enabled Mariner's Instrument for Navigation and Information (GEMINI), Generative Pre-trained Transformer (GPT-4), Large Language Model Meta AI-2 (LLAMA2), and LLAMA3 by employing structured medical data that is used to make the responses accurate.

15.2.1 Dataset

For medical LLM applications, there are three layers in the RAG data structure. Private user information that is regularly updated and kept confidential, like medical reports, is included in top-level data. Patient admissions, diagnoses, treatments, and anonymized clinical notes are all included in the main dataset, *Medical Information Mart for Intensive Care IV (MIMIC-IV)*, which is a publicly accessible electronic health record dataset. *MedC-K* is a comprehensive medical corpus; this includes thirty thousand textbooks and 4.8 million scholarly papers in the field of biomedicine. By including knowledge-intensive medical questions for a thorough assessment of retrieval-augmented models, the *Medical Information Retrieval-Augmented Generation Evaluation (MIRAGE)* dataset improves medical QA even further. It incorporates the *Semantic Scholar Open Research Corpus (S2ORC)* dataset and biomedical research from PubMed Central, resulting in almost 75 billion tokens of medical knowledge. This is an example of medium-level data. *Unified Medical Language System (UMLS)*, which incorporates more than two hundred medical vocabularies, such as *International Statistical Classification of Diseases and Related*

Health Problems-10(ICD-10) and *Systematized Nomenclature of Medicine – Clinical Terms (SNOMED) CT*, makes up bottom-level data. *UMLS* comprises the *SPECIALIST Lexicon* for natural language processing in health information systems, the Semantic Network for organizing medical ideas, and the *Metathesaurus* for standardizing medical terminologies.

15.2.2 Testing Data

The test set consists of multiple-choice questions, fact-verification exercises, and real-world clinical queries from various biological and public health databases. It uses data from the MultiMedQA suite, which contains public health fact verification datasets and a variety of biomedical question-answering standards. Furthermore, Diverse Health, a compiled test set, focuses on health equality and covers a wide range of medical subjects, such as comorbidities, uncommon illnesses, minority health, drug and alcohol use, obesity, suicide, and managing chronic diseases.

15.2.3 Medical Graph Retrieval-Augmented Generation (Med Graph RAG)

MedGraph RAG improves the medical report generation through the combination of structured medical knowledge graphs with LLM. This approach of using verified medical sources and structured relationships helps in getting accurate diagnosing results. Figure 15.1 depicts the workflow of medical graph RAG. There are two stages to a medical graph RAG method [8] for creating diagnostic reports.

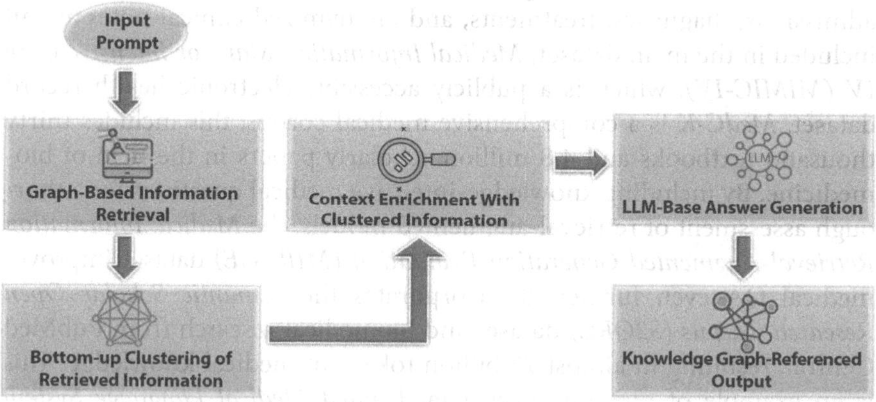

Figure 15.1 Pipeline of medical graph RAG. Source: https://gradientflow.substack.com/p/graphrag-design-patterns-challenges.

Graph-based Retrieval Phase (S)**:** A structured medical knowledge network is used by a retrieval algorithm to find the most pertinent medical information.

LLM-based Generation Phase (N_h)**:** Using recovered graph-based medical information, an LLM produces the final diagnosis report.

The purpose of a prompt q_{naive} is to assist N_h in producing precise medical reports. The retrieval phase finds the most pertinent medical entities and connections (c_s) provided by a query (r), a medical knowledge graph (H), and an embedding model (F). The generative framework utilizes these findings to generate the evaluation result. The following Equations (15.1 & 15.2) represent the process.

$$c_s = S\ (r, H, F) \tag{15.1}$$

$$B = N_h(r, c_s, q_{naive}) \tag{15.2}$$

To improve accuracy, consistency, and safety in medical decision-making, the retrieval component (S) in this case makes sure that medical reports are produced using organized and verified knowledge from the medical knowledge graph (H).

15.2.4 Large Language Models

It includes Gemini, GPT-4, LLAMA 2, and LLAMA 3, which are sophisticated Artificial Intelligence (AI) models made for the creation and comprehension of natural language. To accomplish tasks like text production, question answering, and contextual reasoning across a variety of disciplines, including medicine, these models make use of deep learning and enormous datasets.

GEMINI: RAG enhances and optimizes the LLM skills, incorporating information from the external medical knowledge databases without the need for retraining, and providing accurate, pertinent, and closely related results. The main problem concerning medical LLM distribution is incorrect, general, or expired medical knowledge. Incorporating graph-based retrieval, RAG boosts the degree of accuracy and credibility by extracting evidence-based medical information from documents by leveraging reliable resources such as clinical protocols, articles, or patient files. Consequently, Graph-based RAG initiates medical data into structured knowledge graphs that represent relationships between medical entities such as disease repair, symptoms, treatments, etc. Certain data is then encoded with paid medical embedding models, and the encodings are eventually stored in a vector database. To answer a query, RAG identifies the most similar knowledge by jointly using semantic similarity and a graph search algorithm while maintaining clinical relevance and context awareness. Figure 15.2 (a) depicts the process of GEMINI. Therefore, Gemini [9], with its extensive knowledge base and broad context window, serves as the primary LLM in this framework, addressing the need for more significant and semantically dense medical content to be returned. This keeps surgeons and researchers informed with accurate, context-specific, and safe medical information, preventing hallucinations or misinformative content.

GPT-4: With its sophisticated natural language interpretation and generation capabilities, OpenAI's GPT-4 provides a strong basis for RAG in medical applications. When combined with a medical RAG framework, GPT-4 [10] improves accuracy and reliability by obtaining organized medical information from external knowledge sources, in contrast to traditional LLMs that could produce replies based only on pre-trained knowledge. GPT-4 uses vector databases, embedding models, and structured knowledge graphs to handle medical inquiries in the Medical Graph RAG method. This aids in reducing the possibility of hallucinations and improves the reliability of AI systems in medicine by basing outcomes on clinical guidelines as well as medical literature and knowledge bases from experts. Due to the ability to reason, having a wider context window, and ensuring strong consistency in complex conversational scenarios, GPT-4 can be considered an optimal

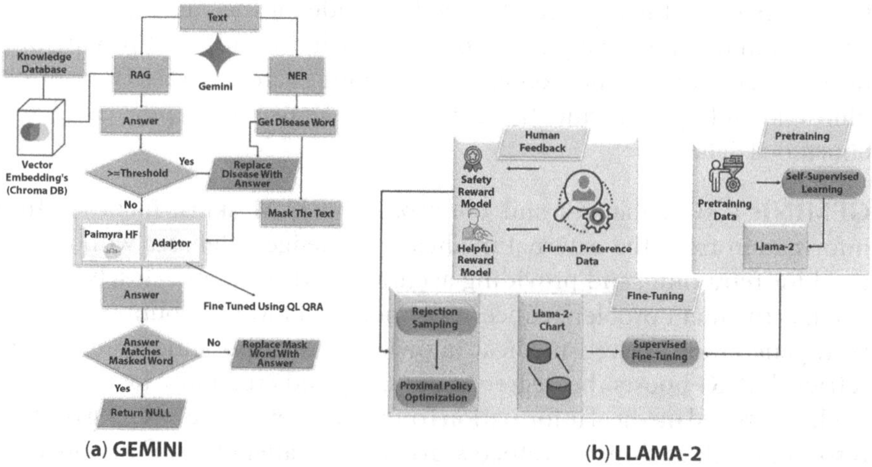

Figure 15.2 Working procedure of (a) GEMINI, and (b) LLAMA 2. Source: (a) [9], (b) https://www.interconnects.ai/p/llama-2-from-meta.

decision for medical applications that require prompt and context-sensitive answers. Safer and more efficient interactions in the healthcare area are ensured by this integration, which enables clinical decision support, medical literature summary, and accurate detection support.

LLAMA2 & LLAMA3: LLAMA2 is highly reliable because it handles a larger dataset and carries out more complex language manipulation tasks compared to LLAMA. By adding medical knowledge sources and connecting to a RAG for Medical Graph architecture, LLAMA2 [11] can get better at finding medical information and providing better medical answers, which will lower the chance of getting answers that are hallucinogenic or not reliable. As natural language generation and understanding improve, the latest version of LLAMA is reliably accurate and contextual for use in medical applications. Figure 15.2 (b) depicts the process of LLAMA2. LLAMA3 [12] shows that graph-based retrieval techniques can improve the processing of medical queries by receiving information from knowledge bases that is relevant to the query domain and making sure that the answers given are in line with biomedical data. When combined with the Medical Graph RAG framework, LLAMA2 and LLAMA3 make LLM-generated medical content more reliable by combining complex contextual reasoning with real-time retrieval. This makes them useful for patient guidance systems, clinical decision-making aids, and medical literature analysis.

15.3 Results

The evaluation of medical RAG with various LLM approaches proves the effectiveness of structured retrieval in increasing the accuracy of medical decision-making. To improve on the results, models using MedGraphRAG outperform the other models, indicating the need to incorporate structured knowledge for better performance. The experimental configuration included a machine with 128GB of RAM, 2TB of SSD storage, and NVIDIA A100 GPUs to speed model training and inference. The framework was built with PyTorch and Hugging Face Transformers, with a medical knowledge network enabling retrieval-augmented generation.

15.3.1 Performance Metrics

It assesses RAG frameworks in a practically scalable environment that closely resembles real-world medical information requirements as feasible. Table 15.1 depicts the evaluation framework for medical RAG systems.

Table 15.1 Comparison of evaluation settings in medical RAG systems.

References	MultiChoice evaluation (MCE)	Retrieval-augmented generation (RAG)	Zero-shot learning (ZSL)	Question-only retrieval (QOR)
[13]	✓	–	✓	–
[14]	✓	–	✓	–
[15]	✓	✓	✓	–
[16]	✓	✓	✓	–
[17]	✓	✓	✓	✓

Source: Own elaboration

Multi-Choice Evaluation (MCE): Multi-choice questionnaires are a popular and workable approach for examining medical quality assurance systems on an immense scale. It also evaluates several systems using a multi-choice scenario in the baseline to be aligned with prior investigations.

Retrieval-Augmented Generation (RAG): It is challenging to respond to the knowledge-based medical questions in MIRAGE without outside assistance. Furthermore, it could be better for medicine to use LLMs as reasoning engines rather than knowledge databases because of the issue of hallucinations. Therefore, to provide precise and dependable responses, RAG is required to gather external data.

Zero-Shot Learning (ZSL): The baseline requires that the RAG techniques be assessed in a zero-shot scenario, whereby in-context few-shot education is prohibited because practical medical inquiries are frequently asked without comparable instances accessible.

Question-Only Retrieval (QOR): To maintain consistency with actual medical quality assurance scenarios, response choices shouldn't be offered as input while retrieving. This is a more practical environment for RAG system evaluation. In their examination, alternatives were employed for retrieval while evaluating LLMs with RAG on medical QA, which is not a realistic environment.

15.3.2 Baselines with Different Retrievals for Medical Large Language Models

The influence of organized retrieval on medical reasoning tasks is demonstrated by the performance evaluation of medical LLMs using various RAG

Table 15.2 Performance of LLMs with MedGraphRAG.

Model	Pub health	MedQA med	Fake health	MMLU col-med	MMLU gene	MCQA pub	MedQA	MMLU col-bio	MMLU pro-med	MMLU anatomy	MMLU clinic
Baselines with MedGraphRAG											
Llama2-70B	69.4	70.1	70.5	74.0	77.5	59.4	77.2	89.5	85.2	70.1	78.5
Llama3-70B	80.0	89.3	82.0	92.0	92.3	80.2	84.6	97.0	94.0	90.5	95.2
Llama2-13B	62.1	66.4	65.3	69.0	68.5	52.3	74.1	77.2	68.0	57.0	71.1
Gemini-pro	77.8	73.0	80.5	87.0	88.5	63.5	77.1	93.8	91.0	86.0	90.2
Llama3-8B	78.5	75.3	80.8	90.1	90.2	62.7	78.8	96.2	92.4	87.2	90.5
GPT-4	84.0	92.5	87.2	92.7	99.0	82.2	84.2	98.5	96.3	94.1	97.1

Source: [19]

Table 15.3 Evaluation of LLMs with RAG.

Model	Pub health	MedQA med	Fake health	MMLU col-med	MMLU gene	MCQA Pub	MedQA	MMLU col-bio	MMLU pro-med	MMLU anatomy	MMLU clinic
Baselines with RAG											
Llama2-13B	55.2	49.0	57.4	63.3	65.2	43.0	69.7	69.1	64.5	52.2	68.3
Llama2-70B	64.1	57.1	65.5	70.5	76.5	50.7	76.0	86.7	78.2	64.0	74.2
Llama3-8B	60.5	65.1	61.3	69.5	86.0	59.0	77.1	85.7	74.1	73.2	78.5
Llama3-70B	73.0	83.1	77.0	87.5	88.0	73.3	81.4	95.1	90.2	85.1	88.7
Gemini-pro	69.2	65.3	73.2	80.1	81.3	58.2	77.8	92.0	87.3	80.2	84.5
GPT-4	78.0	89.2	79.3	82.5	93.5	77.0	78.4	96.2	95.0	84.1	94.2

Source: [19]

Table 15.4 Assessment of LLMs with GraphRAG.

Model	Pub health	MedQA med	Fake health	MMLU col-med	MMLU gene	MCQA pub	MedQA	MMLU col-bio	MMLU pro-med	MMLU anatomy	MMLU clinic
Baselines with GraphRAG											
Llama3-8B	62.0	65.7	62.5	70.2	86.8	60.1	78.0	86.0	75.3	74.0	78.9
Llama2-70B	64.9	56.3	66.5	69.1	74.9	53.1	75.5	87.1	80.0	65.5	76.2
Llama2-13B	58.2	53.2	59.4	65.0	67.5	45.5	73.5	74.1	66.0	53.3	69.0
Llama3-70B	75.1	85.0	78.5	88.3	89.0	74.0	82.2	95.5	91.0	86.0	89.5
Gemini-pro	71.5	66.0	74.5	80.9	82.3	60.0	76.3	91.8	86.7	81.3	85.5
GPT-4	78.5	90.0	79.1	83.5	93.0	78.0	78.9	96.0	95.5	83.7	94.5

Source: [19]

Table 15.5 Performance of LLMs without retrieval.

Model	Pub health	MedQA med	Fake health	MMLU col-med	MMLU gene	MCQA pub	MedQA	MMLU col-bio	MMLU pro-med	MMLU anatomy	MMLU clinic
Baselines without retrieval											
Llama2-13B	50.2	43.8	54.1	61.4	67.1	38.1	69.1	70.2	61.0	53.4	64.5
Llama2-70B	57.5	44.5	59.8	65.0	75.0	36.3	75.1	85.3	76.1	63.2	72.6
Llama3-8B	54.0	60.7	52.2	62.8	83.5	58.1	76.0	79.3	71.1	69.8	75.5
Llama3-70B	62.3	73.0	65.1	73.0	84.5	66.4	78.2	93.0	87.1	73.2	83.5
Gemini-pro	64.5	60.2	61.7	70.1	76.3	55.9	70.5	89.2	78.5	67.4	77.5
GPT-4	71.8	79.1	72.5	77.5	91.5	73.5	76.2	96.0	94.5	82.3	87.3

Source: [19]

techniques [18]. Results for models using MedGraphRAG, regular RAG, GraphRAG, and no retrieval methods are shown in Tables 15.2 to 15.5 and Figures 15.3 to 15.6, which demonstrates that retrieval-based augmentation greatly improves accuracy.

GPT-4 outperforms the baseline models with MedGraphRAG in terms of accuracy, suggesting that structured knowledge retrieval can enhance medical reasoning. Following that, Llama3-70B performs effectively on challenging medical standards. MedGraphRAG's efficacy stems from its capacity to hone contextually relevant data, producing more accurate results. A decrease in performance is noted for models that use regular RAG in contrast to MedGraphRAG. Although retrieval increases model correctness, its efficacy is constrained by the absence of organized integration. Although GPT-4 continues to perform well, the decline in scores emphasizes how organized augmentation could enhance medical accuracy. In particular, the RAG-based GraphRAG techniques perform less effectively than MedGraphRAG but better than a normal RAG model.

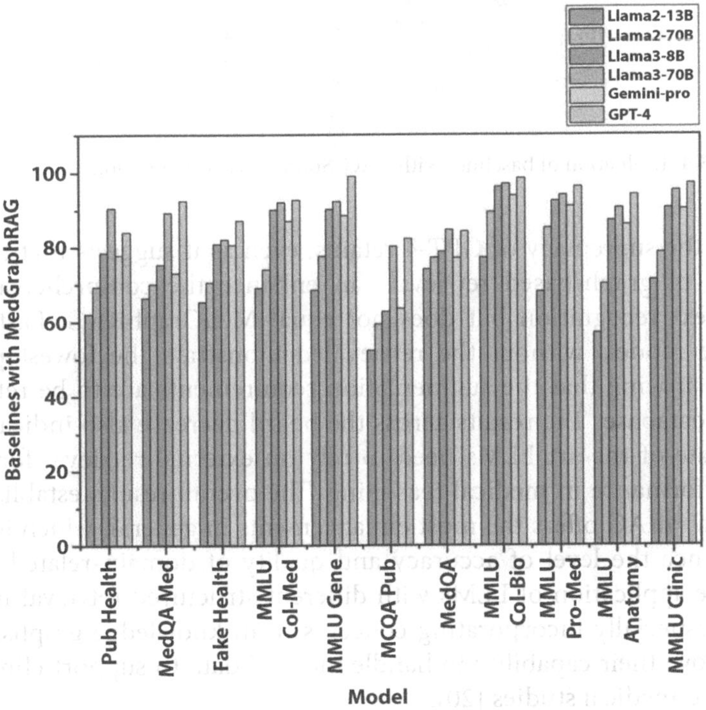

Figure 15.3 Performance comparison of baselines with MedGraphRAG. Source: Own elaboration.

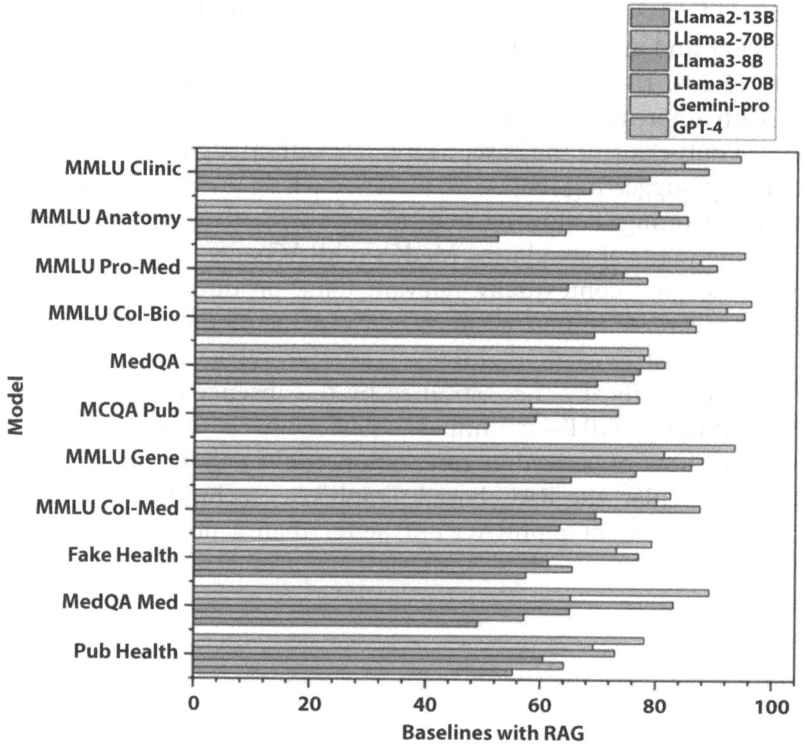

Figure 15.4 Evaluation of baselines with RAG. Source: Own elaboration.

Hence, the supremacy of GPT-4 retains, even as it suggests that the utilization of graph-based retrieval can enhance the comprehensiveness of context recognition but does not equal MedGraphRAG. Lastly, the baseline models without the retrieval demonstrate the lowest performance, proving that the augmentation requirements are to be retrieved from a database. The results across the board decrease also indicate that even state-of-the-art LLMs need to rely on external retrieval for effective performance in medical reasoning. The overall results establish that MedGraphRAG offers the most enhancements in general, which is likely to enhance the level of accuracy and quality of domain-related activities. The application of LLMs with different structured retrieval mechanisms, especially incorporating concepts from knowledge graphs, helps to improve their capability to handle medical data to support clinical or advanced medical studies [20].

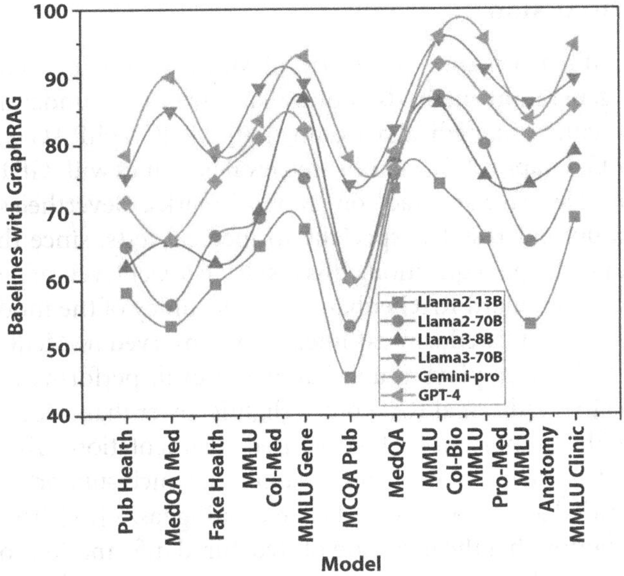

Figure 15.5 Analysis of baselines with GraphRAG. Source: Own elaboration.

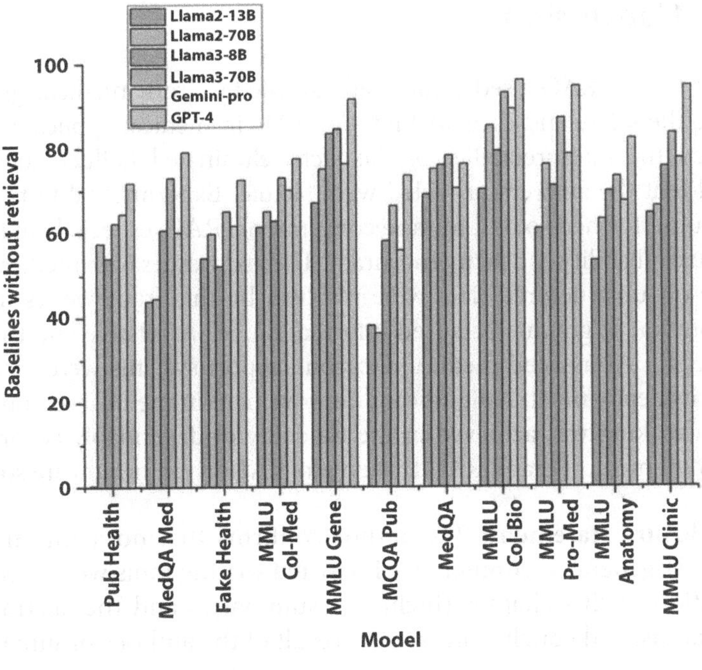

Figure 15.6 Results of baselines without retrieval. Source: Own elaboration.

15.3.3 Discussion

The compared performance of medical LLMs across the different retrieval-augmented generation methods shows that retrieval is fundamental when improving accuracy in medical reasoning [20]. MedGraphRAG is superior to standard RAG, GraphRAG, and non-retrieval baselines with GPT-4, achieving the highest average accuracy on all benchmarks. Nevertheless, Llama3-70B realizes upright results, especially in medical tests, since they require structured knowledge acquisition. This results in lower levels of performance since, although Standard RAG enhances the accuracy of the models, it does not have the sophisticated context integration observed in MedGraphRAG. GraphRAG, which employs graph-based retrieval, performs better when compared to the traditional RAG but is slightly lower than MedGraphRAG, establishing the importance of structured augmentation. The least performing models are the non-retrieval baselines, which support the need for external knowledge retrieval in medical reasoning tasks [21]. These findings support the notion that the inclusion of structured information sources such as knowledge graphs adds value to LLM systems, making them suitable for use in clinical practice as well as in conducting medical research.

15.4 Conclusion

Medical Graph RAG used structured knowledge from medical graphs to improve the safety and dependability of LLMs in medical applications. This improved the interpretability of the facts, eliminated hallucinations, and ensured that the answers provided were factual. Experimental tests showed that it outperformed solo LLMs and conventional RAG, especially in terms of contextual reliability and factual accuracy. The main issues with medical LLMs' reliance on unstructured data were resolved by this framework's dynamic incorporation of graph-structured information. More reliable and therapeutically useful AI-assisted medical decision support systems were made possible by its deployment. A significant improvement in medical reasoning and decision-making was achieved in the modality of dependably accurate and transparent medical graph RAG that employs AI-driven healthcare solutions.

AI disclosure statement: The author confirms that no artificial intelligence (AI)-generated content or AI-assisted writing tools were used in the preparation of this chapter (including summaries and the abstract). All text, analysis, and conclusions are the result of the author's original work.

References

1. Safranek, C.W., *et al.*, The role of large language models in medical education: Applications and implications. *JMIR Med. Educ.*, 9, e509455, 2023, https://doi.org/10.2196/50945.
2. Asgari, E., *et al.*, A framework to assess clinical safety and hallucination rates of LLMs for medical text summarisation. *medRxiv*, pp. 2024–09, 2024, https://doi.org/10.1101/2024.09.12.24313556.
3. Galway, M., *et al.*, The mitigation of excessive retrieval augmentation and knowledge conflicts in large language models, 2024, https://doi.org/10.21203/rs.3.rs-5263949/v1.
4. Afrose, S., Retrieval-augmented generation based doctor recommendation system using knowledge graph, Diss. Brac University, 2024, http://hdl.handle.net/10361/25267.
5. Taleb, I., Navaz, A.N., Serhani, M.A., Leveraging large language models for enhancing literature-based discovery. *Big Data Cognit. Comput.*, 8, 11, 146, 2024, https://doi.org/10.3390/bdcc8110146.
6. Varshney, D., *et al.*, Knowledge graph assisted end-to-end medical dialog generation. *Artif. Intell. Med.*, 139, 1025355, 2023, https://doi.org/10.1016/j.artmed.2023.102535.
7. Alkhalaf, M., *et al.*, Applying generative AI with retrieval augmented generation to summarize and extract key clinical information from electronic health records. *J. Biomed. Inf.*, 156, 1046625, 2024, https://doi.org/10.1016/j.jbi.2024.104662.
8. Bora, A. and Cuayáhuitl, H., Systematic Analysis of Retrieval-Augmented Generation-Based LLMs for Medical Chatbot Applications. *Mach. Learn. Knowl. Extr.*, 6, 4, 2355–2374, 2024, https://doi.org/10.3390/make6040116.
9. Jadhav, S., *et al.*, Maven at MEDIQA-CORR 2024: Leveraging RAG and Medical LLM for Error Detection and Correction in Medical Notes. *Proceedings of the 6th Clinical Natural Language Processing Workshop*, 2024, https://doi.org/10.18653/v1/2024.clinicalnlp-1.36.
10. Fernández-Pichel, M., Pichel, J.C., Losada, D.E., Search Engines, LLMs or Both? Evaluating Information Seeking Strategies for Answering Health Questions, *arXiv preprint arXiv:2407.12468*, 2024, https://doi.org/10.48550/arXiv.2407.12468.
11. Agrawal, A.M., *et al.*, Conversation AI Dialog for Medicare powered by Finetuning and Retrieval Augmented Generation, *arXiv preprint arXiv:2502.02249*, 2025, https://doi.org/10.48550/arXiv.2502.02249.
12. Nguyen, Q., *et al.*, Advancing Question-Answering in Ophthalmology with Retrieval-Augmented Generation (RAG): Benchmarking Open-source and Proprietary Large Language Models, medRxiv, pp. 2024–11, 2024, https://doi.org/10.1101/2024.11.18.24317510.

13. Nori, H., *et al.*, Capabilities of gpt-4 on medical challenge problems, *arXiv preprint arXiv:2303.13375,* 2023, https://doi.org/10.48550/arXiv.2303.13375.
14. Singhal, K., *et al.*, Large language models encode clinical knowledge. *Nature,* 620, 7972, 172–180, 2023, https://doi.org/10.1038/s41586-023-06291-2.
15. Liévin, V., *et al.*, Can large language models reason about medical questions? *Patterns,* 5, 3, 100943, 2024, https://doi.org/10.1016/j.patter.2024.100943.
16. Lála, J., *et al.*, Paperqa: Retrieval-augmented generative agent for scientific research, arXiv preprint arXiv:2312.07559, 2023, https://doi.org/10.48550/arXiv.2312.07559.
17. Xiong, G., *et al.*, Benchmarking retrieval-augmented generation for medicine. *Findings of the Association for Computational Linguistics ACL 2024,* 2024, https://doi.org/10.18653/v1/2024.findings-acl.372.
18. Woo, J.J., *et al.*, Custom Large Language Models Improve Accuracy: Comparing Retrieval Augmented Generation and Artificial Intelligence Agents to Noncustom Models for Evidence-Based Medicine. *Arthrosc. J. Arthroscopic Relat. Surg.,* 41, 3, 565–573, 2025, https://doi.org/10.1016/j.arthro.2024.10.042.
19. Wu, J., *et al.*, Medical graph rag: Towards safe medical large language model *via* graph retrieval-augmented generation, *arXiv preprint arXiv:2408.04187,* 2024, https://doi.org/10.48550/arXiv.2408.04187.
20. Jeong, M., *et al.*, Improving medical reasoning through retrieval and self-reflection with retrieval-augmented large language models. *Bioinformatics,* 40, Supplement_1, i119–i129, 2024, https://doi.org/10.1093/bioinformatics/btae238.
21. Wang, D., *et al.*, Enhancement of the performance of large language models in diabetes education through retrieval-augmented generation: comparative study. *J. Med. Internet Res.,* 26, e580415, 2024, https://doi.org/10.2196/58041.

16

Real-Time Cognitive Load Prediction in Digital Environments

Monika Joshi[1]*, Pushpa J.[2], Sharon M.[3] and Manoranjan Dash[4]

[1]*Maharishi School of Pharmaceuticals, Maharishi University of Information Technology, Uttar Pradesh, India*
[2]*Department of CSIT, Jain (Deemed-to-be University), Bangalore, Karnataka, India*
[3]*Department of Computer Science & Engineering, Presidency University, Bengaluru, Karnataka, India*
[4]*Department of Management, Siksha 'O' Anusandhan (Deemed to be University), Bhubaneswar, Odisha, India*

Abstract

Real-time cognitive load prediction in digital environments is essential for adaptive learning, driver assistance systems, and human–computer interaction. This chapter explores machine learning (ML) and deep learning (DL) approaches for cognitive load prediction using multimodal datasets. The chapter utilizes three datasets; First, a student engagement dataset integrating electroencephalogram (EEG) signals, eye-tracking measures, and contextual features; second a multidimensional cognitive workload supervised data collection combining EEG, visual focus detection, and driver input signals; and third a dataset with EEG recordings using the Neurosky Mindwave device. These data allow examination of cognitive load differences based on physiological and behavioral measures. The key challenges in cognitive load prediction include handling multimodal data, real-time processing constraints, and ensuring high prediction accuracy across different tasks. To address these challenges, ML models, such as logistic regression (LR), support vector machines (SVM), ridge regression (RR), and random forest (RF) were applied for cognitive load prediction to analyze

**Corresponding author*: monika.joshi@muit.in; ORCID: 0000-0002-3708-9446
Pushpa J.: ORCID: 0009-0005-7321-4047
Sharon M.: ORCID: 0009-0008-0205-5757
Manoranjan Dash: ORCID: 0000-0003-3510-3299

Sudesh Yadav, Pethuru Raj, Satya Prakash Yadav and Victor Hugo C. de Albuquerque (eds.) Natural Language Processing in Mental Health Care: Methodologies and Clinical Practice, (233–250) © 2026 Scrivener Publishing LLC

student e-learning. Additionally, DL models including convolutional neural network-recurrent neural networks (CNN-RNN) and deep neural networks (DNN), were implemented for enhanced feature extraction and pattern recognition during simulated driving tasks. The performance evaluation demonstrated strong correlations between cognitive load levels and physiological signals. For the ML approach the SVM archive $accuracy$ (98.9%), $precision$ (98.9%), $recall$ (94.25%), and $F1-score$ (98.9%) are significant performance compared to other methods. Similarly, for the DL approach, the best CNN-RNN model attains $accuracy$ (92.02%,) $precision$ (92.03%), $recall$ (92.02), $F1-score$ (92.02%), and AUC (93.82%). The results indicated superior accuracy in real-time cognitive load prediction. The chapter contributes to real-time adaptive systems by providing an efficient framework for cognitive load assessment, improving personalized learning experiences, and driving safety applications.

Keywords: Cognitive load, learning, prediction, machine learning, deep learning

16.1 Introduction

The growth of online and home-based connections and the broad application of technology to everyday activities and many workplaces result in the growing burden of mental labor and declining physical labor on workers. Mental workload (MWL) or cognitive load (CL) is a concept that thirty years ago became a research field, and today is still actively developing. It has been observed by a number of authors of different fields such as; psychology, neurology and education that there may be slight variations in the difference between cognitive loading and mental effort [1]. To enhance understanding of the interaction of individuals with their environments and also help in reducing workload the long-standing studies conducted on physical ergonomics shall be complemented by looking into the cognitive aspects of a human being. Furthermore, several studies have indicated that psychological variables can play a major role in the emergence of musculoskeletal disorders (MSDs). For example, mental strain, exhaustion, and work-related stress can change the biomechanical control mechanisms for the upper extremities (the arms, hands, shoulders, and neck) and low back extension, as well as enhance the variability of gait and control. This condition can ultimately end in occupational injury and even muscle discomfort for the worker [2]. The purpose of educational technology is to improve student engagement, efficacy, and accessibility. Digital learning environments improve learning through the use of glossaries, hyperlinks, multimedia resources, and other forms of feedback. Digital learning environments should ideally support students' cognitive processes by minimizing the demand for cognitive resources while increasing retention and meaningful learning [3]. However, educational interventions should focus on optimizing the entire cognitive effort required to improve learning efficiency, because learning is impossible without activating cognitive resources. In this context, recent research examines new prospects to promote learning through the effective use of cognitive resources that could emerge from the introduction of artificial intelligence (AI) into educational systems [4]. To be effective, digital learning must direct students' mental activity and teach them how to regulate their own learning. A digitally facilitated variation of conventional in-person cooperation, online collaborative learning focuses on knowledge co-construction, collaborative competency development, and emotional communication [5]. Deeper connections and better teamwork are shown to be strongly facilitated by the continuous development of technologically advanced online environments. Compared to traditional collaboration, the dynamic and virtual nature of the internet makes ongoing communication challenging. Furthermore, online collaboration becomes more complicated when there is a lack of clear direction and communication [6].

By generating a high psychological effort and mental load, these factors impede the development of teamwork skills, learning engagement, and individual efficiency, resulting in cognitive overload and a decrease in teamwork awareness, attributed to the cognitive load prediction [7]. The quantity of stress an activity exerts on a person's remembered knowledge, also known as short-term memory, is often related to as cognitively strain. The importance of cognitive load has been extensively studied in the past since it is utilized in many different contexts, such as problem solving, learning layout, online media, and automation [8]. One popular method for incorporating self-evaluation into teaching is to provide students rubrics, which are intended to educate them about the quality levels and valuation standards related to a task assignment [9]. Performance, exhaustion, and stress levels are predicted by mental effort, measurement an intellectual work desired that finish assignment [10]. Through the real-time detection and monitoring of cognitive load stages, cognitive load identification seeks to enhance human performance. Poor performance on a range of tasks, including educational procedures and related thought or reflection, is mostly caused by cognitive load [11].

This chapter investigates ML and DL techniques in cognitive load prediction utilizing multimodal datasets. The work utilizes three datasets, the first of which is student engagement dataset including EEG signals, eye-tracking measures and contextual features, the second is a multisource mental effort classification system that includes EEG, visual attention monitoring, and Driver performance information, and the third one is an EEG recording dataset with the Neurosky Mindwave device. These datasets provide insights into cognitive load variations based on physiological and behavioral signals.

Organization of the chapter: Section 16.2 demonstrates the suggested method includes ML and DL methods in cognitive load prediction. Section 16.3 presents the performance evaluations. Section 16.4 represents the final conclusion of the chapter.

16.2 Methodology

To forecast cognitive load during simulated driving by applying ML and DL algorithms to multimodal data. The student engagement dataset is utilized initially, and that of the Neurosky Mindwave EEG headset for real-time processing. Multimodal cognitive load classification dataset is employed in DL, and it has EEG, fNIRS, eye track, and driving data. The ML technique of assessing the e-learning of students, and the DL methodology is applied to investigate the extent of cognitive tension in performing driving simulation tasks.

16.2.1 Dataset

Three datasets are used within this chapter, using a ML technique on two datasets to examine e-Learning, for instance, student engagement, and Neurosky Mindwave (EEG) Device Dataset. Lastly, a DL technique is used on the third dataset, the multimodal cognitive load classification dataset, to evaluate levels of cognitive load when performing a simulated driving task.

Student Engagement Dataset: Student engagement metrics for this data set were first built on eye-tracking recordings and EEG activity [12]. It is modelled for forecasting actual involvement, as shown in Table 16.1, in learning and adaptive learning environments.

Multimodal cognitive load classification dataset: For the purpose of to compare the degrees of mental stress in virtual vehicle activities, this multifaceted psychological strain categorization collection combines information on driving actions, visual tracking, fNIRS, and EEG [13]. A one-subsequent multifunctional informational segment is represented by each of the 86,435 data points in the collection. Table 16.2 shows the description of the multimodal cognitive load classification dataset.

Neurosky Mindwave (EEG) Device Dataset: The file contains 300 examples of various people who collected data using the Neurosky Mindwave

Table 16.1 Features of the student engagement dataset.

Feature category	Description
EEG Data	Beta, Gamma, Theta, Alpha, and Delta frequency bands' power spectral densities (PSDs).
Eye-Tracking Data	Includes pupil dilation, blink rate, fixation duration, and saccade velocity.
Contextual Features	Learning content type (Video, Text, Interactive) and difficulty levels (Easy, Medium, Hard).
Engagement Levels	Labeled as Medium (1), Low (0), and High (2) based on cognitive and visual measures.
Real-Time Analysis	Suitable for ML models to assess and predict student engagement dynamically.

Source: [12]

Table 16.2 Description of the multimodal cognitive load classification dataset.

Feature category	Number of features	Description
EEG Features	384	Power Spectral Density (PSD) & statistical measures across 24 channels
fNIRS Features	20	Oxygenated & deoxygenated hemoglobin levels
Eye-Tracking Features	4	Pupil dilation, blink rate, fixation, saccades
Driving Behavior Features	6	Speed, acceleration, steering, braking
Target Variable	1	Cognitive load classification (0-back, 1-back, 2-back)

Source: [13]

EEG Device with 2 electrodes for a maximum of 10–12 minutes. It is useful for people who work with EEG device datasets [14]. The reader will find the file to be highly helpful and easy to understand. The raw data collected by this device was not entered; instead, it was transformed into an EEG standard format using the Neurosky website's formula. The Neuroexperimenter program divides the values into several bands, such as alpha, beta, gamma, and theta, so that the frequency is separated into more manageable bands that allow the user to determine the band's minimum and maximum frequencies.

Cognitive Load Prediction using Machine Learning (ML) for e-Learning
The cognitive load prediction in simulated e-Learning using ML on a student engagement dataset.

Support vector machine (SVM): The examination of students' brainwave data and using the SVM technique to anticipate their education actions in an online educational setting. To differentiate between the attentive and inattentive groups according to quite efficiently things might be distinguished from other groups, the SVM approach employed a decision threshold. Support vectors are parallel lines representing characteristics along the decision border. Predicting attentive and inattentive states is difficult when characteristics are close to the decision border. The grouping of two classes and support vectors is depicted in Figure 16.1. Cognitive EEG data from online learning to develop an expression for an SVM classifier that is used to direct a person's level of concentration. The SVM classifier's Equation (16.1) is shown below.

$$g(w_j) = \begin{cases} +1 & if\ x.w + a \geq 0 \\ -1 & x.w + a < 0 \end{cases} \tag{16.1}$$

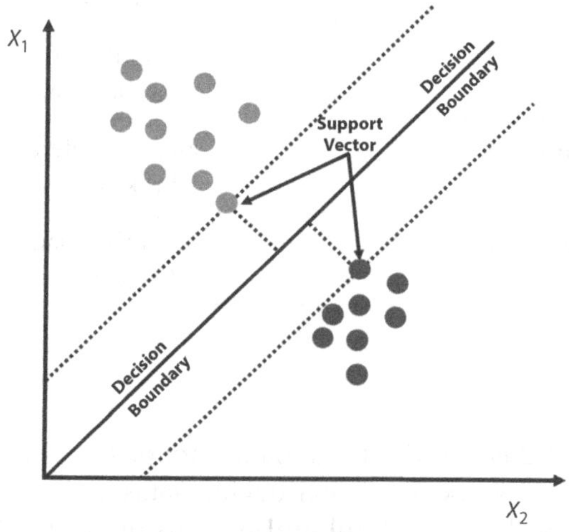

Figure 16.1 Framework of the SVM method. Source: [15].

When a point is on or above the hyperplane, the value is +1, and when a point is below the hyperplane, the value is −1. Equation (16.1) uses the letter g to indicate a hypothesis. By contrasting it with alternative classification algorithms, the SVM algorithm's precision and effectiveness in forecasting students' online learning habits will be evaluated [15, 16].

Logistic regression (LR): The LR approach uses cognitive EEG signals to model the relationship among incoming parameters that an outcome binary parameter in order to assess whether or not a student is paying attention in electronic instruction settings. The coefficient of each feature determines its effect on the classification, and the input characteristics are converted into the output variable using a logistic function. The likelihood that the output variable will rely on the input attributes is determined by the sigmoid function. The sigmoid is provided by Equation (16.2).

$$logostic\,(\eta) = \frac{1}{1+\exp(-\eta)} \tag{16.2}$$

The logistic function maximizes the likelihood of observed data by minimizing the cost function. Once the ideal values for the coefficients are determined, the algorithm may used for predict that output variable's probability according to new input data. The outcome is considered inattentive if the probability decreases below a certain threshold, which is typically 0.5 [15, 16].

Ridge regression (RR): When applied to e-learning, RR accurately predicts student attention based on cognitive EEG data, particularly when there are many highly correlated input criteria in the dataset. Through incorporating a penalty component into the cost function, RR enhances the noise resilience of the model and avoids overfitting. The extra term optimizes the coefficients and alters the conventional least squares term to assess how each characteristic affects classification. The exponential factor (θ_i) is used to evaluate the coefficients. RR not only generates easily understood coefficients but also aids in assessing each feature's relative importance. For forecasting students' attention in online classes, RR is a useful technique. Using Equation (16.3), the adjusted cost function is provided.

$$MSE(\hat{\beta}) = var(\hat{\beta}) + \left(F(\hat{\beta} - (\beta))\right)^2 \tag{16.3}$$

In RR, the ridge estimator is derived by constraint-maximizing the likelihood. RR is further accomplished by adding an extra penalization element, equations (16.4–16.5), and reducing the residual sum of squares.

$$\sum_{j=1}^{m}\left(z_j - \beta_0 - \sum_{i=1}^{o}\beta_i w_{ji}\right)^2 + \lambda\sum_{i=1}^{o}\beta_i^2 \tag{16.4}$$

$$\alpha = \beta \underline{A} + \underline{f} \tag{16.5}$$

The dependent variable is represented by α, the independent variable by β, the regression coefficient that is required to be estimated by $\underline{A}$, and the errors are provided by $\underline{f}$ [15].

Random forest (RF): One supervised ML algorithm composed of decision trees (DT) is called Random Decision (RD). Regression and classification are essentially how it operates. The application builds several DT and adds up their output. Because of this, RD is expected to perform better than standard models like LR, which is why it is considered [16].

Cognitive Load Prediction using Deep Learning (DL) for Driving
The dataset supports DL-established cognitive load prediction to analyze driving task.
Convolutional neural network-recurrent neural network (CNN-RNN): To examine different physiological data, CNN-RNN is integrated into recent advances in the field of cognitive load classification. When it comes to deciphering intricate physiological signals, CNNs excel at identifying spatial patterns in data.

Convolutional neural network (CNN): A subset of DL architectures known as CNN has demonstrated exceptional performance in the analysis and classification of data having grid-like patterns, including images and videos. A CNN variation created for one-dimensional signals, including time-series data, is called a 1D-CNN. The convolution process is the CNN central function. Equation (16.6) provides the mathematical expression for the convolution operation for a 1D input time series w of length n that has been processed using a filter (or kernel) x of size l.

$$z[j] = \sum_{i=0}^{l-1} w[j+i].x[i] + a \tag{16.6}$$

$z[j]$ represents the output at location j, whereas a represents the bias term in cognitive load prediction. Through this process, the model is identifying local patterns in the incoming information. After the convolution, a Rectified Linear Unit (RLU) with an additional trigger perform are used. The initialization variable aids in the system's discovery of ever-more complex patterns by introducing irregularity. Equation (16.7) stated as follows, the sigmoid function is another popular activation function that is actually helpful in binary classification problems.

$$\sigma(z) = \frac{1}{1+f^{-z}} \tag{16.7}$$

The function in Equation (16.7) reduces the input z to a range of 0 to 1, allowing the result to be interpreted as a probability [17].

Recurrent neural network (RNN): For handling and assessing sequence data, the RNN kind of neural system is especially well-suited. Recurrent connections, which distinguish RNNs from conventional feedforward neural networks (FNNs), allow them to preserve an internal state, hence enabling the network to retain memory of prior inputs. Because of this feature, RNNs are especially strong at positions requiring time-dependent signals, where accurate prediction depends on the context of previous data points.

The capacity of the RNN to process sequential information is highly valuable for driving behavior data and fNIRS signal analysis. The cognitive load of a driver and the physiological reactions that accompany it change over time, making these kinds of data intrinsically temporal. The temporal interdependence in the fNIRS signals and driving behavior patterns are captured by RNNs by utilizing the recurrent connections, offering a more accurate and nuanced assessment of the cognitive load of the driver. An input w_s and a hidden state $g_s - 1$ are sent into the RNN at each time step s. Equations (16.8–16.9) provide the updated hidden state g_s.

$$g_s = \theta(X_w w_s + X_w w_s + a) \tag{16.8}$$

$$p_s = \Phi\left(X_p g_s + a_0\right) \tag{16.9}$$

Both Equations (16.8–16.9) use weight matrices, $X_w, X_g, X_p,$ and a_0, whereas a is the bias term and σ is a non-linear activation function, like tanh. With f being the activation function, p_s is the output at each time step [17].

Deep neural network (DNN): The framework of the employed DNN model is displayed in Figure 16.2. One layer of the DNN design has 200 fully linked neurons, while the other layer has 100 fully connected neurons.

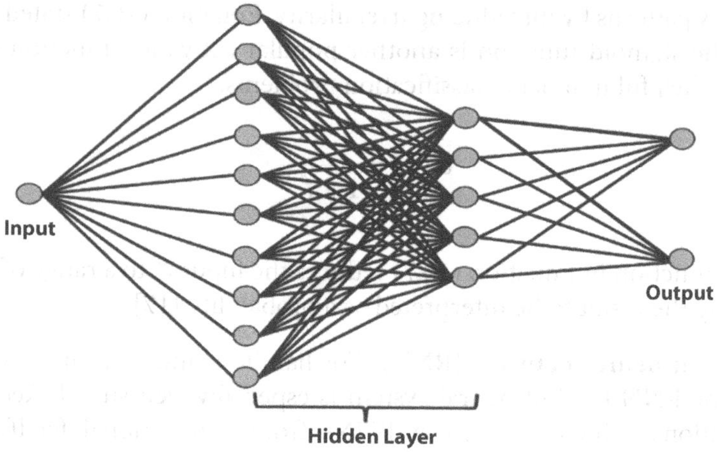

Figure 16.2 Structure of the DNN model. Source: [18].

The four-class assignment has four classes with four output levels, while the three high-low functions have two classes as well as two output layers. Each final stage used a quadratic activating factor for every task. Furthermore, the Keras Adam optimizer and a binary classification loss were used that address 2-class to 4-class classification problems. Relu was each activation function of the second layer, whereas linear was that of the first [18].

16.3 Result and Discussion

The performance evaluation demonstrated high accuracy in real-time cognitive load prediction within digital environments, leveraging ML and DL models. Results assessing criteria including F1-score, recall, accuracy, and precision showed that physiological signals and task complexity were strongly correlated. The discussion highlights practical implications challenges in dynamic settings, and future improvements for adaptive learning and work environments.

16.3.1 Performance Evaluation

Consideration is given to the following performance indicators to assess how well ML and DL models anticipate cognitive overload. Every statistic listed above will provide a thorough explanation of how effectively each algorithm handles the categorization of cognitive load levels and which model makes the most accurate real-time predictions.

Accuracy: Measure that is frequently used for classification tasks is accuracy. The cognitive load evaluates the percentage of accurate predictions among all of a model prediction. The measures is the anticipated cognitive load circumstances were accounted for throughout all computations (Equation 16.10).

$$Accuracy = \frac{TP + TN}{TP + FP + TN + FN} \tag{16.10}$$

Note: true negative *(TN)*, false positive *(FP)*, False negative *(FN)*, and true positive (TP).

Precision: The portion of factual affirmative overflow cases among all predictable overload cases is known as precision. The percentage of true positive forecasts against all positive predictions is determined by a model's performance, or cognitive load. The number of anticipated positive values that are positive is used to evaluate the accuracy of positive forecasts, as follows in Equation (16.11).

$$Precision = \frac{TP}{TP + FP} \tag{16.11}$$

Recall: The percentage of actual overload cases that the model correctly detects is indicated by the measure. Recall is a performance metric that quantifies the proportion of correct beneficial forecasts relative the actual favorable outcomes in the dataset. Cognitive load evaluates how well the model can distinguish between all of the truly positive occurrences, as follows in Equation (16.12).

$$Recall = \frac{TP}{TP + FN} \tag{16.12}$$

F1-score: The result demonstrates the precision and sensitivity/recall metrics harmonic mean. The outcome of the algorithm is evaluated using a fair methodology. By finding out the periodic average of accuracy and recall, the F1 score offers a fair assessment of the system's effectiveness. Because it takes into account both the model's precision and recall, when there is an uneven distribution of the dataset's positive and negative classes, the statistic is especially helpful, as in the following Equation (16.13).

$$F1\ score = \frac{2 \times Precision \times Recall}{Precision + Recall} \tag{16.13}$$

AUC: The ROC curve's area under the curve (AUC) ranges from 0.5 to 1. AUC values that are higher indicate that the gadget is operating efficiently in cognitive load prediction, as follows in Equation (16.14).

$$AUC = \int_0^1 ROC(t)dt \tag{16.14}$$

ML approach outcomes for eLearning Environments

Table 16.3 and Figure 16.3 present the presentation of the ML methods, such as LR, SVM, and RR in cognitive load prediction within digital environments. SVM achieves the highest accuracy (91.68%), precision

Table 16.3 Overall predictive analysis for ML methods.

Methods	Accuracy (%)	Precision (%)	Recall (%)	F1-score (%)
LR [15]	86.20	85.41	87.63	86.76
SVM [15]	91.68	91.23	92.11	91.53
RR [15]	85.52	84.89	86.33	85.67

Source: Own elaboration

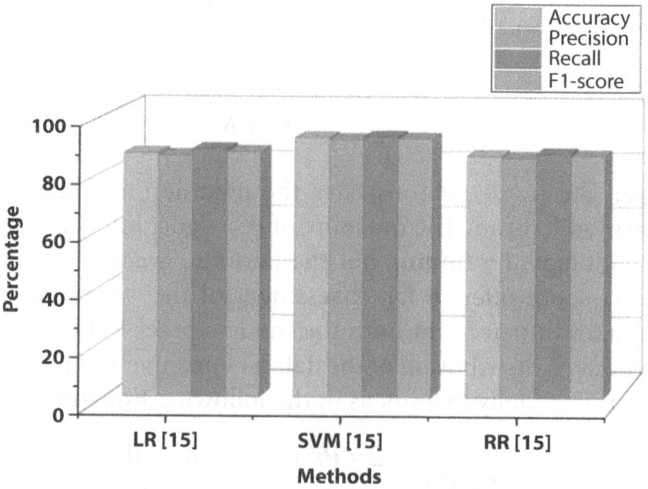

Figure 16.3 Graphical representation of the various metrics. Source: Own elaboration.

(91.23%), recall (92.11%), and F1-score (91.53%), indicating superior predictive capability. LR follows with 86.20% accuracy, 85.41% precision, 87.63% recall, and 86.76% F1-score. SVM is the most efficient approach, with RR performing a little better (85.52% accuracy, 84.89% precision, 86.33% recall, and 85.67% F1-score).

Table 16.4 and Figure 16.4 compare the predictive performance of LR, RF, and SVM in cognitive load prediction in digital environments. SVM achieves the highest accuracy (98.9%), precision (98.9%), and F1-score (98.9%), though its recall is lower at 94.25%. RF follows with 97.86% accuracy, 97.01% precision, 96.28% recall, and 96.64% F1-score. LR performs

Table 16.4 Overall predictive analysis for ML methods (LR, RF, and SVM) in eLearning environments.

Methods	Accuracy (%)	Precision (%)	Recall (%)	F1-score (%)
LR [16]	95.7	95.5	95.7	95.5
RF [16]	97.86	97.01	96.28	96.64
SVM [16]	98.9	98.9	94.25	98.9

Source: Own elaboration

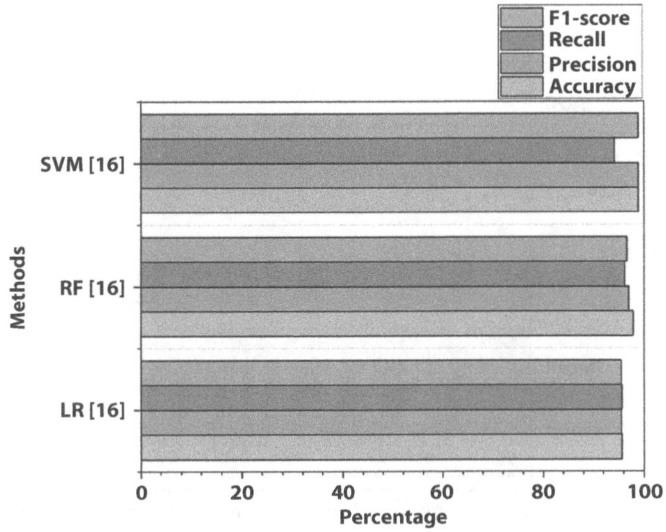

Figure 16.4 Performance evaluation of the ML methods in different metrics. Source: Own elaboration.

slightly lower, with 95.7% accuracy, 95.5% precision, 95.7% recall, and 95.5% F1 score. SVM demonstrates superior overall performance.

DL Method Performance Outcomes for Driving

Table 16.5 and Figure 16.5 present the predictive performance of the CNN-RNN model for driving behavior in cognitive load prediction. Strong predictive capabilities are demonstrated by the model's 92.02% accuracy, 92.03% precision, 92.02% recall, and 92.02% F1-score. Additionally, the area under the curve (AUC) is 93.82%, highlighting its excellent classification performance. These results demonstrate the effectiveness of the CNN-RNN model in accurately predicting cognitive load with high consistency across all evaluation metrics.

Table 16.6 and Figure 16.6 present the performance of DNN classifiers in cognitive load prediction using 10-fold cross-validation on EEG datasets.

Table 16.5 Overall predictive analysis for DL methods in CNN-RNN (driving behavior).

Method	Precision (%)	Recall (%)	F1-score (%)	Accuracy (%)	AUC (%)
CNN-RNN [17]	92.03	92.02	92.02	92.02	93.82

Source: Own elaboration

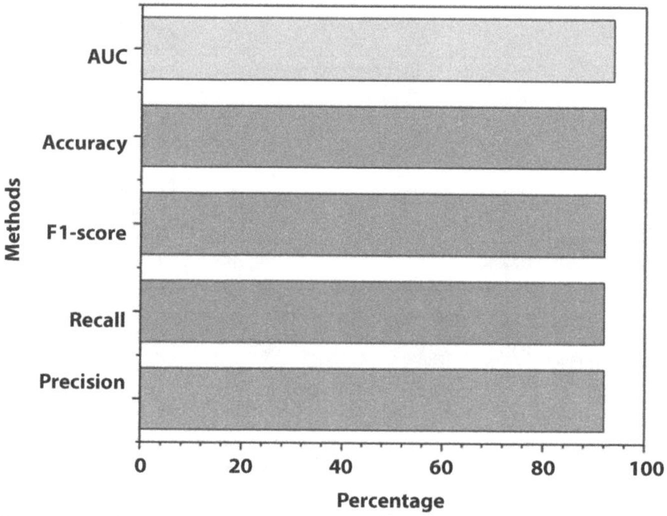

Figure 16.5 Comparison of the DL methods in CNN-RNN. Source: Own elaboration.

Table 16.6 Performance of the DNN classifiers utilizing 10-fold cross validation in EEG dataset.

Method	Classification task	10- fold cross classification		
		Accuracy (%)	**Precision (%)**	**Recall (%)**
DNN [18]	Urban-High-Low	84.26	84.27	84.26
	Motorway-High-Low	90.37	90.37	90.37
	Combined-High-Low	81.65	81.64	81.65
	Four-Class	78.66	77.61	76.70

Source: Own elaboration

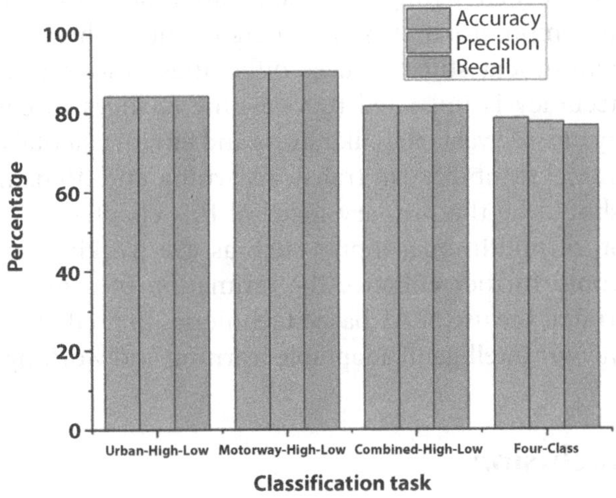

Figure 16.6 Graphical presentation of the classification task in DNN. Source: Own elaboration.

For Urban-High-Low classification, DNN achieves accuracy (84.26%), precision (84.27%), and recall (84.26%). In Motorway-High-Low, it records (90.37%) accuracy, (90.37%) precision, and (90.37%) recall. The Combined-High-Low task shows (81.65%) accuracy, (81.64%) precision, and (81.65%) recall. The Four-Class classification yields 78.66% accuracy, 77.61% precision, and 76.70% recall.

16.3.2 Discussion

This chapter determines how effective ML and DL models are at predicting cognitive load in real-time in digital environments. The high F1 score, recall, accuracy, and precision across experiments show a strong relationship between task complexity and physiological signals. According to these results, the AI-driven cognitive load calculation has the opportunity to improve digital workpieces and adaptive learning. An established evaluation of cognitive load levels when performing e-Learning simulations that used ML techniques such as LR, SVM, RF and RR [15, 16]. The CNN-RNN [17] model improved other cognitive DL techniques based on analyzing driving tasks which highlights the ability to interpret complex temporary correlations in physical information.

The performance of SVM and DNN [18] is investigated in the chapter using the verification of a subscription and 10-fold cross-validation. The results confirmed how well these models classified different cognitive load states of participants. The most effective DL model to predict behavior that was CNN-RNN, which highlights the adaptation of hybrid architecture to identify spatiotemporal patterns. The assignment of these models in the changing environment still produces difficulties despite positive results. Prediction accuracy is impacted by real-time changes in cognitive load brought on by outside variables, like stress and environmental distractions. Improving model flexibility *via* transfer learning and domain adaptation techniques should be the primary focus of this chapter. In addition, the incorporation of multimodal inputs such as eye tracking and heart rate variability would further enhance the estimation of cognitive load. The chapter illustrated the use of AI-based techniques to predict cognitive load paving the way for intelligent, adaptable learning and working spaces.

16.4 Conclusion

Prefers real-time prediction that neural burden in digital environments, problem in user interface design, adaptive learning, and driver support. The greatest challenges are handling multimodal data, real-time processing ability, and provide accurate predictions at any position. The chapter employs DL models such as CNN-RNN and DNN and ML models such as LR, SVM, RR, and RF to solve these issues. The work set a large correlation between cognitive load and physiological signals on multimodal datasets with the integration of eye-tracking, behavioral signals, and EEG signals. The CNN-RNN model can capture high accuracy and precision compared to other DL models. The results suggest a powerful paradigm for quantifying cognitive load, which allows personalized learning and driving safety applications in real-time adaptive systems. Compared to other methods, the SVM archive accuracy (98.9%), precision (98.9%), recall (94.25%), and F1-score (98.9%) of the ML approach are considerable. Accordingly, the most accurate CNN-RNN model for the DL technique achieves accuracy (92.02%), precision (92.03%), recall (92.02%), F1-score (92.02%), and AUC (93.82%). Limitations include mental fatigue, emotional variability, and real-time processing constraints affecting accuracy. Future research can enhance adaptive learning and behavioral analysis by refining real-time cognitive load assessment for personalized and dynamic interactions.

AI disclosure statement: The author confirms that no artificial intelligence (AI)-generated content or AI-assisted writing tools were used in the preparation of this chapter (including summaries and the abstract). All text, analysis, and conclusions are the result of the author's original work.

References

1. Longo, L., Modeling cognitive load as a self-supervised brain rate with electroencephalography and deep learning. *Brain Sci.*, 12, 10, 1416, 2022, https://doi.org/10.3390/brainsci12101416.
2. Lagomarsino, M., *et al.*, An online framework for cognitive load assessment in industrial tasks. *Rob. Comput. Integr. Manuf.*, 78, 1023805, 2022, https://doi.org/10.1016/j.rcim.2022.102380.
3. Khanam, F., Aowlad Hossain, A.B.M., Ahmad, M., Electroencephalogram-based cognitive load level classification using wavelet decomposition and support vector machine. *Brain-Comput. Interfaces*, 10, 1, 1–15, 2023, https://doi.org/10.1080/2326263X.2022.2109855.
4. Zhang, L., *et al.*, A data-driven optimized mechanism for improving online collaborative learning: Taking cognitive load into account. *Int. J. Environ. Res. Public Health*, 19, 12, 6984, 2022, https://doi.org/10.3390/ijerph19126984.
5. Malakul, S. and Park, I., The effects of using an auto-subtitle system in educational videos to facilitate learning for secondary school students: learning comprehension, cognitive load, and satisfaction. *Smart Learn. Environ.*, 10, 1, 4, 2023, https://doi.org/10.1186/s40561-023-00224-2.
6. Wang, C., Fang, T., Gu, Y., Learning performance and behavioral patterns of online collaborative learning: Impact of cognitive load and affordances of different multimedia. *Comput. Educ.*, 143, 1036835, 2020, https://doi.org/10.1016/j.compedu.2019.103683.

7. Šola, H.M., Qureshi, F.H., Khawaja, S., AI Eye-Tracking Technology: A New Era in Managing Cognitive Loads for Online Learners. *Educ. Sci.*, 14, 9, 933, 2024, https://doi.org/10.3390/educsci14090933.
8. Ahmad, M.I., *et al.*, A framework to estimate cognitive load using physiological data. *Pers. Ubiquitous Comput.*, 27, 6, 1–15, 2023, https://doi.org/10.1007/s00779-020-01455-7.
9. Krebs, R., Rothstein, B., Roelle, J., Rubrics enhance accuracy and reduce cognitive load in self-assessment. *Metacogn. Learn.*, 17, 2, 627–650, 2022, https://doi.org/10.1007/s11409-022-09302-1.
10. Yoo, G., Kim, H., Hong, S., Prediction of cognitive load from electroencephalography signals using long short-term memory network. *Bioengineering*, 10, 3, 361, 2023, https://doi.org/10.3390/bioengineering10030361.
11. Liu, J.-C., *et al.*, Assessing perceptual load and cognitive load by fixation-related information of eye movements. *Sensors*, 22, 3, 1187, 2022, https://doi.org/10.3390/s22031187.
12. https://www.kaggle.com/datasets/ziya07/student-engagement-dataset-using-eeg.
13. https://www.kaggle.com/datasets/programmer3/multimodal-cognitive-load-classification-dataset.
14. https://www.kaggle.com/datasets/aimenjaved1/neurosky-mindwaveeeg-device-dataset.
15. Gupta, S., Kumar, P., Tekchandani, R., A machine learning-based decision support system for temporal human cognitive state estimation during online education using wearable physiological monitoring devices. *Decis. Anal. J.*, 8, 1002805, 2023, https://doi.org/10.1016/j.dajour.2023.100280.
16. Ajayi, I.H. and Avksentyeva, E., Machine Learning Methods for Predicting Cognitive Load in eLearning Environments using Eye Tracking Data, *Pak. J. Life Soc. Sci., 22*, 2, 19926–19937, 2024. https://doi.org/10.57239/PJLSS-2024-22.2.001458.
17. Predicting cognitive load in immersive driving scenarios with a hybrid CNN-RNN model, https://doi.org/10.48550/arXiv.2408.06350.
18. Wang, Q., *et al.*, Characterisation of cognitive load using machine learning classifiers of electroencephalogram data. *Sensors*, 23, 20, 8528, 2023, https://doi.org/10.3390/s23208528.

17

NLP-Based Gamification Approaches for Personalized Mental Wellness Support

Samir Sahu[1]*, Trapty Agarwal[2], Sanjeev Kumar Mandal[3], Deepthi S.[4] and Tapasmini Sahoo[5]

[1]*Department of General Medicine, IMS and SUM Hospital, Siksha 'O' Anusandhan (Deemed to be University), Bhubaneswar, Odisha, India*
[2]*Maharishi School of Engineering and Technology, Maharishi University of Information Technology, Uttar Pradesh, India*
[3]*Department of CSIT, Jain (Deemed-to-be University), Bangalore, Karnataka, India*
[4]*Department of Computer Science & Engineering, Presidency University, Bengaluru, Karnataka, India*
[5]*Department of Electronics and Communication Engineering, Siksha 'O' Anusandhan (Deemed to be University), Bhubaneswar, Odisha, India*

Abstract

The individualized features of gamified apps utilize psychological theories combined with advanced artificial intelligence (AI) technologies to develop long-term wellness. Sentiment analysis functions with emotion identification and conversational AI as important natural language processing (NLP) techniques needed to create personalized interventions for individual needs. The retention of user interaction relies on gamified systems through three strategies, including adaptive content delivery with progress metrics and reward structures. User engagement maintenance, along with avoidance of simplification, proper data ethics management and screen time resolution, remain unresolved challenges. This chapter investigates the implementation of gamification in mental health and healthcare to improve both patient engagement and constructive behavioral change and

**Corresponding author*: samirsahu@soa.ac.in; ORCID: 0000-0002-5610-0380
Trapty Agarwal: ORCID: 0009-0007-4081-4999
Sanjeev Kumar Mandal: ORCID: 0000-0002-5562-2486
Deepthi S.: ORCID: 0009-0008-4679-2273
Tapasmini Sahoo: ORCID: 0000-0002-9431-0848

Sudesh Yadav, Pethuru Raj, Satya Prakash Yadav and Victor Hugo C. de Albuquerque (eds.) Natural Language Processing in Mental Health Care: Methodologies and Clinical Practice, (251–268) © 2026 Scrivener Publishing LLC

therapeutic intervention effectiveness. It promotes interdisciplinarity along with adaptive systems as crucial elements for developing responsible gamified health solutions that achieve success.

***Keywords*:** Gamification, mental health interventions, personalized wellness support, natural language processing, AI-powered healthcare, user engagement

17.1 Introduction

The global rise in mental health disorders coincides with society's growing acceptance of technological treatment solutions. An effective mental wellness assistance system emerges when Natural Language Processing (NLP) technology unites with gamification functions. Modern mental health solutions present operational obstacles because of restricted access and associated high costs in addition to weak public reception [1]. Mental health care accessibility and personalization improve with the implementation of digital systems containing sentiment analysis features together with Artificial Intelligence (AI)-powered conversational agents and interactive gamified elements. Through its subfield, AI enables computers to handle human language, therefore empowering mental health solution development. When game-related elements are applied to non-gaming settings, it enhances user involvement and engagement within mental health programs [2]. Mental health treatments gain immersive power and promote enduring engagement through gamification through incentive systems combined with goal-setting tools and interactive challenges and progress tracking. The systematic approach of gamification helps achieve lasting behavioral change because traditional mental health treatments sometimes fail to connect their methods effectively. Personalized engagement, behavior tracking, social interaction, adaptive challenges, progress tracking, and therapeutic feedback are just a few of the gamification features that are utilized to improve mental health interventions, as depicted in Figure 17.1.

The evaluation of text combined with voice data together with nonverbal communication provides NLP with its foremost benefit for mental health applications. Sentiment analysis through NLP technology detects incremental emotional changes in user-submitted written and spoken content, which enables computers to interact with emotional intelligence in real time [3]. Virtual assistants with AI capabilities recommend self-help solutions and mindfulness practices or therapy interactions to users through their understanding of emotional patterns. Through NLP systems, users can receive individualized coping methods because NLP tracks their written and spoken responses throughout time. NLP algorithms detect regular

Figure 17.1 Key dimensions of gamification for mental health support. Source: https://fastercapital.com/content/Behavioral-health-gamification-Level-Up-Your-Mental-Health--How-Gamification-Can-Improve-Well-Being.html.

patterns of mood and stress patterns and mental procedures, which enable them to deliver personalized self-care recommendations that include various techniques, like breathing exercises CBT tools and meditation content [4]. The degree of individual adaptation enhances user commitment and delivers mobile mental health solutions that address personal requirements specifically. Through NLP-based systems, users can detect behavioral patterns that enable them to identify the initial indications of mental health deterioration. Machine tools that analyze linguistic indicators track warning signals of mental health problems through the evaluation of voices for tone and emotional expressions and selected words [5]. Timely detection provides the necessary opportunity to provide swift interventions, thus stopping mental health conditions from advancing. The NLP algorithms enable both users and virtual therapists to carry out meaningful dialogues through teletherapy and virtual counseling by delivering psychological assistance and human-like communication.

The gamification elements guide users to maintain their active involvement leading to an enhanced user experience. NLP-based mental health systems become more appealing to users when they include gamification elements such as interactive storytelling along with mood-based challenges and rewards and personalized goal-setting and community engagement. Users who participate in adaptive goal setting maintain their focus while NLP enables them to build individual wellness objectives such as stress reduction and mindfulness [6]. The usage of NLP supplements specific feedback with motivational implementations that include leaderboards combined with badges and point-based rewards to maintain user commitment. The dynamic aspects of interactive narratives guide players in learning coping skills because their emotional responses trigger specific interactions. Sentiment analysis uses emotional state identification to adjust user tasks, which helps users find stress reduction methods. The digital community space that NLP supports develops a sense of emotional connection through conversation maintenance and pleasant space preservation [7]. Figure 17.2 highlights a consistent increase in research and development while demonstrating the growing use of NLP, gamification, chatbots, AI-powered support, and emotion analysis in mental health apps.

The virtual wellness networks support peer connections and team-based challenges through gamified features, which provide supportive networks to reduce feelings of loneliness. The social features of these platforms combine mood-sharing boards with group mindfulness activities, which support mental health for users. The continued existence of algorithmic prejudice alongside data privacy concerns and AI reliance demonstrates a requirement for ethical standards with human supervision in AI systems. The proper alignment of technological advancement with ethical matters remains vital for the delivery of efficient mental healthcare because NLP and gamification solutions continue to develop [8]. AI and multimodal data processing and adaptive learning algorithm development will result in better NLP-based gamified mental wellness systems, which will become more accessible and personalized while improving user-friendliness.

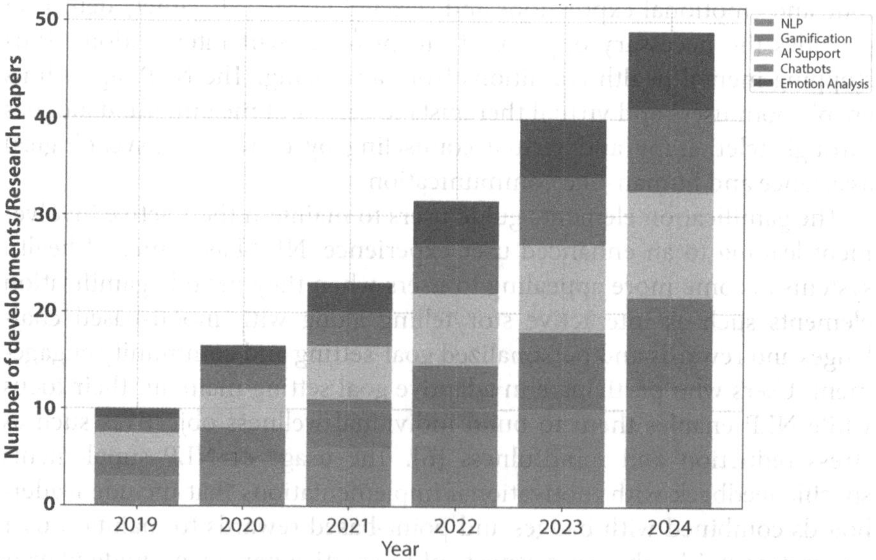

Figure 17.2 Growth of AI, gamification, and NLP in supporting mental health. Source: Own elaboration.

The purpose of this chapter is to explore the application of gamification in mental health and healthcare, examining how it may enhance therapeutic interventions, promote positive behavioral change, and increase patient involvement. The challenges of sustaining user interest, mitigating the risks of oversimplification, and ensuring ethical data processing are also covered. In order to maximize the long-term effectiveness of gamified health solutions, the chapter also highlights the need for adaptable, user-focused tactics.

17.2 Psychological Principles and Theoretical Frameworks

The combination of gamification strategies among various medical fields and age groups produces multiple important psychological findings. Gamification relies on game mechanics to motivate people through internal drives and engage participants because this method combines principles from learning and developmental psychology and motivational theories to achieve positive health outcomes. Due to children and young people's inherent fascination with playing games, it develops gamification systems that promote better mental health treatment adherence and mental fortitude growth [9]. The platform uses psychological development models to include success elements and rewards that give people at younger ages for achieving self-care in mental health through gamified programs. In addition to making therapeutic activities more appealing, this strategy strengthens the psychological requirements for competence and autonomy, which are essential components for the development of resilience in young people [10]. In geriatric psychology, gamification is utilized to improve the social interaction and cognitive function of older adults. Adults can improve their quality of life by combating mental decline and social isolation with activity-based solutions that incorporate gaming elements.

In addition to exploring gamification principles in each specific example, it is essential to recognize the variations and limitations within the existing body of research. Many of the examples in the current literature, especially those about the mental health of children and adolescents, are essentially games, even if gamification entails incorporating game aspects into real-life contexts to improve experiences and outcomes. Although these games offer transferable information and abilities, they don't fully implement the gamification concepts as they are defined [11]. Overall, gamification is a revolutionary approach to healthcare that combines interactive technology and psychological theories to encourage behavior change, improve therapeutic results, and boost the well-being of people of all ages.

17.3 NLP Methods for Personalized Mental Health

Text or voice-based human language can be understood by an NLP module. With roots in linguistics, NLP has been around for more than 50 years. Numerous industries, including business, search engines, healthcare, finance, and marketing, can benefit from its innumerable real-world applications. NLP uses AI to process natural language input (such as English), translate it into a machine-understandable language, and then produce natural language output. Data preprocessing is the first step in a NLP system, which then uses the data to create algorithms. The first stage in creating models is text pre-processing. The procedure entails correctly cleaning and preparing the data so that the machine can analyze it and provide a clear result based on the data processing [12].

This section evaluates multiple NLP methods that support individual mental wellness needs. Text Summarization (TS) supports therapists as it shortens discussions for better oversight, while Sentiment Analysis (SA) together with Emotion Detection (ED) enables the analysis of user emotions. Real-time support and therapeutic interventions through conversational AI are delivered to users by chatbots. Named Entity Recognition (NER) extracts pivotal information that professionals use to generate custom-made recommendations [13]. Speech-to-Text (STT) and Voice Emotion Recognition (VER) systems evaluate vocal signs to detect emotional distress so they can provide quick help. The popularity of sentiment analysis, text summarization, and chatbots is highlighted in Figure 17.3 which shows the number of research publications spanning different NLP approaches used in mental health support.

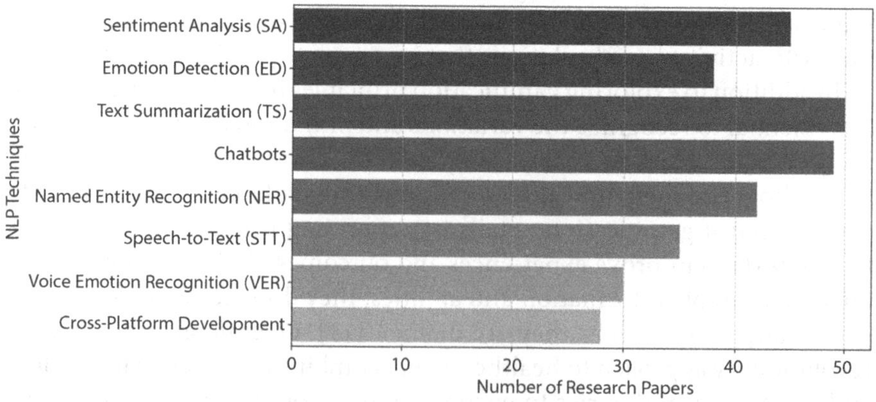

Figure 17.3 NLP techniques in mental health support. Source: Own elaboration.

Sentiment Analysis (SA)

By analyzing emotional tones, the system classifies user responses into three categories: neutral, negative, and positive. Subtle emotional cues are identified for appropriate mental health responses through the use of sophisticated models such as Long Short-Term Memory (LSTM) and Bidirectional Encoder Representations from Transformers (BERT). Sentiment scores provide crucial information for feedback and support by assisting therapists and self-help applications in tracking users' emotional changes over time [14]. The module's primary operating role is to determine the user's emotional state.

SA helps data analysts in big businesses track brand and product notoriety, estimate public opinion, conduct more in-depth market research, and comprehend client experiences. Sentiment analysis is a tool that business organizations can use to analyze direct connections with customers, including emails, chatbot engagements, phone calls, and other exchanges [15]. Text analysis is started to examine the text in the talks by fusing AI and ML. It extracts the text's emotional meaning and context. SA comes in many forms, including aspect-based analysis, fine-grained analysis, intent analysis, graded analysis, and emotion detection analysis. Many texts can be swiftly and automatically identified and examined with the use of sentiment analysis techniques. For instance, because tweets usually contain links, emoticons, and hashtags, it can be challenging for a computer to understand the message being conveyed.

Emotion Detection (ED)

By identifying particular emotions like happiness, sadness, rage, or worry, ED surpasses simple sentiment analysis. Applications can assess text for emotional context by using lexicon-based methods and transformer-based models. This enables sympathetic responses from chatbots and virtual therapists, providing tailored coping strategies or therapeutic activities.

Text Summarization (TS)

In applications related to mental health, TS uses extractive or abstractive approaches to distill long talks into summaries. This makes it easier for therapists to swiftly go over exchanges, spot emotional trends, and track clients' development over time. Maintaining thorough manageable patient records for efficient treatment is another benefit of using summarized content.

Chatbots: Conversational Agents for Mental Health

WOEBOT and Flutter are two examples of mental health chatbots that use NLP to mimic human discussions through sentiment analysis, intent detection, and contextual comprehension. It offers activity from cognitive behavioral therapy (CBT), suggests coping mechanisms, and offers immediate emotional support. Chatbots provide a consistent and encouraging user experience by tailoring responses according to past exchanges.

Through text or voice conversations, a computer program or piece of software called a chatbot mimics human communication. When it comes to AI, people typically think about large systems and intricate architecture; however, the most potent AI is the simplest chatbot. Any system's first focus is user conversations, which must be straightforward, slick, dynamic, and as accurate as possible [5]. Chatbots could assist in achieving these goals with ease. In the past, utilizing a search tool or filling out a form were the only ways to ask a software program to answer a question. The majority of users began using virtual agents to finish simple business-to-business (B2B) and business-to-consumer (B2C) tasks. The path of a chatbot's processing, including receiving user input, analyzing text using NLP, identifying intent, creating responses, and delivering output for interactive communication, is depicted in Figure 17.4.

Virtual assistants used to be text-based and programmed to reply to a limited set of queries with pre-written answers. The developers failed when faced with a challenging question or one they had not even foreseen. The interactive question-answering session showed good performance if it has been trained on the data before. As rule-based approaches and NLP were

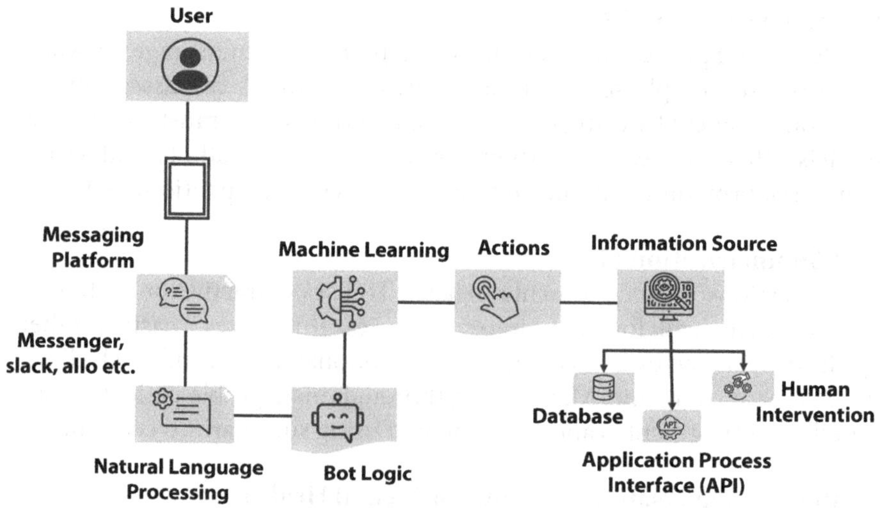

Figure 17.4 Chatbot's processing flow. Source: https://itchronicles.com/artificial-intelligence/the-rise-of-chatbots/.

added over time, it began to behave more like real conversations. These days, chatbots employ several cutting-edge tools and methods to determine the user's needs throughout a conversation. To create ever-more-detailed databases of queries and responses, these technologies mainly rely on ML and DL, two aspects of AI with minor variances.

WOEBOT: An AI-Powered Chatbot for Psychotherapy to Support Mental Health

WOEBOT, a chatbot for psychotherapy, helps users monitor their emotions and gain a better understanding of themselves [16]. It was established in 2017 by a group of AI experts and psychologists from Stanford. WOEBOT asks its users how they are starting to feel and how their lives are doing (maximum) in brief daily chats that last no more than ten minutes. This is achieved by combining psychological expertise, especially in Cognitive Behavioral Therapy, thoughtful writing, a good sense of humor, and NLP. It starts to remember previous exchanges to refine its inquiries and answers after storing all text and emojis. By keeping track of its users' desires and emotions and, when appropriate, providing films and other useful resources *via* chat, the bot promotes mental health.

Developing Flutter-Based Cross-Platform Mental Wellness Applications

An open-source framework called Flutter could be used to create stunning and high-quality apps that work on all cross-platforms, including Windows, iOS, and Android. It was written in the Dart programming language and produced by Google. One code base can be used to operate it. To construct an application that runs on all operating systems, it should write code in two distinct languages and two separate frameworks. Flutter, which is compatible with several platforms including the web, Android, and iOS, is the solution to this problem, as it needs to find a framework that accomplishes the work. Its straightforward and quick technology makes it simple to create applications with beautiful user interfaces. Additionally, Flutter offers a range of pre-made widgets for creating applications. Flutter's features include: The Widget is essentially part of Flutter's core idea. In essence, widgets are User Interface (UI) components that are utilized to create the application's user interface. Flutter has two widgets, the Stateful and Stateless widgets that facilitate state maintenance [17]. The functions, applications, often employed tools with their complete forms, and main advantages in improving mental wellness interventions are highlighted in Table 17.1, which defines the many NLP techniques utilized for individualized mental health support.

Table 17.1 The use of NLP techniques in personalized mental health sport.

NLP method	Primary function	Examples/tools	Key benefits
Sentiment Analysis (SA)	Classifies user emotions (positive, negative, neutral)	LSTM, Bidirectional Encoder Representations from Transformers(BERT), Valence Aware Dictionary and Sentiment Reasoner(VADER), TextBlob	Emotional trend monitoring, timely interventions
Emotion Detection (ED)	Identifies specific emotions like happiness, sadness, anger	Robustly Optimized BERT Pretraining Approach(Roberta), Distilled BERT (DistilBERT), Lexicon-based Models	Enhanced emotional support, personalized coping suggestions
Text Summarization (TS)	Generates summaries of conversations	BART (Bidirectional and Auto-Regressive Transformers), T5 (Text-To-Text Transfer Transformer), GPT (Generative Pre-trained Transformer)	Efficient therapist analysis, reduced data review time
Chatbots	Provides conversational support and therapeutic interventions	WOEBOT (AI-powered CBT Chatbot), Replika (AI Companion Chatbot), Wysa (AI Mental Health Chatbot)	Accessible, cost-effective therapy, immediate support
Named Entity Recognition (NER)	Extracts key information from text	SpaCy (Industrial-Strength NLP Library), Natural Language Toolkit (NLTK), Stanford Named Entity Recognizer (Stanford NER)	Accurate information extraction for personalized care

(Continued)

Table 17.1 The use of NLP techniques in personalized mental health sport. (*Continued*)

NLP method	Primary function	Examples/tools	Key benefits
Speech-to-Text (STT)	Converts speech to text	Google Speech-to-Text (Google STT), Microsoft Azure Speech-to-Text (Azure STT)	Increased accessibility, real-time voice analysis
Voice Emotion Recognition (VER)	Detects emotions through vocal cues	Wave to Vector (Wav2Vec), Multimodal EmotionLines Dataset (MELD), Mozilla DeepSpeech(DeepSpeech)	Enhanced emotional detection, improved voice-based therapy
Cross-Platform Development	Builds applications for various platforms	Flutter (Google's UI Toolkit), React Native (Meta's Open-Source Framework)	Cost-effective development, uniform user experience

Source: Own elaboration.

17.4 Techniques for Gamification to Increase User Engagement

Predictive modeling, data-driven customization, and real-time adaptation are a few advantages that AI offers gamification. A major step forward in producing user experiences that are more captivating and engaging is the integration of AI into gamification. ML-based personalization, predictive analytics, and nm adaptive game mechanics are important AI techniques in gamification. To provide a customized experience; ML algorithms examine user data, including performance, preferences, and activity patterns [18]. Through the use of AI technology, the amount of difficulty, challenges, and incentives can be adjusted respectively to maximize user engagement either by profile-based grouping or reinforcement learning models. System users maintain their motivation through the essential need for customization. AI-learning platforms use user performance data alongside behavioral markers to change question difficulty, which results in maintaining users at their optimal challenge level. An adaptable system models gamification flow by matching game difficulty to user ability levels. Models that use predictive analysis estimate user actions through examination of past behaviors. The technology of AI investigates potential user disengagement to launch specific treatment procedures including reminders and bonus prizes. The predictive algorithms use neural networks and Markov chains together with regression analysis to function. The prevention of user disengagement remains the most efficient approach for maintaining continuous audience engagement. The historical behavior data of users allows a fitness app to predict a forthcoming decrease in user activity [19]. The system can then use limited-time gamified badges as rewards while seeking to continue user engagement. The predictive retention method significantly improves user loyalty to health-related software.

The implementation of adaptive mechanics is enabled by AI in a real-time fashion. The system uses adaptive mechanics, which enhance participation by providing functional reinforcements for positive behavioral outcomes that improved after learning occurs through reinforcement learning. When users demonstrate signs of disengagement, AI systems could both streamline the tasks and extend rewards as two different ways to maintain user interest. Through real-time adjustments, the gamification system adapts to all user skills and provides rewarding yet challenging gameplay because of its feature modifications [20]. User performance data enables AI systems to adjust tip frequency in tutorial games to provide simpler tasks for novices as well as harder challenges for experienced players. The adaptive strategy delivers engaging gameplay across various categories of users to enhance their learning success.

AI-driven gamification's mathematical model

Several mathematical models can be used to organize and enhance AI-driven gamification elements, including user engagement, progression, and adaptive incentives. These frameworks offer a structure for putting individualized and captivating gamification experiences into practice [21]. It introduces several important models and Equations are given below.

Dynamic reward system: By determining the optimal reward frequency and value and adjusting according to user engagement and difficulty, AI models can optimize reward distribution. Reward Frequency is an exponential function that illustrates a system that encourages prolonged participation by increasing reward intervals as users interact more and it is presented in Equation (17.1):

$$Q(s) = Q_o . f^{\alpha s} \quad (17.1)$$

Where, at time s, rewards are represented by $Q(s)$, the starting reward frequency is Q_o, α modifies the incentive scaling according to engagement data.

Diminishing Rewards: Diminishing returns can be used to gradually lower reward value to avoid over-rewarding, as presented in Equation (17.2).

$$U(m) = \frac{U_0}{1+\beta m} \tag{17.2}$$

After m interactions, the reward value is represented by $U(m)$. The initial reward value is U_0. The rate of diminishing returns is adjusted by β.

Adaptive Development and Scaling Difficulties: Models that match task difficulty to user skill level are advantageous for progression systems because they produce an experience that is neither too simple nor too demanding. The logistic advancement model allows for adaptive advancement by modifying task complexity in response to user performance, as shown in Equation (17.3).

$$C(w) = \frac{C_{max}}{1+f^{-\gamma(w-w_0)}} \tag{17.3}$$

$C(w)$ is the level of difficulty (w). The highest level of difficulty is denoted by C_{max}. The rate of advancement is controlled by γ. The basic skill level is w_0. Equation (17.4) can be used to maintain a linear relationship between task difficulty C_{max} and skill level $t(w)$, which will keep users in an ideal flow state.

$$D(w) = t(w) + l \tag{17.4}$$

The challenge level at user skill w is denoted by $D(w)$. The user skill level is represented by $t(w)$. A constant that keeps things in equilibrium is l.

Model for Predictive Engagement and Retention: Retention probability $O(s)$ is calculated using a logistic regression model as a function of time s, engagement variables F, and incentive factors Q (Refer Equation (17.5)).

Table 17.2 AI-powered gamification strategies for enhancing user engagement.

Techniques	Purpose	AI methods/ models used	Key benefits
Predictive modeling	Forecasts user behavior and detects disengagement	Neural networks, Markov chains, regression analysis	Proactive interventions to retain users
Personalized adaptive challenges	Adjusts task difficulty based on user performance	Reinforcement learning, adaptive algorithms	Maintains user in the "flow zone" for sustained engagement
Dynamic reward system	Provides optimal reward frequency and value based on interaction	Exponential functions, Engagement-based scaling	Encourages long-term participation
Diminishing rewards	Prevents over-rewarding by gradually reducing reward value	Diminishing return models	Balances reward distribution and user motivation
Engagement decay management	Tracks and counteracts declining user engagement	Exponential decay Functions	Mitigates user dropout through adaptive re-engagement
Retention prediction	Estimates the likelihood of user retention	Logistic regression	Enables timely incentives to prevent user churn
Real-time adaptation	Adjusts feedback, rewards, and challenges in real-time	Reinforcement learning, adaptive AI models	Ensures a personalized and engaging experience
Flow state management	Maintains optimal challenge level to match user skills	Logistic progression models	Prevents frustration or boredom, maximizing user satisfaction

Source: Own elaboration.

$$O(s) = \frac{1}{1 + f^{-(bF + cQ - c)}} \quad (17.5)$$

The coefficients b and a stand for engagement and reward impact, while d represents a threshold value. Engagement Decay, it is over time, engagement frequently deteriorates. This drop is modeled by an exponential decay function, and Equation (17.6) describes how AI modifies engagement parameters in response.

$$F(s) = F_0 . f^{-\lambda s} \quad (17.6)$$

Engagement at time s is denoted by $F(s)$, initial engagement by F_0, and decay constant by λ. The implementation of AI-driven gamification systems that adjust to the requirements and actions of specific users is made possible by these mathematical models [22]. Developers could produce more successful and captivating gamified experiences that sustain user attention over time by utilizing these concepts. Table 17.2 highlights certain AI-powered gamification strategies that improve user engagement through behavior prediction, challenge personalization, reward management, and real-time experience adaptation, which contribute to long-term user happiness and retention.

17.5 Applicants and Difficulties for Gamified Health Interventions

Within mental and general health psychological services, gamification has proven to be a successful and flexible method for improving health metrics among patients in various treatment settings. As technology advances and psychological understanding deepens, the field of health psychology has even more revolutionary power to propel its further growth. Issues with user retention and medical conditions that could be oversimplified by the technology continue to hinder the development of gamification strategies for health psychology [23]. Future analysis must create sophisticated gamified platforms that offer comprehensive medical intervention value along with prolonged user involvement. When users must provide the system with their confidential medical information, gamification of health applications creates ethical dilemmas and significant privacy concerns. User security necessitates compliance with international data protection laws in order to preserve confidentiality. To reduce safety risks in gamified health programs, strategies that include frequent computer screen breaks and social face-to-face connection are required [24, 25]. As gamification is further developed, research is necessary to maximize its moral practices and demonstrate its effectiveness and long-term health advantages.

AI disclosure statement: The author confirms that no artificial intelligence (AI)-generated content or AI-assisted writing tools were used in the preparation of this chapter (including summaries and the abstract). All text, analysis, and conclusions are the result of the author's original work.

17.6 Conclusion

The implementation necessitates interdisciplinary collaboration between psychologists, healthcare professionals, and technology developers in order to handle ethical data, streamline health interventions, address engagement and retention difficulties, and address screen time concerns. This chapter examined how gamification improves interactions with patients, helps change behavior, and makes it easier to use therapeutic interventions for mental health care. The advancement of AI-driven NLP tools, such as sentiment analysis and emotion detection, as well as conversational AI, has made it possible to provide more accessible, personalized mental wellness solutions. For gamified mental health interventions to be implemented successfully and maintain morality and long-term efficacy, evidence-based design, user feedback integration, and adaptive learning mechanisms are required. Three main shortcomings are highlighted in this section: problems with user retention, simplistic depictions of mental illnesses, and moral dilemmas around data collection privacy. Modifiable gamified platforms that offer individualized feedback throughout sessions will be the focus of future study. The research that was needed to assess the long-term mental health outcomes required a method that examined changes over time.

References

1. Jesuthasan, J., Low, M., Ong, T., The impact of personalized human support on engagement with behavioral intervention technologies for employee

mental health: an exploratory retrospective study. *Front. Digit. Health*, 4, 8463755, 2022, https://doi.org/10.3389/fdgth.2022.846375.

2. Alslaity, A., *et al.*, Personalized Persuasive Technologies in Health and Wellness: From Theory to Practice, in: *A Human-Centered Perspective of Intelligent Personalized Environments and Systems*, pp. 261–292, Springer Nature Switzerland, Cham, 2024, https://doi.org/10.1007/978-3-031-55109-3_10.
3. Shi, L., Li, X., Win, K.T., Investigating mobile persuasive design for mental wellness: A cross-domain analysis. *Int. J. Med. Inf.*, 185, 105353, 2024, https://doi.org/10.1016/j.ijmedinf.2024.105353.
4. Weng, J.H., *et al.*, Mental wellness self-care in Singapore with mindline. sg: A tutorial on the development of a digital mental health platform for behavior change. *J. Med. Internet Res.*, 26, e444435, 2024, https://doi.org/10.2196/44443.
5. Kazi, F.F. and Sandbulte, J., Examining a social-based system with personalized recommendations to promote mental health for college students. *Smart Health*, 28, 1003855, 2023, https://doi.org/10.1016/j.smhl.2023.100385.
6. Alqahtani, F., Winn, A., Orji, R., Co-designing a mobile app to improve mental health and well-being: focus group study. *JMIR Form. Res.*, 5, 2, e18172, 2021, https://doi.org/10.2196/18172.
7. Chaturvedi, A., *et al.*, Content recommendation systems in web-based mental health care: real-world application and formative evaluation. *JMIR Form. Res.*, 7, 1, e38831, 2023, https://doi.org/10.2196/38831.
8. Valentine, L., D'Alfonso, S., Lederman, R., Recommender systems for mental health apps: advantages and ethical challenges. *AI Soc.*, 38, 4, 1627–1638, 2023, https://doi.org/10.1007/s00146-021-01322-w.
9. Turner, R.J., *et al.*, Information extraction from free text for aiding transdiagnostic psychiatry: Constructing NLP pipelines tailored to clinicians' needs. *BMC Psychiatry*, 22, 1, 407, 2022, https://doi.org/10.1186/s12888-022-04058-z.
10. Gil-Aciron, L.A., The gamer psychology: a psychological perspective on game design and gamification. *Interact. Learn. Environ.*, 32, 1, 183–207, 2024, https://doi.org/10.1080/10494820.2022.2082489.
11. Xu, J., *et al.*, How gamification drives consumer citizenship behavior: The role of perceived gamification affordances. *Int. J. Inf. Manage.*, 64, 1024775, 2022, https://doi.org/10.1016/j.ijinfomgt.2022.102477.
12. Behl, A., *et al.*, Gamification and neuromarketing: A unified approach for improving user experience. *J. Consum. Behav.*, 23, 1, 218–228, 2024, https://doi.org/10.1002/cb.2178.
13. Cheng, C. and V. Ebrahimi, O., Gamification: A novel approach to mental health promotion. *Curr. Psychiatry Rep.*, 25, 11, 577–586, 2023, https://doi.org/10.1007/s11920-023-01453-5.
14. Pérez-Jorge, D., *et al.*, The relationship between gamified physical exercise and mental health in adolescence: An example of open innovation in gamified learning. *Healthcare*, 12, 2, 124, MDPI, 2024, https://doi.org/10.3390/healthcare12020124.

15. Kishimoto, T., *et al.*, Understanding psychiatric illness through natural language processing (UNDERPIN): Rationale, design, and methodology. *Front. Psychiatry*, 13, 9547035, 2022, https://doi.org/10.3389/fpsyt.2022.954703.
16. Ahmed, U., *et al.*, EANDC: An explainable attention network-based deep adaptive clustering model for mental health treatment. *Future Gener. Comput. Syst.*, 130, 106–1135, 2022, https://doi.org/10.1016/j.future.2021.12.008.
17. Spruit, M., *et al.*, Exploring language markers of mental health in psychiatric stories. *Appl. Sci.*, 12, 4, 2179, 2022, https://doi.org/10.3390/app12042179.
18. González-González, C.S., *et al.*, Personalized gamification for learning: A reactive chatbot architecture proposal. *Sensors*, 23, 1, 545, 2023, https://doi.org/10.3390/s23010545.
19. Jelassi, M., *et al.*, Enhancing Personalized Mental Health Support through Artificial Intelligence: Advances in Speech and Text Analysis within Online Therapy Platforms. *Information*, 15, 12, 813, 2024, https://doi.org/10.3390/info15120813.
20. Oyebode, O., *et al.*, Machine learning techniques in adaptive and personalized systems for health and wellness. *Int. J. Hum.-Comput. Interact.*, 39, 9, 1938–1962, 2023, https://doi.org/10.1080/10447318.2022.2089085.
21. Rathnayaka, P., *et al.*, A mental health chatbot with cognitive skills for personalized behavioral activation and remote health monitoring. *Sensors*, 22, 10, 3653, 2022, https://doi.org/10.3390/s22103653.
22. Qi, X., Sun, G., Yue, L., Applying self-optimized feedback to a learning management system for facilitating personalized learning activities on massive open online courses. *Sustainability*, 15, 16, 12562, 2023, https://doi.org/10.3390/su151612562.
23. Zhu, Z., Maternal mental health monitoring in an online community: a natural language processing approach. *Behav. Inf. Technol.*, 44, 10, 1–10, 2024, https://doi.org/10.1080/0144929X.2024.2333927.
24. Zhang, L., *et al.*, How to improve user engagement and retention in mobile payment: a gamification affordance perspective. *Decis. Support Syst.*, 168, 1139415, 2023, https://doi.org/10.1016/j.dss.2023.113941.
25. Fadzillah, NH.H., *et al.*, Comparing the effects of gamification to user engagement in stress management application. *J. Adv. Res. Appl. Sci. Eng. Technol.*, 30, 1, 290–302, 2023, https://doi.org/10.37934/araset.30.1.290302.

18

Context-Aware NLP for Early Detection of Cognitive and Emotional Distress

Chandan Das[1]*, Awakash Mishra[2], Preethi D.[3] and Mohammed Mujeerulla[4]

[1]*Department of General Medicine, IMS and SUM Hospital, Siksha 'O' Anusandhan (Deemed to be University), Bhubaneswar, Odisha, India*
[2]*Maharishi School of Engineering and Technology, Maharishi University of Information Technology, Uttar Pradesh, India*
[3]*Department of CSIT, Jain (Deemed-to-be University), Bangalore, Karnataka, India*
[4]*Department of Computer Science & Engineering, Presidency University, Bengaluru, Karnataka, India*

Abstract

Cognitive and emotional distress can significantly impact mental well-being, making early detection crucial for timely intervention. Traditional diagnostic methods primarily rely on self-reported data or clinical evaluations, which can be subjective, inconsistent, and delayed, limiting their effectiveness. This chapter aims to develop a context-aware natural language processing (NLP) model to identify early signs of cognitive and emotional distress using textual data. A dataset was collected from Kaggle, consisting of user-generated content related to mental health concerns. Various machine learning (ML) and deep learning (DL) techniques, including sentiment analysis, were employed to classify distress levels accurately. The results demonstrated that DL models outperformed traditional ML approaches in detecting distress patterns, highlighting their superior ability to capture contextual and linguistic nuances. These findings emphasize the potential of context-aware NLP in mental health assessment, providing an efficient and scalable solution for early detection. By leveraging AI-driven insights, this approach can enhance intervention strategies, assisting mental health professionals in

**Corresponding author*: chandandas@soa.ac.in; ORCID: 0000-0001-7696-1770
Awakash Mishra: ORCID: 0009-0002-5447-7499
Preethi D.: ORCID: 0009-0007-4135-2140
Mohammed Mujeerulla: ORCID: 0000-0003-2615-8888

Sudesh Yadav, Pethuru Raj, Satya Prakash Yadav and Victor Hugo C. de Albuquerque (eds.) Natural Language Processing in Mental Health Care: Methodologies and Clinical Practice, (269–284) © 2026 Scrivener Publishing LLC

identifying individuals experiencing distress at an early stage and enabling timely psychological support and care.

Keywords: Natural language processing, machine learning, mental health assessment, deep learning

18.1 Introduction

The integration of natural language processing (NLP) in healthcare has opened new avenues for early detection of cognitive and emotional distress, offering insights into individuals' mental states through linguistic patterns [1]. Context-aware NLP involves the use of semantic, syntactic, and contextual data, which aid in the precise identification of distress and the use of speech, text, and behavioral signals in real time. In particular, this approach has been useful for detecting the initial symptoms of depression, anxiety, or cognitive decline and enhancing mental health outcomes [2]. Consequently, the improvement in the performance and capabilities of deep learning (DL) and transformer architectures has greatly boosted the efficiency of NLP. These models involve processing massive amount of data, including sentiment, tone, and other minor shifts associated with psychological conditions or phases. In addition, there is a better understanding of the context with the help of multimodal NLP, including speech, facial expressions, and physiological markers, which help to assess the level of, distress more effectively [3]. However, some limitations pose significant challenges to the use of context-aware NLP in distress detection. One of the major issues is that it requires relatively large high-quality datasets for training. Most datasets are imbalanced and this consequently results in promoting bias in the detection model, especially concerning cultural and linguistic diversity [4]. Privacy and moral concerns present challenges, particularly in the collection of sensitive mental health data, where data privacy and user consent are essential [5]. A key challenge is the lack of interpretability in DL models. While these models achieve high accuracy, their decision-making processes remain opaque, making it difficult for clinicians to trust and validate predictions. Real-world implementation also poses a challenge since different people have different language usage, ways of speaking, and even methods of communication [6]. However, although the use of real-time distress detection is highly valuable, it can pose technical issues with integration into existing healthcare systems, which cannot be possible at times. Evolving language patterns and the dynamic psychological indicators further complicate the need for continuous model updates. To overcome such limitations, it is imperative to ensure reliability, fairness, and moral use of context-aware NLP in mental health applications [7]. This chapter aims to develop a context-based NLP model that can predict early signs of stress in the human mind based on textual data. The model seeks to enhance the accuracy and timeliness of mental health assessment by making use of ML and DL paradigms.

18.2 Methodology

Using various kinds of machine learning (ML) and DL approaches, including sentiment analysis, a dataset of user-generated content pertaining to mental health was taken from Kaggle and analyzed to precisely categorize distress levels. It evaluates the emotional and cognitive discomfort recognition after completing training.

18.2.1 Dataset

In this research, three datasets were evaluated: The Emotion Dataset acquired from Kaggle [8] contains labeled emotions in text data, which helps in analyzing diverse emotions. Another dataset was the Emotion Detection from Text Dataset [9], which provided textual data that has been marked with certain emotions to ease the analysis of the sentiment of the text for the discussion of such topics as mental health. Furthermore, the NLP Mental Health Conversations Dataset [10] was included to consider stress, depression, and other psychological aspects of the users. These datasets are highly beneficial in detecting emotions and behaviors to enable DL in the assessment of the patient's mental health.

18.2.2 Data Preparation

It involved the text preprocessing, including tokenization, stop word removal and lemmatization for the textual data that will be used for the analysis. For the supervised learning processes, sentiments and separated emotional categories were assigned to the data. Feature extraction was performed using TF-IDF and word embeddings, which allow the capturing of the contexts of features such as Word2Vec. The collected data was later split for the creation of training and test data samples for the models.

18.2.3 Early Detection Models for Emotional Distress

To examine textual data and identify distress patterns, early detection methods for emotional distress use cutting-edge machine learning and deep learning approaches. Techniques like Multi-Domain Network (MDNet), residual network with 50 layers (ResNet-50), support vector machine (SVM), random forest (RF), multilayer perceptron (MLP), and gated recurrent unit (GRU) improve classification accuracy by encoding contextual data and intricate emotional signals.

18.2.4 Multi-Domain Network

The primary learning module for feature extraction in a context-aware NLP framework intended to identify emotional and cognitive discomfort is the MDNet [11] model. Advances in DL, especially in natural language processing, make it possible to analyze textual material effectively and spot patterns of distress. There are several layers in the architecture and each of them retrieves higher-level language characteristics. Image convolution layers achieve feature maps by sliding small kernels over textual input to determine local patterns, such as word dependencies, context relation, and others. Some of the pooling layers that are used include average and max pooling, which reduce the dimensionality of the feature maps while preserving important information. All these collected characteristics are used in the last layer, a fully connected layer that provides the output for cognition and emotion. The features, such as five dropout layers for regularization, four layers with the convolutional layer, and four max-pooling layers alongside the fully connected layer, are all optimized through various hyperparameters. This structure helps in identifying distress signals in textual data in the earliest stages, with the capability of considering complex linguistic features. The following Equation (18.1) represents the mathematical function of the convolutional process used in the present research to process the input text matrix.

$$E_{j,i}^{k} = \sigma\left(\sum_{n=0}^{N-1} \sum_{m=0}^{M-1} X_{n,m}^{k} W_{(j+n),(i+m)}^{k-1} + a^{k}\right) \quad (18.1)$$

The feature map at layer l in this formulation, which captures the altered characteristics of the input text, is represented as $E_{j,i}^{k}$. A kernel $X_{n,m}^{k}$, of dimension $N \times M$, is used to carry out the convolution process. It looks across the input representation to find patterns and correlations. Contributing to the feature extraction process, the input feature from the preceding layer is represented as $X_{(j+n),(i+m)}^{k-1}$. The learned features are adjusted by adding a bias term a^{k}, and the activation function σ, like ReLU, adds non-linearity, improving the model's capacity to represent intricate language patterns.

Residual Network with 50 layers (ResNet50)

ResNet50 uses a 50-layer convolutional neural network for context-aware NLP tasks, namely for feature extraction. One maxpool and one average pool layer are included in its 48 convolutional layers. The problem of decreasing gradients in deep neural networks is addressed by the deep residual learning system, which forms the basis of the ResNet50 design shown in Figure 18.1.

ResNet50 [12] is operationally efficient because it has more than 23 million trainable parameters, much fewer than other contemporary frameworks. By enabling layers to learn residual mappings rather than direct transformations, residual blocks provide insight into its effectiveness. The residual of a neural network block with input w, whose objective is to resemble the true function $G(w)$, is defined as follows in Equation (18.2).

$$S(w) = G(w) - w \tag{18.2}$$

The Equation (18.2) is rearranged in Equation (18.3):

$$G(w) = S(w) + w \tag{18.3}$$

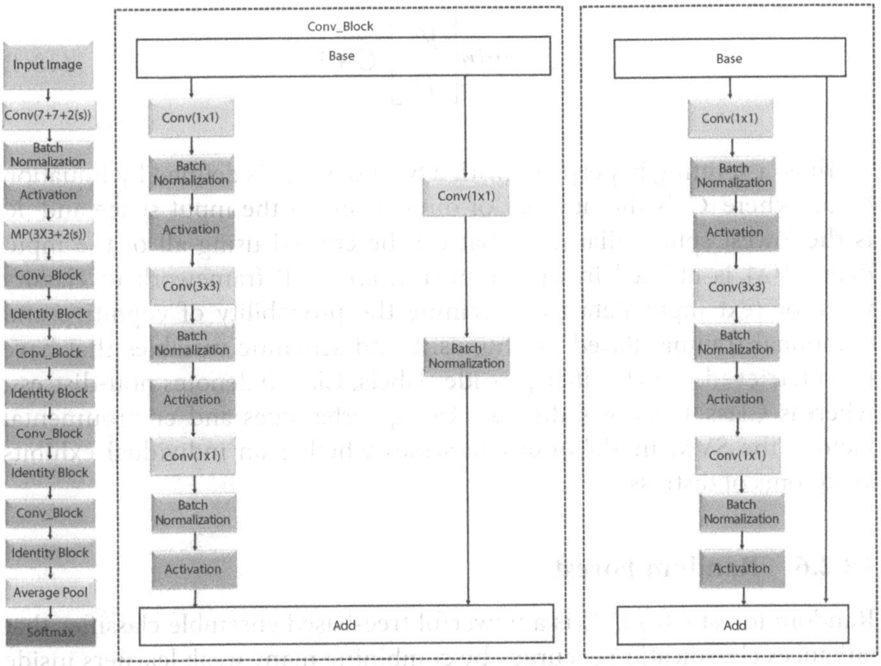

Figure 18.1 Schematic structure of ResNet-50. Source: https://www.scirp.org/journal/paperinformation?paperid=118603.

Here, the residual block uses identity connections that allow for effective gradient flow to learn the function $G(w)$ by concentrating on $S(w)$. While residual networks concentrate on learning $S(w)$, which streamlines the optimization process, traditional networks directly learn $G(w)$. Reusing activations from previous levels is also made simpler by the identity residual model without imposing additional architectural complexity. By utilizing deep residual learning, ResNet50 is combined with pre-trained weights to improve feature extraction for context-aware NLP applications, aiding in the early identification of cognitive and emotional discomfort.

18.2.5 Support Vector Machine

SVM is a supervised learning classifier that uses structural risk reduction to choose the best hyperplane for input data classification. SVM [13] efficiently reduces both training error and generalization error by determining the optimal hyperplane. Better classification performance is achieved by optimizing the gap between the hyperplane and the closest data point, which is linked to the VC dimension. Finding the best hyperplane offers a balance between classification accuracy and processing economy.

$$a \le min\left[\frac{R^2}{f^2}\right], C+1 \tag{18.4}$$

Thus, a splitting hyperplane with a boundary f is defined by Equation (18.4) where C is the number of dimensions in the input space and R is the lowest sphere diameter that can be created using all of the input data. SVM is utilized in this context-aware NLP framework to classify voice or text input data to determine the probability of cognitive and emotional trauma. Based on linguistic and semantic variables that have been retrieved, the classifier provides labels, Class 0 denotes non-distress, whereas Class 1 denotes distress. Using verbal cues and environmental factors, the SVM model's outputassesses whether an individual exhibits symptoms of distress.

18.2.6 Random Forest

Random forest (RF) [14] is a powerful tree-based ensemble classifier that enhances classification accuracy by combining many weak learners inside the context-aware NLP framework for the early identification of cognitive and emotional distress. To lower variance and enhance generalization, it uses bootstrap bagging to train decision trees on various dataset subsamples. The training and test dataset sizes are maintained by training each decision tree on a bootstrap sample. RF uses decision trees, similar to other ensemble classifiers, to make predictions; nonetheless, choosing the best root node at each step is yet a major problem in tree building. The majority voting determines the categorization outcome calculated by Equations (18.5 & 18.6).

$$O = Mode\{S_1(z), S_2(z), S_3(z), \ldots\ldots, S_n(z)\} \tag{18.5}$$

$$o = mode\{\textstyle\sum_{n=1}^{n} S_n(z)\} \tag{18.6}$$

where $S_1(z), S_2(z), S_3(z), \ldots\ldots, S_n(z)$ indicates the individual decision trees and o indicates the final decision obtained by majority voting.

18.2.7 Multilayer Perceptron Classifier

MLP is a DL neural network that nonlinearly maps input vectors to their corresponding output vectors, which is essential to context-aware NLP for the early identification of cognitive and emotional discomfort. MLP can simulate intricate connections in data since it is composed of an input layer, one or more hidden layers, and an output layer. MLP [15] can handle non-linearly separable data efficiently when nonlinear activation functions are applied to all neurons except the input nodes. The network is ideal for examining language patterns suggestive of cognitive and emotional discomfort because it minimizes classification mistakes by adjusting link weights by taking into account both the intended and actual outputs. The error is calculated using the following Equation (18.7), where z is the output node at the mth data point:

$$f_z(m) = s_z(m) - o_z(m) \tag{18.7}$$

Where the target value is denoted by s and the perceptron's output is denoted by o. To reduce the total error, the node weights are adjusted iteratively and are illustrated by Equation (18.8).

$$\in(m) = \frac{1}{2}\textstyle\sum_z f2z(m) \tag{18.8}$$

To maximize weight modifications, gradient descent is used. It is computed as follows in Equation (18.9).

$$\Delta\omega_{zw}(m) = \eta \frac{\delta\varepsilon(m)}{(\delta v_z(m))} o_w(m) \tag{18.9}$$

where o_w is the output from the previous neuron and η is the learning rate. When calculating derivatives, the local induced field uz assists in Equation (18.10).

$$\frac{\delta\varepsilon(m)}{(\delta v_z(m))} = f_z(m)\varphi'(u_z(m)) \tag{18.10}$$

Where φ stands for the activation function's derivative. Furthermore, weight updates follow Equation (18.11).

$$\frac{\delta\varepsilon(m)}{(\delta v_z(m))} = f_z(m)\Sigma_l \frac{\delta\varepsilon(m)}{(\delta v_z(m))} \omega_{lz}(m) \tag{18.11}$$

18.2.8 Gated Recurrent Unit

The GRU optimizes the vanishing gradient problem of generally existing recurrent neural networks (RNNs) in the context of NLP for the early diagnosis of cognitive and emotional distress. Long Short-Term Memory (LSTM) and GRU function similarly; however, GRU's design is simplified by combining the input and forget gates into a single update gate and mixing the hidden and cell states. This enables GRU to effectively learn long-range associations in sequential text input, which makes it perfect for spotting patterns connected to cognitive and emotional distress. Multiple regularly performed operations, any of which might be a neural network operation, comprise a GRU [16] unit. The GRU structure, which consists of an update gate, reset gate, and current memory content, allows the network to choose to communicate important contextual information to future states and store it for a predefined amount of time. The model's capacity to evaluate sequential language input indicative of distress-related signals is improved by this process. In the GRU framework, the update gate is represented by y_s. It produces an output between 0 and 1 by multiplying the input w_s and the hidden state from the previous unit g_{s-1} by the weight X_y, adding them together, and then running through a sigmoid activation function. The update gate mitigates vanishing gradient issues by regulating the amount of information that is kept or carried forward. Similar to the input gate, the reset gate (shown by q_s) selectively erases historical data that is no longer pertinent to the current forecast. The input w_s is multiplied by X, and q_s is element-wise multiplied by g_{s-1} to filter pertinent information. This signifies the current memory content, which is represented by g_s'. The summation is then subjected to a $\tan g$ activation function. The last memory state, denoted by g_s, propagates the data throughout the network while retaining the information required for the current unit. The following Equation (18.12) applies to the computations.

$$\begin{aligned} y_s &= \sigma(X_y.|g_{s-1}.w_s|) \\ q_s &= \sigma(X_q.|g_{s-1}.w_s|) \\ \overline{g}_s &= \tan g(X.|q_s g_{s-1}.w_s|) \\ g_s &= (1-y_s)g_{s-1} + y_s.g_s \end{aligned} \tag{18.12}$$

The network mostly depends on historical data when y_s is near 0, as shown in the final equation, which implies that $(1-y_s)$ is close to 1. Most of the current material becomes unimportant at this point. On the contrary, new content receives priority if y_s is near 1. Through sequential text analysis, GRU's adaptive mechanism enables early detection of cognitive and emotional suffering, making it a useful model for context-aware natural language processing.

18.3 Results

The performance metrics were used to evaluate the context-aware models to detect cognitive and emotional distress. The results demonstrate the ability of different ML and DL approaches in detecting the distress patterns with varying degrees of reliability. The experimental setup utilized a system with an *Intel Core i9 processor, 32GB RAM,* and an *NVIDIA RTX 3090 GPU* for efficient model training. The environment was configured on *Python* with *TensorFlow* and *PyTorch* frameworks, leveraging a *2TB SSD* for high-speed data processing and storage.

18.3.1 Comparative Analysis

The efficiency of the individual ML and DL models is determined in the identification of cognitive and emotional distress. Using recall, precision,

F1 score, and accuracy indicators, it is possible to determine the advantages and disadvantages of each model that can be identified. It assists in establishing the mode of identifying the most effective model in the early detection of distress levels, ensuring optimal intervention strategies.

Accuracy: The percentage of correctly classified distress levels out of all instances is used to represent the overall accuracy of the NLP model. Overall categorization performance improves with increasing exactness. Figure 18.2 and Table 18.1 show the accuracy results. In comparison to other models, the SVM model demonstrated its better capacity to recognize distress patterns, with the greatest accuracy of 78.97%.

Precision: It reduces false alarms by calculating the proportion of distress situations that the model accurately predicts. Reliable distress detection is ensured by a high precision value. Table 18.1 and Figure 18.3 depict the precision result. With a maximum precision of 81.45%, the SVM model reduced the number of inaccurate distress classifications and increased prediction trust, making it especially helpful for early intervention in mental health evaluations.

Recall: It calculates the percentage of true positives among genuine distress instances to assess the model's accuracy in identifying all actual distress situations. A higher rate of recall ensures that more people in distress are identified by lowering false negatives. Table 18.1 and Figure 18.4 depict the recall evaluation. With the greatest recall of 78.94%, the GRU

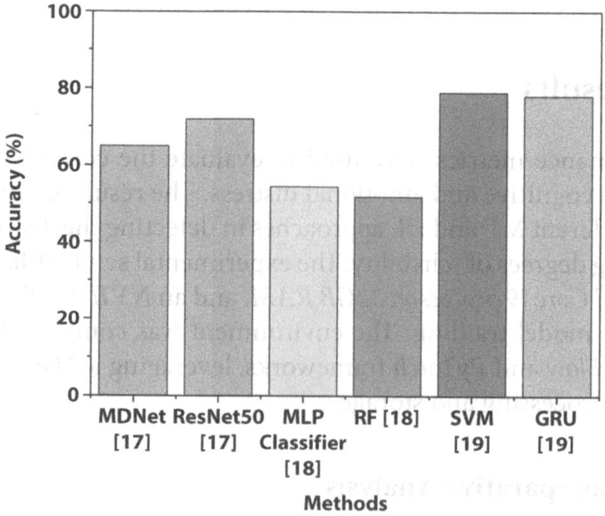

Figure 18.2 Comparison of model accuracy for cognitive and emotional distress detection. Source: Own elaboration.

Table 18.1 Evaluation metrics of context-aware models for cognitive and emotional distress detection.

Methods	Precision (%)	F1-score (%)	Recall (%)	Accuracy (%)
MDNet [17]	61	58	59	65
ResNet50 [17]	71	69	68	72
MLP Classifier [18]	48.31	44.48	44.51	54.32
RF [18]	42.49	31.77	36.68	51.71
SVM [19]	81.45	79.67	78.36	78.97
GRU [19]	78.37	78.65	78.94	78.02

Source: Own elaboration

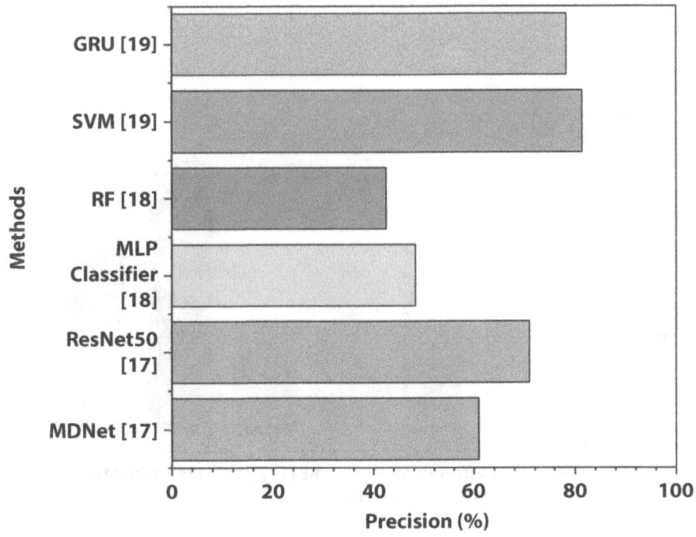

Figure 18.3 Precision analysis of context-aware models for distress classification. Source: Own elaboration.

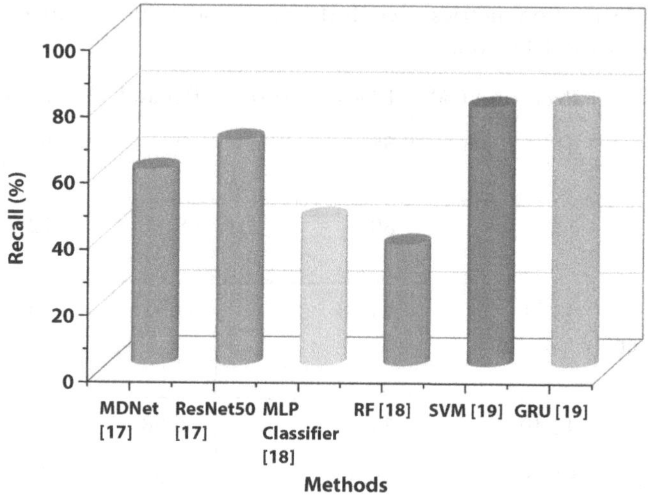

Figure 18.4 Recall performance of various models in detecting emotional and cognitive distress. Source: Own elaboration.

model proved to be successful in spotting patterns linked to distress with few examples overlooked.

F1 Score: It ensures that the model maintains dependable detection without placing too much emphasis on one measure by striking a balance

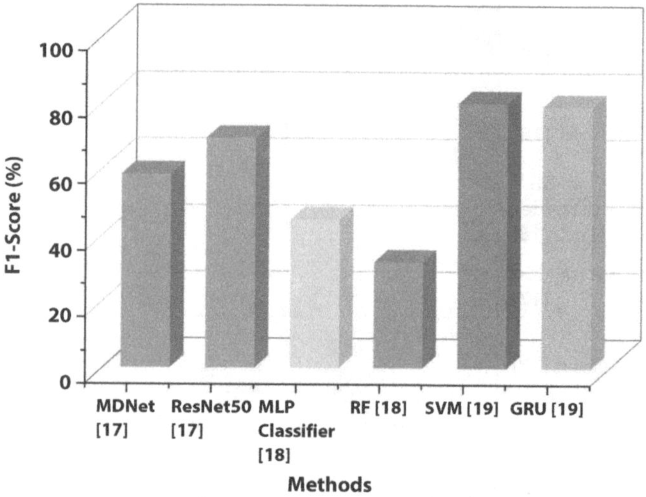

Figure 18.5 F1 score evaluation of ML and DL models. Source: Own elaboration.

between precision and recall. To manage uneven distress levels, this is essential. The F1 score results are shown in Table 18.1 and Figure 18.5. With the greatest F1 score of 79.67%, the SVM model demonstrated its overall efficacy in identifying distress levels while preserving the ideal ratio of false positives to false negatives.

18.3.2 Discussion

The comparison of context-aware models for identifying cognitive and emotional signs of distress has the advantages and disadvantages of the examined approaches. Overall, the highest performance was obtained from the SVM model [19], concerning both accuracy and precision, which means that it offers the lowest false positive rate, which is very important when analyzing the level of distress and beginning early intervention. In terms of recall, the GRU [19] model was more effective, as it offers less chance of overlooking distress instances, crucial for providing help to those struggling. Nonetheless, SVM [19] proved rather competent in terms of recall and F1-measure as it robustly balances between precision and recall. Other models such as MDNet [17], ResNet50 [17], MLP Classifier [18], and RF [18] demonstrated relatively weaker performance across various metrics, highlighting their challenges in accurately identifying distress patterns. These results have highlighted the need to consider all the performance measures while choosing the models to detect and intervene early on in the mental health assessments.

18.4 Conclusion

Context-aware NLP has the potential to be used in detecting cognitive, and emotional distress in the proposed model for mental health assessment. Employing ML and DL approaches, the model accurately extracts the distressed patterns from textual data as compared to conventional methods. ML and DL models demonstrate better performance that results in early detection caused by the models' capability to capture contextual and linguistic features. This technology permits mental health experts to recognize people suffering distress at an early period, enabling timely interventions and personalized care. It is also important that the presented approach applies at different levels, from clinical to online environments, to serve as a valuable asset for enhancing the individuals' mental well-being. In general, the development of context-aware NLP to be incorporated into the assessment of mental health patients simplifies the psychological treatment significantly.

AI disclosure statement: The author confirms that no artificial intelligence (AI)-generated content or AI-assisted writing tools were used in the preparation of this chapter (including summaries and the abstract). All text, analysis, and conclusions are the result of the author's original work.

References

1. Ismail, L., *et al.*, ML-NLPEmot: Machine Learning-Natural Language Processing Event-Based Emotion Detection Proactive Framework Addressing Mental Health. *IEEE Access*, 11, 144126–144149, 2023, https://doi.org/10.1109/ACCESS.2023.3343121.
2. Mascio, A., *et al.*, Cognitive impairments in schizophrenia: a study in a large clinical sample using natural language processing. *Front. Digit. Health*, 3, 711941, 2021, https://doi.org/10.3389/fdgth.2021.711941.
3. Ibitoye, A.O.J., Oladosu, O.O., Onifade, O.F.W., Contextual emotional transformer-based model for comment analysis in mental health case prediction. *Vietnam J. Comput. Sci.*, 1–23, 2024, https://doi.org/10.1142/S2196888824500192.
4. Taiwo, O. and Al Bander, B., Emotion aware psychological first aid: Integrating BERT-based emotional distress detection with Psychological First Aid Generative PreTrained Transformer chatbot for mental health support. *Cognit. Comput. Syst.*, 7, 1, e12116, 2025, https://doi.org/10.1049/ccs2.12116.
5. Henry, S., Yetisgen, M., Uzuner, O., Natural language processing in mental health research and practice, in: *Mental Health Informatics: Enabling a Learning Mental Healthcare System*, pp. 317–353, 2021, https://doi.org/10.1007/978-3-030-70558-9_13.
6. Singh, N.K., *et al.*, Deep Learning Model for Interpretability and Explainability of Aspect-Level Sentiment Analysis Based on Social Media. *IEEE Trans. Comput. Soc. Syst.*, 12, 3, 1307–1318, 2024, https://doi.org/10.1109/TCSS.2023.3347664.
7. Rokhsaritalemi, S., Sadeghi-Niaraki, A., Choi, S.-M., Exploring emotion analysis using artificial intelligence, geospatial information systems, and extended reality for urban services. *IEEE Access*, 11, 92478–92495, 2023, https://doi.org/10.1109/ACCESS.2023.3307639.
8. Emotion Dataset for Emotion Recognition Tasks: https://www.kaggle.com/datasets/parulpandey/emotion-dataset/data.
9. Emotion Detection from Text Dataset: https://www.kaggle.com/datasets/pashupatigupta/emotion-detection-from-text/data.

10. NLP Mental Health Conversations Dataset: https://www.kaggle.com/datasets/thedevastator/nlp-mental-health-conversations/data.
11. Tzirakis, P., *et al.*, Facial Emotion Recognition using Deep Residual Networks in Real-World Environments, *arXiv preprint arXiv:2111.02717*, 2021, https://doi.org/10.48550/arXiv.2111.02717.
12. Mishra, S., *et al.*, Deep residual learning for facial emotion recognition, in: *Mobile Computing and Sustainable Informatics: Proceedings of ICMCSI 2021*, Springer Singapore, Singapore, 2022, https://doi.org/10.1016/j.ijcce.2021.02.002.
13. Sujanaa, J., Palanivel, S., Balasubramanian, M., Emotion recognition using support vector machine and one-dimensional convolutional neural network. *Multimed. Tools Appl.*, 80, 18, 27171–27185, 2021, https://doi.org/10.1007/s11042-021-11041-5.
14. Alsubai, S., Emotion detection using deep normalized attention-based neural network and modified-random forest. *Sensors*, 23, 1, 225, 2022, https://doi.org/10.3390/s23010225.
15. Kumar, S., *et al.*, Multilayer Neural Network Based Speech Emotion Recognition for Smart Assistance. *Comput. Mater. Continua*, 75, 1, 2023, https://doi.org/10.32604/cmc.2023.028631.
16. Prakash, P.R., *et al.*, A novel convolutional neural network with gated recurrent unit for automated speech emotion recognition and classification. *J. Control Decis.*, 10, 1, 54–63, 2023, https://doi.org/10.1080/23307706.2022.2085198.
17. Aina, J., *et al.*, A hybrid Learning-Architecture for mental disorder detection using emotion recognition. *IEEE Access*, 12, 91410–91425 2024, https://doi.org/10.1109/ACCESS.2024.3421376.
18. Abeera, V.P., Kumar, S., Soman, K.P., Social media data analysis for Malayalam YouTube comments: sentiment analysis and emotion detection using ml and dl models. *Proceedings of the Third Workshop on Speech and Language Technologies for Dravidian Languages*, 2023, https://doi.org/10.26615/978-954-452-085-4_006.
19. Bharti, S.K., *et al.*, Text Based Emotion Recognition Using Deep Learning Approach. *Comput. Intell. Neurosci.*, 2022, 1, 2645381, 2022, https://doi.org/10.1155/2022/2645381.

19

Deep Learning Techniques for Analyzing Mood Variability in Patients

Pritam Keshari Sahoo[1]*, Awakash Mishra[2], Suneetha K.[3], Smitha S. P.[4] and Laxmidhar Maharana[5]

[1]Department of Electronics and Communication Engineering, Siksha 'O' Anusandhan (Deemed to be University), Bhubaneswar, Odisha, India
[2]Maharishi School of Engineering and Technology, Maharishi University of Information Technology, Uttar Pradesh, India
[3]Department of CSIT, Jain(Deemed-to-be University), Bangalore, Karnataka, India
[4]Department of Computer Science & Engineering, Presidency University, Bengaluru, Karnataka, India
[5]Department of Pharmaceutical Sciences, Siksha 'O' Anusandhan (Deemed to be University), Bhubaneswar, Odisha, India

Abstract

Investigating mood variability is essential for comprehending emotional changes and advancing mental health assessments. Traditional approaches have difficulty assessing the spatial and time dependencies of mood data. There is potential for deep learning (DL) methods to improve emotion classifications. The chapter focuses on using DL-based models to classify moods to analyze mood variability in patients. Using a multi-modal dataset with speech spectrograms, facial expressions, and text-based sentiment data improves accuracy in classification. Before training the DL models the dataset receives preprocessing steps that involve noise elimination and variable normalization to achieve quality input data. Deep learning methods effectively capture emotional patterns, demonstrating high accuracy in sentiment and mood recognition. The research highlights the significance of

**Corresponding author*: pritamkesharisahoo@soa.ac.in; ORCID: 0000-0001-5509-6431
Awakash Mishra: ORCID: 0009-0002-5447-7499
Suneetha K.: ORCID: 0000-0001-6738-3921
Smitha S. P.: ORCID: 0000-0002-1161-6770
Laxmidhar Maharana: ORCID: 0000-0002-0424-0875

Sudesh Yadav, Pethuru Raj, Satya Prakash Yadav and Victor Hugo C. de Albuquerque (eds.) Natural Language Processing in Mental Health Care: Methodologies and Clinical Practice, (285–302) © 2026 Scrivener Publishing LLC

integrating spatial and temporal dependencies in mood analysis. The models enhance emotion classification, contributing to AI-driven affective computing and real-time mental health monitoring, aiding in early intervention strategies.

Keywords**:** Mood variability, deep learning, emotion classification, mental health monitoring, affective computing

19.1 Introduction

The evaluation of mood fluctuations can help clarify psychiatric disorders, such as depression, bipolar disorder, and anxiety [1]. Traditional approaches that include self-report and clinical assessments typically present subjective data without the possibilities of objective assessment or real-time evaluations. Deep Learning (DL) [2] Ground-breaking advancements have allowed for the construction of intelligent algorithms capable of recognizing trends and advanced computation of high-dimensional data, thus improving the accuracy and efficacy of mood analysis. (DL has also been demonstrated to provide orders of magnitude performance improvement when processing multimodal data [3], such as text, audio, and biological indicators (facial emotions, biosignals, etc.). These models promote automated and scalable mental health surveillance by detecting complex mood-related phenomena using the nonlinear transformations and extraction of hierarchical features [4]. Real-time mood tracking receives enhancement through DL methods, which simultaneously decrease the requirement for subjective evaluations [5]. Studies examining emotional instability become more effective when implemented at an early stage because this approach enables superior mental illness management through machine learning mood analysis systems. DL helps improve the accuracy levels of classifications, according to research [6]. Models using big data sets combined with processing capacity, which enables reliable and flexible monitoring [7]. To further develop prediction abilities, real-time data streams are incorporated to facilitate real-time evaluation of a medication, and indeed a patient without requiring continuous clinical supervision [8]. More recently, developments in AI-assisted systems have offered possibilities to reconsider the monitoring of mental disorders by furnishing data-driven evidence that is not clouded by clinical bias [9]. The use of DL technology in mood variability analysis leads to enhanced treatment monitoring and improved patient results, while technological improvements have revolutionized digital mental healthcare [10]. The objective of this chapter is to explore the use of Deep Learning models for classifying mood variability in patients by analyzing multi-modal data. The work aims to improve emotion recognition accuracy and enhance real-time mental health monitoring for early intervention.

19.2 Methodology

Multiple DL models work together to detect mood patterns in compound data streams according. eXtreme Language Net (XLNet) performs sentiment identification on textual inputs but Convolutional Neural Network (CNN) together with Bidirectional Long Short-Term Memory (BiLSTM) analyses sequential mood patterns. The Convolutional Neural Network-Bidirectional Long Short-Term Memory (CNN-BiLSTM) model merges spatial and temporal characteristics but Residual Network (ResNet-50) serves to detect facial emotional expressions. The updated system boosts accuracy in mood evaluations so that experts can conduct continuous psychological health monitoring through advanced DL methods.

19.2.1 Dataset

The dataset includes emotional data defined by the mood states happy, sad, angry, neutral, fear, disgust and surprise. The dataset consists of three main components: text-based internet and conversation data, audio files of varying types, and screen captures or video recordings of faces. Along with the data objects are given the mood descriptors and timestamps that track the items and their associated time. The dataset boasts various emotional reactions due to a diverse participant sample representing different demographics. The mood variation analysis is more powerful when the materials contain high-definition audio sources and text from several languages. This organized data, combined with emotional computing, enables ample mood variability and smart mental health tracking.

19.2.2 Data Preprocessing Steps

The preparation procedure of preparing raw multimodal data provides a better environment for completing mood variability density analysis. Cleaning procedures are applied to raw inputs to generate quality data by correcting data inconsistencies. The data preparation process removes unnecessary data elements while extracting important aspects that yield meaningful data outputs. Standardization processes are used to make the data format somewhat standardized. Temporal structuring arranges sequential data along a time axis, allowing for the identification of mood patterns. The data are prepared for analysis formatting, which can also improve classification performance and identify variability in moods with potential for mental health indicators.

19.2.3 Convolutional Neural Networks and Bidirectional Long Short-Term Memory (CNN-BiLSTM)

Emotion variation studies advance using the CNN-BiLSTM [11] employed in this research project. The CNN implementation effectively discards spatial features of the combined modalities of facial expression and audio spectrogram along with EEG signals yet retains the key information regarding mood. Using the model, temporal emotional patterns can be assessed since the BiLSTM component tracks of temporal relationships. Time series combined with geographic information creates a method that enables maximal accuracy in mood analysis tasks. The model utilizes the storage capabilities of BiLSTM and the hierarchical feature extraction of CNN, providing real-time detection of small fluctuations in mood. This technology is invaluable when healthcare organizations require continuous monitoring of changes in emotional state so that they can identify disruptions early. The CNN-BiLSTM system provides a scalable and automated approach for AI-driven emotional calculating, allowing for impartial and dependable mood variability analysis using Equation (19.1).

$$Z_{i,j,k} = \sum_{m=0}^{M-1} \sum_{n=0}^{M-1} X_{i+m,j+n} . W_{m,n,k} + B_k \tag{19.1}$$

Equation (19.2) signifies the convolution process in CNN, where X is the input feature map, W is the filter, and B_k is the bias term. The output feature map is denoted as $Z_{i,j,k}$.

$$f(Z) = max(0, Z) \tag{19.2}$$

Here Z is the input, and the ReLU function applies a threshold process, where negative values are substituted with zero, safeguarding nonlinearity using Equation (19.3).

$$C_t = f_t \odot C_{t-1} + i_t \odot \grave{C}_t \tag{19.3}$$

In Equation (19.4), C_t is the cell national at times, f_t is the forget gate, i_t is the input gate, and C_t is the applicant memory cell. The element-wise increase operator is denoted by $\odot$.

$$h_t = Concat(\vec{h}_t, \overleftarrow{h}_t) \tag{19.4}$$

The final hidden state h_t is obtained by concatenating the onward hidden state $\overrightarrow{h_t}$ and the backward hidden state $\overleftarrow{h_t}$, enabling bidirectional context learning.

19.2.4 Convolutional Neural Networks (CNN)

CNNs are extensively used for mood variability studies because these networks efficiently work with structured information, including speech spectrograms, facial images, and EEG signals. Common Neural Networks process information through their convolutional layers to generate hierarchical patterns which move to pooling layers for feature reduction of essential mood-related features. The CNN [12] architecture allows it to obtain spatial representations that enable the detection of mood changes from complex input data. Automated feature extraction enables mental health applications to work without manual preprocessing for CNNs and thus supports their scalability. Improved learning of complex spatial characteristics in the model structure produces better classification outcomes that enable precise mood detection. Successful application of CNNs exists in emotion recognition, where the model detects micro-expressions from facial characteristics or varying vocal tones. Figure 19.1 presented the

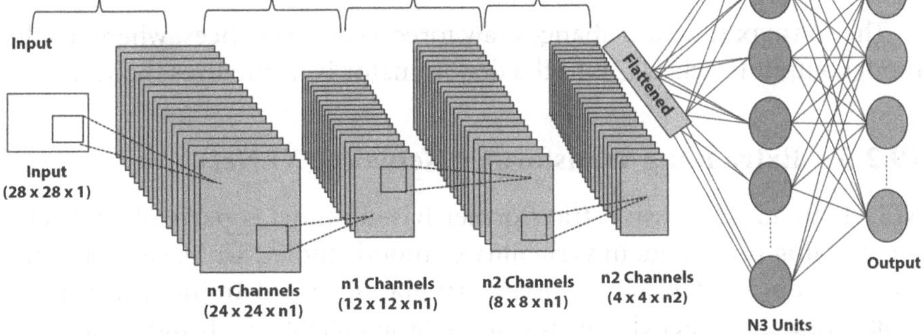

Figure 19.1 CNN architecture. Source: https://medium.com/analytics-vidhya/on-vectorization-of-convolution-layer-in-convolution-neural-networks-cnns-1775cb4d30e6.

CNN architecture diagram. The system uses these tools to execute real-time mental health status assessment capabilities.

The capabilities of large data processing and meaningful semantic generation enable CNNs to become an optimal methodology for automated mood variability assessment using Equation (19.5).

$$Z_{i,j,k} = \sum_{m=0}^{M-1} \sum_{n=0}^{M-1} X_{i+m,j+n}.W_{m,n,k} + B_k \tag{19.5}$$

Equation (19.6) describes how effort is applied to extract spatial features, where X is the input feature map, W is the convolutional kernel, and B_k is the bias term.

$$P_{i,j} = \max(Z_{i',j'}), i' \in [i,i,+s], j' \in [j, j+s] \tag{19.6}$$

Here, $P_{i,j}$ signifies the pooled output, where the extreme value is taken from a gap of size s over the feature map Z using Equation (19.7).

$$y = W_h.h + b \tag{19.7}$$

Equation (19.8) signifies the final classification layer, where W_h is the weight matrix, h is the input vector, and b is the bias term.

$$\sigma(y_t) = \frac{e^{y_t}}{\sum_j e^{y_t}} \tag{19.8}$$

The softmax function changes raw forecasts into chances, where y_t the model output for class i, and the denominator is normalizes the values.

19.2.5 Extra Long Transformer Network (XLNet)

XLNet, an autoregressive, transformer-based model is particularly useful for studying prose data in variability of mood studies. Unlike a traditional bidirectional model, XLNet uses permutation-based training to capture long-range dependencies in textual data associated with mood, such as patient journals, therapy transcripts, or social media data. The framework improves sentiment classification and emotion recognition while enhancing mood changes over time. Because of XLNet's [13] dynamic attention mechanism, the model gains the ability to understand complex relationships within the context, supporting natural language analysis to monitor mental health. XLNet's capacity to manage sequential emotional patterns enables a more precise interpretation of mood changes based on text. This is increasingly important given that XLNet's accuracy in emotion detection is superior to traditional NLP models, thereby developing an effective method for automation in mood variation measurement by AI. Figure 19.2 shows the XLNet, which strengthens research opportunities through its implementation of context-aware text analysis while it contributes to artificial intelligence development for affective computing research of immediate mental health tracking as Equation (19.9).

$$h_t = \Sigma_{t \le t} \alpha_i V_i \tag{19.9}$$

Equation (19.10) represents attention calculation, where h_t is the hidden state at time t, α_i are care weights, and V_i are value vectors.

$$\alpha_i = \frac{\exp(QK^T)}{\Sigma_j \exp(QK_j^T)} \tag{19.10}$$

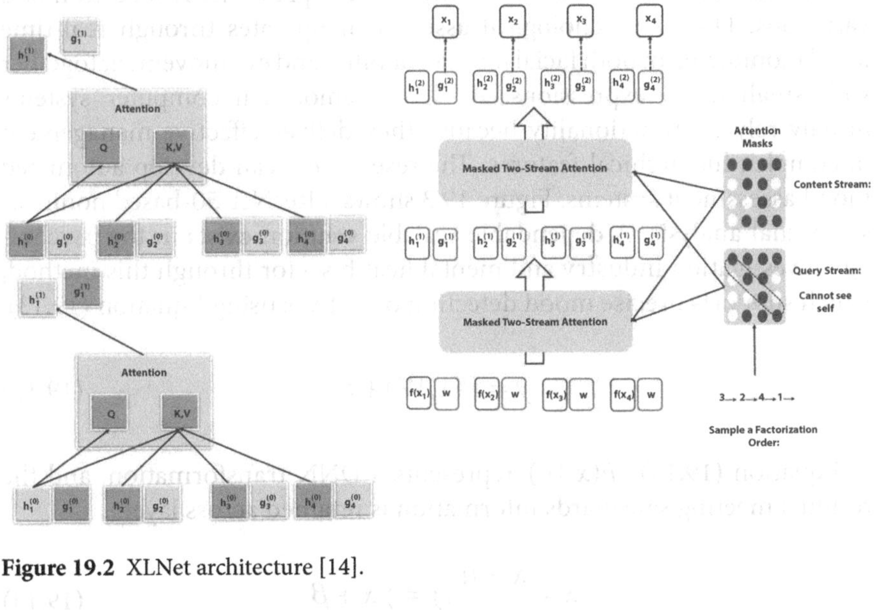

Figure 19.2 XLNet architecture [14].

Here, Q signifies the inquiry matrix, K is the key medium, and devotion weights α_i are computed using a softmax function as Equation (19.11).

$$FFN(h) = \max(0, hW_1 + b_1)\, W_2 + b_2 \tag{19.11}$$

Equation (19.12) defines the feed-forward system, where h is the input, W_1 and W_2 are weight media, and b_1 are bias terms.

$$y = Softmax(W_h h + b) \tag{19.12}$$

Here, the final organization is achieved using a softmax function, where W_h is the weight matrix, h is the input, and b is the bias term.

19.2.6 Residual Network

ResNet-50, or a deep residual network, is very important in image-based mood analysis, especially when the image is a facial expression. The residual learning framework enables the model to train effectively in deep networks while also mitigating the challenges posed by the vanishing gradient problem while allowing meaningful feature learning from high-resolution images. Over its analysis of refined emotional indicators, ResNet-50 [15] enables accurate identification of tiny facial expressions related to mood variations. Digital psychological assessment operates through real-time facial monitoring of both facial muscle mobility and eye movement together with small facial expressions. AI-driven emotional computer systems heavily rely on functionality because they deliver effective management of complex hierarchical features. The researchers can develop automated mood assessment systems. Figure 19.3 shows a ResNet-50-based noninvasive visual analysis. A dependable scalable solution exists in the psychology investigation industry and mental health sector through this method, which supports precise mood detection objectives using Equation (19.13).

$$y = F(x, W) + z \tag{19.13}$$

Equation (19.14), $F(x, W)$ represents a DNN transformation, and the residual meeting safeguards information is retained across layers.

$$\hat{x} = \frac{x - \mu}{\sigma}, y = \gamma \hat{x} + \beta \tag{19.14}$$

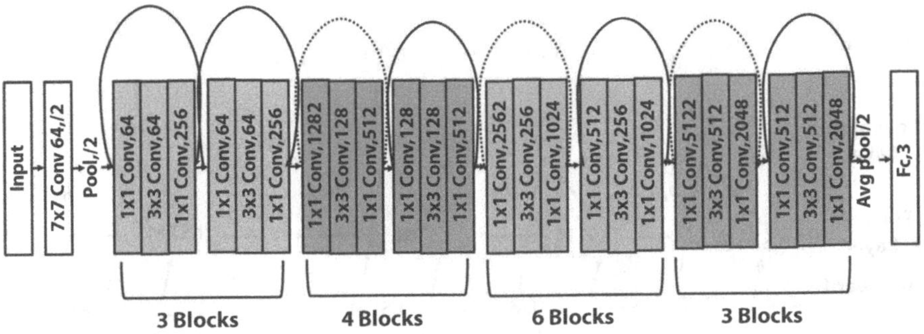

Figure 19.3 ResNet architecture. Source: Own elaboration.

Batch standardization normalizes the input x using mean μ and standard eccentricity followed by a scaling operation with limits γ and β using Equations (19.15 and 19.16)

$$f(x)\max(0,x) \tag{19.15}$$

$$y = W_h.h + b \tag{19.16}$$

The final fully associated layer maps removed features to mood classes using weight matrix W_h and bias b.

19.2.7 Bidirectional Long Short-Term Memory

BiLSTM networks function well for sequential mood analysis because they process time-series emotion data using context dependencies from both preceding and succeeding time points. Regular LSTMs operate in a one-way direction, but BiLSTMs [16] advance mood tracking by processing information from forward and backward time points. This capability is particularly useful for exploring textual data, audio recordings, and biological signals, all three of which are extremely time-dependent. BiLSTMs improve predicted accuracy and ensure confident mood classification in real-time situations by detecting small emotional variances. A two-way architecture within BiLSTM models enables better recognition of emotional states, which makes them a suitable choice for mental health monitoring applications. Figure 19.4 presented the BiLSTM architecture. AI has sufficient potential to detect mood fluctuations through its capability of processing long-term dependencies in patient data, which results in accurate monitoring of mood changes. The contextual understanding of

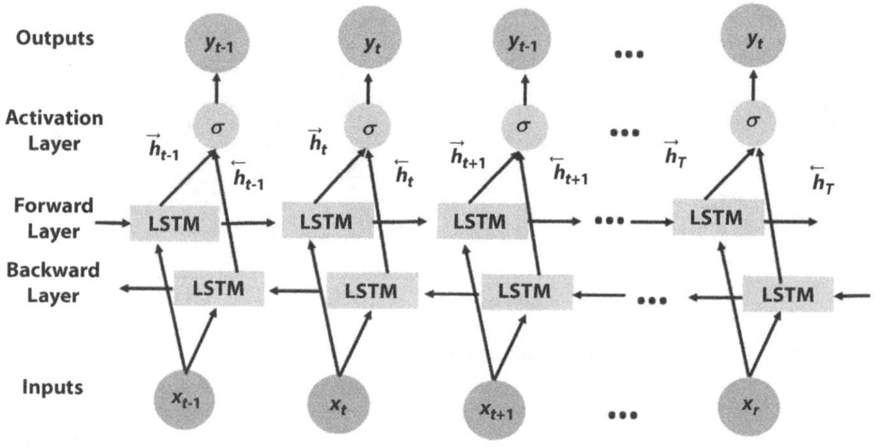

Figure 19.4 BiLSTM architecture. Source: https://www.themoonlight.io/en/review/integrating-medical-imaging-and-clinical-reports-using-multimodal-deep-learning-for-advanced-disease-analysis.

BiLSTM models surpasses that of sequential models and thus makes these models essential components for automated systems that measure mood variability changes as Equation (19.17).

$$f_t = \sigma(W_f.[h_{t-1}, x_t] + b_f) \tag{19.17}$$

The forget gate controls the retaining of past info, where f_t is the forget vector, W_f is the heaviness matrix, and x_t is the input at time t as Equations (19.18 and 19.19).

$$i_t = \sigma(W_i.[h_{t-1}, x_t] + b_i) \tag{19.18}$$

Here, i_t represents the input gate, W_i is the weight matrix, and x_t is the input.

$$C_t = f_t \odot C_{t-1} + i_t \odot \grave{C}_t \tag{19.19}$$

The cell state C_t is updated using forget gate f_t and input gate i_t, where C_t is the candidate state as in Equation (19.20).

$$h_t = concat(\vec{h}_t, \overleftarrow{h}_t) \tag{19.20}$$

19.3 Results

The experimental design employs DL methods for mood regulatory analysis while processing combinations of speech, text, and facial expression data. The research uses Python as its programming language and TensorFlow together with PyTorch as framework implementations for building the models. Testing occurs on a computing system equipped with an NVIDIA RTX 3090 GPU supported by an Intel Core i9 processor and 32GB RAM for maximizing computational speed. The system functions on Ubuntu 20.04 while it optimizes its hyperparameters for better classification accuracy and real-time mood evaluation. DL techniques succeed in mood variability analysis through their achievement of effective spatial and temporal emotion pattern detection. The results demonstrate improved accuracy in detecting subtle mood fluctuations, safeguarding reliable classification for mental health monitoring. The examination validates the possibility of DL for precise and automatic mood variability assessment, enhancing real-time emotional state recognition. These insights contribute to the advancement of intelligent systems for mental health applications, improving early detection and intervention strategies. Figure 19.5 illustrates the confusion matrix for mood classification, depicting the model's ability to distinguish emotional states. It highlights correct and misclassified predictions across different emotions, providing insights into classification performance. The distribution of values indicates the model's strengths and weaknesses in recognizing various emotional expressions, aiding in performance evaluation.

The accuracy of several DL models in mood variability analysis is shown in Table 19.1. BiLSTM shows its efficacy in capturing sequential dependencies by achieving the best accuracy. CNN uses spatial feature extraction to achieve good results. The CNN-BiLSTM hybrid model combines both methodologies to achieve balanced performance. Textual mood data is processed effectively by XLNet, but image-based mood identification restrictions cause ResNet-50 to perform less accurately. These accuracy comparisons are shown graphically in Figure 19.6 for easier understanding.

Multiple models in mood variability analysis are shown in Table 19.2. CNN demonstrates its capacity to reliably categorize moods with few false positives, achieving the greatest precision of 97.28%. CNN-BiLSTM, which gains from both geographical and sequential feature extraction with 96.99%. A precision of 79.4% is recorded by BiLSTM, suggesting some misclassification. Recall achieved 97% at CNN and 92.66% at CNN-BiLSTM

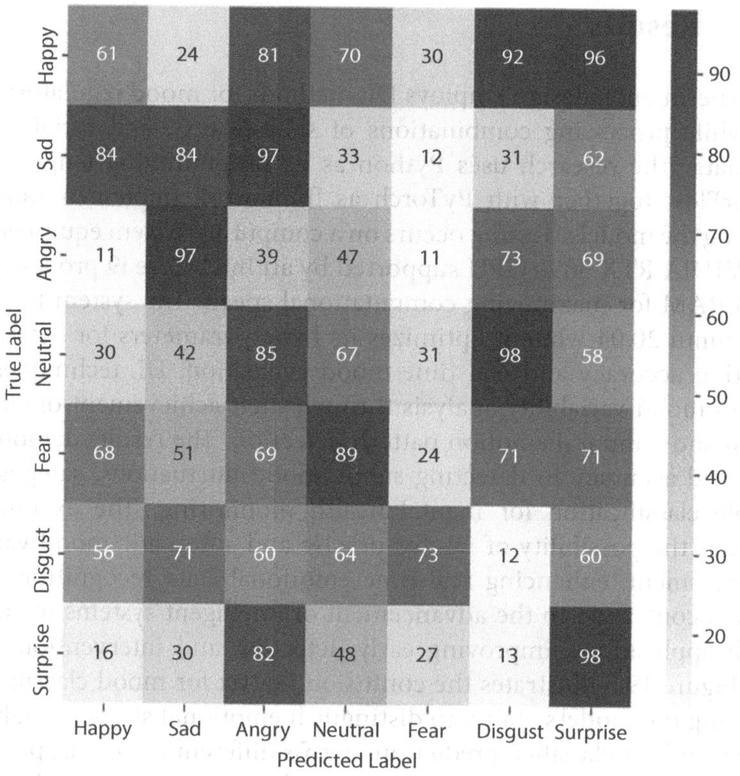

Figure 19.5 Confusion matrix. Source: Own elaboration.

Table 19.1 Accuracy comparison of deep learning models.

Methods	Accuracy (%)
CNN-biLSTM [17]	94.28
CNN [18]	96.78
XLNet [19]	94.78
ResNet-50 [20]	77.20
BiLSTM [21]	97.10

Source: Own elaboration.

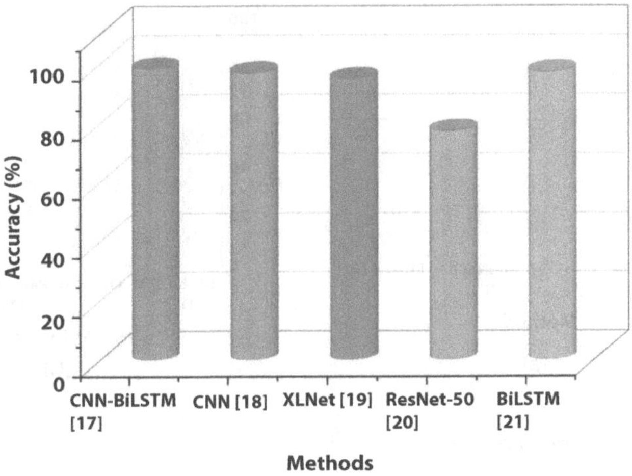

Figure 19.6 Comparison of the accuracy. Source: Own elaboration.

Table 19.2 Performance metrics evaluation for individual models.

Methods	Precision (%)	Recall (%)	F-1 score (%)
CNN-biLSTM [17]	96.99	92.66	94.28
CNN [18]	97.28	97	97.36
ResNet-50 [20]	79.72	74.45	76.99
BiLSTM [21]	79.4	73.5	76.3

Source: Own elaboration.

comes in second, guaranteeing reliable sequential mood identification. With a recall of 73.5%, BiLSTM demonstrates a decent ability to identify mood shifts. The 74.45% recall of ResNet-50 is the lowest, demonstrating difficulties with image-based mood detection. CNN consistently and accurately detects mood due to its highest F1 score of 97.36%. CNN-BiLSTM, which gains from the integration of spatial-temporal features, comes in second with 94.78%. With an F1 score of 76.3% with 76.99%, accordingly, BiLSTM and ResNet-50 demonstrate a reasonable level of classification reliability. Figure 19.7 of mood variability.

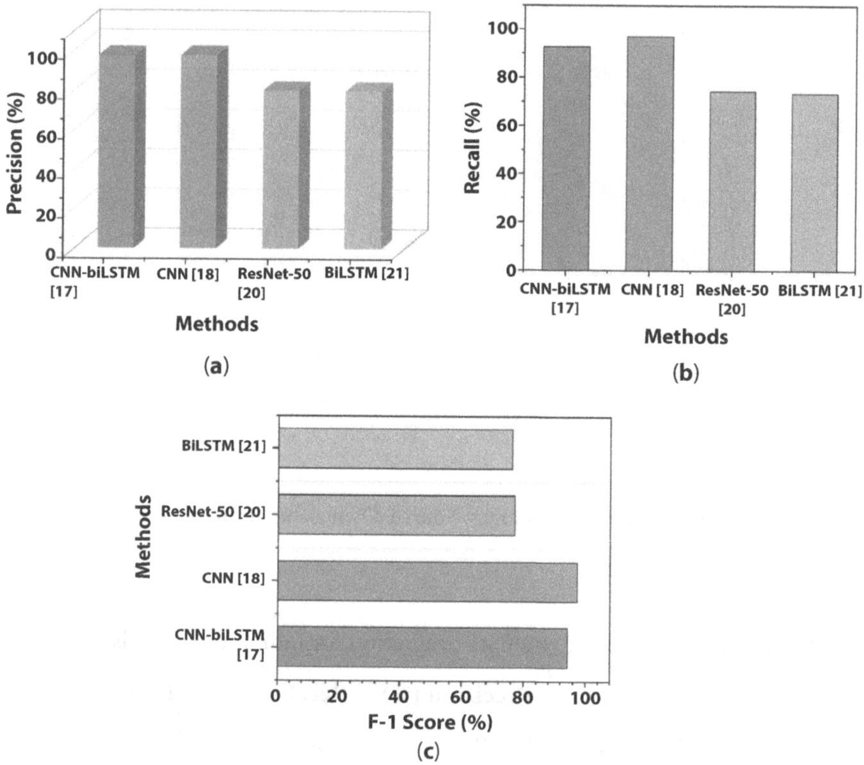

Figure 19.7 Performance evaluation of mood variability. (a) Precision, (b) Recall, (c) F-1 score. Source: Own elaboration.

19.4 Discussion

DL methods combined with mood variability analysis offer a revolutionary way to comprehend emotional swings. Combining CNNs [18] for spatial feature extraction with BiLSTMs [21] for temporal recognition of patterns improves the capacity to model dynamic feelings. The hybrid CNN-BiLSTM [17] architecture improves the visualization of features by capturing complex connections among spatial and chronological information, making it extremely successful in mood pattern identification. With the use of transformer-based frameworks, such as XLNet [19], textual mood analysis has advanced significantly, allowing for reliable contextualization from social interactions and client narratives. ResNet-50 [20] is nevertheless useful for extracting deep features from high-dimensional face and EEG data, even if it has trouble catching subtle emotional changes.

Together, these structures aid in the development of sophisticated systems for detecting mood variations, providing noninvasive, data-driven knowledge into the tracking of emotional wellness. Problems including noisy sensibility, data variation, and generalization issues call for more developments in preprocessing techniques and model optimization. Multi-modal data fusion, which combines textual inputs, visual data, and bodily signals, can improve the resilience of frameworks for assessing mood.

19.5 Conclusion

The DL methods for evaluating mood fluctuation are a highly effective way to monitor mental well-being. With the maximum accuracy of 97.10%, next to CNN at 96.78% and XLNet at 94.78%, the suggested framework performs better in categorization. At 94.28% accuracy, the hybrid CNN-BiLSTM models also show good predictive power. Even with its reduced accuracy of 77.20%, ResNet-50 is useful for deep extraction of features based on picture mood evaluation. The use of CNNs for geographical extraction of features, BiLSTMs for behavioral pattern identification, and XLNet for text mood analysis enables comprehensive emotion modeling. By combining these designs, mood variability detection accuracy is increased, allowing for automated and real-time emotional health evaluations. The findings demonstrate how well DL captures intricate emotional patterns, providing an affordable and noninvasive alternative for cutting-edge mental health monitoring apps.

AI disclosure statement: The author acknowledges the use of AI-based tools for minor language editing or grammatical correction. However, all intellectual contributions, analyses, and conclusions presented in this chapter are entirely the author's own.

References

1. Nan, J., *et al.*, Personalized machine learning-based prediction of wellbeing and empathy in healthcare professionals. *Sensors*, 24, 8, 2640, 2024, https://doi.org/10.3390/s24082640.
2. Sandulescu, V., *et al.*, Integrating IoMT and AI for Proactive Healthcare: Predictive Models and Emotion Detection in Neurodegenerative Diseases. *Algorithms*, 17, 9, 376, 2024, https://doi.org/10.3390/a17090376.

3. Jangir, D., *et al.*, Mood Prediction Using Social Media Data, in: *Emerging Trends in IoT and Computing Technologies*, pp. 277–285, CRC Press, London, 2024, https://doi.org/10.1201/9781003535423-47.
4. Uddin, M.S. and Chowdhury, M., A user-friendly anger and anxiety disorder prediction scheme using machine learning and a mobile application for mental healthcare. *Int. J. Data Anal. Tech. Strat.*, 16, 1, 47–81, 2024, https://doi.org/10.1504/IJDATS.2024.137466.
5. Yu, X., *et al.*, A novel prediction model for the probability of aggressive behavior in patients with mood disorders: Based on a cohort study. *J. Psychiatr. Res.*, 177, 420–428, 2024, https://doi.org/10.1016/j.jpsychires.2024.07.041.
6. Jilka, S. and Giacco, D., Digital phenotyping: how it could change mental health care and why we should all keep up. *J. Mental Health*, 33, 4, 439–442, 2024, https://doi.org/10.1080/09638237.2024.2395537.
7. Kumar, S., *et al.*, Depression Prediction Using Machine Learning Techniques, in: *Artificial Intelligence in Healthcare*, pp. 241–265, CRC Press, London, 2024, https://doi.org/10.1201/9781003522096-12.
8. Cirillo, F., *et al.*, Variability of excessive daytime sleepiness and cataplexy according to seasonality: A study in central disorders of hypersomnolence. *J. Sleep Res.*, 34, 4, e14451, 2025, https://doi.org/10.30574/wjarr.2024.23.1.2258.
9. Khaled, S.M., *et al.*, Lifetime prevalence, risk, and treatment of mood and anxiety disorders in Qatar's national mental health study. *Int. J. Methods Psychiatr. Res.*, 33, S1, e2011, 2024, https://doi.org/10.1002/mpr.2011.
10. Mason, A.J.C., *et al.*, Applying neural network algorithms to ascertain reported experiences of violence in routine mental healthcare records and distributions of reports by diagnosis. *Front. Psychiatry*, 15, 1181739, 2024, https://doi.org/10.3389/fpsyt.2024.1181739.
11. Lamichhane, A. and Karn, G., CNN-BiLSTM based Facial Emotion Recognition. *Int. J. Eng. Technol.*, 2, 1, 227–236, 2024, https://doi.org/10.3126/injet.v2i1.72579.
12. Chatzimina, M.E., *et al.*, A comparative sentiment analysis of Greek clinical conversations using BERT, Roberta, GPT-2, and XLNet. *Bioengineering*, 11, 6, 521, 2024, https://doi.org/10.3390/bioengineering11060521.
13. Mao, K., *et al.*, Prediction of depression severity based on the prosodic and semantic features with bidirectional LSTM and time distributed CNN. *IEEE Trans. Affective Comput.*, 14, 3, 2251–2265, 2022, https://doi.org/10.1109/TAFFC.2022.3154332.
14. https://www.kdnuggets.com/2019/10/research guide-transformers.html.
15. Aravindan, A.A., *et al.*, Prediction of arousal and valence state from electrodermal activity using wavelet-based resnet50 model. *Curr. Dir. Biomed. Eng.*, 9, 1, 555–558, 2023, https://doi.org/10.1515/cdbme-2023-1139.
16. Sun, Q. and Duan, S., User Intent Prediction and Response in Human-Computer Interaction *via* BiLSTM. *J. Comput. Sci. Softw. Appl.*, 5, 3, 2025, https://doi.org/10.5281/zenodo.14985042.

17. Kour, H. and K. Gupta, M., A hybrid deep learning approach for depression prediction from user tweets using feature-rich CNN and bi-directional LSTM. *Multimed. Tools Appl.*, 81, 17, 23649–23685, 2022, https://doi.org/10.1007/s11042-022-12648-y.
18. Pradhan, S.N., *et al.*, Evaluation of stress based on multiple distinct modalities using machine learning techniques. *Int. J. Public Health*, 13, 2, 944–954, 2024, https://doi.org/10.11591/ijphs.v13i2.23577.
19. Pyrovolakis, K., Tzouveli, P., Stamou, G., Multi-modal song mood detection with deep learning. *Sensors*, 22, 3, 1065, 2022, https://doi.org/10.3390/s22031065.
20. Suparatpinyo, S. and Soonthornphisaj, N., Smart voice recognition based on deep learning for depression diagnosis. *Artif. Life Rob.*, 28, 2, 332–342, 2023, https://doi.org/10.1007/s10015-023-00852-4.
21. Bhat, P., *et al.*, Mental health analyzer for depression detection based on textual analysis. *J. Adv. Inf. Technol.*, 13, 1, 2022, https://doi.org/10.12720/jait.13.1.67-77.

20

Text-Based Cognitive Bias Identification for Assessing Negative Thinking Patterns

Jyoti Ranjan Das[1]*, Savita[2], Kannagi Anbazhagan[3] and Sridevi S.[4]

[1]*Department of Management, Siksha 'O' Anusandhan (Deemed to be University), Bhubaneswar, Odisha, India*
[2]*Maharishi School of Engineering and Technology, Maharishi University of Information Technology, Uttar Pradesh, India*
[3]*Department of CSIT, Jain (Deemed-to-be University), Bangalore, Karnataka, India*
[4]*Department of Computer Science & Engineering, Presidency University, Bengaluru, Karnataka, India*

Abstract

Text-based analysis of cognitive biases offers valuable insights into negative thinking patterns, which can significantly impact mental well-being. However, identifying these biases remains challenging due to the subjective nature of text interpretation and the complexity of linguistic nuances. This chapter aims to develop an automated approach for detecting negative thinking patterns by leveraging computational techniques. Various natural language processing (NLP), machine learning (ML), and deep learning (DL) methods are employed to analyze textual data, classify cognitive distortions, and identify recurring negative biases. The results demonstrate the effectiveness of these techniques in accurately detecting cognitive biases, providing a foundation for automated psychological assessments. The results demonstrate the possibility of AI-driven techniques to improve mental health diagnostics, providing a scalable and objective solution for recognizing negative thinking patterns through textual analysis.

**Corresponding author*: jyotiranjandas@soa.ac.in; ORCID: 0000-0001-9556-8229
Savita: ORCID: 0000-0002-4826-4721
Kannagi Anbazhagan: ORCID: 0000-0003-3810-7500
Sridevi S.: ORCID: 0009-0003-4898-7481

Sudesh Yadav, Pethuru Raj, Satya Prakash Yadav and Victor Hugo C. de Albuquerque (eds.) Natural Language Processing in Mental Health Care: Methodologies and Clinical Practice, (303–318) © 2026 Scrivener Publishing LLC

Keywords: Deep learning, negative thinking patterns, machine learning, natural language processing

20.1 Introduction

Mental health issues like anxiety and depression are often exacerbated by negative thought patterns, which are frequently connected to cognitive distortions. These tendencies impact people's emotional reactions and decision-making and can take many forms, such as overgeneralization, catastrophizing, and black-and-white thinking [1]. Conventional techniques for evaluating cognitive biases, such as clinical interviews and self-report questionnaires, mostly depend on subjective answers, which are susceptible to recall and social desirability biases [2]. Recent developments in machine learning (ML) and natural language processing (NLP) have created new opportunities for text analysis-based cognitive distortion detection. Automated algorithms can more accurately identify negative thinking tendencies by examining linguistic patterns in spoken or written text [3]. Nevertheless, there are some challenges associated with several approaches that use NLP for citation analysis. This debate is far from easy due to several factors, including the use of a particular word or phrase with another meaning from another context [4]. Although current models of NLP, particularly the general NLP, fail to understand the unduly complicated cognitive distortions in the discourse of psychologists. Finally, the patients' individuality, culture, and language also hinder the effectiveness of model implementation across the board [5].

Another disadvantage of the deep learning (DL) model is interpretability. While these models could be used to categorize text-based cognitive biases, it can be difficult to understand the reasoning process and application in clinical practice, where there must be a form of accountability for the decision-making process performed by the intelligent system [6]. There are some limitations to bias and generalizability in such models and the concerned datasets with which these are trained and tested are generally small and disparate. When using personal text data for psychological analysis, some other factors, such as privacy and security of data, are also important factors. To maintain confidence and moral standards in mental health applications, it is imperative to ensure that NLP technologies are used appropriately and with the prior consent of the subject [7]. The main goal of this chapter is to develop an automated approach that can identify negative thinking patterns using computational methods. It uses NLP, ML, and DL algorithms to process text-based information, categorize cognitive distortions, and recognize redundant negative biases for psychological evaluation.

20.2 Methodology

An incorporation of NLP, ML, and DL methods is used to process text and recognize distortions in cognition. Data cleaning, feature selection, extraction methods, and classification models are utilized to achieve the intended better detection rates. The identified technique focuses on the automation of the analysis of the negative thinking patterns.

20.2.1 Dataset

The datasets for cognitive bias identification are often text data samples that originate from text annotation of posts on social media and news, texts of therapies and transcripts, or responses of users provided through open-ended questions. These datasets include documenting and categorizing negative thoughts such as catastrophizing, overgeneralizing, splitting things into black and white, and reasoning with emotion. It frequently includes labeled examples of biased remarks for comparison with neutral or corrected versions. Concepts like sentiment polarity, context of the comments and words, word embedding and syntactical structures, and patterns are used for bias identification. However, demographic data, context and credibility of the information source can also be other features to be considered while making the analysis. They are mainly used for training machine learning models intended for the identification and elimination of cognitive bias within textual data.

20.2.2 NLP Techniques

In this chapter, NLP methods are used to facilitate the cognition of biases that include identifying negative thought patterns using textual information. Techniques like GloVe-300, Count Vectorization (CV), and bigram assists in feature extraction as well as representation that positively impact the cognitive bias.

20.2.3 Global Vectors for Word Representation

The Global Vectors for Word Representation (GloVe) model [8] was used to train the 300-dimensional word embeddings, which are referred to as GloVe 300. This model captures semantic relationships in text by combining predictive and count-based methods. Unlike word2vec, which focuses on local context, GloVe employs word co-occurrence statistics from a corpus to learn word associations efficiently. To ensure that the dot product of word vectors roughly equals the logarithm of their co-occurrence probability, the model factorizes a co-occurrence matrix, as expressed in Equation (20.1).

$$x_j^S \tilde{x}_l + a_j + a_l = \log\left(W_{jl}\right) \tag{20.1}$$

where x_j and $\tilde{x}_l$ are word and context vectors, a_j and a_l are bias variables, and W_{jl} is the co-occurrence counts of word j in the context of word l. A weighting function $e\left(W_{jl}\right)$ is used to balance common and rare word pairings. GloVe improves the detection of cognitive biases in the text by preserving semantic links that represent negative thought patterns by collecting word associations broadly.

20.2.4 Count Vectorization

CV [9], commonly referred to as the term frequency, determines the number of times each unique token is used in a text. A token's frequency can be expressed mathematically as follows in Equation (20.2).

$$TF(s,c) = \Sigma_{j=1}^{M} e\left(s_j, c\right) \tag{20.2}$$

Where $TF(s,c)$ indicates the term frequency of token s in document c and $e\left(s_j, c\right)$ indicates the count of token s_j in document c. A higher score helps identify recurrent patterns linked to cognitive biases since it suggests that the token is more prevalent in the text.

20.2.5 Bigrams

The bigram model [10] simplifies the conditional probability given the prior word $O(x_m|x_{m-1})$ is the only statistic that can be utilized to estimate the likelihood of a word given all the previous words $O(x_m|x_{1:m-1})$. The Bigram model for cognitive distortions is approximately calculated by Equation (20.3):

$$O(x_m|x_{1:m-1}) \approx O(x_m|x_{m-1}) \tag{20.3}$$

This helps also in the search of cognitive biases because the function reveals how often particular words appear often together, which could reflect some biases in the cognitive processes. It can identify language patterns that can be considered as cognitive distortions within the texture of the text by analyzing word combinations.

20.2.6 Negative Thinking Patterns Using ML and DL Techniques

ML and DL methods improve the identification of cognitive biases by categorizing negative thinking styles in textual information. Models like long short-term memory (LSTM), convolutional neural network (CNN), logistic regression (LR), support vector machine (SVM), bidirectional LSTM (Bi-LSTM), and random forest (RF) are effective for pattern recognition, and their effectiveness is reflected in higher reliability in detecting bias.

20.2.7 Long Short-Term Memory

A subset of recurrent neural networks (RNNs) called LSTM neural networks is made specifically to handle long-term dependencies in sequential input. Because of its structure, LSTMs [11] are specifically effective at examining textual patterns, such as spotting cognitive biases and pessimistic thought patterns in text. A memory cell and three gates, including the forget, input, and output gates, make up an LSTM unit. The cell state, which serves as a conveyor belt and allows information to flow through with minimum alteration unless specifically changed by the gates, is the fundamental part of an LSTM. Although irrelevant data is removed, this structure ensures that key features related to cognitive biases remain. The forget gate decides, which historical data should be kept or removed. With an input sequence w_s and a concealed state from the previous time step g_{s-1}, the forget gate modifies the cell state D_{s-1}, by calculating with the use of Equation (20.4).

$$e_s = \sigma(X_e.[g_{s-1}, w_s] + a_e) \tag{20.4}$$

The output is scaled between 0 (totally forget) and 1 (fully retain), with σ serving as the sigmoid activation function. The new information that should be stored in the cell state is determined by the input gate. A hyperbolic tangent (tan_g) layer creates candidate values for updating the cell state, while a sigmoid layer filters the incoming data are illustrated in Equations (20.5 to 20.7).

$$j_s = \sigma(X_j.[g_{s-1}, w_s] + a_j) \tag{20.5}$$

$$\ddot{D}_s = \tanh(X_D.[g_{s-1}, w_s] + a_D) \tag{20.6}$$

$$D_J = e_s * g_{s-1} + j_s * \ddot{D}_s \tag{20.7}$$

By identifying patterns linked to cognitive biases, this process enables the model to choose preserve important elements in textual material. Furthermore, the output gate decides whatever pertinent data should be sent to the following state. The filtered output is managed by a sigmoid layer and then subjected to further processing by a tan_g activation function is calculated by Equations (20.8 & 20.9).

$$P_s = \sigma(W_{jP}.[g_{s-1}, w_s] + a_O) \tag{20.8}$$

$$g_s = P_s * \text{tang}(D_s) \tag{20.9}$$

LSTMs are well suited to identifying biased thought processes like confirmation bias, overgeneralization, and catastrophizing in written content because of their gated design, which allows them to learn intricate relationships in textual data.

20.2.8 Convolutional Neural Network

CNN [12] uses feature representations (FE) as input and extracts patterns related to cognitive biases by processing them through convolutional, pooling, and fully connected layers. Multiple filters are used by the convolutional layer to capture crucial feature mappings, which are calculated as follows in Equation (20.10).

$$H^{e_k}_{e_a, e_b, e_c} = w^{e_k{}^T}_{e_c} * EF + F^{e_k}_{e_c} \tag{20.10}$$

$w^{e_k{}^T}_{e_c}$ is the weight during training, and $e_k{}^T$ is the weight. $F^{e_k}_{e_c}$ Represents the bias term. Activation functions, which are calculated as Equation (20.11), add non-linearity into multi-layered networks.

$$\alpha^{e_k}_{e_a, e_b, e_c} = \phi(H^{e_k}_{e_a, e_b, e_c}) \tag{20.11}$$

where the activation function is represented by $\phi(\cdot)$.

Pooling Layer: To decrease feature dimensions while keeping important patterns, the pooling layer downsamples. The pooled feature value $\lambda^{e_k}_{e_a,e_b,e_c}$ is computed by Equation (20.12).

$$\lambda^{e_k}_{e_a,e_b,e_c} = @\left(\alpha^{e_k}_{e_a,e_b,e_c}\right), \forall(e_p,e_q) \in \Omega_{e_p,e_q} \tag{20.12}$$

The pooling function performed across an area Ω is denoted by $@(\cdot)$. CNN's optimization target is represented by the loss function, which is expressed by Equation (20.13).

$$Loss = \frac{1}{D_e}\sum_{e_q=1}^{C_e} l(\theta, \lambda_{e_q}, OT_{e_q}) \tag{20.13}$$

Where θ stands for trainable parameters, λ_{e_q} for feature mappings, and OT_{e_q} for CNN output. This approach allows recognizing negative attitudes and cognitive biases in the text with a high degree of efficiency.

20.2.9 Logistic Regression

An effective method for identifying cognitive biases in text is LR [13], which separates biased from unbiased patterns. Based on linguistic and psychological elements that have been retrieved, LR is a binary classification model that forecasts the likelihood of negative thought patterns. Given l characteristics, the log-odds of cognitive bias present $W = w_1, w_2, \ldots, w_l$ is represented by the following Equations (20.14 & 20.15).

$$\log\left(\frac{o}{1-0}\right) = \sum_{i=1}^{l} \beta_i z_i \quad \leftrightarrow \quad 0 = \frac{1}{1+f^{-\sum_i \beta_i z_i}} \tag{20.14}$$

$$k\beta \sum_{j=1}^{m}[w_j z_j \beta - \log\left(1+f^{y_j \beta}\right)] \tag{20.15}$$

Lasso penalization reduces parameter β values to fine-tune feature selection by setting some coefficients to zero is expressed in Equation (20.16).

$$k\beta \sum_{j=1}^{m}[w_j z_j \beta - \log\left(1+f^{z_j \beta}\right)] \tag{20.16}$$

Using the likelihood ratio test, which maintained significant main effects if their p-values were less than 0.05, feature relevance was assessed. Second-order interactions that had p-values less than 0.10 were included in the systematic evaluation of interaction terms. Also, higher-order interactions were adopted to boost categorization capacity. To enhance the accuracy of identifying cognitive bias in textual data, the Lasso and Ridge techniques were applied. The optimized function can be written as the following Equation (20.17).

$$k_{\lambda}^{\omega} = \Sigma_{j=1}^{m}[x_j y_j \beta - \log\left(1 + f^{y_j \beta}\right)] - \lambda \Sigma_{i=1}^{l} |\beta_i|^{\omega} \quad (20.17)$$

This LR framework provides a methodical way to evaluate cognitive bias in literature by identifying negative thought patterns through the analysis of language elements and contextual clues.

20.2.10 Support Vector Machine

Support vector machine (SVM) is a supervised learning classifier that finds the best hyperplane for classifying text data by using structural risk reduction. SVM [14] lowers training error and generalization error by determining the hyperplane that optimizes the margin. Ensuring the maximum distance between the hyperplane and the nearest data points, expressed as follows, establishes the connection between the ideal hyperplane and the Vapnik-Chervonenkis (VC) dimension are illustrated by Equation (20.18).

$$a \leq min\left[\frac{R^2}{f^2}\right], C+1 \quad (20.18)$$

where R is the lowest sphere diameter that contains all feature embeddings (FE), and C is the number of dimensions in the feature space. A better generalization result from increasing the margin since it reduces the VC dimension. SVM divides the text into groups that represent various negative thought patterns to identify cognitive bias. The model assesses whether or not a particular text demonstrates cognitive bias.

20.2.11 Bidirectional LSTM

Sequential behavioral data is analyzed by RNNs; however, because of memory constraints and vanishing gradient problems, RNNs have difficulty handling long-term relationships. These issues are addressed by Long Short-Term Memory (LSTM) networks, which use memory cells controlled by three gates: input, forget, and output. The forget gate for cognitive distortions decides whether to maintain or reject previous negative thinking patterns, which are represented by Equation (20.19).

$$f_t = \sigma(W_t[g_{t-1}, y_t] + c_i) \tag{20.19}$$

The input gate changes pertinent data are illustrated by Equation (20.20).

$$i_t = \sigma(W_t[g_{t-1}, y_t] + c_i) \tag{20.20}$$

Cell state update is calculated by Equation (20.21).

$$D_t = f_t \odot D_{t-1} + i_t \odot tanh(W_d[g_{t-1}, y_t] + c_d) \tag{20.21}$$

The hidden state is determined by the output gate and expressed by Equation (20.22).

$$g_t = o_t \odot \tanh(D_t) \tag{20.22}$$

By analyzing language patterns both forward and backward, Bi-LSTM [15] improves LSTM as illustrated in Equation (20.23).

$$g_t = \overrightarrow{g_t} \oplus \overleftarrow{g_t} \tag{20.23}$$

By collecting contextual dependencies from past and future words, this bidirectional technique enhances the identification of cognitive biases and makes it easier to identify emotional signals, stress indicators, and cognitive distortions in textual data.

20.2.12 Random Forest

RF [16] is an ensemble classifier using a set of weak classifiers that provide improved prediction accuracy. To train distinct decision trees on different bootstrap samples taken from the training dataset while preserving the training and testing dataset sizes as identical, RF uses bootstrap bagging. To anticipate, RF builds decision trees, just as other ensemble classifiers.

Knowing which root node to use at each step for optimal tree growth is a crucial problem in this procedure. Several decision trees are used to determine the final categorization choice, which is illustrated by Equations (20.24 & 20.25).

$$O = Mode\{S_1(z), S_2(z), S_3(z), \ldots\ldots, S_n(z)\} \tag{20.24}$$

$$o = mode\{\textstyle\sum_{n=1}^{n} S_n(z)\} \tag{20.25}$$

where $S_1(z), S_2(z), S_3(z), \ldots\ldots, S_n(z)$ the individual decision tree is involved in the classification process, and o is the final decision which is derived by the process of voting. The random state in RF is used as an input to control the randomness of sample selection during the training phase for better stability of the model. This technique is used to identify cognitive biases to improve the overall accuracy of classification by identifying extended negative word patterns.

20.3 Results

The evaluation of these models for identifying cognitive bias from text reveals disparities in their performance in recognizing negative thoughts. The performance indicators include accuracy, precision, recall, and F1-score that capture the effectiveness and drawbacks of each method. These results highlight the need for appropriate models for improving the accuracy of identifying cognitive distortions in textual content. The experimental setup consisted of an Intel Core i7 processor alongside 32GB RAM and 1TB SSD storage while operating Ubuntu 20.04. An implementation system used Python, TensorFlow and Scikit-learn for executing NLP combined with ML and DL models to detect cognitive bias. Table 20.1 depicts the comparative analysis of ML and DL methods with NLP techniques.

Accuracy: Accuracy provides an overall assessment of the model's performance by indicating the percentage of accurately categorized biased and unbiased text samples. Better generalization is indicated by higher accuracy. Figure 20.1 shows the accuracy results. SVM demonstrated its exceptional capacity to accurately identify cognitive bias across various textual samples, with the greatest accuracy of 96%.

Precision: By calculating the percentage of accurately predicted biased text across all detected biased instances, it reduces false positives. A higher

Table 20.1 Performance comparison of different models for cognitive bias detection.

Model	Recall (%)	Accuracy (%)	F1-score (%)	Precision (%)
SVM [17]	96	96	96	96
LSTM [17]	90	90	90	90
CNN-GloVe300d [18]	42	-	55	82
LR-CV [18]	95	-	95	95
Bi-LSTM [19]	86	86	88	90
RF-bigram [19]	94	94	92	91

Source: Own elaboration.

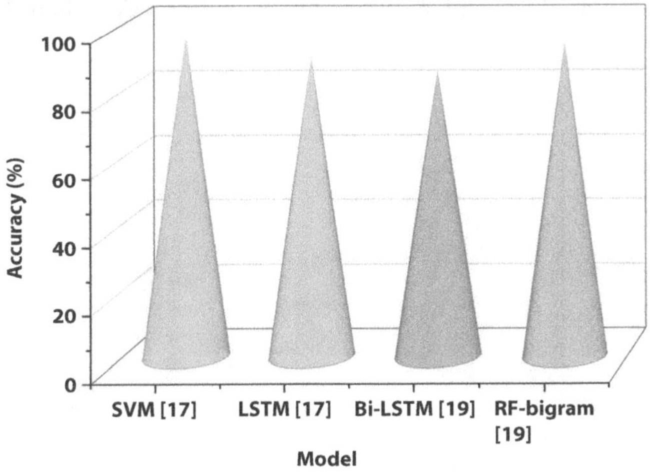

Figure 20.1 Accuracy performance of cognitive bias detection models. Source: Own elaboration.

precision means that bias and neutral text are successfully separated by the model. Figure 20.2 depicts the precision result. The most accurate bias predictions were made by SVM (96%) with the least amount of misclassification.

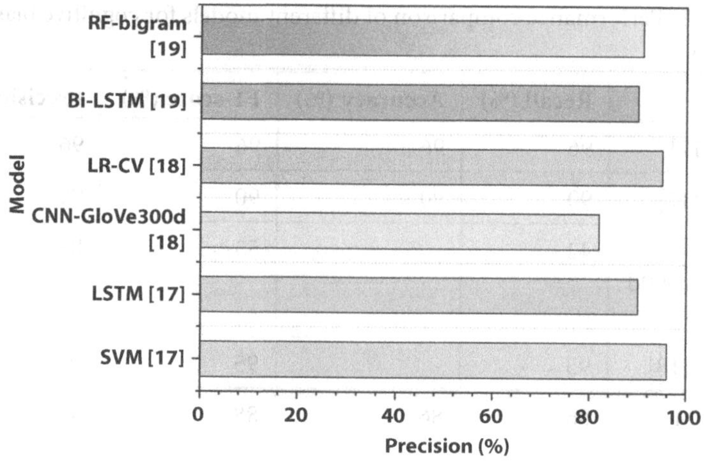

Figure 20.2 Precision analysis of various computational models. Source: Own elaboration.

Recall: Recall assesses the model's ability to identify all real biased cases, minimizing false negatives. When it pertains to biased content, high recall is critical. Figure 20.3 depicts the recall evaluation. SVM had the highest

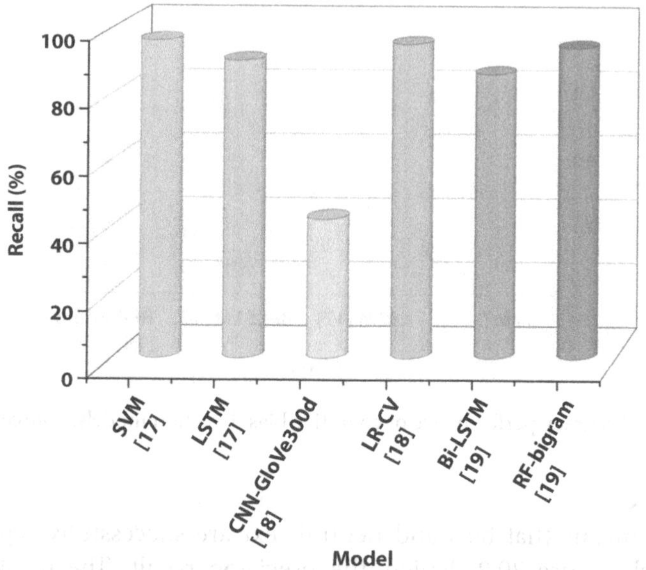

Figure 20.3 Recall evaluation for text-based cognitive bias identification. Source: Own elaboration.

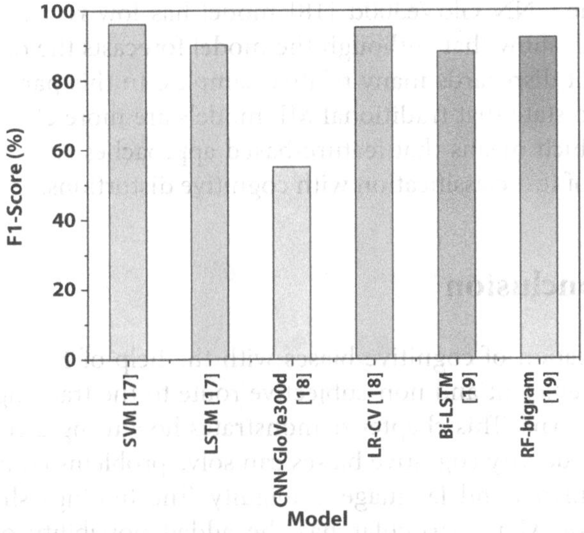

Figure 20.4 F1 score comparison of different AI approaches for bias detection. Source: Own elaboration.

recall (96%), guaranteeing that the majority of biased samples were properly recognized, making it extremely effective at detecting cognitive bias.

F1-Score: F1-score is essential for models that deal with class imbalances because it strikes a compromise between accuracy and recall. Strong performance is indicated by a higher F1 score. The F1 score results are shown in Figure 20.4. To improve detection reliability, SVM (96%) achieved the most effective balance between detecting biased events and reducing false positives.

20.3.1 Discussion

The evaluation with other models also shows that there are several differences in their ability to recognize cognitive biases from texts. The model results show that both SVM [17] and the LR [18] with the count vectorization have the highest values of recall, accuracy, F1 score, and precision, which means that those models are the most accurate with low false positive and false negative rates when it comes to negative thinking styles classification. RF with bigrams [19] also produces effective results; the lower F1-score is explained by the lower precision rate and recall rate. Conversely, LSTM [17] and Bidirectional LSTM [19] provide slightly lesser results, which can deduce its strengths in capturing the sequential dependencies while exhibiting slight drawbacks in terms of precision-recall balance.

However, the CNN-GloVe300d [18] model has low recall and F1-score values, which show that, although the model forecasts the outcomes with confidence, it disregards many relative samples. In this particular case, it is possible to state that traditional ML models are more efficient than DL methods, which means that feature-based approaches are yet valuable in the context of text classification with cognitive distortions.

20.4 Conclusion

The identification of cognitive biases with the help of NLP, ML, and DL provides an efficient and non-subjective route to the tracking of negative thinking patterns. This chapter demonstrates how using a computational approach to identify cognitive biases can solve problems concerning subjective judgments and language ambiguity. The findings show how the application of AI in particular has the added possibility of improving psychological testing and bringing about more efficient early detection in the field of mental health. It can enhance the reliability and effectiveness of detecting negative thought patterns since it entails a logical and thorough approach to analyzing textual data. Further developments of these approaches should target improvement of the applicability of these models in diverse linguistic and cultural contexts to comprise a wide range of practical uses in mental health evaluations and treatment.

AI disclosure statement: The author confirms that no artificial intelligence (AI)-generated content or AI-assisted writing tools were used in the preparation of this chapter (including summaries and the abstract). All text, analysis, and conclusions are the result of the author's original work.

References

1. Mercan, N., Bulut, M., Yüksel, C., Investigation of the relatedness of cognitive distortions with emotional expression, anxiety, and depression. *Curr. Psychol.*, 42, 3, 2176–2185, 2023, https://doi.org/10.1007/s12144-021-02251-z.
2. Giromini, L., Young, G., Sellbom, M., Assessing negative response bias using self-report measures: New articles, new issues. *Psychol. Inj. Law*, 15, 1, 1–21, 2022, https://doi.org/10.1007/s12207-022-09444-2.
3. Guanghui, F.U., *et al.*, Evaluating the Efficacy of Supervised Learning vs. Large Language Models for Identifying Cognitive Distortions and

Suicidal Risks in Chinese Social Media, 2023, https://doi.org/10.21203/rs.3.rs-3355484/v1.
4. Naseem, U., *et al.*, Transformer based deep intelligent contextual embedding for twitter sentiment analysis. *Future Gener. Comput. Syst.*, 113, 58–69, 2020, https://doi.org/10.1016/j.future.2020.06.050.
5. Chen, Z., Lu, Y., Wang, W.Y., Empowering psychotherapy with large language models: Cognitive distortion detection through diagnosis of thought prompting, *arXiv preprint arXiv:2310.07146*, 2023, https://doi.org/10.48550/arXiv.2310.07146.
6. Sharma, A., *et al.*, Cognitive reframing of negative thoughts through human-language model interaction, *arXiv preprint arXiv:2305.02466*, 2023, https://doi.org/10.48550/arXiv.2305.02466.
7. Fadda, M., *et al.*, Ethical issues of collecting, storing, and analyzing geo-referenced tweets for mental health research. *Digit. Health*, 8, 20552076221092539, 2022, https://doi.org/10.1177/20552076221092539.
8. Ding, L., Assessing and Mitigating Social Bias in Text and Natural Language Processing Systems, 2024, https://doi.org/10.7939/r3-s1rm-bc07.
9. Dewangan, D., Selot, S., Panicker, S., The accuracy analysis of different machine learning classifiers for detecting suicidal ideation and content. *Asian J. Electr. Sci.*, 12, 1, 46–56, 2023, https://doi.org/10.51983/ajes-2023.12.1.3694.
10. Dyulicheva, Y.Y., Identification of affective states based on automatic analysis of texts of comments in social networks. *Autom. Remote Control*, 83, 12, 1877–1885, 2022, https://doi.org/10.1134/S00051179220120025.
11. Lee, J.E. and Yoo, S.K., Recognition of negative emotion using long short-term memory with bio-signal feature compression. *Sensors*, 20, 2, 573, 2020, https://doi.org/10.3390/s20020573.
12. Zhang, W., *et al.*, CNN-LSTM neural network model for fine-grained negative emotion computing in emergencies. *Alexandria Eng. J.*, 61, 9, 6755–6767, 2022, https://doi.org/10.1016/j.aej.2021.12.022.
13. Ayyalasomayajula, M.M.T., Agarwal, A., Khan, S., Reddit social media text analysis for depression prediction: using logistic regression with enhanced term frequency-inverse document frequency features. *Int. J. Electr. Comput. Eng. (IJECE)*, 14, 5, 5998–6005, 2024, https://doi.org/10.11591/ijece.v14i5.pp5998-6005.
14. Wibawa, A.D., *et al.*, Rules Extraction of Relevance Vector Machine for Predicting Negative Emotions from EEG Signals. *Int. J. Intell. Eng. Syst.*, 15, 1, 42–54, 2022, https://doi.org/10.22266/ijies2022.0228.05.
15. Wu, J.-L., *et al.*, Identifying emotion labels from psychiatric social texts using a bi-directional LSTM-CNN model. *IEEE Access*, 8, 66638–66646, 2020, https://doi.org/10.1109/ACCESS.2020.2985228.
16. Li, M., *et al.*, A clinical-oriented non-severe depression diagnosis method based on cognitive behavior of emotional conflict. *IEEE Trans. Comput. Soc. Syst.*, 10, 1, 131–141, 2022, https://doi.org/10.1109/TCSS.2022.3152091.

17. Macias, C., *et al.*, Modeling the Depressive Mind: A Machine Learning Approach to Deciphering Beck's Cognitive Triad.
18. Mostafa, M., El Bolock, A., Abdennadher, S., Automatic Detection and Classification of Cognitive Distortions in Journaling Text. *WEBIST*, 2021, https://doi.org/10.5220/0010713000003058.
19. Marshan, A., *et al.*, Comparing machine learning and deep learning techniques for text analytics: Detecting the severity of hate comments online. *Inf. Syst. Front.*, 27, 1–19, 2023, https://doi.org/10.1007/s10796-023-10446-x.

Index

Printed in the USA/Agawam, MA
September 16, 2026

910660.005